English I: . . . P–K4

CONTEMPORARY CHESS OPENINGS
GENERAL EDITOR: R. G. WADE

English I: . . . P–K4

JOHN L. WATSON

B. T. Batsford Ltd. *London*

To my mother

First published 1979
© John L. Watson 1979
ISBN

Film set by Willmer Brothers Limited, Birkenhead, Merseyside
Printed in Great Britain by
Billing & Son Ltd.,
London, Guildford and Worcester

for the publishers

B. T. Batsford Limited
4 Fitzhardinge Street, London W1H 0AH

Batsford Chess Series
General Editor: R. G. Wade

CONTENTS

AUTHOR'S PREFACE

APPROACH

Opening books can be categorized as 'encyclopaedic' or 'illustrative'. The first type emphasizes variations and specific analysis, while the second concentrates on the characteristic ideas and themes of an opening. *The English Opening* combines general theory, discussion, and examples, but tends toward the encyclopaedic, at least insofar as the reader is given the chance to track down particular subvariants and move orders without having to rely on an analogy with a more'standard' line.

In my own experience, many misconceptions about variations arose because I based my understanding on one or two sample games, or on some positional generality. I suffered more than one disillusionment because a simple transposition denied me time or opportunity to achieve the prescribed positional goals. I feel that only by careful comparison of numerous examples does one achieve a subtler comprehension of a variation, i.e. an understanding which could hardly be rendered in less than several pages of bewilderingly qualified prose. The alternative of diagramming the characteristic pawn structure and listing the 'ideas' of a system may unify material, but is literally a superficial view. Moreover, such an approach is in a sense authoritarian, i.e. it *tells* the reader a generalization he should find for himself if he is to know in what sense it is valid. To put it bluntly, almost anyone can master opening principles, but one aim of an opening book should be to show precisely where and how that principle applies. For this purpose, prose is simply no substitute for games and specific analysis. What I have tried to do is: (a) to select spritely and instructive examples; (b) to organize them so that, in combination with notes, they show the results of *distinct* strategies and timing; (c) to interrupt the monotony of long variations and games with discussion of the themes and goals of each; and (d) to include as many new ideas and original analysis as possible, indicating thereby both unsolved problems and interesting territory for further exploration.

ACKNOWLEDGEMENTS

I should like to express my gratitude to everyone who assisted me with the writing of *English I: . . . P–K4*. In particular, Ken Rogoff and Evàn Michaelides provided analysis and encouragement, while Jon Frankle and Chris Chase offered their books and madcap hospitality on numerous occasions. I am also indebted to Eric Helmreich of the Boston Chess Studio for his generous provision of books and magazines, to Burt Hochberg for his counsel and to Kevin O'Connell for the use of his games files. Bob Wade did a consummate job of checking game sources, while David Friedgood earns credit for proof-reading.

My deepest thanks goes to Kenneth J. Case, who read and criticized the entire manuscript, and most importantly, to Cindy Royce for several years of dedication to every phase of its preparation. Without her help and friendship, the book would never have seen the light of publication in its present form.

INTRODUCTION

The English Opening is divided into four books:—

English I: ... P–K4 deals with 1 P–QB4 P–K4;

English II: ... N–KB3 deals with 1 P–QB4 N–KB3 and for the sake of convenience excludes variations in which Black plays early either ... P–K4 or ... P–QB4. Thus a game which begins 1 P–QB4 N–KB3 2 N–QB3 P–Q4 3 P×P N×P 4 P–KN3 P–QB4 may be found in *English III: ... P–QB4* under the order 1 P–QB4 P–QB4 2 N–QB3 N–KB3 3 P–KN3 P–Q4 4 P×P N×P;

English III: ... P–QB4 deals with 1 P–QB4 P–QB4;

English IV is made up with other important variations like 1 ... P–K3, 1 ... P–KN3, 1 ... P–KB4, 1 ... P–QB3 and 1 ... P–QN3.

WHO PLAYS THE ENGLISH?

The best players in the world! Korchnoi, Larsen, Polugaevsky, and Uhlmann have used 1 P–QB4 (or 1 N–KB3 and 2 P–QB4) as their main weapon over many years; and Smyslov, Petrosian, Tal, Portische, Hübner, and Hort have shown a marked liking for it. Also, no discussion of English Opening greats can exclude Mikhail Botvinnik; while of the other world champions, even Spassky, Fischer, and Karpov (normally 1 P–K4 adherents) have had recourse to the English in key situations. Newer devotees are many, Andersson and Miles being prominent examples.

The cause for such enthusiasm may be found in the intriguing balance of tactical and strategical challenges offered by the English. Hardly any other opening is so assured of increasing popularity in the years to come.

In my opinion there are three other outstanding players whose creative contributions to the theory of 1 P–QB4 deserve special notice: Pal Benko, Ludek Pachman, and Mark Taimanov. Each of these has had his influence on innumerable variations through the years and has brought respectability to many hitherto disreputable lines.

TRANSPOSITIONS

While almost every chess opening can be confusing with regard to move order and the crisscrossing of variations, the English is likely the most convoluted of all. Even 1 P–QB4 regulars are often manouvered into lines they wished to avoid, and the whole subject is rendered even more complicated by the existence of multitudinous 'reversed variations', in which White adopts a normal Black set-up, or vice-versa (see below).

Books on the English Opening have generally tended to ignore transpositions and left the reader to his own devices.* In this book, transpositional possibilities are mentioned throughout the text for immediate reference; but the important tool in this regard is the Index of Variations and Transpositions (page 236). By use of the Index, the reader should be able to locate the pages of the book which analyze any logical sequence of early moves, without having to thumb through five or six chapters in hopes of finding the author's move order.

The Index also explains much that is not apparent in the Table of Contents. After 1 P–QB4 N–KB3, for example, there are countless games every year with 2 N–KB3 (or with 1 N–KB3 N–KB3 2 P–QB4). Where does one find analysis on this sequence? Of course that depends on what happens next, and one can find a specific answer in the Index at the beginning of *English II:* . . . N–KB3 in the section on alternatives to 2 N–QB3.

Finally, one may find the Index useful in forming a comprehensive personal repertoire for either colour.

REVERSED POSITIONS

One of the trickiest aspects of the English Opening is that White can often be found playing the Black side (or Black the White side) of another English system, or of another opening. I have tried to note these 'reversed positions' when they occur, and recommend studying both lines together (e.g. 1 P–QB4 P–K4 2 N–QB3 N–KB3 3 P–KN3 B–N5 4 B–N2 0–0 5 P–K4 P–B3 with 1 P–K4 P–QB4 2 N–KB3 N–QB3 3 B–N5 P–KN3 4 0–0 B–N2 5 P–B3 P–K4).

A word of warning to the reader: simply because White has an extra tempo on some normal Black defensive system by no means indicates that he should stand better. More often than not, the extra tempo brings with it the drawback of committing oneself before one's opponent, and thus opening oneself to possible counterattacks and equalizing plans. A general case of this paradoxical situation is that throughout Part 1 (1 P–QB4 P–K4), White has so difficult a time in many variations where he plays a normal Sicilian Defence formation. Thus we find, e.g. Karpov, Korchnoi, Spassky, Mecking, Portisch etc. regularly using 1 . . . P–K4 as a dynamic defence to 1 P–QB4, despite the excellent reputation of 1 . . . P–QB4 versus 1 P–K4.

---

* Schwarz's work does make a respectable (if incomplete) attempt to deal with transpositions. However, he tends to treat 'irregular' move orders as though they inevitably lead to main lines (by e.g. having one side or the other make feeble or unnecessary moves).

WHY PLAY THE ENGLISH

Hopefully this book will provide the answer. I would add that some of the finest games of modern chess, both positional and tactical, have begun with 1 P–QB4, and that the English, by virtue of its extraordinary flexibility, makes for the most open-ended and creative play of any first move. If the claim that the English is a 'dull, drawish opening' still needs refutation, one observes that Larsen, Tal, Uhlmann, Korchnoi, et al are hardly inclined toward dullness. *One Thing Is Certain:*

No one can stop you from playing 1 P–QB4!

BIBLIOGRAPHY

I have tapped many sources over the last several years, including older theoretical works (e.g. Pachman, Euwe), games collections, and particularly many magazines and tournament books. The references I relied most heavily on were:

Books:

Keene, R. *Flank Openings* (2nd Edition, Sussex 1970)

Schwarz, R. *Englisch/Bremer Partie* (Hamburg 1963)

Shatskes, B. A. *The English Opening,* translated from Russian by Ralph Lawrence (Chicago 1973)

Taimanov, M. *Slawisch bis Reti-Eröffnung* (1st Edition, Berlin 1971); 3rd Edition, Berlin 1976)

Cafferty, B. *English Opening* (1st Edition, Nottingham 1973; 2nd Edition, Nottingham 1977)

Comment on the last three books is unavoidable, for even the casual browser may be confused by the fact that the text and diagrams of all three bear a striking resemblance. In fact, Shatskes' is an original work, and the title page of the first edition of Cafferty states that it is a translation of *'English Opening* by B. Shatskes.' I used it as such, since Cafferty's few revisions and addition were easily distinguishable from the original.

In the case of Taimanov's book, one observes the collaboration of Shatskes, whose work on the 1 P-QB4 section (slightly over a third of the book) doubtless accounts for the similarity of exemplary games, analysis, and conclusions.

Periodicals and Pamphlets:

Chess Archives
Chess Life and Review
Modern Chess Theory
The reti (Weinstein; Dallas 1976)
Sahovski Informator (1–25)
Shakmatny Bulletin
Shakmatny v SSSR
The Chess Player (1–15)

All analysis in the book is the author's unless otherwise indicated. Very elementary notes (or variations pointed out by all annotators) I have sometimes left unaccredited.

SYMBOLS

ch	Check
Δ	With the idea of
±(∓)	Some advantage for White(Black) (sometimes convertible to a win)
±(∓)	Clear advantage for White(Black) (usually convertible to a win)
±±(∓∓)	White(Black) has a clearly won position
=	The position is balanced or equal
∞	The position is complicated and unclear
!	Strong move
!!	Excellent move
!?	Interesting move
?!	Not the best move, although with some value (e.g. trickiness)
?	Weak move
??	Blunder
(!)	Probably a good move (e.g. could use more tests)
(?)	Probably a bad move (e.g. could use more tests)
½–½	Draw agreed
1–0	Black resigns
0–1	White resigns
(1–0, 75)	White went on to win in 75 moves
Ch	Championship
TU	Trade Union
corres	Correspondence game
Top L	Top League
W or B	beside each diagram indicates which player is to move

1 THE CLOSED ENGLISH: 3 P–KN3 P–KN3

1 P–QB4 P–K4 2 N–QB3 N–QB3 3 P–KN3 P–KN3 4 B–N2 B–N2 is one of the oldest systems of the English Opening. Of the various appellations given it, 'Closed English' seems the most appropriate, inasmuch as White is playing the Black side of a Closed Sicilian, and vice versa. Clearly then, a study of the Closed Sicilian will be no hindrance to understanding these analogous positions. But White's extra tempo obscures the issues, and both sides must take particular care with the specifics of move order. In practice, overconfident Whites are regularly mated (certainly more frequently than defenders of the Closed Sicilian), often as a consequence of overshifting their forces to fuel a queenside attack. Leading players of 2 . . . N–QB3 like Spassky, Hort, and Liberzon have been winning such games for years.

With that admonition in mind, one nevertheless prefers White's prospects. Black has denied himself the option of . . . P–QB3 and subjected himself to harassment from N–Q5, P–QN4–N5, etc.. Presumably because of such considerations, Geller actually queried 2 . . . N–QB3 and called 3 P–KN3 '±'!

1	P–QB4	P–K4
2	N–QB3	N–QB3
3	P–KN3	P–KN3

3 . . . N–B3 (?) 4 B–N2 is analysed in Chapter 4 (introductory material, note (a)). Another renegade variation is **3 . . . B–B4?!**, transgressing the old Alekhine axiom that . . . B–QB4 is only suitable when White's P–Q4 can be prevented. In the case before us, P–Q4 will come supported by P–K3 and thus win central territory with a gain of tempo: 4 B–N2 **P–Q3** (4 . . . **N–B3**, see Chapter 4, introduction, note (b)) 5 P–K3 and:

a) **5 . . . B–B4** (bishops before knights!) 6 P–Q3 KN–K2 7 KN–K2 Q–Q2 8 P–KR3! P–KR4 9 P–R3 B–QN3 10 P–QN4 P–R4 11 P–N5 N–Q1 12 P–K4 B–KR2 13 N–R4 B–QB4 14 P–B4! ± Benko-Pogats, Hungarian Ch 1954;

b) **5 . . . KN–K2** 6 P–QR3 P–QR4 7 KN–K2 0–0 8 0–0 (or 8 P–Q4 B–N3 9 0–0 B–Q2 10 P–Q5 and 11 P–R3 ±-Alekhine) **8 . . . B–Q2** (On **8 . . . N–B4**, to stop 9 P–Q4, White plays 9 P–N3 Δ B–N2, N–Q5, and P–Q4. In the meantime, Black has closed off his main source of counterplay: . . . P–KB4.) 9 P–KR3! Q–B1 10 K–R2 ±. White controls the centre and will station his troops with P–Q4, P–N3, B–N2, N–Q5 etc. Black can do little that is affirmative; perhaps he should try to remain as obstinate as possible in the centre, e.g. 10 . . . P–B3 11 P–Q4 B–R2 12 P–N3 N–Q1 13 B–N2 (13 N–Q5 R–B2) 13 . . . N–B2 14 N–Q5 R–K1 ±.

Other third moves are direct transpositions: **3 . . . P–B4** is Chapter 10, C; **3 . . . P–Q3** is Chapter 9, D1 (or this chapter if . . . P–KN3 follows).

    4 B–N2   B–N2 (*1*)

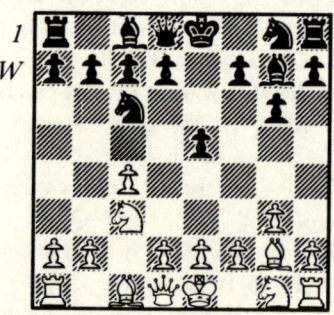

A crossroads. White has:
A 5 N–B3
B 5 P–K3
C 5 P–Q3
D 5 R–N1
E 5 P–K4

The choice is an important one, for each fifth move introduces a distinct strategy. Transpositions are explained in the text.

A

    5 N–B3

Development of the king's knight serves to prepare P–Q4 and encourages in response the kind of Closed Sicilian in Reverse where Black plays . . . P–KB4 and/or . . .

KN–K2 (i.e. leaving his dark-squared bishop 'unmasked' against d4). Taimanov and Shatskes use 5 N–B3 as the introductory move to a position arising after 5 N–B3 N–B3 6 P–Q3 P–Q3 7 0–0 0–0 8 R–N1, one of the 'main lines' of the English Opening. This is misleading, however, because that position is hardly likely to occur (or should not occur) after 5 N–B3, or indeed in any of the lines of the Closed English excepting 5 P–Q3. (I have given that variation as coming about by 1 P–QB4 N–KB3 2 N–QB3 P–KN3 3 P–KN3 B–N2 4 B–N2 0–0 5 N–B3, etc, to be dealt with in *English II*, Ch 5, though other move orders are also plausible.) In the order of this chapter, after 5 N–B3 **N–B3 (?)**, White has 6 P–Q4! P×P (6 . . . P–Q3 7 P×P!) 7 N×P 0–0 8 0–0 R–K1 9 N×N (or 9 N–B2), a variation dealt with in Chapter 7, A (4 . . . P–KN3), and known to favour White. Even the milder treatment 5 . . . N–B3(?) 6 0–0 0–0 7 P–Q4 P–Q3 gives us the 'Uhlmann Variation' of the King's Indian Defence, when 8 P–Q5 N–K2 9 P–K4 (or even 9 P–B5!?) generally results in a game going more White's way than Black's. Note that **5 . . . P–Q3** 6 0–0 N–B3(?) 7 P–Q4! is just as good. So Black should play a sequence not involving an early . . . N–B3 (at least not before White's P–Q3 or Black's . . . P–KB4). That brings us to:
A1 5 . . . KN–K2
A2 5 . . . P–B4

    5 . . . P–Q3 will transpose, but see the note to 7 0–0 in A1.

A1

5 ...	**KN–K2**
6 P–Q3	P–Q3

6 ... 0–0 reduces Black's options. See the next two notes.

7 0–0

For **7 B–Q2**, see C2. **7 R–QN1** will often transpose to Section C or D, or back to the text, but has independent value, to wit: after 7 0–0, Black has the choice of lining up his queen and queen's bishop on c8 and d7 respectively, or (following 7 . . . P–KR3) on d7 and e6; but after 7 R–QN1,

a) **7 . . . P–KR3** 8 P–QN4 B–K3 9 P–N5 leaves Black a tempo short of being able to retreat to d8, while 9 . . . N–Q5 10 N–Q2! Δ P–K3 is definitely better for White.

b) Nor does **7 . . . B–K3** solve Black's problems: 8 P–QN4 Q–B1 (or 8 . . . Q–Q2? 9 N–KN5) 9 P–N5 N–Q1 10 N–N5 B–Q2 11 P–KR3 P–KR3 12 N(5)–K4 P–KB4 13 N–Q2 N–B2 14 P–QR4 ±. Thus 7 R–QN1 tends to discourage the . . . P–KR3, . . . B–K3 plans.

Finally, for the record, **5 . . . P–Q3** 6 P–Q3 P–KR3(!) 7 R–QN1 B–K3 (or 7 . . . P–QR4 8 P–QR3 B–K3) avoids this fine point, after which the game will usually enter the next note.

7 . . .   0–0

Black waives the chance for
a) **7 . . . P–KR3**, by which he could achieve the aforementioned regrouping e.g. 8 R–N1 and now:
a1) **8 . . . P–QR4** 9 P–QR3 B–K3 10 P–QN4 P×P 11 P×P Q–Q2 12 R–K1 (12 P–N5 N–Q1 13 P–K4!? ∞) 12 . . . B–R6 13 B–R1 P–B4 14

P–N5 N–Q1 15 N–Q5? (Better is 15 B–QN2 or 15 Q–N3!?) 15 . . . 0–0 16 N–Q2 N×N 17 P×N P–N3! (Now Black has a free hand on the kingside.) 18 P–B4 N–B2 19 N–B3 QR–K1 20 B–QN2 P–N4 ∓ Lewi-Hort, 1970;
a2) **8 . . . B–K3** 9 P–QN4 Q–Q2 10 P–N5 N–Q1. Schwarz calls this position equal, whereas Taimanov quotes Barcza-Joksić, Belgrade 1966: 11 B–QR3 P–KB4?! 12 N–Q2 P–KR4 13 P–B5! P–Q4 14 P–B6! P×P 15 N–N3 N–N2 16 B×N K×B 17 P×P Q×P 18 R–B1 Q–Q2 19 P–K4! when White has excellent play (though ½–½, 38). That should not be the last word: after **11 B–QR3**, Black has the simple riposte 11 . . . P–QR3! e.g. 12 Q–R4 0–0 13 P–B5? P–Q4 14 P–B6 P×BP 15 P×BP N(1)×P, or if here 14 KR–B1 (directed against . . . P–K5) 14 . . . P–QB3. If White attempts to prepare B–QR3 by **11 P–QR4**, then 11 . . . B–R6 12 B–R3 P–N3! or 12 P–R5 0–0 is satisfactory. Lastly, 11 R–K1 0–0 12 P–QR4 P–KB4 (Δ . . . P–K5) 13 Q–B2 R–B2 is unclear and potentially exciting. These are themes which recur throughout this chapter.
b) An immediate **7 . . . B–Q2** is similar to A11 below, unless Black goes for broke, e.g. 8 R–N1 Q–B1 9 R–K1 B–R6 10 B–R1 P–KR4?! 11 P–QN4 P–R5 12 B–N5? P–B3 13 B–Q2 P×P 14 BP×P Stolyar-Zereteli, Moscow 1964, and here 14 . . . Q–B4! would have been dangerous. But such wild-eyed charges are usually refutable: a natural counter-thrust with 12

P–N5 N–Q1 (12 ... N–Q5 13 N×N P×N 14 N–K4) 13 P–Q4! N–K3 14 P×P P×P 15 N–Q5 (Taimanov) would have revealed White's superiority.

8 R–N1(*2*)

A parting of ways:

A11 8 ... B–Q2
A12 8 ... P–QR4
A13 8 ... P–B4

The alternatives are slightly dubious:

a) **8 ... B–K3** 9 N–KN5! B–N5 10 P–B3 (or 10 P–B4) 10 ... B–Q2 11 P–B4 grants White the better of it. Another strategy was (8 ... B–K3:) 9 P–QN4 Q–B1 10 P–N5 N–Q1 11 B–Q2 B–R6 (11 ... P–KR3 is more circumspect.) 12 N–Q5 N×N 13 P×N P–QR3?! (13 ... B×B) 14 B×B! Q×B 15 Q–B2 Q–Q2 (15 ... R–B1!?) 16 KR–B1 P×P 17 Q×P Q×Q 18 R×Q R×P 19 B–N4! ±± Matera-Balashov, Student Teams, 1974.

b) **8 ... P–KR3** is similar to A12: 9 P–QN4 B–K3 10 P–N5 N–N1 11 N–Q2! Q–B1 12 R–K1 N–Q2 and here Schwarz recommends 13 N–N3 ±. In general, White stands

well if the knight must retreat to b8 instead of d8.

A11

8 ...   B–Q2

This can also be preceded by 8 ... P–QR4 9 P–QR3, but Black's intended queen placement (on c8) makes it likely that White will be the beneficiary of the open QR file. The problems related to this file – its control and even the advantage of ridding oneself of a potential target in one's QRP – crops up again and again in the English, and is comparable to the 'which rook' problem in so many openings.

9 P–QN4   Q–B1
10 P–N5   N–Q1

10 ... N–Q5 11 N×N (or 11 N–Q2) 11 ... P×N 12 N–Q5 N×N 13 P×N B–R6 14 B×B! Q×B 15 Q–B2 Δ R–N4–B4, B–QN2, etc.

11 R–K1   B–R6

Korchnoi-Lisitsin, 22nd USSR Ch 1955, took another course: **11 ... P–KR3** 12 Q–B2 (or P–Q4, but Korchnoi has a different notion) 12 ... B–R6 13 B×B?! (13 B–R1) 13 ... Q×B 14 N–Q5 N×N 15 P×N (In such a position, time is vital; 11 R–K1 could have been dispensed with. Now Black consolidates:) 15 ... Q–Q2 16 B–Q2 P–KB4 17 R(K)–QB1   R–B2   18   R–N4 (Progress is hard to make: if 18 P–QR4, 18 ... P–N3! 19 R–N4 N–N2 20 R–B4 N–B4 21 B–N4 QR–KB1-Schwarz)   18   ... P–QR4! 19 P×Pe.p. (19 R–QB4 Q×P   20   R×P   Q×P(4)   ∓—

Schwarz) 19 ... R×P 20 Q–N3
P–B4! 21 R–N6 R×R 22 Q×R
P–K5 23 N–K1 R–K2 24 B–K3
N–B2 ∓ (0–1, 35).

12 B–R1   P–KR3(3)

13 P–Q4

Alternate strategies are
P–QR4–R5, B–QR3, etc. and
Q–B2 Δ N–Q5. Black would in
either case be able to advance on
the kingside, but it will take many
moves before there are actual
threats in that sector.

13 ...   N–K3
14 P×P   P×P

15 N–Q5 N×N 16 P×N R–Q1 17
B–QN2 P–K5! 18 B×B N×B 19
N–Q4 (19 N–K5? Q–B4) 19 ...
R×P 20 B×P R–Q3 21 R–N4!
N–K3 22 Q–R1 P–QB4! 23
P×Pe.p. P×P 24 R–QB1 N×N 25
R×N R×R 26 Q×R Q–Q2 27
Q–K3 R–Q1! Pachman-Penrose,
1954. By inspired defence, Black
has achieved an ending which
should have been drawn (but 1–0,
41).

A12

8 ...   P–QR4
9 P–QR3   P–R3

9 ... B–B4 10 P–R3 P–R3 11
P–QN4 P×P 12 P×P Q–Q2 13
K–R2 B–K3 14 P–N5 N–Q1
Lipnitsky-Averbach, 19th USSR
Ch 1951, and instead of 15 N–Q2,
White could have played 15 B–N2
Δ R–R1 ±.

10 P–QN4   P×P
11 P×P   B–K3

12 P–N5 N–Q5 (12 ... N–N1 13
B–N2 Δ R–R1-Taimanov) 13
N–Q2! B–B1 (13 ... P–QB3 14
P–K3 N(5)–B4 15 N(2)–K4—
Taimanov) 14 P–K3 N–K3 15
Q–B2 P–QB3 16 N–R4! Nikolaev-
sky-Peterson, USSR TU Ch 1967.
White is making inroads on the
queenside.

A13

8 ...   P–B4

Black plays to gain space on the
kingside and, by the tactical point 9
P–QN4?? P–K5, to commit White
to a passive piece disposition.

9 B–Q2

White acquiesces. In view of the
next note, **9 Q–B2** deserves
consideration, for instance 9 ...
P–KR3 10 P–QN4 P–KN4 11
P–N5 N–Q5 (11 ... N–N1 12
P–QR4 Δ B–QR3) 12 N×N P×N
13 N–Q5 N×N (else P–B5) 14 P×N
P–QR4   (White   threatened
R–N4–QB4, B–N2, KR–B1, etc.)
15 P×Pe.p. R×P 16 R–N4 and
Black has difficulties (16 ... P–N3
17 P–QR4! B–Q2 18 B–N2).

9 ...   P–KR3?!

Now that White's bishop is not
headed for b2 (and thus protecting
a1), I think Black should play **9 ...
P–QR4!**. If White then follows his

plan in the text, Black is simply more active and controls the QR-file for some time. Of course, 9 . . . P–QR4 allows 10 Q–B1, an attempt to stifle Black's kingside advance, but 10 . . . B–K3! is a clever rejoinder, since 11 B–R6 Q–Q2 12 B×B K×B 13 N–KN5 B–N1 (á la Hort!) 14 P–B4 P–R3 15 N–B3 P–R5 or 11 N–KN5 B–Q2 12 P–B4 P–R3 13 N–B3 P×P 14 P×P B–K3 Δ . . . P–Q4 is quite equal.

10 P–QN4   Q–K1?!

Black follows the natural idea of vacating a square for his queen's knight with an eye toward . . . P–KN4, . . . P–B5, . . . Q–R4, etc . . . But too much is left unprotected! Better **10 . . . K–R2** or **10 . . . P–KN4** 11 P–N5 N–Q5 12 N–K1 P–B5 13 P–K3, although White would keep the upper hand (in the latter case he dominates the light squares, particularly e4).

An (unsuccessful) attempt to neutralize White's queenside activity was **10 . . . P–QR3** 11 P–QR4 P–QR4 12 P×P N×P (12 . . . R×P!? 13 N–Q5 R–R2) 13 N–Q5 (13 N–K1!?) 13 . . . N(4)–B3 14 B–B3 N×N 15 P×N N–K2 16 N–Q2 P–N3 17 P–R5! ± Malpert-Shamkovich, Ohio 1977.

11 N–Q5!   N×N
12 P×N   N–K2

We are following Stolyar-Hasin, ½F 24th USSR Ch 1956: 13 Q–B1 (double attack) 13 . . . P–K5 14 N–K1 N×P 15 B×RP N–B6? (15 . . . Q–K4! Δ 16 B×B K×B is better, but White's king would still be the safer one. Had Black played 9 . . . P–QR4!, his position would now be

much more active.) 16 R–N2 B×B 17 Q×B P–QR4 (too late!) 18 P×KP P×NP 19 P×P R×BP 20 R×P Q–B2 (20 . . . R–KR4 21 Q–Q2) 21 Q–Q2 N×RP 22 R–KR4 Q–B3 23 N–Q3 N–B6 24 P–K4 R–R7 25 Q–R6 N–K7ch 26 K–R1 R–B6 27 Q–R7ch K–B1 28 N–N4 R×BP 29 Q–R8ch Q×Q 30 R×Qch K–N2 31 R×B ±±,

CONCLUSION:

In this . . . KN–K2 system, Black lacks positive play on the kingside, in part because his knights do not easily find their way to effective posts there. The second player's hopes would seem to lie in . . . P–KR3, . . . B–K3, and . . . Q–Q2 before castling. White should confidently pursue his queenside and central incursions, being careful to place his pieces as energetically as possible in support of them (e.g. the queen's bishop goes to a3 or b2, not d2).

A2

5 . . .   P–B4

A natural response to 5 N–B3: Black employs a system which has had excellent results with colours reversed in the Closed Sicilian. Here White's extra tempo roughly balances things and makes for terrific complications.

The move **5 . . . P–Q3** can also introduce a . . . P–KB4 plan, but White can delay his own P–Q3 longer and thus avoid some of the embarrassing variations (e.g. A23) where Black organizes his forces to good effect before castling, i.e. 6

0–0 P–B4 7 R–N1! P–QR4 8 P–QR3 N–B3 (8 . . . P–K5? 9 N–K1 N–B3 10 P–Q3 ±) 9 P–QN4 P×P 10 P×P 0–0 11 P–Q3, the actual move order of the game in A22.

    6 P–Q3   P–Q3

Black too can omit this move for the time being, as in Taimanov–Aronin USSR Team Ch 1954 (by transposition): **6 . . . N–B3** 7 R–QN1 P–QR4 8 0–0 0–0 9 P–QR3 Q–K1 10 B–N5!? P–Q3 11 P–QN4 P×P 12 P×P Q–B2 with tough play ahead.

    7 0–0

a) As in A1, **7 R–N1** may be more forcing, e.g. **7 . . . N–B3** 8 P–QN4 0–0 9 P–N5 N–K2 10 P–B5!? (10 0–0 is normal) 10 . . . N–R4 (10 . . . P–K5!∞) 11 Q–N3ch P–Q4 12 P–B6! ± Gik–Zlotnik, 1973. Keres–Gufeld, Tallinn 1969, saw (after 7 R–N1) **7 . . . P–KR3** 8 P–K4!? **N–B3?!** 9 N–KR4! N–K2 10 P×P P×P 11 P–Q4 (11 P–B4!) 11 . . . 0–0 12 0–0 ±. An original concept, but **8 . . . KN–K2!** was a better test of White's idea.

b) Karaklaić suggests **7 N–Q5** N–B3 8 B–N5 Δ P–QN4.

    7 . . .   N–B3
    8 R–N1(*4*)

The situation is shaping up as a race between respective flank attacks. Black usually prefaces his pawn expansion by one of these moves:

A21 8 . . . B–K3
A22 8 . . . P–QR4
A23 8 . . . 0–0

8 . . . P–KR3!? tries to put the tempo normally spent on . . . 0–0 to better use. Pfleger–Larsen, Manila 1974 continued 9 P–QN4 P–KN4 10 P–N5 N–K2 11 P–QR4 (11 B–N2 Δ P–B5—Karaklaić) 11 . . . N–Q2 12 N–K1 N–B4 13 P–K3 0–0 14 P–Q4 N–K3 15 N–B2? (15 P×P) 15 . . . P×P 16 P×P P–B5 ∓.

A21

    8 . . .   B–K3

Why not? **9 N–KN5** would now be a harmless sortie: 9 . . . B–N1 10 P–B4 P–KR3.

    9 P–QN4   Q–Q2
    10 P–N5   N–Q1
    11 P–QR4

Since . . . P–QN3 loses to N×KP, the immediate **11 B–QR3** Δ P–B5 is logical. Then 11 . . . P–QR3 12 Q–R4 is better for White than it was in A1, because . . . P–Q4 in response to White's P–B5 will allow N×KP. Even **11 P–B5!?** at once could be tried, Δ 11 . . . P×P? 12 N×P Q–Q5 13 B–N2 Q×KN 14 N–K4. But in both cases, P–B5 must be followed up by time-consuming queenside manoeuvres before White achieves specific threats.

    11 . . .   P–KR3
    12 B–QR3

Halfdanarsson-Kupreichik, Dresden 1969. Dynamically equal.

A22
8 ...   P–QR4

Black treats the position as Smyslov used to handle the White side of a Closed Sicilian. 8 ... P–QR4 is often suggested but seldom played.

```
 9 P–QR3      0–0
10 P–QN4      P×P
11 P×P        P–KR3
```
12 P–N5 N–K2 13 B–N2! (Geller's move versus Spassky in the corresponding Sicilian line; here Black is a tempo – ... B–K3 – behind. 13 P–B5 B–K3 14 P–N6 P–B3 achieves less.) 13 ... P–B5!? (Trying to seize the initiative perforce. The Spassky plan of ... P–QN3 is unplayable here because of 14 N×KP.) 14 P–B5! (or 14 R–R1 ±) 14 ... P×NP (14 ... B–K3 15 NP×P KP×P 16 N–Q4) 15 RP×P N–N5 16 P×P P×P 17 Q–N3ch K–R2 18 B–QR3 N–B4 19 N–K4 Q–N3 20 B–R3 ± Watson-J. Meyer, USA (telephone) 1977.

A23
8 ...   0–0

```
 9 P–QN4      P–KR3
```
9 ... P–QR3 10 P–QR4 P–R3 11 P–N5 P×P 12 RP×P is A22.
```
10 P–N5       N–K2(5)
11 N–K1?!
```
White's best here is not known. Leaving the knight on f3 to support a central pawn attack makes sense, but watch this: 11 P–B5 B–K3 12 B–QR3 R–B1! (A beautiful defensive idea!) 13 Q–R4 P–N3 14 P×QP (14 P–B6? leaves it all up to the kingside, where Black is better.) 14 ... P×P 15 R(N)–B1 Q–Q2 16 Q–QN4 R–B4 (not 16 ... KR–Q1? 17 N×P!) 17 P–Q4? (17 N–QR4 R×R 18 R×R R–B1 =) 17 ... N(3)–Q4 18 N×N N×N 19 Q–Q2 R×R 20 R×R P–K5 21 N–K1 Q×P 22 B×QP R–B1! ∓ Rajković-Rukavina, Yugoslavia Ch 1975. Rajković must still be wondering what went wrong!

The most accurate continuation is probably **11 P–QR4** or **11 N–Q2**, especially in view of:
```
11 ...        P–N4
12 N–B2
```
Matulović-Uhlmann, 1968, continued similarly but unhappily for White: **12 P–QR4?!** (better with the knight still on f3) 12 ... R–N1 13 N–B2 P–B5 ('!∓'-Uhlmann) P–R5 B–B4 15 N–N4 Q–Q2 16 P–R6? (the right idea, but White should wait a move: 16 B–Q2) 16 ... P–B4! 17 P×Pe.p. P×BP 18 Q–R4? P–B4! 19 Q×Q B×Q 20 N–B2 R×R 21 N×R, and instead of 21 ... B–B1?! ∓ (later White actually *won*), Black had 21 ... R–N1 ∓.

12	...	P–B5
13	N–N4	N–B4
14	P–QR4	N–Q5
15	P–R5	P–N5?
16	P–R6! ±	

Besser-Minić, Halle 1967 (1–0, 35). But **15 ... P–N5?** was a blunder: **15 ... Q–K1!** turns the tables, as 16 P–R6? Q–R4! 17 P×NP B×P! 18 B×B N–N5 19 P–R4 P×NP 20 BP×P P×RP! is crushing, and 16 P–K3 P–B6! likewise tears into White's kingside: 17 B×P N×Bch 18 Q×N B–R6 19 R–K1 P–Q4! etc. (based on analysis by Minić).

CONCLUSION:

After 5 N–B3, 5 ... P–B4, with the development of the king's knight to f6, grants Black much freer piece play than 5 ... KN–K2. White must be careful about the safety of his king, and it is unlikely that he should gain any significant advantage here.

B

5 P–K3

The most popular of White's alternatives (though often leading to positions which can equally well be introduced by 5 P–Q3). The problems of a Black kingside pawn avalanche, which caused the White KN to lose time in A1, are here avoided, and the diagonal of the bishop on g2 is unobstructed. White plays KN–K2 and either directly pushes forward in the centre with P–Q4 or more discreetly expands on the queenside. In the latter case, he counts on his increased control of

f4 to ward off a Black attack on the opposite wing.

5	...	P–Q3	.

The almost universal response. **5 ... P–B4, 5 ... N–R3**, and **5 ... KN–K2** are occasionally played, but usually transpose to B2, B4, and B7 respectively. The following examples, not terribly critical, had independent significance:

a) **5 ... P–B4** 6 KN–K2 P–K5?! (Conceding d5 to White, when he might fight for it by 6 ... N–B3 e.g. 7 P–Q3 0–0 8 R–QN1 N–K2 9 P–K4 – else ... P–Q4 – 9 ... P–Q3 10 0–0 N–R4 – 10 ... P–B3!? – 11 P–B4 ± Averbach-Aronin, Moscow TU Team Ch 1961.) 7 P–Q3 P×P 8 Q×P N–B3 9 P–N3 P–Q3 10 0–0 0–0 11 B–QR3 P–QR4 12 QR–Q1 ± Smyslov-Kotov, USSR Training 1953;

b) **5 ... KN–K2** (or **5 ... N–R3**) 6 KN–K2 N–B4 (? Black prevents P–Q4, but deprives himself of a plan.) 7 P–N3! (intending an eventual P–Q4 anyway) 7 ... P–Q3 8 B–N2 0–0 9 0–0 B–K3 10 P–Q3 (also not bad is 10 N–Q5, but White wants to build up with Q–Q2 and either QR–Q1 or P–B4) 10 ... N(4)–K2 (back again, but waiting was futile) 11 P–Q4 P×P 12 P×P P–Q4 13 N–B4! ± Furman-Bannik, 1957.

6 KN–K2(6)

Again, alternatives like **6 R–N1** will usually transpose, although **6 P–Q3** allows 6 ... N–B3 and a fiasco for White was **7 R–N1** B–N5 8 Q–R4 0–0 9 P–N4? P–QR4! 10 P–N5 N–N5 11 B–B1 P–K5! 12 P–B3 (12 P×P N–Q2!) 12 ...

P×QP! 13 B–Q2 R–K1 ∓ Kupka-Razuvaev, Vilnus 1969. Here **7 KN–K2** 0–0 8 0–0 might have been answered by 8 . . . N–K2 Δ . . . P–Q4, . . . P–B3.

Now Black has a wealth of ideas to choose from:

B1 6 . . . N–B3
B2 6 . . . P–B4
B3 6 . . . P–KR4
B4 6 . . . N–R3
B5 6 . . . B–Q2
B6 6 . . . B–K3
B7 6 . . . KN–K2

Of these, B6 and B7 are most often encountered.

B1

6 . . .   N–B3
7 P–Q4

The most direct. **7 P–Q3** is more like a Closed Sicilian. For example: **7 . . . 0–0** 8 0–0 R–N1?! (Tal mentions **8 . . . N–KR4**!? and **8 . . . B–K3**. For **8 . . . N–K2**, see the end of this note.) 9 R–N1 P–QR3 10 P–QN4 N–K2 11 P–QR4 P–Q4 12 P×P N(3)×P 13 P–N5 P×P 14 P×P R–R1 15 Q–B2 B–K3 16 N–K4 B–N5 17 R–N3! Tal-Gulko, USSR Ch 1974. With the ideas of N–B5 and B–QR3, White stands excellently. In Aronin-Terpugov,

Moscow Ch 1949, 7 P–Q3 was answered by **7 . . . N–K2**!? Δ . . . P–Q4. Aronin replied 8 P–Q4, and Black after **8 . . . P–B3** 9 0–0 0–0 10 P–K4 P×P 11 N×P P–Q4! 12 BP×P P×P 13 P–K5 N–K5 had achieved equality. But 9 P×P P×P 10 Q×Qch K×Q 11 P–N3 is certainly not pleasant for the second player (d6 is vulnerable). In the Tal-Gulko game, however, Black could have tried the same idea with **8 . . . N–K2**(!), when 9 P–Q4 P–B3 10 P×P P×P is innocuous and here 10 P–N3 allows 10 . . . P×P 11 N×P P–Q4 =. The alternative 9 P–K4 P–B3 also gives White worries about . . . P–Q4. Black therefore appears to gain equality after 8 . . . N–K2.

7 . . .   0–0
8 0–0   B–Q2

9 P–KR3 P–QR3 10 P–N3 R–N1 11 P–QR4 P–QR4 (Now Black has an outpost on b4, but White is better centralized and owns d5. Of course 10 . . . P×P 11 P×P R–K1 12 B–K3 would surrender the centre.) 12 B–N2 R–K1 13 Q–Q2 P–KR4 (Δ . . . P–K5) 14 P×P P×P 15 KR–Q1 ± Polugaevsky-Lutikov, Harkov 1967 (1–0, 40).

B2

6 . . .   P–B4
A move White is specifically prepared to meet, and rather a luxury when Black has so many pieces undeveloped. Yet this central constellation has its advantages, because White must play carefully to avoid a sudden breakthrough to his king.

7 P–Q3

7 R–QN1 will transpose. White can also stake out a claim on the centre by **7 P–Q4** e.g. 7 . . . P–K5 8 P–QN4! N–B3 9 R–QN1 N–K2 10 P–B3 (before . . . P–Q4 equalizes) 10 . . . P×P 11 B×P 0–0 12 0–0 K–R1 13 P–N5 N(2)–N1 (13 . . . P–Q4 14 Q–N3 forces capitulation in the centre.) 14 N–B4 R–K1 15 R–N2! N–R3 16 B–N2 N–B2 17 N(4)–Q5 ± Spassky-Hort (3), 1977. White has shaken Black's grip on e4.

7 . . .   N–B3

8 R–QN1

8 0–0 0–0 9 P–N3 is like Matulovic's plan in the equivalent Closed Sicilian e.g. 9 . . . P–KN4?! (Black generally lacks time for this.) 10 B–N2 N–K2 11 P–B4 N–N3 12 Q–Q2 NP×P 13 KP×P P–B3 14 P–KR3 P–KR4 15 P×P P×P 16 P–Q4 ± Garcia-Padron-Browne, Lanzarote 1977. Moves like . . . P–KN4 and . . . P–KR4 are too loosening.

8 . . .   0–0

a) **8 . . . P–QR4** 9 0–0 0–0 10 P–B4 (Thematic, stopping . . . P–B5 and hindering . . . P–Q4.) 10 . . . B–K3 11 P–N3 B–B2 (so that N–Q5 can be met with . . . N×N) 12 P–KR3 P–Q4? 13 P×KP N×P 14 N–B4 ± Masic-Zinn, Baja 1971. Better 12 . . . Q–Q2.

b) **8 . . . B–K3** 9 N–Q5 Q–Q2 10 N(2)–B3 (or 10 0–0 N–Q1 11 P–N3! ±) 10 . . . N–Q1 11 P–K4 P–B3 12 N×Nch B×N 13 0–0 0–0 14 P×P P×P 15 P–B4 ± Watson-Brobie, Canada 1975. A typical central resolution in that 14 . . .

B×P?! would have given up e4, but now Black has to worry over an eventual P–Q4, or play against his hanging pawns if White decides on P×P at the right moment.

9 P–QN4

9 0–0 B–K3 10 N–Q5 Q–Q2 11 P–QN4 N–KR4! 12 P–N5 N–Q1 13 P–B4 P–B3 14 P×BP NP×P 15 N(5)–B3 R–K1 16 Q–R4 R–QB1 = Rukavina-Uhlmann, Leningrad 1973. 9 P–QN4 denies Black time for this reorganization.

9 . . .   K–R1

a) **9 . . . P–QR3** 10 0–0 (10 P–QR4) 10 . . . B–Q2?! (10 . . . K–R1 Δ . . . P–KN4-Browne. 10 . . . B–Q2 reaches, by transposition, Smyslov-Liberzon, Riga 1968:) 11 P–QR4! R–N1 12 P–N5 P×P 13 RP×P N–K2 14 B–QR3 B–K3 15 Q–N3 P–N3 16 P–Q4! P–K5 17 P–Q5 B–B2 18 N–Q4 ±.

b) **9 . . . P–QR4** 10 P–N5 N–K2 11 P–B4 P×P 12 N×P N–N5 13 N(3)–Q5 N×N 14 B×Nch K–R1 15 0–0 ± Sokolsky-Kupreichik, Spartakovtsev Ch, Minsk 1966.

10 P–N5	N–K2
11 0–0	P–N4
12 P–B4	NP×P
13 KP×P	N–N3
14 N–Q5	N×N
15 B×N ±	

Simagin-Schmulkin, corres 1966. Shatskes comments that the White king's bishop is a stronger piece than its light-squared counterpart (Black's QB), a remark that holds true for most of the lines after 6 . . . P–B4.

B3

    6 . . .   **P–KR4!?**

Played intermittently; White's best plan is not obvious.

7 P–Q4

a) **7 P–KR3** P–R5 (not 7 . . . P–B4? 8 P–KR4! Averbakh-Sokolsky, ½ F 28th USSR Ch 1960) 8 P–KN4 P–B4! ∞ (Mikenas).

b) **7 P–KR4** B–N5 (7 . . . N–R3!?) 8 P–Q3 (8 Q–R4 N–K2 9 P–N4 P–R3 10 B–N2 0–0 11 Q–N3 B–K3! 12 P–QR4 P–R4! 13 P–N5 N–N5 ∓ Etruk-Stein, Tallin 1969) 8 . . . N–B3 9 N–Q5? (9 P–B3 B–K3 10 P–K4!?) 9 . . . N×N 10 P×N N–K2 11 Q–N3 Q–B1 12 N–B3 0–0 13 B–Q2 P–QB4! with a nice game, Larsen-Spassky Match (2), 1968.

c) **7 0–0** is untried. Taimanov gives 7 . . . P–R5 8 N–Q5 P×P 9 BP×P! with good play, but 8 . . . P×P? would of course be a mistake. Black should develop by **8 . . . B–K3** △ . . . Q–Q2 ∞.

    7 . . .   P–R5

'**7 . . . P×P!**' (Razuvaev). Then 8 N×P N(1)–K2 does little, so 8 P×P P–R5 9 B–K3 looks best (±). The text (**7 . . . P–R5**) made its point after 8 P–N3? P–R6! 9 B–B3 Q–B3 10 B×Nch P×B 11 P–B4 P×BP 12 KP×P N–R3 ∓ Akopian-Gufeld, USSR 1975.

    8 P–Q5!   N(3)–K2
    9 P–K4   N–KB3
    10 P–KR3   P–B4

Lein-Razuvaev, 40th USSR Ch 1972. Now 11 B–K3! would have kept White well on top.

B4

    6 . . .   **N–R3**(7)

Formerly employed by Taimanov. Development of a knight 'to the rim' is not bad here, since . . . P–B4–B5 remains an option; and if necessary, the knight can hop back to f7 to support the centre.

    7 0–0

7 R–QN1 gains a tempo for storming the queenside: **7 . . . B–K3** (7 . . . 0–0 8 P–QN4 P–B4 9 P–Q4 N–B2 10 P–N5 N–K2 11 P–QR4 P–B3 12 B–QR3 P–K5 13 P–R4! ± Quinteros-Schmid, Mar del Plata 1970, although Black later won) 8 P–Q3 0–0 9 P–QN4 Q–Q2 10 P–KR4 P–B4 11 P–N5 N–Q1 12 N–Q5 P–B3 13 N(5)–B3 N–N5 = /∞ Larsen-Spassky, Match (4) 1968.

    7 . . .   0–0
    8 P–QR3?!

a) **8 P–Q4?** is what Black wants: 8 . . . P×P 9 P×P R–K1 (9 . . . N–B4!? is B7) 10 N–K4 B–N5! 11 P–B3 R×N! 12 P×B R×NP 13 P–KR3 R–N4! 14 B×R Q×B 15 Q–Q3 R–K1 16 R–B4 N–B4 ∓ Roizman-Zidkov, Leningrad 1969.

b) **8 P–Q3** is consistent e.g. 8 . . . B–K3 9 P–KR3! Q–Q2 10 K–R2 P–B4 11 P–N3 QR–K1 12 P–Q4 B–B2 13 P×P! N×P 14 B–N2

P–KN4!? 15 P–B4 N(K)–N5ch!? 16 P×N N×Pch Forintos-Taimanov, Skopje 1970. Black's attack should not succeed, but White missed the proper defence and lost.

8 ...	B–K3
9 N–Q5	Q–Q2
10 P–Q3	B–R6
11 P–K4	B×B
12 K×B	P–B4
13 P–B3	

This game is worthy of study, in that a typical situation after the exchange of light-squared bishops is produced. White's queen's bishop is 'better' than Black's king's bishop, and his knight looks imposing on d5. Despite this, Black now secures the advantage. Although 'correctly' on light squares, White's kingside pawns cannot productively advance, whereas Black can chase back the invading knight and then strike in the centre or the kingside as he prefers. In either case, his g7 bishop will eventually be unleashed.

13 ...	N–Q1!
14 B–K3	

In later examples, the White pawns are on b5 and perhaps a4 at this point, so White has B–QR3, after which Black's . . . P–B3 drives back the knight only at the cost of opening the QN-file and weakening the QR3–KB8 diagonal. The situation before us arose because (a) White's KP took two moves to get to e4; (b) the move 8 P–QR3 was wasteful; and (c) Black could play . . . B–R6 directly (without prior protection of his QBP) because 11 B×B Q×B 12 N×P?? would have

failed to 12 . . . N–KN5, a tactical point which is not the case in, say, B6, B7, or many lines of C, D, and E.

The text follows Schmidt-Taimanov, Helsinki 1966, instructive in all its aspects: 14 . . . P–B3 15 N(5)–B3 N–K3 16 Q–Q2 N–KB2 17 QR–N1 P–QR3! 18 P–QR4 P–QR4 19 P–QN4 P×P 20 R×P N(2)–Q1 21 N–B1 P–R4! 22 N(1)–K2 P–B5 23 P×P P×P 24 B–B2 N–N4 25 N–KN1 N×BP! 26 N×N Q–N5ch 27 B–N3 P×B 28 P×P P–R5 29 N×P R×R 30 K×R Q×NP 31 N–N2 Q–B6ch 32 K–N1 B–Q5ch (see note to 13 P–B3) 33 K–R2 Q–R4ch 34 K–N3 Q–K4ch 0–1.

B5

6 ...	**B–Q2**

Fairly common in the past, but d7 seems an inferior square for this piece, as Black now lacks room in which to manoeuvre.

7 P–Q4!

Other moves are less precise:

a) **7 0–0** P–KR4!?. and if 8 P–KR4, 8 . . . P–KN4! is undesirable for White (Mikenas' idea). Best is 8 N–Q5 P–R5 9 N(2)–B3. A surer course for Black after 7 0–0 might be 7 . . . Q–B1 8 N–Q5 N(3)–K2!.

b) **7 P–KR3** Q–B1 8 P–N3 KN–K2 9 B–N2 0–0 10 P–Q3?! R–K1 11 Q–Q2 P–QR3 12 0–0–0? (12 K–B1 Δ K–N1–R2!) 12 . . . P–QN4 ∓ Goldberg-Smyslov, 17th USSR Ch 1949. Of course 10 P–Q4 is more to the point, but White can hardly claim any advantage.

c) **7 N–Q5** Q–B1 may transpose, but not if White plays 8 P–QN4?! N(3)–K2! 9 N(2)–B3 N×N 10 P×N N–B3 11 B–N2 0–0 12 0–0 B–R6 = Donner-Pachman, Buenos Aires 1955.

    7 . . .   Q–B1

    8 N–Q5!

Or **8 P–Q5** N(3)–K2 9 P–K4 P–KR4?! 10 N–KN1! N–R3 11 Q–K2 ('? 11 P–B4; **11 . . . P×P** 12 P×P P–KB4 13 P–K5 P×P 14 P×P B×P 15 N–B3; or **11 . . . 0–0** 12 P×P P×P 13 N–B3'-Korchnoi, with White better in both cases) 11 . . . P–KB4 12 P–B4 N–B2 13 N–B3 0–0 14 0–0 ± Korchnoi-Polugaevsky, USSR Ch 1963. But the move 8 P–Q5 is less convincing than the text:

    8 . . .   N–Q1

8 . . . N(3)–K2 9 P×P P×P 10 N(2)–B3 P–QB3 11 N–K4! (Shatskes). **8 . . . N–Q1** follows Ilivitsky-Alatortsev, USSR Ch 1948: 9 P×P P×P 10 P–N3 P–QB3 11 N(5)–B3 P–KB4 12 B–QR3 N–B2 13 0–0 Q–B2 14 R–B1!. Since 14 . . . 0–0–0? would allow 15 N–Q5 ±±, Black's position is critical.

B6

    6 . . .   **B–K3**

The move Hort has preferred; it is tricky and unclear. White has several methods of meeting the threat to his QBP:

B61 7 P–Q4
B62 7 N–Q5
B63 7 P–Q3

    7 P–QN3 was awarded a '?' in Smederevac-Smejkal, Polanica

Zdroj 1970: 7 . . . Q–Q2 8 P–KR3 **P–B4** 9 P–Q4 B–B2 10 0–0 P–K5 and Black indeed built up an attack (0–1, 29). But a great improvement is 10 P×P!: 10 . . . B×P 11 B–N2, or 10 . . . P×P 11 Q×Qch K×Q 12 B–R3. On the other hand, **8 . . . KN–K2!**, and if 9 P–Q4, 9 . . . P×P 10 P×P P–Q4 (or here 10 N×P N×N 11 P×N P–Q4) leaves White little to boast of.

B61

    7 P–Q4(*8*)

If there is a 'refutation', this is it. Black has two replies:
B611 7 . . . P×P
B612 7 . . . B×P

B611

    7 . . .   **P×P**

The 'normal' move, not so consequent as 7 . . . B×P, but playable.

    8 N×P

8 P×P? B×BP! and:

a) **9 Q–R4** P–Q4 10 N–B4 N–K2 11 P–N3 B×QP 12 B–N2 P–QN4 ∓∓;

b) **9 B×Nch** P×B 10 Q–R4 B–K3 11 Q×Pch B–Q2 12 Q–K4ch N–K2 ∓;

c) **9 P–Q5** N–K4 10 0–0 N–K2 11 P–B4 N–Q2 12 P–KN4 P–KR4 ∓∓ Pachman-Emma, Mar del Plata 1959.

    8 ...   N×N

8 ... B–Q2 9 0–0 KN–K2 10 P–N3 0–0 11 B–N2 R–N1 12 N–Q5 N–B4 13 N×N(6) P×N 14 B×B N×B **15 N–B4!** and White has a pull, e.g. with Q–Q2–R5 (Taimanov). Here **15 N–B3?!** N–K3! 16 Q–Q2 P–KB4 is equal.

    9 P×N   Q–Q2

Benko–Emma, Skopje 1972, continued **9 ... N–K2** 10 P–Q5! (A nice idea; not 10 B×P?! 0–0! 11 B×R Q×B 12 P–Q5 B–R6 ∞– Benko) 10 ... B–Q2 11 0–0 0–0 12 N–K4 (Black just can't level the game; now if 12 ... N–B4, 13 B–N5!) 12 ... P–KR3 13 B–Q2 P–KB4 14 N–B3 P–KN4!? 15 N–K2 ±.

    10 0–0!

10 B×P R–N1 11 B–Q5 P–QB3 12 B×B Q×Bch =.

    10 ...   N–K2

10 ... B×BP? is a blunder: 11 R–K1ch N–K2 12 B×NP R–N1 13 B–Q5 ±±.

    11 R–K1   0–0
    12 P–Q5   B–B4

13 P–KR3! (As in Benko-Emma, the pawn structure favours White. Now **13 ... P–KR4** -Quinteros-should be tried.) **13 ... Q–Q1?** 14 B–N5 P–KB3 15 B–K3 B–Q2 16 P–B4 N–B4 17 B–B2 P–KR4 18 Q–Q3 K–R2 19 R–K2 P–R3 20 QR–K1 R–B2 21 P–KN4! P×P 22 P×P N–R3 23 P–B5! P×P 24 R–K6! ±± Quinteros-Hort, Vinkovci 1972 (1–0, 37). Black's king was too exposed.

B612

    7 ...   **B×P!**
    8 P–Q5

The natural response, although Black seems to have a good game after the forced series of moves which follows. Perhaps White could experiment with **8 Q–R4!?**, e.g. **8 ... B×N** 9 B×Nch P×B 10 Q×Pch K–B1 11 N×B N–K2 12 Q–B2 ∞. A wild answer to 8 Q–R4 would be **8 ... P–Q4(!)** 9 P–K4! N–K2! (9 ... Q–Q2 10 P×QP N×P 11 Q×B N–B7ch 12 K–Q1 ±±) 10 P×QP (10 B–N5 0–0! 11 P×QP P–N4) 10 ... B×P 11 N×B N×N 12 N–B3 N–N3 13 B×Nch P×B 14 Q×Pch Q–Q2 = /∞.

    8 ...   B×N
    9 Q×B   N–N1
    10 Q–N5ch   N–Q2

11 Q×P R–N1 (Even 11 ... N–B4 12 Q–B6ch K–B1 gives Black a fair game.) 12 Q–R6 (12 Q×RP?? N–B4 13 Q–R3 R–R1 14 Q–N4 N–Q6ch) 12 ... N–B4 13 Q–K2 P–B4 14 P–K4 N–B3 15 P×P P×P 16 B–R3 0–0 (or 16 ... Q–Q2 17 Q–B2 P–K5, or here 17 Q–B3 N–N5) 17 0–0 N(3)–Q2 18 K–R1 K–R1 19 B–K3 P–B5 (19 ... P–K5!) 20 B×N(5) P–B6 21 Q–B4 P×B 22 Q–KN4 N–B3 23 Q×P R×P 24 QR–Q1 R–N5! 25 Q–K2 R–Q5 26 B–N2 P–K5! ∞ Larsen-Suttles, Palma de Mallorca 1970. A valuable game for theory, eventually drawn.

B62

    7 N–Q5   N(3)–K2!

Another idea from the Closed Sicilian (Black being a surprisingly insignificant tempo down). An example of the older set-up is **7 ... Q–Q2** 8 Q–R4 N–B3? (8 ... KN–K2 or 8 ... P–B4) 9 0–0 0–0 10 N(2)–B3 N–K1 11 P–B4 P–B4 12 P–Q3 N–Q1 13 Q–R3! N–B2 14 B–Q2 Q–Q1 15 P×P P×P (? 15 ... N×P ±) 16 N–K7ch K–R1 17 B×P ± Tal-Tcheskovsky, USSR Ch 1969.

8 P–Q4

8 N×N N×N 9 B×P R–QN1 10 B–N2 B×P is terrific for Black.

8 ...   P–QB3
9 N×N   N×N
10 P–Q5

The game Panno-Hort, Palma de Mallorca 1969 (with the moves 5 R–QN1 P–QR4 included), took another course: **11 P–N3** P–KB4 12 B–N2 0–0 13 0–0 B–B2 (∆ ... P–K5) 14 P–Q5 P×P 15 P×P P–QN4 16 P–K4 Q–N3 17 N–B3 QR–B1 ∓.

10 ...   B–N5
11 P–B3?

11 P–KR3 (Hort)′ =.

11 ...   B–Q2
12 N–B3   P×P
13 P×P   P–QN4! ∓

With this characteristic thrust, Black wins space on the queenside, and has superior prospects on both wings, Benko-Hort, Venice 1969 (0–1, 59).

B63

7 P–Q3   Q–Q2

With the moves 5 P–QR3 P–QR4 included, Larsen-Gerusel, Büsum 1969 illustrated another Black strategy: 8 ... KN–K2 9 N–Q5 0–0 10 N(2)–B3 Q–Q2 11 B–Q2 N–Q1 12 0–0 N–B1 13

P–K4, and now 13 ... P–QB3 14 N–K3 P–KB4 was best.

8 0–0

8 N–Q5 N–Q1 9 P–K4 P–QB3 10 N–K3 B–R6 = Benko-Hort, Wijk an Zee 1970.

8 ...   P–KR4!
9 P–KR4   N–R3
10 N–Q5 N–Q1 11 P–K4 (11 P–N3! is more flexible.) 11 ... P–QB3 12 N–K3 N–N5 13 P–B3 N×N 14 B×N P–KB4 (similar to B4. Black holds some advantage due to his prospective pawn breaks on all fronts. White's structure is essentially static, as was confirmed by:) 15 P–B4? N–B2! 16 Q–B2 N–R3 17 QR–Q1 N–N5 18 B–B1 Q–QB2 (∆ ... Q–N3ch) Jankovič-Hort, Czechoslovakia 1970. Black's edge is already decisive.

B7

6 ...   KN–K2(9)

In accordance with 'ancient' principles: knights before bishops and attention to the centre prior to action on the wings. However suspect such generalities, this versatile developing move is Black's most popular choice after 6 KN–K2.

B71 7 P–Q4
B72 7 0–0
B73 7 R–QN1

B71

   7 P–Q4   P×P
   8 P×P

More ambitious than **8 N×P** because it frees the QB and keeps pieces on the board. Nevertheless, Black must play carefully after 8 N×P:

a) **8 ... N×N?** 9 P×N 0–0 10 0–0 N–B4 11 P–Q5 R–K1 (maybe 11 ... B×N!?) 12 N–K4! (Black has problems similar to those in B612; 13 B–N5 threatens.) 12 ... P–KR3 13 Q–Q3 K–R2 14 R–N1 N–K2 15 B–Q2 P–KB4 16 N–B3 N–N1 17 KR–K1 B–Q2 18 N–K2 Δ N–Q4 ± Reinfeld-Adams, 1941.

b) **8 ... R–QN1** is not well-tested, but was successful in Dubinin-Ivashin, corres 1940: 9 0–0 0–0 10 P–KR3 P–QR3 11 N(4)–K2 P–QN4 12 P×P P×P 13 P–K4 P–N5 14 N–Q5 B–QR3 15 R–K1 N–K4 ∓. Nor is 8 ... R–QN1 9 P–N3 N×N 10 P×N N–B4 any problem, so White should try 9 N(4)–K2 e.g. 9 ...0–0 10 0–0 B–K3 11 P–N3 Q–Q2 12 B–N2 P–QR3 13 P–QR4 B–R6 14 Q–Q2 with a bare advantage.

c) **8 ... B–Q2!** 9 0–0 0–0 10 N(4)–K2 (preferable to 10 P–KR3 N×N 11 P×N N–B4 12 N–K2 – 12 P–Q5 B×N 13 P×B Q–B3 is now appropriate – 12 ... Q–B3 13 B×NP QR–K1 14 B–N2 N×QP ∓ Goldberg-Lissitsin, 1956) 10 ... Q–B1 11 N–B4 N–K4 12 Q–K2 R–K1 13 B–Q2 P–QB3 14 N–K4 Q–B2 15 B–QB3 QR–Q1 16

P–KR3 P–Q4!? = /∞ Smyslov-Radovic, Tel Aviv 1964.

   8 ...   0–0

A case might be made for inserting 7 0–0 0–0 before trying 8 P–Q4 because now, instead of 8 ... 0–0, Black can cause a disturbance with **8 ... B–N5!?** e.g. 9 P–KR3 B×N 10 N×B N–B4 11 P–Q5 N–K4 12 R–QN1 P–QR3 13 Q–R4ch?! P–QN4! 14 P×P N–Q6ch 15 K–B1 0–0 16 B–B3 Q–N1 ∓ Tukmakov-Wright, Hastings 1969 (but ½–½, 29).

   9 0–0   B–N5

The most difficult move to contend with, but Black has two other continuations of interest:

a) **9 ... R–K1** (Black strengthens his position before deciding on ... N–B4 or the development of his queen's bishop.) 10 P–KR3 N–B4 11 P–Q5 N–R4! (awkward to meet, e.g. 12 P–N3? R×N!) 12 Q–Q3 P–B4 13 P–KN4?! N–R5 14 B–K3 N×B ∓ Müller-Nilsson, corres (0–1, 26).

b) **9 ... N–B4** (somewhat discredited by a game of Botvinnik's, yet this move too is reasonable) 10 P–Q5 N–K4 (Gheorghiu opines that 10 ... N(3)–Q5 11 N×N N×N is equal, but 12 B–K3 N–B4 13 B–Q2 is suspiciously akin to Benko-Emma in B612 and to Reinfeld-Adams above.) 11 P–N3 P–QR4? (Too static. Botvinnik suggests **11 ... P–QR3!** 12 B–N2** P–QN4 13 P×P P×P 14 Q–B2 P–N5 15 N–K4 B–QR3. This was tested in Roizman-Livshits, Belorussia Ch 1970, but White answered **12**

P–QR4(!), preventing . . . P–QN4, and then **12 . . . P–KR4?!** 13 P–R3 N–Q2 14 R–N1 P–R4 15 N–K4 N–B4 16 N(2)–B3 led to White's control of the ensuing play. **12 . . . P–QR4** 13 R–N1 N–Q2 14 N–K4 P–KR3 15 N(2)–B3 P–N3 looks like a solider move order.) 12 B–N2 N–Q2 13 P–QR3 N–B4 (? Useless, but in contrast to the last note, White's mobile pawns on the queenside are´a valuable asset in any case.) 14 P–QN4 N–Q2 15 Q–N3 N–Q5 16 N×N B×N 17 QR–Q1 B–N2 18 KR–K1 P×P 19 P×P N–B3 20 P–R3 P–R4 21 P–B5! ± Botvinnik-Reshevsky, AVRO 1938.

10 P–B3

10 P–KR3 B×N 11 N×B N–B4 12 P–Q5 N–K4 (12 . . . N(3)–Q5 13 N×N – 13 N–B3 – 13 . . . N×N 14 B–Q2 R–K1 = Nikitin-Uusi, Spartakiade 1967. 14 R–N1 ±- Gheorghiu) 13 Q–B2 R–K1 (a position from analysis by Botvinnik) 14 B–Q2 P–QR4 15 QR–K1 N–Q2 16 B–K4 N–Q5 17 N×N B×N 18 P–N3 N–B4 19 B–KB3 P–N3 = Saidy-Gheorghiu, Los Angeles 1974.

.   10 . . .   B–B4

10 . . . B–B1 11 P–Q5 N–K4 12 P–N3 P–QR3?! (12 . . . P–QB3!? confronts the issue, at any rate) 13 B–N5! P–R3 14 B–K3 N–B4 15 B–B2 R–K1 16 Q–Q2 ± Averbakh-Bannik, USSR Ch 1954.

11 P–KN4   B–B1

12 P–Q5

Consequent. **12 B–B4** met a vigorous response in Larsen-Spassky, Belgrade 1964: 12 . . .

P–Q4! 13 P–B5 P–N3! 14 N–N5 B–QR3 15 N×BP B×N 16 Q×B N×P 17 Q–Q3 R–B1 18 P×P P×P 19 B–K3 N(2)–B3 ∓.

12 . . .   N–K4
13 P–N3 P–QB3 14 B–K3 Q–R4 15 Q–Q2 P–QN4! 16 P×NP P×NP 17 P–QR3 B–N2 18 P–R3 N×QP ∓ Sadomsky-Murei, corres 1965. If 19 N×N Q×Q 20 N–K7ch K–R1 21 B×Q, 21 . . . KR–K1!.

CONCLUSION:

7 P–Q4 P×P 8 P×P is more dangerous for White than Black.

B72
    7 0–0
White doesn't hurry to commence operations as he did in B71.
    7 . . .   0–0 (10)
a) **7 . . . P–KR4!?** storms the ramparts, and White must take the invasion seriously:
a1) **8 P–KR3?!** (the only move examined by Schwarz, who therefore awards 7 . . . P–KR4 an '!') 8 . . . P–R5 9 P–KN4 P–B4 10 P×P (10 P–B3? B–K3 11 P–Q3 P–Q4) 10 . . . B×P 11 P–Q4 P×P 12 N×P N×N 13 P×N Q–Q2 14 R–K1 (Schwarz), is about equal;
a2) **8 P–KR4.** Now Shatskes suggests '**8 . . . P–KN4!** 9 P×P P–R5 with good attacking chances.' After 10 N–K4!, however, it seems that Black is struggling to keep those chances alive. Better might be **8 . . . B–N5**, holding back White's P–Q4 (9 P–B3 B–K3); the idea is to continue with . . . Q–Q2 and in some cases . . . 0–0–0 and . . . P–KN4;

a3) **8 P–Q4** P–R5?! (8 . . . P×P 9
P×P P–R5 10 B–B4 B–B4 or 9 N×P
P–R5 ∞) 9 P×KP? (9 P–Q5! ±) 9 . . .
N×P 10 P–B4 N(4)–B3 11 P–K4?
P×P 12 N×P (12 P×P B–N5 ∓) 12
. . . B–Q5ch 13 K–R1 N–KN1! (Δ
. . . R×Pch) ∓∓) Batchelder-
Watson, Los Angeles 1975;
a4) **8 N–Q5** P–R5!? (8 . . . N×N 9
P×N N–K2 Δ 10 P–Q4 P–R5 11
P×KP B×P! ∞ or 10 P–KR4 B–N5
11 P–B3 B–Q2 12 N–B3 P–QB3 =)
9 N(2)–B3 P×P (9 . . . B–K3 or 9
. . . B–B4 is preferable.) 10 BP×P
B–R6 11 B×B R×B 12 N–K4! ±
(Shatskes / Taimanov). Not 12
R×P!? R×Pch! 13 P×R K×R =.

A thorny variation! Black has a
calmer alternative in
b) **7 . . . B–K3** 8 N–Q5 Q–Q2, a
position that could transpose to B62
i.e. 9 Q–R4 etc.

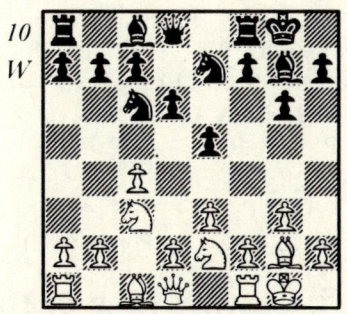

10
W

8 R–N1

The diagrammed position is a
popular one; some informative
examples:

a) **8 P–N3** B–K3 9 N–Q5 P–B4 10
N×Nch Q×N 11 P–Q4 P–B5! 12
P–Q5? (12 NP×P P×QP =) 12 . . .
B–N5 13 P–B3 P–K5! 14 P×B
P B6! with a powerful attack,

Goldin-Murei, Moscow 1966.
b) **8 N–Q5** N×N 9 P×N N–K2 10
P–Q4 N–B4! 11 P×P P×P 12 P–K4
N–Q3 ∓ (A 'Nimzowitsch knight'!)
Alexander-Reshevsky, Nottingham
1936. As Botvinnik pointed out,
N–Q5 is not often desirable or
necessary before . . . B–K3 has been
played.
c) **8 P–Q3** is a common move (see
also Section C). Then **8 . . . P–B4** 9
P–B4! merely limits Black's QB, so
we examine:
c1) **8 . . . P–KR3** 9 R–N1 P–KN4?!
10 P–QN4 N–N3 11 P–N5
N(B)–K2 12 Q–N3 K–R1 13
P–QR4 R–QN1 14 N–Q5 P–KB4
15 P–B4! B–K3 16 N×N Q×N 17
Q–B2 Q–Q2 18 P–Q4 NP×P 19
KP×P P×QP 20 B–N2 ± Szabo-
Damjanović, Beverwijk 1966 (1–0,
34). White is particularly well-
situated to meet a kingside pawn
storm in this variation;
c2) **8 . . . B–K3** exhibited a Sicilian-
ish look in Robatsch-Boey, Nice
1974: 9 N–Q5 Q–Q2 10 R–N1
N–Q1 11 P–QN4 N–B1?! (11 . . .
P–QB3 12 N×Nch ±) 12 P–N5
P–QB3 13 N(5)–B3! P–Q4? (13 . . .
B–R6 14 B–R3 ±-Robatsch) 14
B–QR3 R–K1 15 NP×P NP×P
16 Q–R4! ±:
c3) **8 . . . B–B4(!)** discourages 9
N–Q5 (9 . . . N×N). If 9 P–K4, 9 . . .
B–K3 transposes to E32 below
(about equal).

| 8 . . . | P–QR4 |
| 9 P–QR3 | B–B4 |

Usually superior to . . . B–K3,
because White's N–Q5 can still be
answered by . . . N×N.

| 10 P Q3 | Q–Q2 |

11 R–K1

To save his king bishop, White exposes himself to an attack. **11 P–QN4** P×P 12 P×P B–R6 13 P–N5 B×B 14 K×B N–Q1 15 B–N2 is safer, but does not promise much.

11 ...   B–R6

Against **11 ... N–Q1(!)**, White has no simple way to make inroads. Shatskes gives **12 P–QN4** P×P 13 P×P P–QB3! 14 P–N5 P–Q4, when 15 P×QP P×QP 16 N–R4?! allows 16 ... R×N! 17 Q×R B×P. And **12 N–Q5** is harmless: 12 ... N×N 13 P×N P–B4! 14 P×Pe.p. N×P 15 N–B3 N–K2 16 P–QN4 KR–B1 = Selesniev-Gratvoll, Perm 1967.

12 B–R1

12 B×B? would resemble Korchnoi-Lisitsin in A11.

12 ...   P–B4

13 P–QN4?

If White wants to allow ... P–B5 at all. **13 Q–R4** would at least keep his QN protected. Natural is **13 P–B4**, but Taimanov thinks that 13 ... P–KN4! 14 P×NP N–N3 15 N–Q5 P–KR3 16 P×P B×P △ ... P–B5 would be strong.

13 P–QN4? follows Bakulin-Murei, Moscow 1968: 13 ... P×P 14 P×P P–B5 15 P–N5 P×NP 16 N×P (if 16 RP×P or 16 BP×P, 16 ... Q–B4 ∓∓) 16 ... N–Q1 17 N(B)–K4 N–N3 18 P–B3 P–R4! ∓.

CONCLUSION:

After 7 0–0, Black may continue speculatively with **7 ... P–KR4!?** or await events by **7 ... 0–0.** In the latter case, he does well to avoid early kingside pawn charges, and to develop by ... B–KB4! rather than

by ... B–K3 (which encourages N–Q5).

B73

7 R–QN1 (*11*)

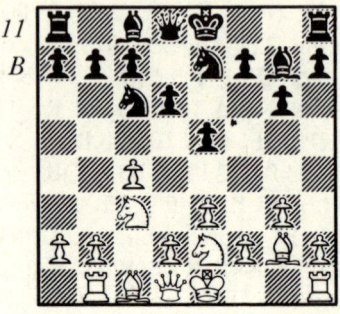

7 ...   B–K3

Again

a) **7 ... B–B4!** probably equalizes: 8 P–Q3 Q–Q2 9 N–Q5 (9 P–KR4 0–0 10 P–QN4 N–Q1 11 P–K4 B–K3 12 P–R5 P–KB4 13 RP×P N×P = /∞ Korchnoi-Holmov, Leningrad 1967) 9 ... P–KR4?! (But 9 ... 0–0! △ 10 0–0 N×N = or 10 N(2)–B3 N–Q1 11 N–K4 N×N 12 P×N B–R6 =) 10 P–KR4 0–0 11 N(2)–B3 N–Q1 12 N–K4 P–KB3 13 P–QN4 P–B3 14 N×Nch Q×N 15 P–N5 ± Popov-Nikitin, 1970.

b) The moves **7 ... P–QR4** 8 P–QR3 are often inserted here e.g. b1) **8 ... B–K3** 9 N–Q5 Q–Q2 (9 ... N–B4?! 10 P–QN4 P×P 11 P×P N–N1!? 12 P–K4 N–K2 13 P–Q4 N(2)–B3 14 B–N5! P–B3 15 B–K3 ± Benko-Keres, Candidates 1959. ... N–B4 worked badly because Black could not undertake anything positive.) 10 P–Q3 0–0 11 0–0 K–R1 12 B–Q2 P–B4 13 P–B4

B–N1 14 Q–R4! (Δ Q–N5) 14 . . .
N×N 15 P×N N–N1 16 Q–B2 ±
Gulko-Smyslov, USSR Ch 1977;
b2) **8 . . . 0–0** 9 P–Q3 **B–Q2?!**
(More pointed was **9 . . . B–N5!** 10
P–R3 B×N 11 Q×B P–B4 12 P–B4
K–R1 13 B–Q2 N–KN1!? Δ . . .
N–B3 Skiba-Cylwik, Poland 1975)
10 P–QN4 P×P 11 P×P Q–B1 12
P–R4 P–R4 13 B–Q2 N–Q1 14
Q–B2 P–QB3 15 P–B5! Q–B2 (15
. . . P–Q4 16 N–R4 ±) 16 P×P
Q×P 17 N–K4 Q–B2 18 P–N5
N–Q4 Korchnoi-Gheorghiu, Buch-
arest 1966, and instead of 19
P–N6?!, White could have main-
tained the pressure by 19 0–0.
c) The unhurried **7 . . . 0–0** 8 P–Q3
B–B4 has its points: 9 P–QN4
Q–Q2 10 P–KR3 P–KR3 11 Q–B2
P–QR4!? (11 . . . N–Q1!) 12
P–QR3 P×P 13 P×P N–Q1 14
N–Q5 B–K3 15 N(2)–B3 N–B1 16
P–N5 P–QB3 17 N–N4! N–K2 18
N–R4 Q–B2 ∞ Janicki-Watson,
Canada 1975.

8 N–Q5

Appears forced, but a corres-
pondence game Heemsoth-Hunter
showed a different and remarkable
idea for White: **8 P–Q3!** P–Q4 (the
natural response; if 8 . . . Q–Q2 9
N–Q5, Black has lost his chance to
play . . . B–N5 as below. So 9 . . .
0–0 10 0–0 N–Q1 11 P–QN4 N×N
12 P×N B–R6 13 Q–N3 B×B 14
K×B P–QB3 – Averbach-Szabo,
Budapest 1970 – 15 P–K4! ±) 9
P–N3! 0–0 (**9 . . . P×P** 10 NP×P ±
or **9 . . . P–Q5** 10 P×P P×P 11
N–K4 Δ B–N5, P–QN4, N–B5 etc;
9 . . . P–QR4!?) 10 B–QR3 R–K1 11
0–0 P–QR4 12 P–K4! Altogether a

very pretty sequence! White
forces either **12 . . . P–Q5** 13
N–Q5, after which P–QN4
and/or P–B4 are positional
threats; or **12 . . . P×KP** 13 P×P,
when with or without the
exchange of queens, White's
N–Q5 is a move to contend with.
Petrosian-like craftiness!

8 . . .	0–0
9 P–Q3	B–N5!

9 . . . Q–Q2 10 0–0! is the
Averbach-Szabo game of the last
note.

10 P–B3?!

Black was ready to capture the
knight on d5. Correct but harmless
was **10 P–KR3** B–Q2 11 0–0 N×N
12 P×N (the point of Black's ninth
was to compel this recapture.) 12
. . . N–K2 followed by . . . P–QB3
or . . . P–QB4.

10 . . .	B–Q2
11 0–0	N×N

12 P×N N–K2 13 P–B4 P–QB3 14
P×BP B×P 15 Q–N3 B×B 16 K×B
Q–Q2 17 B–Q2 P–KR4! 18
P–KR3 P–Q4 19 R(N)–B1
KR–K1 20 P×P B×P ∓ Kagan-
Spassky, Winnipeg 1967.

CONCLUSION:

7 R–QN1 B–B4 or **7 . . . 0–0** 8 0–0
B–B4 seems level. **7 . . . B–K3** 8
P–Q3! deserves more tests.

In general, 5 P–K3 has proven
sound and fairly flexible; on the
other hand, Black's opening moves
are much too logical to be bad, and
he has a choice of equalizing
variations. In particular, **6 . . .
B–K3** and **6 . . . KN–K2** qualify on
that account, when the problems of

White's loose QBP and inability to play P–K4 without loss of time are highlighted. With correct play, a verdict of '=' must be arrived at. Most other Black replies (such as **6 ... P–B4** and **6 ... B–Q2**) leave something to be desired, although **6 ... N–R3** is a creditable attempt and could have good surprise value.

The body of material with 5 P–K3 is very extensive; only a fraction of it is presented here. The important thing is to become intimate with the applicability and timing of both sides' typical ideas. Naturally too, practical experience is invaluable for clarifying the distinctions between subvariations.

C

5 P–Q3

Logical, emphasizing the light squares and leaving the KN and KP uncommitted.

5 ...   P–Q3

Alekhine once opined that **5 ... KN–K2** was weaker because of 6 R–N1. Theory does not deal with this possibility; but in the author's own experience, Black has indeed had problems getting his knights coordinated:

a) **6 ... 0–0** 7 P–QN4 P–Q3 8 P–K3 (Δ P–N5) 8 ... N–B4 9 KN–K2 (or 9 P–N5!? N(3)–K2 10 Q–R4!-Frankle) 9 ... N(3)–K2 10 0–0 P–QB3 11 P–N5 B–K3 12 B–QR3 Q–B2 13 Q–R4 KR–Q1 14 KR–B1 ± Watson-Frankle, Boston 1977;

b) **6 ... P–QR4** 7 P–QR3 P–Q3 8 P–QN4 P×P 9 P×P 0–0 10 P–K3

P–B4 11 KN–K2 P–KN4!? 12 P–N5 N–N1 13 Q–B2?! (13 N–Q5! ±) 13 ... QN–Q2 14 P–B4 NP×P 15 KP×P N–B4 (=) 16 0–0 P–B3 17 B–K3 N–K3 18 K–R1 N–Q5? 19 B×N P×B 20 P×P (±) ½–½ Watson-Shamkovich, London 1978.

Among 5 P–K3, 5 P–Q3, 5 R–N1, and 5 P–K4, there are naturally many transposition. This section deals with:

C1 6 P–B4
C2 6 B–Q2
C3 6 N–R3
C4 6 P–K3
C5 6 R–N1

Of course, C4 examines variations not already considered in B, and C5 only concerns lines in which White plays P–QN4 as soon as possible thereafter. The move 6 P–K4 is investigated in E.

C1

6 P–B4

Schwarz calls this move 'the best next to **6 R–N1.**' Back in the 1930's, Salo Flohr employed the move with good results. White often gets active piece play from 6 P–B4, but at the cost of weakened central squares (e.g. d4, e3). This kind of 'positional trade,' makes sense only if White acquires lasting pressure (e.g. along the KB-file or on the dark squares around the enemy king), or if he can mobilize his centre pawns. Black can attack the loose White centre with minor pieces and swing his rooks to the open central files. His ease of development accounts for the infrequency of moves like 6 P–B4 in grandmaster praxis today.

6 ... KN–K2

Of course, **6 ... P×P** is possible, but it can also wait. An annoying counterthrust is **6 ... P–KR4!?**: **7 N–B3?!** P–R5! 8 P×RP (8 P×KP P–R6!; 8 N×RP P×P 9 N–B3 P×P 10 P×P R×Rch 11 B×R B–N5 Δ ... N–R3–B4) 8 ... N–Q5 9 P×P P×P! 10 B–N5 P–KB3 11 B–K3 N–R3 ∓ Goldberg-Soloviev, USSR 1969 (0–1, 31). **7 P–KR3** only improves a little after 7 ... N–R3!; best is **7 N–R3!**, transposing to C3.

7 N–B3 0–0

a) **7 ... B–Q2?** gives us a look at White's plan realized: 8 P×P P×P 9 N–K4! N–B4 10 0–0 P–KR3 11 R–N1 Q–K2 12 P–QN4 ∓ Flohr-Muller, 1933.

b) **7 ... B–N5** is better, yet: 8 0–0 0–0 9 P–KR3 B×N 10 B×B N–B4 11 K–R2 P×P 12 B×P R–K1?! (weakens f7) 13 Q–Q2 R–N1 14 B–K4 N(4)–Q5 15 B–Q5! N–K3 16 B–R6 Δ N–K4 ± Flohr-Euwe, Match (3) 1932 (but ½–½, 33).

c) Rather than insist upon giving up the light squares, Black has a logical set-up with **7 ... P–KR3** 8 0–0 B–K3 9 B–Q2 and now, instead of **9 ... 0–0** 10 Q–B1 K–R2 11 R–N1 Q–Q2 12 P×P Flohr-Steiner, 1933, **9 ... P×P!** puts a finger on the weak points of White's strategy: 10 B×P P–Q4 (also **10 ... 0–0** 11 Q–Q2 P–KN4 12 B–K3 P–Q4) 11 P×P (11 N–QN5 R–QB1) 11 ... N×P 12 B–Q2 0–0 13 N×N B×N 14 B–B3 P–B4. Then White's centre is immobilized and exposed to attack

from Black's rooks.

8 0–0 P–KR3

8 ... B–N5 9 P–KR3 B–Q2 10 B–Q2 Q–B1 11 K–R2 P–QR4 12 P–QR3 P–B3 13 P–K3 ± Stoyko-Mansang, 1977).

9 P–K4 P–B4?!

Rather cooperative. Again, the simple **9 ... P×P** 10 P×P (10 B×P B–N5!) 10 ... P–B4 is available, or **9 ... B–K3** 10 B–K3 Q–Q2 11 Q–Q2 K–R2 12 P–QN4! N–Q5 13 B×N P×B 14 N–K2 P–QB4 15 N–R4 P–B4 16 P×QBP P×KP = /∞ Kirilov-Avrosimov, Latvian Ch 1970.

10 N–Q5 N×N
11 BP×N N–Q5
12 P×KP N×Nch
13 B×N ±

Alekhine-Tarrasch, Vienna 1922. White has good prospects on the queenside.

C2

6 B–Q2 and:

C21 6 ... N–B3
C22 6 ... KN–K2

Otherwise:

a) **6 ... P–KR4?!** 7 N–B3 B–Q2 8 P–QR3 Q–B1 9 P–R3 N–R3 10 N–Q5 N–Q1 11 N–N5! N–K3 (Obviously 11 ... P–QB3 12 N–K4! is unpalatable.) 12 N×N B×N 13 B–R5! (similar to Geller's idea in the Closed Sicilian) 13 ... P–N3 14 B–Q2 P–QB3 15 N–B3 ± Petrosian-Ree, Skopje 1972. Typically, Petrosian's manoeuvres resulted in emphasizing the strength of his king's bishop.

b) **6 ... P–B4** 7 R–N1 (White could adapt Black's Closed Sicilian strategy of **7 N–R3** N–B3 8 P–B4 0–0 9 0–0 P–KR3 and now 10 N–Q5 △ B–B3; his extra tempo is handy.) 7 . . . N–B3 8 P–QN4 0–0 9 P–N5 N–Q5 10 P–K3 N–K3 11 P–B4 N–B4 12 Q–B2 R–K1 13 KN–K2 ½–½, Bilek-Dely, Hungary 1959.

c) **6 . . . B–K3** 7 N–B3 (**7 P–QN4!?** Q–Q2 8 P–N5 N–Q1 9 P–QR4 has a certain charm.) 7 . . . P–KR3 8 0–0 Q–Q2 9 R–K1 (questionable, since Black has a standard attack and White's B–Q2 gets in his own way) 9 . . . B–R6 10 B–R1 N–B3 11 Q–B1? (And this is downright feeble. White must play aggressively e.g. 11 P–QN4, 11 Q–R4, or 11 N–Q5.) 11 . . . N–KN5 12 N–Q5 P–B4 13 R–N1 0–0 14 B–B3 QR–K1 15 P–K3 P–KN4 16 P–N4 P–K5 ∓ Naranja-Schiffer, Bad Pyrmont 1970. The Black attack played itself.

C21
6 . . .	**N–B3**

7 N–B3

7 R–N1 △ P–QN4–N5 has lost its impact, since White's bishop is no longer headed for a3.

7 . . .	P–KR3

Schwarz criticizes this preventive move, but offers no alternative. On **7 . . . 0–0,** 8 Q–B1 gives the game a different character e.g. 8 . . . R–K1 (8 . . . N–Q5!?) 9 B–N5! N–Q5 (What else? 9 . . . B–B4 10 N–KR4 B–K3 11 0–0 etc.) 10 N×N P×N 11 N–K4 B–B4 12 0–0 ±.

8 Q–B1	B–K3
9 0–0	Q–Q2

10 P–K4 (White has no simple plan at hand. **10 R–K1** B–R6 11 B–R1 N–KN5 is risky, while **10 R–N1** B–R6 11 N–Q5 B×B is equal.) 10 . . . N–KN1? (Irresolute. **10 . . . B–R6!** 11 N–Q5? B×B 12 K×B 0–0–0 13 N×N B×N 14 B×P? R×B! 15 Q×R R–R1, etc. ∓∓-Schwarz) 11 N–Q5 KN–K2 12 P–QN4 ± Carls-Grünfeld, 1920 (1–0, 39).

C22
6 . . .	**KN–K2** (*12*)

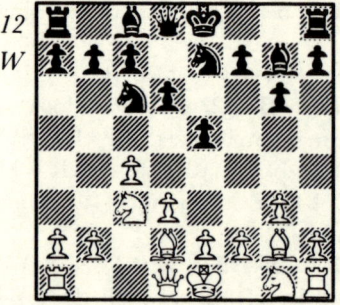

As in B, this deployment of the KN is logical and strong.

7 N–B3

With ideas similar to A1. The most consistent independent idea is **7 Q–B1**. Then Black can play the reliable **7 . . . P–KR3**; or **7 . . . N–Q5!?**, as in the instructive encounter Suttles-Liberzon, Venice 1974: 8 P–KR4 (probably a mistake. If White does not rid himself of Black's knight, he suffers in the centre. Therefore **8 P–K3** N–K3 9 KN–K2 and if 9 . . . 0–0 10 0–0 P–QB3 11 P–K4 N–Q5 12 N×N P×N 13 N–K2 with a fairly effective 'Botvinnik' position – compare E) 8 . . . P–KR3 9 R–N1

P–QR4 ('∓'-Liberzon) 10 P–N3
P–QB3 11 N–R3 P–R4 12 N–KN5
(Perhaps White should pause a
move for the less whimsical **12
P–K3** N–K3 13 N–K4) 12 . . . 0–0
13 N–R4 P–N3 ('∓'-Liberzon.
Black is harmoniously centralized.)
14 B–K3 B–Q2 15 B×N P×B 16 0–0
N–B4 17 B–K4 R–B1 18 Q–K1
R–K1 19 N–N2 Q–B3 20 P–R3
B–R3 21 N–B3 N–K2 ! ∓.

    7 . . .   0–0
    8 0–0

8 Q–B1 N–B4 9 P–KR4 (? **9 0–0**
is stauncher.) 9 . . . P–B3! 10 N–Q5
B–K3 11 P–R5 Heinicke-Stephan,
1953, and now 11 . . . Q–Q2!
(Schwarz), when White's attack is
dead.

    8 . . .   B–Q2
    9 R–N1   Q–B1
10 P–QN4 B–R6 11 P–N5 N–Q5
12 P–R4 B×B 13 K×B Q–Q2 =
Petrosian-Boleslavsky, Candidates
1953. **13 . . . N–K3** (Schwarz) was
also interesting, as White's bishop
on d2 interferes with his desire to
play P–Q4.

CONCLUSION:

6 B–Q2 lacks the impetus to achieve
much.

C3
   6 N–R3
   I feel that this move deserves
closer attention. White does not
move an already effective piece (6
B–Q2), nor block off one or the
other of his fine bishops (6 P–K3, 6
P–K4, 6 N–B3). He is prepared to
block a Black pawn rush on the
king's wing with P–KB4, and for his

own part has a variety of positive
plans among which he will choose
according to how Black deploys his
pieces:
C31 6 . . . P–KR4
C32 6 . . . KN–K2

  6 . . . P–KR3 covers g5 and
prepares . . . B–K3: 7 0–0 B–K3 8
P–B4 Q–Q2 (**8 . . . KN–K2** 9
N–Q5 P–B4 10 B–Q2 0–0 11
B–QB3 ±) 9 N–B2 KN–K2 (**9 . . .
N–B3** 10 P×P P×P 11 K–R1 Δ
N(2)–K4 ±) 10 N–Q5 (10 P×P!?)
10 . . . B×N 11 P×B N–Q1 12 P×P
B×P 13 N–K4 P–KB4 14 N–B3 ±.

C31

  6 . . .   **P–KR4!?** (*13*)

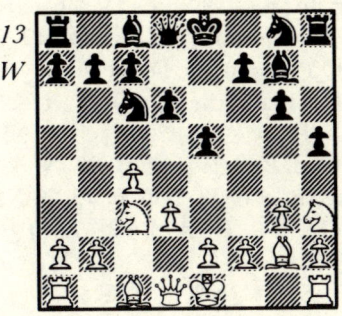

13
W

A very important try, since White
cannot stop . . . P–R5.
    7 P–B4
   After this push, Black's attacking
chances may seem intimidating,
although the author, who has
played both sides, feels that White is
objectively safe. For those who wish
to approach the situation more
cautiously, **7 P–N3** makes a good
impression. Then **7 . . . P–R5(?)** 8
B–N2 B×N?! 9 B×B P×P 10 RP×P

Q–B1!? 11 B–N2! R×Rch 12 B×R Q–R6 13 K–Q2! achieves nothing for Black but the weakening of his light squares. Better is **7 . . . B–Q2** 8 B–N2 Q–B1 9 N–KN1! (or **9 N–KN5** P–B3 10 N–KB3 B–R6 11 B×B Q×B 12 N–Q5 with a very slight plus) with an interesting position in which White's loss of time is balanced by Black's weakening . . . P–KR4 and passively-placed queen and bishop e.g. **9 . . . P–R5** (?) 10 P–K3 KN–K2 11 N–Q5 $\pm$ or **9 . . . KN–K2** 10 N–Q5 0–0 11 P–K3 (or 11 Q–Q2) 11 . . . B–K3 12 N–K2.

    7 . . .   P–R5
    8 N–B2   KN–K2

Watson–C. Evans, Vancouver 1977, continued **8 . . . N–R3** 9 N–Q5 (probably better simply 9 R–QN1 as in the text) 9 . . . N–K2! 10 N–K4 N(2)–B4?? (10 . . . N×N!) 11 P×KP P–R6 12 B–B3 N–N1 (forced; else 13 B–N5) 13 B–N5 Q–Q2 14 P×P P×P 15 0–0 $\pm\pm$.

    9 R–QN1!   B–K3
    10 N(3)–K4   Q–Q2

11 P–QN4 N–Q5 12 P–K3 P×NP 13 RP×P N(5)–B4 14 N–N4?! (White has imperturbably set about his business, and **14 R×Rch!** B×R 15 N–N4 N–N1 16 B–B3 – against 16 . . . N×NP – would have kept some advantage.) 14 . . . R×Rch 15 B×R 0–0–0! 16 N(K)–B6 R–R1 17 B–KN2 Q–Q1 18 Q–B3 P–QB3 19 P–N5?! Q–R4ch 20 B–Q2 Q×RP 21 Q–Q1 B×N $\mp\mp$ Stoyko–Watson, New York 1975.

C32

    6 . . .   **KN–K2**
    7 P–B4

7 0–0 is riskier due to 7 . . . P–KR4!

    7 . . .   0–0

Now **7 . . . P–KR4** 8 P×P P×P 9 N–K4 P–R5 10 B–N5, or here 9 . . . P–B4 10 N–B3! (e.g. 10 . . . P–R5 11 B–N5) only emphasizes White's positional assets.

    8 0–0   P–B4

Black can play **8 . . . P–KR3** as above. Then 9 N–B2 P–B4 10 B–Q2 K–R2 11 R–N1 N–Q5 12 P–K3 N–K3 13 P–QN4 P–B3 14 P–N5 P–B4 15 P–QR4 R–QN1 16 N–Q5 Q–K1 17 B–QB3 B–Q2 18 Q–Q2 was Golombek–Broadbent, British Ch, Play-off 1947. Black played **18 . . . Q–B2?** 19 P×P P×P 20 Q–N2 $\pm$; but even after the better **18 . . . R–B2** or **18 . . . P×P**, White would be nicely centralized.

    9 B–Q2   K–R1
    10 R–N1

10 P–K3 forms a reliable pawn structure à la the Sicilian Defence.

    10 . . .   P–QR4
    11 P–QR3   B–K3

12 N–Q5 (12 **P–QN4** P×NP 13 P×NP P–Q4!? 14 P–N5 N–QN1 15 P×KP P×P! ∞) 12 . . . Q–Q2 13 P–QN4 (Here **13 B–QB3** makes a good impression, too.) 13 . . . P×NP 14 P×NP N–Q1 (**14 . . . P–K5!?** 15 P–N5 N–Q1 16 Q–N3 $\pm$ or 14 . . . R–R7 15 P–N5 N–Q1 16 N–N4 R–R1 17 B–QB3 $\pm$) 15 P–N5 and White's is the easier position to play. 15 N×N Q×N 16 P–N5 Δ P×P, B–N4 is also moderately advantageous.

C4

6 P–K3

Yet another attempt to achieve a Closed Sicilian Reversed. Now **6 ... P–B4** is B2, and **6 ... N–B3** (not a bad idea versus White's P–Q3 and P–K3) is B1. We look at:
C41 6 ... P–KR4!?
C42 6 ... KN–K2

C41

6 ... P–KR4!?
7 P–KR4?!

Often a mistake when played this early. **7 P–KR3** should be right, when Black may try to tie White to the defence of his KRP, e.g. 7 ... B–K3 **8 KN–K2!?** Q–Q2 9 R–QN1 (9 N–Q5 N–Q1) 9 ... KN–K2 10 P–QN4 (Δ 10 ... P–Q4 11 P–N5 N–Q1 12 P×P N×P 13 N–K4) 10 ... P–R5 11 P–N5 N–Q1 12 P–N4 P–KB4 with good counterplay. **8 R–N1** would be more foresighted, intending 8 ... Q–Q2 9 P–QN4 KN–K2 (9 ... P–R5 10 P–N5 N–Q1 11 P×P! R×P 12 N–K4) 10 P–N5 N–Q1 11 P–QR4, but such positions are far from clear.

7 ...   N–R3
8 KN–K2   B–N5
9 Q–Q2   0–0

10 P–N3 Q–Q2 11 B–N2 QR–K1 12 0–0–0 (rather than 'castle into it,' but White can be attacked on the queenside too:) **12 ... P–QR4** ∓ Hug-Calvo, Palma de Mallorca 1972 (½–½, 86). Or here **12 ... P–QR3!?** ∓.

C42

6 ...   KN–K2
7 R–N1

7 KN–K2 B–K3 (7 ... P–KR4 is still plausible) 8 N–Q5 0–0 9 0–0 R–QN1!? Δ ... P–QR3 is best met by 10 R–QN1 **P–QR3** 11 P–QN4 P–QN4 12 B–Q2, or here **10 ... P–QN4!?** 11 B–Q2, or **10 ... B×N** 11 P×B N–N5 12 P–K4! (12 Q–N3 P–QB4!) 12 ... P–QB4 13 P–QR3 N–R3 14 B–N5 P–B3 15 B–K3 P–R3 16 Q–Q2 K–R2 17 P–KR4 ±.

7 ...   P–QR4
8 KN–K2 (*14*)

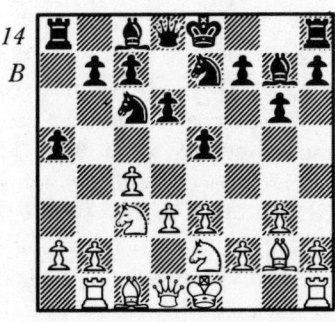

14
B

'Normal-looking' but leading to obtuse problems is **8 P–QR3**, e.g. 8 ... B–K3 9 N–Q5 Q–Q2 10 P–QN4 P×P 11 P×P 0–0 12 P–N5 N–Q1 13 Q–B2 (White plays to prevent ... B–R6 as long as possible.) 13 ... N–B1 14 N–K2 P–QB3 15 P×P P×P 16 P–R3! Q–R2 (16 ... P×N 17 P×P ±) 17 N–N4 N–K2 18 N(2)–B3 P–KB4 19 0–0 (19 P–B4!?) 19 ... P–N4! 20 K–R2 (The influence of the queen on a7 is felt.) **20 ... R–B1?** (trying to enforce ... P–Q4, but ... P–B5 is more important: **20 ... P–B5!** 21 Q–K2 Q–Q2 with a double-edged struggle) 21 P–B4 NP×P 22 KP×P N–N3 23 N–K2 P–Q4 (positionally suspect, but otherwise White will take over the queenside files) 24 P×KP P×P 25 N–B4! P×P 26 N(N)×QP N×P 27 N×N B×N 28 R–K1 Q–R7 29 B–N2 B×N 30 P×B Q–B5 31 Q–B2 R–KB2 32 R(N)–QB1 Q–R5 33 Q–N3ch K–B1 34 B–R3ch ±± Watson-S. Ball, Vancouver 1977.

8 . . .   P–R4(!)

Apparently this idea gains in effectiveness from White's P–K3 and KN–K2.

9 N–Q5?!   N×N
10 P×N   N–K2

11 P–KR4 0–0 12 N–B3 P–QB3 (White's advanced QP is liquidated and his queenside chances are correspondingly reduced. **9 N–Q5** should have been replaced by **9 P–KR3.**) 13 0–0 B–N5 14 Q–N3? (14 Q–Q2) 14 . . . Q–Q2 15 K–R2 N×P! 16 N×N P–R5 (A tactical device which forces White to relinquish his hold on d5.) 17 Q–B4 P×N 18 Q×P R–R2! ∓ Barcza-Polugaevsky, Sochi 1966. Black's centre cannot be restrained (. . . B–K3) and he also has attacking possibilities (0–1, 34).

CONCLUSION:

6 P–K3 is solid, and even promising against the wrong plan; but either **6 . . . N–B3** or **6 . . . KN–K2** will equalize if handled properly.

C5

6 R–N1

Condemned by Taimanov and Shatskes as an inaccurate move order. Yet 6 R–N1 is in one way more cunning than 5 R–N1: Black can no longer play for . . . P–Q4 in one jump! (Compare D4). If nothing else, White can use 6 R–N1 to transpose into positions already discussed or to various other systems that Black employs in the Closed Sicilian. For example, on **6 . . . P–B4**, both 7 P–K3 and 7 P–K4 are productive continuations; also, **6 . . . B–K3** 7 P–K4 (or 7 N–B3, as in A1) and **6 . . . N–B3 7 P–QN4** yield standard positions. Finally, **6 . . . N–B3 7 N–B3** is *English II*, or White could choose **7 P–K4.** We look into:

C51 6 . . . P–QR4
C52 6 . . . B–K3

a) **6 . . . B–Q2** can transpose after **7 N–B3** or **7 P–QN4** Q–B1 8 N–B3 to A1, or acquire its own character by 7 P–QN4 Q–B1 **8 P–N5** N–Q1 9 P–QR4 Δ B–QR3, P–B5. Also worth notice is **7 P–B4!?**, as in C1, where the development of Black's bishop to d7 may not be best, e.g. 7 . . . Q–B1 8 P×P P×P (8 . . . N×P 9 B–B4) 9 N–K4! Δ 9 . . . P–N3 10 P–QN4.

b) **6 . . . KN–K2** makes less sense here than in any other system, as Black's QN will lack a good retreat: 7 P–QN4 (Other moves give time for . . . B–K3, . . . Q–Q2, etc.) 7 . . . N–Q5 (Pachman) 8 P–K3 N–K3 9 KN–K2 0–0 10 0–0. Black stands solidly enough, but lacks definite counterchances.

C51

6 . . .	P–QR4
7 P–QR3	B–K3

Similar to C53. The text features White's attempts to profit by the

... P–QR4 /P–QR3 insertion:

8	P–QN4	P×P
9	P×P	Q–Q2
10	P–N5	N–Q1
11	N–Q5!	

One benefit of ... P–QR4 for White is that there is no pawn on a7 to stop N–N6 should Black play ... P–QB3. We are following Smyslov-Nicevsky, Zagreb 1970, where Black was soon forced to cede the bishop pair: 11 ... KN–K2 12 B–N5! B×N 13 P×B P–N3 (A knight heads for c5 as White expands in the centre.) 14 P–K4 0–0 15 N–K2 N–N2 16 0–0 N–QB4 17 P–Q4 P×P 18 N×P R–R5 (Using the file, but ...) 19 N–B6 N×N 20 NP×N Q–B1 21 B–K3 R–R4 22 K–R1 R–K1 23 B×N! (White will either win in the centre or accrue dividends from the QR-file.) 23 ... R×B 24 P–B4 R–K2 25 R–N4 R–R4 26 R–R4! Q–K1 (26 ... R×R lets White's queen penetrate.) 27 R×R P×R 28 Q–B2 P–KB4? (28 ... B–Q5 offers more hope.) 29 P–K5!! P×P 30 P–Q6 P×P 31 P–B7 Q–QB1 32 R–B1 P×P (32 ... P–K5 33 B–B1 ±±) 33 Q–N3ch K–B1 34 Q–N8 R–K1 35 Q×Q R×Q 36 B–N7 R×P 37 R×R P×P 38 P×P 1–0.

C52
6 ... **B–K3**

The most important move, giving Black time to free d8.

7 P–QN4

Considering the rather listless game White can easily slip into after the text move, **7 N–R3(!)** deserves mention. The themes are the same as in C3 e.g. 7 N–R3 P–KR3 8 P–B4 Q–Q2 9 N–B2 KN–K2 10 N–Q5 N–Q1 11 0–0 P–QB3 12 N×N Q×N 13 P×P P×P 14 P–QN4 0–0 15 B–K3 P–N3 16 Q–Q2 K–R2 17 P–QR4 P–KB4 18 N–Q1 R–QN1 19 N–B3 Q–Q2 20 P–B5 P×P 21 B×P ± Barcza-Taimanov. Black has weak pawns (though $\frac{1}{2}$–$\frac{1}{2}$, 51).

| 7 ... | Q–Q2 |
| 8 P–N5 | N–Q1 (*15*) |

15
W

9 P–QR4

A parting point:

a) **9 P–KR4** P–KR3 10 P–R5 P–N4 11 P–K4 P–KB4 12 P×P B×P(4) 13 KN–K2 N–KB3, excellent for Black, was Bukić-Polugaevsky, Sarajevo 1964.

b) **9 Q–R4!?** is Larsen's idea, which Shatskes claims gives Black good play by 9 ... N–K2 **10 N–B3** P–KR3 11 0–0 0–0. But 9 ... N–K2 can also be answered **10 N–Q5!.** Then **10 ... P–QB3?** (which would have repulsed the knight on 9 N–Q5?) 11 N–N6 and 10 ... N–B1 11 B–N5 are undesirable, while **10...0–0** might meet with 11 B–QR3 or even 11 Q–R5!?. Many ideas here!

c) **9 N–B3** P–KR3 10 0–0 N–K2 11 N–K1 0–0 12 N–B2 is the sort of scheme we saw in A24. Arnaudov-Mesing, Varna 1973 delivered a familiar verdict: 12 ... B–R6 13 N–N4 B×B 14 K×B P–KB4 15 N(4)–Q5 (better 15 N(3)–Q5, according to Ghizdavu) 15 ... N–K3 16 P–QR4 P–B3 17 P×P P×P 18 N×Nch Q×N 19 P–R5 P–K5 20 N–R4?! P–Q4 ∓ (0–1, 33).

9 ...   N–K2
10 B–QR3   P–KR3

Perhaps by the design of his opponent, Liberzon was found on the other (i.e. White) side of this position against Maslov at Aktiubinsk 1970. He tried a different strategy for White, but did not render the variation more attractive: **10 ... 0–0** 11 P–R5 R–B1 (else P–R6) 12 N–B3 B–R6 13 B×B Q×B 14 N–Q5!? N×N 15 P×N, and now Black entered into the seductive continuation **15 ... P–K5!?** 16 P×P B–B6ch 17 N–Q2 Q–N7 18 R–KB1 Q×KP 19 R–B1 B×P 20 B×P! R–K1 21 B×P! R×B! (Otherwise the QP advances.) 22 R×R Q×QP 23 R–B8 Q×NP 24 P–B4?! R–K3 25 R–KB2 K–N2? (25 ... Q–Q4! ∞) 26 K–B1 ± (1–0, 50). 15 ... P–K5!? may have been adequate, but **15 ..P–N3!** (Δ ... N–N2–B4) 16 P–R6 P–KB4 was simpler, when White still has problems getting his king into safety.

11 N–B3   0–0
12 0–0 P–KB4! 13 N–Q2 R–B1 14 Q–B2 P–B5 15 QR–K1 B–R6 16 P K3 B×B 17 K×B N–K3 18

N(3)–K4 R–B2 ∓ Botvinnik-Liberzon, Moscow 1968 (½–½, 30).

CONCLUSION:

6 R–N1 has definite merits, but should sometimes be used as a transpositional tool, because an immediate P–QN4–N5 push is not always best (e.g. versus 6 ... B–K3).

D

5 R–N1

'A dynamic, modern treatment.' Thus Taimanov describes 5 R–N1 and indeed, there was a time when it seemed every 1 P–QB4 regular was playing it. The idea is maximum flexibility; White reasons that R–QN1 will be desirable against any defensive set-up. But Black has his own thoughts about that:
D1 5 ... P–QR4
D2 5 ... P–Q3
D3 5 ... N–R3
D4 5 ... N–B3

5 ... KN–K2 has evident problems discussed in C (note to 5 ... P–Q3).

D1

5 ...   **P–QR4**
6 P–QR3   P–Q3

Not successful was the foray **6 ... P–R4?!** 7 N–B3 P–Q3 8 P–Q3 KN–K2 9 0–0 N–B4 10 P–KR4! 0–0 11 P–QN4 ± Taimanov-Reshko, USSR 1973.

Actually, any of Black's fifth-move ideas may be tried in conjunction with 5 ... P–QR4, but especially deserving attention is **6**

...N–B3! (see the discussion in D4 5 ... N–B3). White can answer **6 ...P–B4** by **7 P–Q3** N–B3 8 N–B3, probably transposing to A22, or by **7 P–QN4** e.g. 7 ... P×P 8 P×P N–B3 9 P–Q3 0–0 10 P–N5 N–Q5 11 P–K3 N–K3 12 KN–K2 N–R4 13 P–B4 ± Polugaevsky-Nikitin, USSR Ch 1969 (1–0, 50).

 7 P–QN4 P×P
 8 P×P B–B4

8...P–B4 9 P–K3?! (9 P–N5 △ P–Q3) 9 ... N–B3?! (9 ... P–K5!- Sigurjonsson-clearing e5 for the QN) 10 KN–K2? P–K5! ∓ Jacobsen-Sigurjonsson, Denmark 1973.

 9 P–Q3 Q–B1
 10 P–N5 N(3)–K2

11 P–K4 B–N5 12 P–B3 B–Q2 13 KN–K2 B–R6 14 0–0 B×B 15 K×B ('White stands somewhat better,' says Taimanov, not quoting any game. It turns out that Pachman played this position as White versus Szabo in Solingen 1968. The game concluded:) 15 ... N–KB3 16 N–Q5?! (16 B–N5! ±) 16 ... N(2)×N 17 BP×N P–B3! ½–½.

D2

 5 ...   P–Q3
 6 P–QN4
6 P–Q3 is C5.
 6 ...   P–B4

Black may also choose:

a) **6...P–QR3** (a tardy attempt to get back into D1) 7 P–K3 (**7 P–QR4** N–B3; not 7 ... P–QR4 8 P–N5 N–N5? 9 B–QR3) 7... P–B4 8 KN–K2 N–B3 9 P–Q3 0–0 10 0–0 B–Q2 11 P–QR4, reaching Smyslov-Liberzon of B2 above;

b) **6 ... N–B3** 7 P–K3 B–N5!? 8 KN–K2 Q–B1 9 0–0 B–R6 10 P–N5 N–K2 (10 ... N–Q1!- Pachman) 11 P–K4 B×B (11 ... P–KR4!?) 12 K×B Q–K3 13 N–Q5 N(2)×N 14 BP×N Q–K2 = /∞ Ilivitsky-Pachman, Match 1956;

c) G. Meyers-Watson, Lone Pine 1976, illustrates a traditional Black method: **6 ... B–B4** 7 P–Q3 Q–Q2 8 P–N5 N–Q1 9 P–K3 N–K2 10 N–Q5 0–0 11 N×Nch Q×N 12 N–K2 Q–Q2 13 0–0 B–K3 14 Q–B2? P–Q4 ∓.

 7 P–N5 N(3)–K2
 8 P–K3

8 P–Q3 N–KB3 9 P–K4 0–0 10 KN–K2 P–QR3 11 P–QR4 RP×P 12 RP×P P×P 13 N×P N×N 14 B×N P–B3 = Evans-Spassky, Lugano 1968.

 8 ...   N–KB3
 9 P–Q4

9 KN–K2 0–0 10 0–0 P–N4 11 P–B4 NP×P (11 ... P–KR3) 12 KP×P N–N3 13 P–Q3 was aesthetically pleasing and ± in Averbach-Ciocaltea, Bucharest 1971; but by **10 ... B–K3!**, Black could have caused confusion in the ranks, e.g. **11 P–Q3** P–Q4 or **11 B×NP** R–N1 12 B–KN2 B×P 13 Q–R4 B–Q6, etc.

 9 ...   P–K5

a) **9...P×P** 10 P×P 0–0 11 KN–K2 P–Q4 12 Q–R4! ± Smyslov-Ungureanu, Lugano 1968.

b) **9 ... 0–0** 10 N–B3 P–K5 11 N–Q2 P–B3 12 0–0 with White for preference (Shatskes/Taimanov).

 10 KN–K2 0–0

11 0–0 B–K3 12 P–Q5 B–B2 13 N–Q4 (Smyslov is always getting

his pawn to d5 and knight to d4!) 13
... N–Q2 14 P–B3 P×P 15 Q×P
R–N1 16 B–N2 ± Smyslov-Levy,
Hastings 1969/70 (1–0, 31).

D3

5 ...   **N–R3**

Taimanov's conception. Black
develops a piece, leaves e7 free for
his retreating QN, and awaits
events.

6 P–K3

Naturally, **6 P–QN4** is also seen.
Then 6 ... 0–0 7 P–N5 **N–Q5** 8
P–K3 N–K3 9 KN–K2 P–Q3 10
P–Q3 P–KB4 11 N–Q5 (Black
threatened ... P–B5) 11 ... B–Q2
12 0–0 P–B3 13 N–N4 Q–B1 was
Smyslov-Taimanov, Moscow 1968.
White may have a bit the better of
it. **7 ... N–K2** 8 P–K3 P–QB3 is
another valid plan.

6 ...   P–Q3

6 ... 0–0 7 KN–K2 P–Q3 8
P–QN4 P–B4 (? 8 ... B–B4 Δ 9
P–Q3 Q–Q2) 9 P–N5 N–K2 10
P–B4 N–B2 11 P–Q4 P–K5 12
P–N4! P×P 13 0–0 ± Spiridonov-
Daskalov, Bulgaria 1969.

7 P–QN4   0–0

As above, **7 ... B–B4** 8 P–Q3
Q–Q2 is an acceptable alternative.

8 P–N5   N–K2
9 KN–K2   P–QB3
10 P×P   P×P
11 Q–R4   Q–B2

12 0–0 B–Q2? (Natural enough,
but from now on White has a pull.
The centre should be watched, i.e.
with ... P–KB4 and ... N–B2.) 13
P–Q4! P×P 14 P×P N(3)–B4 15
P–B5! N–Q4 16 N×N P×N 17
Q–R3 and White went on to win in

only ten more moves in Portisch-
Schmid, Monaco 1969.

D4

5 ...   **N–B3**

This puts a finger on the weak
point of 5 R–N1, i.e. that it does
nothing for the centre. Here Black
intends ... N–K2 and ... P–Q4; it
is worth noting again that the entire
conception works even better with
5 ... P–QR4 6 P–QR3 thrown in.

6 P–QN4

Consistent. On **6 P–Q3, 6 ...
P–Q3** transposes to C5, but **6 ...
P–QR4!** 7 P–QR3 0–0 8 P–QN4
P×P 9 P×P R–K1 10 P–N5 N–Q5
11 P–K3 N–B4 12 KN–K2 P–B3
would be a sample of Black
exploiting the tempo he has saved
by withholding his QP.

6 ...   0–0
7 P–K3   N–K2! (*16*)

16
W

8 N–B3

8 P–K4 P–B3 can only be worse
for White.

8 ...   P–Q4!
9 N×KP

White needs a pawn to compensate for his efforts on the queenside.

9 ...	B–B4
10 R–N3	N–K5

Encircling the White knight on e5.

11 N×N	B×N
12 B×B	P×B
13 P–B4	P–KR4

14 P–Q4?! (14 P–QB5!?) 14 ... P–KB3 15 N×P N×N 16 Q×P N–K2 17 P–KB5 P–N4! 18 P×P P–R3 19 P×P R×P 20 P–QR3 R–B3 21 0–0 Q–Q4 22 R–N2 N×P! ∓∓ Kapengut-Gulko, USSR 1970 (0–1, 40). The game itself is not completely convincing; yet I believe that, with the move order 5 ... P–QR4 6 P–QR3 N–B3, the same strategy would force White to revise his play, perhaps as early as move 7.

CONCLUSION:

There is nothing wrong with 5 R–N1, nor is anything amiss about the Black positions which arise after straightforward replies. More particularly, **5 ... N–R3** and **5 ... P–QR4** 6 P–QR3 N–B3 keep things complicated; while a safe system is **5 ... P–Q3** 6 P–QN4 B–B4 △ ... Q–Q2.

E

5 P–K4 (*17*)

The 'Botvinnik System,' which is encountered in the Symmetrical Variation, as well as in the King's Indian formations. White clears e2 for his KN, secures his hold on d5, and leaves open his plan of action; which may be N–Q5, B–K3, and a

central advance, but usually involves P–KB4 and attack on the king's wing.

In return, Black gains the square d4, which he can post a knight on or simply gloat over the possession of. Moreover, now that White has voluntarily blocked off his own king's bishop, Black should have no difficulties developing his queenside pieces. He too can consider breaking with ... P–KB4.

Under the microscope go:

E1 5 ... N–B3
E2 5 ... P–Q3
E3 5 ... KN–K2

E1

5 ... **N–B3**

Not advisable. For one thing, Black can no longer blockade White's P–KB4–B5 plan with ... P–KB4 unless he moves the knight again. The same goes for **5 ... P–Q3** 6 KN–K2 N–B3.

6 KN–K2	P–Q3

An independent try was **6 ... 0–0** 7 0–0 P–QR3, from (by transposition) Hecht-Westerinen,

Montilla 1973: 8 P–B4 (or 8 P–Q3) 8 ... P–Q3 9 P–Q3 R–N1 10 P–QR4 N–Q5 11 P–KB5 (11 P–R3-Marić) 11 ... P–B3 12 P–R3. Now, instead of 12 ... **P–Q4?!** 13 BP×QP BP×P 14 P×NP BP×P 15 N×N ±, Marić suggests **12 ... N–Q2!** Δ ... P–QR4, ... N–B4. Unclear!

7 0–0

Occasionally seen is **7 P–Q3** 0–0 8 P–KR3 Δ B–K3 and P–Q4. But the game Piazzini-Panno, Argentina 1953, demonstrated an effective defence: 8 ... N–Q2! 9 B–K3 N–B4 10 0–0 (10 P–Q4 P×P 11 N×P N–K4!) 10 ... N–K3 11 Q–Q2 N(K)–Q5 (the fifth move with this piece, threatening 12 ... B×RP!) 12 P–B4 B–K3 13 N–Q5 (13 R–B2!?) 13 ... N×Nch 14 Q×N N–Q5 15 Q–KB2 P–QB3 16 N–B3 P–KB4 ∓. Now Black has two approaches:
E11 7 ... B–K3
E12 7 ... 0–0

E11

7 ...	**B–K3**
8 P–Q3	Q–Q2

8 ... 0–0 9 P–KR3! Q–Q2 10 K–R2 N–K1 (else White plays P–B4) 11 P–KN4! P–B4 12 NP×P P×P 13 P×P R×P 14 N–N3 R–B2 15 N(B)–K4 P–KR3, and instead of **16 Q–R5?!** ∞, simply **16 B–K3** would have kept a clear advantage in Watson-Nikitovich, Colorado 1975.

9 P–N3

A recurring theme, protecting the QBP in order to play P–Q4 and in some cases B–QN2. Less

challenging was **9 P–B4** 0–0 10 N–Q5 N–K1! 11 B–K3 P–B4 = Szabo-Yanofsky, Dallas 1957

9 ...	0–0
10 N–Q5	N–KR4(?)
11 B–N2	QR–K1
12 P–Q4 ±	

Filip-Westerinen, Havana 1967 (1–0, 35).

E12

7 ...	**0–0** (*18*)

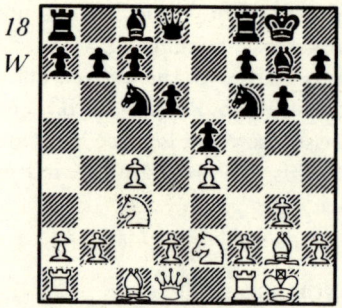

8 P–Q3!?

This has led to some nice wins, but objectively White should play **8 P–B4!** before Black is able to meet that move with ... P–KB4. On 8 P–B4 **N–Q5** 9 P–Q3 P–B4, White has 10 P–B5! N–K1 (10 ... P×P 11 B–N5 ±) 11 P–KN4 P–KN4 12 N–Q5 P–B3 13 N×N KP×N 14 P–QN4 with an attack on both flanks i.e. via P–QN4 and P–KR4, Ojanen-Lihflaender, Finland 1955. Against 8 P–B4, Black may as well try **8 ... P×P**, ceding the centre for piece play. Then if **9 N×P,** 9 ... N–Q5 is reasonable; so White might continue **9 P×P** N–KR4 10 P–Q4 (10 P–KB5 Q–R5!) 10 ... B–N5 11 B–K3 e.g. 11 ... P–B4 12 P–K5 (12

P–Q5 N–K2) 12 . . . P×P 12 QP×P
(13 BP×P P–B5) and Black may
not yet relax (13 . . . P–KN4!?).

8 . . .   N–Q5(?)

Occupying d4 doesn't seem to be
the right idea with the other knight
on f6. After

a) **8 . . . R–K1** 9 R–N1, Black did
even worse with 9 . . . N–Q5? 10
N×N P×N 11 N–K2 N–Q2 12
P–QN4 P–QR4 13 P–N5 N–B4 14
B–N2 ± Sanguinetti–Schweber,
Mar del Plata 1968.

b) **8 . . . N–KR4** is better, but with
9 N–Q5! (not **9 B–K3** N–Q5 or **9
P–KR3** P–B4 10 P×P P×P 11 P–B4
N–K2 =) White keeps an initiative
e.g. 9 . . . P–B4 10 P×P B×P (10 . . .
P×P 11 N(2)–B3 N–B3 12 B–N5
etc.) 11 B–K3 Q–Q2 12 Q–Q2
R–B2 13 N(2)–B3 B–R6 14 N–K4
B×B 15 K×B N–K2 16 N×Nch
R×N 17 P–B3! (Δ P–Q4) 17 . . .
N–B3 18 B–N5 R–B2 19 QR–K1
P–Q4 20 N×Nch B×N 21 B×B
R×B 22 Q–B3 P–Q5 L. Popov–
Dely, Amsterdam 1974, and now
23 Q–R5! would have been ±±.
Best is simply

c) **8 . . . N–K1** 9 B–K3 (9 P–B4
P–B4) 9 . . . N–Q5 10 K–R1 P–B4
= Botvinnik–Blau, Moscow
1956.

9 N×N

9 P–B4 is the note to 8 P–Q3.
Petrosian elects a different method.

9 . . .   P×N
10 N–K2   P–B4

Keene queries this move, which
he says creates a 'dead point' in the
centre. True enough, but after his
10 . . . N–Q2 White has 11 P–QN4
and Black cannot do without . . .

P–QB4 for very long. If he tries to
defend with pieces, i.e. 11 . . .
P–QR4 12 P–N5 N–B4 13 B–N2
N–K3, then 14 P–B4! P–KB4 15
P×P Δ B–Q5 wins the important QP.

11 P–QN4!   N–Q2
12 P×P   P×P
13 P–B4   .

With a mobile kingside majority.

13 . . .   P–B3
14 P–QR4 P–QR4 15 P–N4 N–N1
16 N–N3 N–B3 17 R–B2 B–Q2 18
B–B3 R–R2 19 P–R4 P–R3
Petrosian–Bertok, Zagreb 1965.
After lengthy manoeuvring, White
ultimately sacrificed a pawn with
P–K5 and after . . . P×P, played
P–KB5 to capture the light squares
in the centre, which proved enough
to win! A brilliant game which
deserves a look and can be found
with Keene's excellent notes in his
book *Flank Openings*.

E2

5 . . .   P–Q3

Here we consider sixth moves other
than . . . N–KB3 or . . . KN–K2:
E21 6 KN–K2
E22 6 P–Q3

E21

6 KN–K2   P–KR4!?

Eccentric. Now, after 7 P–KR3,
White's KRP may become a target;
nevertheless he should consider
playing it that way.

7 P–KR4   N–R3
8 P–Q3   0–0
9 P–B3!?

An interesting way to prepare
B–K3.

9 . . .   B–K3

9...K-R2 10 B-K3 N-KN1! Δ
... B-R3.

10	N-Q5	K-R2
11	B-K3	P-B4?

Thus far Black's 6 ... P-KR4
has not fared badly, but **11 ...
P-B4?** is too weakening. Attending
to the centre with **11 ... N-K2** was
called for. Then 12 Q-Q2 P-QB3
13 N×N (13 N-B6ch B×N 14 B×N
B-N2 Δ ... P-Q4 =) 13 ... Q×N
14 N-B3 and now 14 ... P-KB4
makes sense (or 14 ... P-QR3 15
P-QR4 QR-K1, since White's
P-KN4 will run into ... P-KB4!).

11 ... P-B4? was played in
Portisch-Gulko, Biel 1976: 12
Q-Q2 Q-Q2 13 R-QB1 N-K2 14
N-N1! (so simple; g5 is weak ...)
14 ... P-B3 15 N×N Q×N 16
N-R3 (... so prepare its
occupation!) '±' (Forintos); at any
rate, White has the better of it and
won handily.

E22

6	P-Q3	P-B4

6...N-Q5 (with drawish intent)
7 N(3)-K2 N×N 8 N×N P-QB4 9
0-0 N-K2 10 R-QN1 P-QR4 11
P-B4 gives White a slight lead in
tempi. After 11 ... P×P 12 B×P
N-B3 13 Q-Q2 B-K3 14 B-N5
Q-Q2 15 B-B6, White had some
initiative, but eventually drew in
Timman-Popov, Tallin 1973.

7	KN-K2	N-B3
8	0-0	0-0
9	P×P!	

A purposeful move, and perhaps
best. **9 K-R1** and **9 P-KR3** would
also be logical, but actual praxis has
seen:

a) **9 R-N1** P-QR4 10 P-N3 B-K3
11 N-Q5 K-R1 12 B-N2 R-B2 13
P×P B×P 14 P-B4 B-N5 =
Furman-Korchnoi, Leningrad
Spartakiad 1964) (0-1, 27);
b) **9 N-Q5** B-K3 10 B-N5 Q-Q2
11 Q-Q2 R-B2! 12 QR-K1 (12
QR-B1 is Shatskes' idea, preparing
exchanges and P-Q4.) 12 ...
R(1)-KB1 13 P-B3 = Liberzon-
Smyslov, Moscow 1967.

9 ...	P×P

9...B×P 10 P-KR3, and Black
either gives up both central light
squares (11 P-KN4), or tries 10 ...
P-KR4 11 B-N5 ±.

10	B-N5	B-K3
11	Q-Q2 ±	

A rather standard English
position in which White can
continue P-KB4 and/or play P-N3
Δ P-Q4.

E3

5	...	KN-K2
6	KN-K2	0-0
7	P-Q3	P-Q3
8	0-0	

Black's most popular forma-
tion. Now:
E31 8 ... P-B4
E32 8 ... B-K3
Minor alternatives:
a) **8 ... N-Q5** 9 N×N P×N 10
N-K2 P-QB3 11 P-QN4(?!)
P-QR4 12 P-N5 P×P 13 P×P
P-Q4 14 B-QR3 P×P 15 B×P
R-K1 16 N-B4 B-R3! = Portisch-
Smyslov, Monte-Carlo 1968. 11
P-N3 would have been more
circumspect.
b) **8 ... B-Q2** 9 N-Q5 R-N1 10
B-N5 P-B3 11 B-K3 P-B4 12

Q–Q2 N×N 13 BP×N N–Q5 14
N×N P×N 15 B–N5 Q–B1 16
QR–B1 R–B2 17 B–R6 B×B 18
Q×B B–N4 19 KR–Q1 P–B4! =
Botvinnik-Spassky, Leiden 1970.

Better was 17 KR–K1.

E31

8 ... **P–B4**
9 N–Q5

9 P–B4 BP×P 10 QP×P B–K3 11
N–Q5 Q–Q2 = Reshevsky-Alexander, Munich 1958. 9 P–KR3
(Hort) has insidious effects – see E322.

9 ... P–KR3!

9 ... K–R1 10 B–K3 B–K3 11
Q–Q2 Q–Q2 12 QR–K1 (12
P–QN4! ±) 12 . . . QR–K1 (12 . . .
R–B2!?) 13 P–B4 KP×P 14 N(2)×P
B–N1 15 N×N N×N 16 B–R3! with
much pressure, Botvinnik-Petrosian, USSR Team Ch 1966;
for **9 . . . B–K3**, see E321.

10 R–N1 K–R2
11 P–B4 BP×P!

12 QP×P P×P 13 P×P B–N5 14
B–K3 Q–Q2 15 Q–Q2 QR–K1 16
R(N)–K1 N–KN1! ∓ Barcza-Simagin, Salgó-Tarjań 1967. He
should have preferred **10 .P×P!**
P×P (**10 . . . B×P** 11 P–KR3 or **10
. . . N×P** 11 N(2)–B3 Δ 12 N–K4)
11 P–B4 ±.

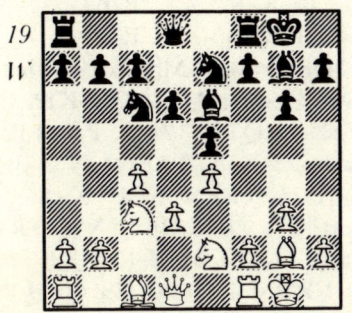

E32

8 ... **B–K3** (*19*)
With this significant breakdown:
E321 9 N–Q5
E322 9 P–KR3

E321

9 N–Q5
The customary continuation,
now that Black can't capture on d5
with his knight.

9 ... P–B4

9 ... Q–Q2 10 B–K3 N–Q5?!
(10 . . . P–B4) 11 N×N P×N 12
B–R6! P–QB4 13 B×B K×B 14
Q–Q2 N×N 15 BP×N B–R6 16
B×B Q×B 17 P–B4 Q–Q2 18 P–B5
P–B3 19 P–KR4 with a menacing
kingside attack that should have led
to a win in Botvinnik-Geller,
Moscow 1966 ($\frac{1}{2}$–$\frac{1}{2}$, 59).

In this line (9 . . . Q–Q2 10
B–K3), **10 . . . K–R1?** is quite as
bad, giving White the opportunity
for 11 P–Q4! N–KN1 12 N×BP!
Q×N 13 P–Q5 N–Q1 14 P×B N×P
15 R–B1 N–K2 16 Q–Q2 N–B3 17
P–B4! N(B)–Q5 18 P–B5! ±
Uhlmann-Adorjan, Arandelovac
1976. Typical power-play chess by
Uhlmann!

10 B–K3

'?' (Shatskes). The alternative is
interesting: **10 R–N1** Q–Q2 11
P–QN4 **QR–K1** (The idea of . . .
R–B2, . . . QR–KB1 – usually
appropriate – is bad here: **11 . . .
R–B2** 12 P–N5 N–Q1 – 12 . . .
N–Q5 13 N×N P×N 14 N–B4 – 13
B–N5! etc.) 12 P–N5 N–Q1 13
B–QR3. Analysis by Taimanov,
who states that White's chances are
preferable. But that would be
extremely hard to prove: White

must contend still with ´ his opponent's kingside-oriented forces.

10 ...   Q–Q2
11 Q–Q2

Csom-Gulko, Biel 1976, illustrated another and perhaps superior plan: **11 R–B1** R–R2 12 Q–Q2 QR–KB1 13 P–B3! (The difference; White stabilizes the king's wing before undertaking anything.) 13 ... K–R1 14 P–N3 N–KN1 15 P×P P×P? (15 ... B×P 16 P–Q4 ±-Csom) 16 P–B4 ± (1–0, 42).

11 ...   R–B2!

The standard procedure ... ever since the text game.

12 QR–K1

a) **12 N×Nch** R×N! (12 ... Q×N? 13 P×P! ±) 13 N–B3 R–KB1 14 P×P B×P 15 QR–K1?! B–R6! ∓ Filip-Geller, Curaçao 1962. Better 15 KR–K1 B–R6 16 B–R1 (Schwarz).

b) **12 QR–B1** R(1)–KB1 13 P–QN4 N–B1 (compare comments to the text) 14 P–N5 N–Q1 15 P–Q4!? brought about a complex situation, hard to assess, in Uhlmann-Timman, Nikšić 1978 (½–½, 33).

12 ...   QR–KB1
13 P–B4   BP×P

Against Schmidt in Leipzig 1973, Ribli substituted **13 ...N–Q5?** for the text move, and found himself in hot water after 14 P×KP! QP×P 15 N×N P×N 16 B–N5 N–B1 (16 ... N–B3 17 N–B4 ±-Schmidt) 17 P–K5 P–B3 18 N–B6ch B×N 19 P×B R–K1 20 R–K5! ±±.

14 QP×P   N–B1(!)

Black prepares ... B–R6 by defending his QBP along the second rank. This is Benko-Botvinnik, Monaco 1968, one of the classic English games: 15 P–QB5 (15 P–QN4!?) 15 ... B–R6 16 P–QN4 B×B 17 K×B KP×P 18 NP×P R–K1 19 N–N3 (19 N(2)–B3 has been suggested. With his next move, Black launches an attack and risks the opening of his kingside. This game has been so often analysed and discussed, with such contradictory conclusions, that here we merely give the moves. By this point, however, it does seem that White is hoping for equality.) 19 ... P–KR4! 20 P–N5 N(3)–K2 (20 ... N–Q1!?) 21 P–B5 P–R5 22 P×NP R×R 23 R×R P×N 24 R–B7 B–K4! 25 B–Q4 Q–N5 26 R–B4? Q–R4 27 B×B Q×Pch 28 K–B3 Q×Q 29 N–B6ch K–N2 30 N×Rch K×P 31 R–B6ch K–R2 32 B×NP Q–Q6ch 33 K–B2 Q×NP 34 P×P Q×N 0–1.

E322
9 P–KR3

A move employed recently by Hort.

9 ...   Q–Q2
10 K–R2   P–B4
11 N–Q5   R–R2

Hort-Browne, Manila 1976, had several lessons: **11 ... QR–K1?!** 12 B–K3 N–Q5?! (12 ... P–KR3!?-Hort) 13 B×N! P×B 14 N(2)–B4 N×N 15 KP×N (or 15 N×B ±-Hort) 15 ... B–B2 16 Q–N3! K–R1 (16 ... Q–B1 17 N–K6! ±±) 17 Q×NP R–QN1 18 Q–B6! Q×Q 19

P×Q R×NP 20 QR–N1 R(1)–N1 21 R×R R×R 22 B–Q5 P–N4 23 N–K6! B×N 24 B×B B–K4 25 B×BP ±. The move . . . R–KB2 is better, when feasible, than . . . QR–K1.

    12 B–K3   QR–KB1
    13 P–B4   N–Q5!

Fine, now that the White knight has no access to f4 after 14 B×N?.

    14 N×N   P×N
15 B–Q2 N–B1 (As in the Benko-Botvinnik game above) 16 Q–B3 P–B3 17 P–N3 (Since taking the knight loses the piece back and cedes key central squares; 17 N–N4 P×P 18 Q×P P–QR4 Δ 19 . . . P–Q4 =) 17 . . . P–KN4!

(threatening 18 . . . P×KP 19 P×KP P–N5 ∓∓) 18 Q–R5! P×KP 19 P×KP P×P 20 P×P P×N 21 BP×P Q–N4 22 P–QR4 Q×NP 23 KR–QN1 Q–B5 24 R–QB1 Q–N6 25 R(B)–N1, etc. ½–½ Hort-Spassky (4), 1977.

CONCLUSION:

The Botvinnik System is rich in ideas and calls for delicate handling. Black should not expect full equality from the systems involving . . . N–KB3 (either before or after . . . P–KB4); but the variations with . . . KN–K2, currently undergoing tests, have not lost their good reputation.

2 THE THREE KNIGHTS SYSTEM: 3 N–B3 P–KN3

1	P–QB4	P–K4
2	N–QB3	N–QB3
3	N–B3	P–KN3

3 N–B3 will usually transpose to the Main Line (after **3 . . . N–B3**), or to Chapter 10, B (after **3 . . . P–B4**). With **3 . . . P–KN3**, Black attempts to increase his control over e5 and d4 immediately, aiming for the Closed English (4 P–KN3 B–N2, 5 B–N2 etc. See Chapter 1,A). But White's third has taken note of these central dark squares, so plans based on P–Q4 must be considered.

3 . . . KN–K2 is a bizarre minor alternative, when White can choose either **4 P–KN3** with normal development, or **4 P–Q4(!)** P×P 5 N×P P–KN3 6 P–KN3 (6 **B–N5!** B–N2 7 N×N NP×N 8 P–K4 P–KR3 9 B–K3 0–0 10 Q–Q2 ± is given by Schwarz, but 10 . . . K–R2 Δ . . . P–KB4, . . . P–Q3, . . . P–QB4 looks complicated.) 6 . . . B–N2 7 N×N N×N (7 . . . NP×N 8 B–N2 ± is B2b below), and we have transposed to B2, note to 5 . . . B–N2, below.

After 3 . . . P–KN3:
A 4 P–K3
B 4 P–Q4

A

4	**P–K3**	**B–N2**

4 . . . P–B4 5 P–Q4 P–K5, see Chapter 10, B2.

5	P–Q4	P–Q3!

5 . . . P×P 6 P×P KN–K2 (6 . . . P–Q3 7 B–N5!) 7 P–Q5 N–K4 8 P–Q6 (8 N×N B×N 9 N–K4 ±) 8 . . . N–B4 9 N×N B×N 10 P×P Q×P 11 N–Q5 Q–Q1! 12 B–Q3 = Nimzovich–Stolz, Bled, 1931.

6 P–Q5

6 B–K2 P–B4 7 P×P ('!'-Schwarz) 7 . . . P×P 8 Q×Qch N×Q =.

6	. . .	N(3)–K2

7 B–K2 P–KB4 8 Q–B2 N–KB3 9 0–0 0–0 10 R–Q1 P–KR3 11 P–B5 P–KN4 12 P×P P×P 13 N–Q2 P–B5 14 N–B4 N–B4 15 P–QR4 P–KR4 with a double-edged game, Tolush–Smyslov, Bucharest, 1953.

B

4	**P–Q4!**	P×P (20)

20
W

Inferior are:

a) **4 ... P–Q3** 5 P×P N×P 6 N×N P×N 7 Q×Qch K×Q 8 B–N5ch and 0-0-0 (Taimanov)

b) **4 ... N×P?** 5 N×N P×N 6 Q×P Q–B3 7 Q–K3ch Q–K2 (7 ... Q–K3 8 N–Q5 B–Q3 9 Q–Q4 P–KB3 10 B–B4) 8 N–Q5 Q×Q 9 B×Q threatening 10 N×Pch and 10 B–Q4.

Now White has tried:
B1 5 N–Q5
B2 5 N×P

B1
5 N–Q5

Most players prefer to avoid the complications which stem from this move; **5 N×P** is 'more thematic'. Nevertheless, 5 N–Q5 is very dangerous and deserves examination.

    5 ...   B–N2

5 ... P–KR3 6 B–B4 P–Q3 7 N×P (Δ 8 N–N5 and 8 N×N P×N 9 Q–Q4).

    6 B–N5   N(3)–K2(!)

Certainly **6 ... N(1)–K2??** 7 N×P B×N 8 Q×B! N×Q 9 N–B6ch K–B1 10 B–R6 MATE is no better; but Black can curl up with **6 ... P–B3!?** 7 B–B4 P–Q3 8 N×P N×N (8 ... P–QR3?! 9 P–KR4 P–KR3? – 9 ... N–R3! 10 Q–Q2 N–B4 - Pachman – 10 P–KN3 P–B4 11 N×N P×N 12 N–B3 ± Szabo-Pachman, Marianski Lázne 1954.) 9 Q×N N–K2! 10 P–KR4 0-0 11 Q–Q2 and White is only slightly better.

    7 N×P   P–KR3

The most active continuation. **7 ... P–QB3** 8 N×N (Schwarz's **8 N–QB3** keeps more pieces on) 8 ... N×N 9 Q–Q2 P–Q4 10 P–K3 0-0 11 B×N (**11 P×P** Q×P! 12 B×N R–K1 13 B–R3 – *best* – 13 ... Q×N 14 Q×Q = Mikenas-Poljak, Leningrad 1947) 11 ... Q×B 12 P×P P×P 13 B–K2 ± (Mikenas).

    8 B–R4   P–KN4
    9 B–N3   N×N
    10 P×N   P–QB4!

10 ... P–Q3? 11 R–B1. **10 ... P–QB4** frees Black's queen to strike at the dark squares. Now 11 P×Pe.p.? and 11 N–N5? lose to 11 ... Q–R4ch, while 11 ... B×NP will refute all other knight moves except:

    11 N–B5   B×NP
    12 N–Q6ch

According to analysis by Shatskes:

a) **12 P–K4** Q–R4ch 13 K–K2 P–QN3! ∓.

b) **12 Q–B2** Q–R4ch 13 K–Q1 B×R 14 Q–K4ch K–Q1 15 N–Q6 N–K2 16 N× BPch is a draw.

c) **12 Q–R4** Q–B3! 13 Q–K4ch N–K2. Though it may transpose to the text,

d) **12 P–B3** seems to retain more options.

    12 ...   K–B1
    13 P–B3   P–KR4

Taimanov claims that White has enough compensation after **13 ... B×R** 14 Q×B R–R2 15 P–K3. Black's situation would be awkward, to say the least! After **13 ... P–KR4**, Sedov-Choernov, Moscow 1961, continued 14 P–KR4 N–R3 15 K–B2?? Q–B3 ∓∓. Instead, 15 R–QN1 Q–R4ch 16 K–B2 Q×RP is a 'sharp position', according to Taimanov. However, White seems hard-pressed to justify his two-pawn deficit; so the draw after 12 Q–B2 may be his soundest course in this variation.

B2

    5 N×P   **B–N2**

    5 . . . KN–K2 6 P–KN3 B–N2 7 N×N N×N 8 B–Q2 (Perhaps **8 Q–Q2!** Δ B–N2, P–N3, B–QN2, etc.) 8 . . . P–Q3 9 B–N2 0–0 10 0–0 B–N5 (10 . . . R–K1) 11 P–KR3 B–K3 12 P–N3 ± Petrosian-Botvinnik (7), 1963.

    6 N×N

    6 N–B2 bears down on d5: 6 . . . P–Q3 7 Q–Q2 (**7 P–K3** is passive: 7 . . . B–K3 8 B–K2 KN–K2 9 N–Q5 0–0 10 0–0 N–K4 = Florian-Ragozin, Moscow-Budapest 1949. Also **7 . . . B×Nch!?** 8 P×B N–B3 is attractive.) 7 . . . N–B3 (Taimanov suggests **7 . . . KN–K2**, to meet 8 P–K4 with 8 . . . 0–0 9 B–K2 P–B4. Of course 8 P–KN3 is more consistent with the position and probably ±.) 8 P–K4 P–QR3?! (Closer to equality would be **8 . . . 0–0** 9 B–K2 R–K1 10 P–B3 N–KR4) 9 B–K2 R–QN1 10 0–0 0–0 11 R–K1 with space and a bind on Black's centre, Flohr-Johner, Bern 1932.

    6 . . . NP×N 7 P–KN3 (*21*)

White intends to exert pressure on the centre by B–KN2, 0–0, and bringing his rooks to the queenfile. From the diagram, Black has tried three strategies, none of them quite satisfactory:

B21 7 . . . N–B3

B22 7 . . . Q–K2

B23 7 . . . N–K2

B21

    7 . . .   **N–B3**

    8 B–N2   0–0

    8 . . . N–N5?! 9 Q–B2 0–0 10 0–0 N–K4 11 P–N3 B–N2 12 B–N2 P–Q3 13 P–KR3 R–N1 14 P–B4 N–Q2 15 P–K4 N–B4 16 QR–Q1 (with a terrific preponderance in space) 16 . . . Q–K2 17 P–K5! P–QR4 (17 . . . P×P 18 B–QR3) 18 B–QR3 P–B3 19 P×QP P×P 20 N–R4 ±± Gheorghiu-Keene, Hastings 1967/8.

    9 0–0

This is a position from Chapter 7, A (4 . . . P–KN3), which favours White.

B22

    7 . . .   **Q–K2**

Polugaevsky's **7 . . . P–KR4!?** (presumably with the idea 8 P–KR3 N–R3) might have similar intent, i.e. e7 is left free for the queen.

    8 B–Q2

Safest, although **8 B–N2** saves a tempo in some variations, since 8

... Q–N5!? neglects Black's development: 9 0–0! B–QR3 (9 ... Q×BP 10 B–B4 P–Q3 11 R–B1 B–Q2 12 N–Q5; 9 ... N–K2 10 Q–Q3 B–R3 11· N–N5! P×N 12 B×R P×P 13 Q–K3 Q–N3 14 B–B3 ± Smyslov-Szabo, Buenos Aires 1970) 10 N–N5! B×N 11 P×B Q×P(4) 12 ˙B–B4 R–B1 13 P–QR4 Q–N5 14 B–R3 with good compensation for the pawn, Renter-Flohr, Parnu 1947.

8 ...   R–N1
8 ... Q–K3 9 P–N3 N–K2 10 R–QB1 B–N2 11 B–N2 R–QN1 (11 ... P–Q4 12 P×P P×P 13 N–R4-Taimanov) 12 0–0 0–0 13 P–K4 P–Q3 14 Q–B2 P–QB4?! 15 N–Q5 Holmov-Goldenov, USSR Ch 1960.

9 QR–N1   N–B3
10 B–N2
We are following Kavalek-Taimanov, Harrakov 1966, which continued 10 ... 0–0 11 0–0 P–Q4 12 P×P P×P 13 P–N3? P–Q5! 14 N–Q5 N×N 15 B×N R–Q1 ∓. But **13 B–N5!** P–B3 14 P–K4 (Taimanov) would have conferred White an indisputable superiority.

B23
7 ...   **N–K2**
Cozy, but also rather passive.
8 B–N2   0–0
9 0–0   R–N1
9 ... P–Q3 (9 ... **P–Q4** 10 B N5-Shatskes) 10 B–N5 P–B3 (or **10 ... B–Q2** 11 Q–Q2 ± Euwe vs.

Milner-Barry, Hastings 1934 /5) 11 B–Q2 B–K3 12 Q–R4 B–Q2 13 P–B5! ± Larsen-Torre, Leningrad 1973.

After 9 ... R–N1, White may proceed with:
a) **10 Q–R4!?** P–QR3 (Gheorghiu recommends **10 ... P–Q3!** Δ 11 Q×RP B–K3 12 Q–R4 P–QB4 13 P–QR3 ∞) 11 Q–B2 N–B4?! (11 ... P–QB4 is a solider approach.) 12 P–K3 P–B4 13 R–N1 B–N2 14 N–Q5 B×N 15 P×B Q–K2 16 B–Q2 KR–B1 17 KR–B1 B–B1 (17 ... P–Q3 18 B–R3) 18 Q–Q3 R–N3 19 P–N3 P–QR4 20 R–B4 Polugaevsky-Taimanov, Moscow 1974. White will win one of the weak centre pawns. A nice exploitation.
b) **10 Q–B2** P–Q3 (10 ... N–B4?! 11 P–K3 Q–B3 12 R–N1 R–Q1 13 R–Q1 ± Larsen-Hübner, Busum 1969) 11 P–N3 P–QB4 12 B–N2 B–N2 13 B×B R×B 14 N–K4! N–B3 15 B×B K×B 16 Q–N2ch P–B3 17 QR–Q1 Q–K2 18 N–B3! Gheorghiu-Suba, Rumania Ch 1977. White has emerged with the better pawn structure and pressure down the queen file (1–0, 41).

CONCLUSION:

3 N–KB3 P–KN3 4 P–K3 B–N2 is probably satisfactory for Black, but 4 P–Q4! P×P 5 N×P gives White enduring pressure. The variations thereafter are instructive, but not recommended for the second player.

3 THE KERES SYSTEM:
3 P–KN3 P–B3

1 P–QB4	P–K4
2 N–QB3	N–KB3
3 P–KN3	P–B3

For many years, the English Opening was taken lightly; most players felt it to be too passive for serious winning chances. *Modern Chess Openings*, for example, which devotes very little space to 1 P–QB4, blandly assumes that every defence equalizes. One way this idea started was that the majority of English theory (such as it was) concentrated on 1 . . . P–QB4 or 1 . . . P–K4. The Symmetrical Defence was held to be drawish to begin with (a facile assumption, as it turns out; and after 1 . . . P–K4 2 N–QB3 N–KB3, White was supposed to play either **3 N–B3** N–B3 4 P–Q4(?!), when 4 . . . P–K5 and 4 . . . P×P were good (see Chapter 8), or **3 P–KN3** (hoping for 3 . . . P–Q4), when Keres' move 3 . . . P–B3!, taking a big share of the centre by force, disheartened many prospective English players.

Times have changed; and most of these judgements have been overturned; but the Keres System is still a respected defensive tool for Black. Unfortunately for this chapter, **3 . . . B–N5** has superseded **3 . . . P–B3** as the usual move versus

3 P–KN3; and **3 P–KN3** itself is being seen less in international chess since **3 N–B3** N–B3 4 P–KN3 (or 4 P–K3) has proved itself a dependable White system. Therefore, many of the problems related to Keres' continuation have never been solved, and for certain positions there are not enough high-quality examples. The last nine Informants (as of 1978), for example, contain only three games with 3 . . . P–B3.

White's best chance of securing an advantage, and the most promising territory for new ideas, is almost certainly in the play after 4 N–B3. We examine in turn:

A 4 P–Q4
B 4 B–N2
C 4 N–B3

There is also the bizarre **4 Q–R4**, which discourages the immediate . . . P–Q4, but does little else. Black may answer by **4 . . . P–Q3** e.g. 5 B–N2 QN–Q2 6 N–B3 P–KN3 (or **6 . . . B–K2** and Black's normal Old Indian plan of . . . 0–0, . . . P–QR3, and . . . P–QN4 has gained force) 7 P–Q4 B–N2 8 0–0 0–0, when White's queen is badly placed, or **4 . . . N–R3** 5 P–Q3 B–K2 6 N–B3 P–Q3 7 B–N2 0–0 8 0–0 N–B4 9 Q–B2 P–QR4 = Mirkovich-Turukin, 1970.

A
4 P–Q4

If 3 . . . P–Q4 is playable for Black in the Alapin Sicilian (e.g. 1 P–K4 P–QB4 2 N–KB3 N–QB3 3 P–B3 P–Q4), why not for White here, with the extra tempo P–KN3? As usual, it's not so simple: in that system, Black plays either . . . P–K3 or an early . . . P×P and . . . P–K4; in other words, the KB comes out along its original diagonal. Pursuing the identical strategy here, White would not only 'waste' the move P–KN3, but seriously weaken his kingside.

But if White cannot play P–K3, . . . P–Q4–5 is difficult to restrain, after which Black obtains an aggressive position with effortless development.

```
4 . . .          P×P
5 Q×P          P–Q4 (22)
```

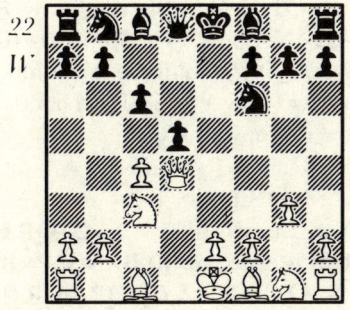

White has tried several approaches at this point:

A1 6 P×P
A2 6 B–N5
A3 6 B–N2
A4 6 N–B3

A1
6 P×P?

Universally queried. Black's . . . N–QB3 and . . . P–Q5 come too fast.

```
6 . . .          P×P
```

Leading to:
A11 7 N–B3
A12 7 B–N2
A13 7 B–N5

A11

```
7 N–B3          N–B3
8 Q–QR4        P–Q5
9 N–QN5        B–QB4
```

Also **9 . . . B–N5ch** 10 B–Q2 B×Bch 11 N×B 0–0 12 B–N2 R–K1! is better for Black (Schwarz).

```
10 B–N2          0–0
```

11 0–0 P–QR3! (threatening 12 . . . P×N! 13 Q×R Q–K2, with a queen trap) 12 Q–B2 Q–K2 13 N–R3 N–QN5 14 Q–Q1 R–Q1 15 B–N5 B–B4 16 N–K1 P–R3 17 B×N Q×B ∓ Uhlmann-Gligorić, Moscow 1956.

A12

```
7 B–N2          N–B3
8 Q–Q1
```

8 Q–QR4 P–Q5 9 N–N5 B–N5ch ∓ (Euwe).

```
8 . . .          P–Q5
9 N–K4          N×N
10 B×N          B–N5ch
```

11 B–Q2 0–0 12 B×B (**12 B–N2** R–K1 13 N–B3 P–Q6! 14 P–K3 B–N5; **12 B×N** B×Bch 13 Q×B P×B 14 N–B3 P–B4 15 0–0 Q–Q4 and Black threatens . . . B–N2, . . . P–Q6 and/or . . . QR–Q1, . . . KR–K1-Schwarz) 12 . . . N×B 13

Q–Q2 R–K1 (or 13 ... Q–N3 Δ
... R–K1) 14 B–N1 (**14 B–N2**
Q–K2 15 P–QR3 N–B3 and White
has trouble developing; or **14 Q×N**
R×B 15 R–Q1 P–QR4! 16 Q–Q2
B–K3! 17 P–B3 R–K4-Euwe.) 14
... Q–Q4 15 P–B3 Q–QB4 16
P–QR3 N–B3 17 B–K4 B–B4! 18
R–B1 Q–K4 19 B×B Q×B 20 K–B2
R–K6 Baumbach-Fuchs, Berlin
1960. Black won in a few moves.
Not a critical variation, but the
kind of thing White has to watch
out for.

A13

7 B–N5   N–B3
   Simplest, although 7 ... B–K2! 8
B–N2 N–B3 is A2.
   8 Q–QR4
   8 B×N? N×Q 9 B×Q N–B7ch 10
K–Q1 N×R 11 B–N5 B–KB4 12
B–N2 P–B3 13 B–Q2 P–Q5 14
N–N5 0–0–0! (Shatskes).
   8 ...   P–Q5
   9 0–0–0   B–Q2
10 B–R3 B–K2 11 B×N B×B(3) 12
B×Bch Q×B 13 P–K3 0–0–0 14
KN–K2? (14 P×P ∓) 14 ... P–Q6
∓ Laaman-Keres, corres 1935. On
15 N–B4, 15 ... P–Q7ch and ...
B×N follows.
   Thus 6 P×P? frees Black's pieces
(especially his queen knight) before
Black can cope with them.

A2

6 B–N5   B–K2
   Or **6 ... P×P** 7 Q×Qch K×Q 8
P–K4 P–KR3! 9 0–0–0ch K–K1 10
B×N P×B B–K3 = (Shatskes).
   7 P×P
a) **7 0–0–0?** P×P! 8 Q×Qch (8 Q×P
Q–R4! ∓) 8 ... B×Q 9 N–K4

B–K2 10 N–Q6ch B×N 11 R×B
B–K3 and Black is a pawn up.
b) **7 B–N2** P×P 8 Q×P B–K3 9
Q–R4 Q–N3 10 B–Q2 (forced: ...
Q×NP and ... N–N5 were threats)
10 ... QN–Q2 11 N–B3 N–B4 12
Q–B2   P–QR4   (Schwarz)   is
obviously more comfortable for the
second player.
c) **7 N–B3** 0–0 8 B–N2 P–KR3 9
B–B4 P–B4 (or 9 ... P×P =) 10
Q–Q3 P–Q5 11 N–QN5? (better 11
N–Q5! – Δ *11 ... N–B3 12 P–K4!* –
11 ... N×N 12 P×N Q×P 13
N–N5! Q–B4 14 B–K4 Q–Q2 15
B–B6 Q–B4 16 B–K4 = – Shatskes)
11 ... N–B3 12 B–B7 (12 N–B7?
P–KN4!) 12 ... Q–K1 13 0–0
B–N5 14 P–KR3 B–R4 15 N–K5
P–QR3 16 N×N NP×N 17 N–R3
B–Q1! 18 B×B B×P! 19 Q–Q2 B×R
∓∓ Rejfir-Keres, Moscow 1956.
   7 ...   P×P
   8 B–N2
   8 N–B3 N–B3 9 Q–QR4 P–Q5
10 R–Q1 B–Q2 (Shatskes), or **8
R–Q1** N–B3 9 Q–QR4 0–0 10
B–N2 Q–N3! Goldberg-Antoshin,
Moscow 1956. A typical and handy
move to unpin the QP.
   8 ...   N–B3
   9 Q–Q2
   Not surprisingly, **9 Q–QR4
P–Q5!** is effective: 10 B×Nch P×B
11 R–Q1 0–0 12 Q×QP Q–R4!
(Shatskes). But here not **9 ...
B–K3?** 10 P–K3 0–0 11 KN–K2 ±
Kraidman-Lederman, Beer-sheva
1976.
   9 ...   P–Q5
   10 B×N
   10 N–N5? Q–N3 11 B×N P×B Δ
... B–QN5.

10 ... B×B 11 N–Q5 0–0
Taimanov-Shamkovich, Leningrad 1955. Black is better, according to Shamkovich, who gives . the following remarkable analysis:
a) 12 N×Bch Q×N 13 N–B3 B–N5 14 0–0 KR–K1 15 QR–Q1 QR–Q1 16 KR–K1 P–Q6! ∓;
b) 12 N–B4? B–B4 13 N–B3 R–K1 14 0–0 B–K5 ∓;
c) 12 N–R3 P–Q6!! 13 0–0 *(13 P×P B×N 14 N×Bch Q×N 15 B×B N–Q5! ∓; 13 Q×P B×P 14 R–QN1 B–Q5! 15 N(3)–B4 Q–R4ch 16 Q–Q2 B×Pch ∓∓)* 13 ... P×P 14 Q×P N–Q5 15 Q–Q1 B×N 16 N×Bch Q×N 17 B×B QR–Q1 18 B–N2 KR–K1 19 K–R1 R–K7 etc.

A3
6 B–N2   B–K3!
6 ... P×P 7 Q×P (but Shamkovich gives 7 Q×Qch K×Q 8 P–K4! B–K3 9 P–B4! ±) 7 ... B–K3 8 Q–QR4 N–Q4 9 N×N B×N 10 N–B3 N–Q2 11 0–0 B–K2 12 P–K4 B–K3 13 R–Q1 0–0 = Hecht-Polugaevsky, Siegen 1970.
7 P×P
Otherwise 7 ... P×P or 7 ... P–B4 Δ ... P–Q5.
7 ...   P×P
8 N–B3
Still another example of the power of the isolated pawn is **8 B–N5** B–K2 9 N–B3 0–0 10 R–Q1 Q–R4 11 0–0 N–B3 12 Q–Q2 KR–Q1 ∓ 13 N–Q4 N×N 14 Q×N P–KR3 15 B–Q2 Q–R3! 16 Q–QR4? Q×Q 17 N×Q QR–B1 18 R–B1 N–K5 19 B–K3 P–QN4! ∓ Madsen-Jezek, corres 1959 (0–1, 38).

8 ...   N–B3
9 Q–QR4   B–QB4
a) **9 ... Q–N3** 10 0–0 0–0–0? (better **10 ... B–K2**; Black's queenside is airy) 11 N–QN5 P–Q5? 12 B–B4 N–Q4 13 QR–B1 N×B 14 N×Pch! K–Q2 15 P×N B–Q3 16 N×N P×N 17 R×P! R–R1 18 Q×R 1–0 Bakonyi-Szilayi, Hungarian Ch 1951.
b) **9 ... B–K2** 10 N–K5?! (10 **0–0** 0–0 11 N–Q4 =-Shatskes) 10 ... Q–N3! 11 0–0 0–0 12 N×N? P×N 13 P–N3 B–QN5! ∓ Zotkin-Ravinsky, Leningrad 1966.

10 0–0   0–0
11 B–N5 P–KR3 12 B×N Q×B 13 P–K4 P×P 14 N×P Q–K2 15 N×B Q×N 16 KR–Q1 QR–Q1 = Pirc-Keres, Yugoslavia-USSR 1956. Quickly drawn.

A4
6 N–B3
The most interesting attempt to make headway.
6 ...   B–K2
The point is that **6 ... B–K3** can be answered with 7 N–KN5.
7 B–N2   0–0
A simple plan is **7 ... P–B4(!)** 8 Q–Q3 P–Q5 **9 N–K4** N–B3 10 N×Nch B×N 11 0–0 0–0 12 P–QR3 B–K3 13 B–B4 R–K1 ∓ Pfleger-Keres, Bamberg 1968. Possibly **9 N–QN5** was better, but this game makes 6 N–B3 and 7 B–N2 look bad as a winning try.
8 0–0   P–B4
8 ... P×P 9 Q×P P–QN4!? unbalances the situation: 10 Q–Q4 P–N5 11 N–K4 B–R3 12 R–K1 QN–Q2 Yogyale-Mikenas, Pri-

Baltic 1965, with rapid development in return for weaknesses.

9 Q–Q3   P×P

9 ... P–Q5 10 N–Q5! was Stahlberg-Keres, Stockholm 1967, when **10 ... N×N** 11 P×N Q×P? 12 N–N5 Q–B4 13 Q×Q and 14 B×NP is winning. After Keres' **10 ... N–B3**, White still would have been better had he played 11 P–K4!.

10 Q×P   N–B3
11 R–Q1   Q–R4 =

Analysis by Shatskes.

CONCLUSION:

4 P–Q4 lacks punch, and can be a perilous course for White. To get equality, he should play **6 B–N2** or perhaps **6 N–B3** (although after 6 N–B3 he must face 6 ... B–K2 7 B–N2 P–B4).

B

4 B–N2   P–Q4

Of course **4 ... P–Q3** is plausible, transposing into a King's or Old Indian, for example. Also **4 ... B–N5** may yield positions from Chapter 4. But the text is ideal.

5 P×P

Else **5 ... P–Q5** is strong, e.g. 5 P–Q3 P–Q5 6 N–K4 N×N 7 B×N N–Q2 8 B–N2 B–B4 9 N–B3 0–0 10 0–0 P–QR4 11 P–K4 P×Pe.p. 12 P×P B–R2 13 P–Q4? P×P 14 P×P N–K4! ∓ Norcia-Keres, Munich 1958.

5 ...   P×P
6 Q–N3

6 P–Q3 is timid: 6 ... N–B3 7 N–B3 (**7 B–N5** P–Q5; **7 P–B4?** P–Q5 8 P×P N–KN5 9 N–K4

B–N5ch 10 K–B1 N(5)×P 11 N–R3 0–0 ∓ Hugolf-van Perlo, corres. 1958) 7 ... B–K2 (**7 ... P–Q5!** 8 N–K4 N×N 9 P×N B–N5ch ∓-Gavlikovski and Plater) 8 0–0 0–0 9 P–Q4 P–K5 10 N–K5 B–K3 11 N×N P×N 12 N–R4 N–Q2 13 B–K3 Q–R4 14 R–B1 N–N3! 15 N–B5 N–B5! 16 N×B P×N ∓ Szabo-Keres, Moscow 1956. The usual verdict of '=' after 12 N–R4 is likely an accurate one, but Black's position is the easier to play.

6 ...   N–B3!

Lively but dubious is **6 ... P–K5?!** 7 P–B3! (**7 P–Q3?!** P×P 8 N×P N×N 9 B×N B–N5ch! 10 K–B1 P×Pch 11 N×P 0–0 ∞ Wexler-Bazon, Buenos Aires 1960) **7 ... P×P?!** 8 B×P N–B3 9 N×P N–Q5 10 Q–K3ch (Shatskes). After 7 P–B3!, Black should probably try something speculative like **7 ... N–B3!?** 8 P×P P–Q5 9 N–Q5 B–K3 10 Q×P R–B1, which stirs up trouble, anyway.

7 N×P

Too late for **7 P–Q3?** P–Q5 8 N–Q5 N×N 9 B×N B–N5ch 10 K–B1 Q–K2 ∓ Peterson-Tal, Riga 1958.

7 ...   N–Q5

Interesting though probably not sound was **7 ... N×N!?** 8 Q×N (**8 B×N** N–Q5 9 B×Pch K–K2 10 Q–B4 B–B4 etc.) 8 ... Q×Q 9 B×Q N–Q5 10 K–Q1?! (**10 B–K4!** or **10 R–N1** seems better) 10 ... B–B4 11 P–Q3 (11 B×P!?) 11 ... R–Q1 12 B×P P–K5 13 B–QR6 P×P 14 B×P N×P 15 N×N R×Bch with a strong attack, Petters-Carlson, Colorado 1973.

8 N×Nch
Obligatory.

a) **8 Q–R4ch** B–Q2 9 Q–Q1 N×N
10 B×N Q–R4 11 B–N3 (else 11 . . .
B–R5!) 11 . . . B–B3 12 P–B3 B–B4
∓ Maslov-Mikenas, Vilnus 1961.

b) **8 Q–B4** N×N 9 B×N P–QN4! 10
B×Pch (**10 B–B6ch** B–Q2 11
B×Bch Q×B 12 Q–Q3 Q–B3 ∓∓)
10 . . . K–K2 11 Q–Q5 N–B7ch 12
K–Q1 N×R 13 P–N3 (13 Q×R
Q–B2! ∓∓) 13 . . . Q–B2 14
B–R3ch K–B3 15 Q–B3ch B–B4
0–1 Bydev-Pirc, Rogaska-Slatin
1957.

8 . . .   P×N (23)

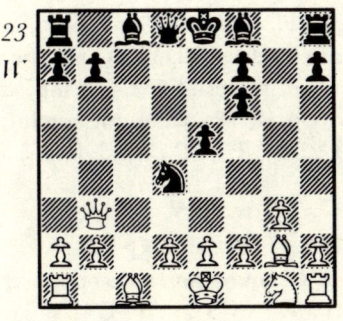

23

The old move was **8 . . . Q×N**
and:

a) **9 Q–Q1?!** B–KB4 10 P–Q3 (10
P–K4 Q–B3!) 10 . . . R–B1 11
R–N1 (11 K–B1 Q–QR3! is very
strong) 11 . . . B–N5ch 12 K–B1 (**12
B–Q2** B×Bch 13 Q×B R–B7 14
Q–R5 B×P! ∓∓) 12 . . . 0–0 13
N–B3 N×N 14 B×N KR–Q1 15
P–K4 B–R6ch 16 B–N2 B–QB4! 17
Q–K2 B–KN5 18 P–B3 Nazari-
Perez, Mar del Plata 1961, and now
18 . . . B–Q2 Δ . . . B–N4 was
decisive. But better is

b) **9 Q–Q3!** B–KB4 (**9 . . . B–QB4**

10 P–K3 B–B4 11 B–K4 B×B 12
Q×B ± Gurgenidze-Panteleev,
Sofia 1958) 10 B–K4 B–Q2 (or **10
. . . B×B** 11 Q×B R–B1!? 12 Q×NP
Q–K3 13 K–B1 B–Q3 14 P–K3
N–B7 15 R–N1 and Black is 'very
active . . . but two pawns down'-
Shatskes) 11 B×NP! (**11 P–K3**
N–K3 12 Q–K2 N–B4 13 B–B2
P–K5! ∓ Novak-Trapl, Prague
1959) 11 . . . R–QN1 12 N–B3! (**12
B–N2** R–B1 13 K–B1 B–QB4 ∓∓-
Shatskes) 12 . . . R×B 13 N×N
B–QB4 (13 . . . P×N 14 Q–K4ch)
14 N–B3 B–B3 15 Q–B2 Sazonov-
Litvinov, BSSR 1963, and correct
was 15 . . . B×N! 16 P×B Q×P 17
0–0 R–B2 when Black stands no
worse, according to Shatskes and
Taimanov.

9 Q–Q3
9 Q–Q1 Q–B2 10 K–B1 B–K3 11
P–N3 N–B7 12 R–N1 R–B1! 13
B–N2 (on **13 P–Q3** or **13 N–B3**, 13
. . . N–R6! 14 B×N B×B-Shatskes)
13 . . . B–QR6! 14 B–QB3 N–N5 15
B×N (15 R–R1 N–Q4) 15 . . . B×B
and Black penetrates on c2
(Taimanov).

9 . . .   B–KB4
10 B–K4   B×B
11 Q×B   Q–B2
12 K–B1 P–B4! 13 Q–Q3 B–N2 14
P–K3 Q–B3! 15 P×N Q×R 16 P×P
0–0 17 Q∓KB3 Q×P 18 P–Q4
KR–Q1 ∓ Zamikovsky-Zurakhov,
Kiev 1958.

CONCLUSION:

4 B–N2 P–Q4 5 P×P P×P 6 P–Q3
N–B3 looks at best equal for White,
whereas 6 Q–N3 N–B3! is worse
still.

C

4 N–B3

Upon which the fate of the Keres System hangs! White attacks the Black KP which cannot be defended without some kind of concession.

4 ...   P–K5

Of course **4 ... P–Q3** is possible with another transposition to an Old or King's Indian; but **4 ... Q–B2** 5 P–Q4 P×P 6 Q×P is very good for White who can play B–B4 and bear down on d6.

5 N–Q4 (*24*)

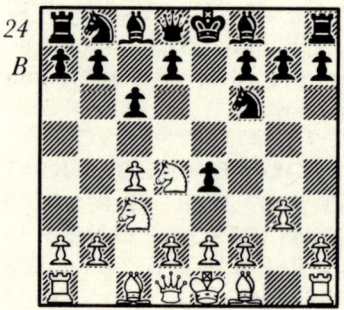

24
B

As in an Alapin Sicilian or Alekhine's Defence; White hopes the advanced Black centre will be weak, while Black intends to cramp White's game and develop his own pieces aggressively. Now:

C1 5 ... B–B4
C2 5 ... Q–N3
C3 5 ... P–Q4

C1

5 ...   B–B4!?
6 N–N3   P–Q3

Bronstein's idea. If White takes the bishop, then Black has the queen-file and his pawns control important central squares. e4 is to be supported by pieces.

7 B–N2   B–B4
8 0–0   QN–Q2
9 P–Q3   P×P
10 P×P   0–0

11 B–B4 R–K1 12 Q–Q2 N–B1 (Both sides are developing logically. Black's last is directed against 13 P–Q4 B–QN5 14 P–QR3; now on 13 P–QR3, the bishop retreats to b6.) 13 N–R4 N–K3 14 P–Q4 B–QN3 15 N×B P×N 16 P–Q5 (16 B–K3!?) 16 ... N×B 17 Q×N B–Q6? (17 ... B–K5! = was correct—Smyslov) 18 KR–Q1 N–R4 19 Q–Q2 B–K7 20 P×P! ± Smyslov-Bronstein, Monte Carlo 1969. White is either winning material or getting a deadly passed pawn on the seventh after 21 B×R P×P etc. (1–0, 27).

C2

5 ...   Q–N3

Tal's move, the most popular alternative to **5 ... P–Q4**. What White should do is not clear:
C21 6 N–N3
C22 6 N–B2
C23 6 P–K3

C21

6 N–N3

Natural, but allowing a sharp reply:

6 ...   P–QR4!

One of the few times in the Keres System when this move is genuinely effective. Black threatens to win a piece.

7 P–Q4
7 N–R4!? Q–N5 8 N–Q4 B–B4! 9

P–K3?! ('**9 N–B5!** Q×BP 10 N–N6
B×Pch ∞'-Tompa. *Not* 10 . . .
B×N? 11 *N–Q6ch.* After 10 . . .
B×Pch(!) 11 K×B Q–B4ch 12
K–N2 Q×N(3), however, one
prefers Black.) 9 . . . B×N 10 P×B
N–R3! 11 P–N3 P–Q4 12 P–QR3
Q–K2 13 N–N6 B–N5 14 B–K2 B×B
15 Q×B R–Q1 and Black had the
better chances, Forintos-Tompa,
Hungary Ch 1976 (0–1, 57).

     7 . . .   P–R5
     8 P–B5   Q–N5
9 N–Q2 P–Q4! (9 . . . Q×QP? 10
N(2)×P ±) 10 P–K3 (**10 P×Pe.p.**
Q×P(5) 11 N(2)×P Q×Qch 12
K×Q N×N 13 N×N B–B4 etc.-
Shatskes) 10 . . . P–KN3 11 P–KR3
B–N2 = Bagirov-Tal, Moscow
1963. An interesting, double-edged
situation.

C22
     6 N–B2   P–Q4
     Or **6 . . . B–B4** 7 N–K3 B×N!? 8
QP×B 0–0 9 B–N2 R–K1 10 P–N3,
unclear, Raicević-Judović, Yugo-
slavia Ch 1978 (½–½, 43).
     7 B–N2   B–KB4
     8 0–0
     8 P×P P×P 9 P–Q3 B–N3 10 0–0
QN–Q2 11 B–K3 Q–R3 12 P×P
P×P 13 N–Q4 B–Q3 14 N(4)–N5
B–N1 15 Q–N3 0–0 = Huguet-
Darga, Las Palmas 1973 (0–1, 31).
     8 . . .   P×P?!
This works out badly; **8 . . .
P–Q5?!** 9 N–R4 Q–Q1 10 P–Q3
P×P 11 P×P B–K2 12 P–QN4! also
looks dubious, but **8 . . . B–K2** and
8 . . . B–N3 are legitimate
alternatives.
     9 N–K3   B–N3

     10 N×BP   Q–B4
     11 P–N3   N–R3
12 P–Q4 Q–KR4 13 P–B3 R–Q1
14 Q–K1! B–N5 (14 . . . R×P? 15
P–KN4!) 15 P–N4 B×N 16 Q×B
Q–Q4 17 B–QR3! ± Saharov-
Timman, corres 1970. After 17 . . .
Q×Pch? 18 Q×Q R×Q 19 QR–Q1,
White won in 6 more moves.

C23
     6 P–K3   P–Q4
     7 Q–B2
     Played by Najdorf. White
threatens 8 P×P P×P 9 N×QP! etc.
     7 . . .   B–Q2
a) **7 . . . QN–Q2?** 8 P×P P×P 9
N(3)–N5! (Tajmanov). That looks
strong, for if **9 . . . B–B4**, 10 P–QN4
B×N 11 N–B7ch or **9 . . . N–B4 10
P–QN4 N–R3 11 P–QR3 ±**.
b) **7 . . . P–B4?** 8 N×QP N×N 9
P×N ± ±.
     8 P–QR3   B–K2?!
     8 . . . P–QR4 Δ . . . N–R3 would
defend queenside territorial rights.
     9 P–QN4   0–0
10 B–QN2 N–R3 (criticized by
commentators, but White is better
regardless) 11 P–B5 Q–B2 12 P–B3!
± Najdorf-Rossetto, Buenos Aires
1968. White's pieces are finding
excellent squares, while Black is
cramped (1–0, 23).

C3
     5 . . .   P–Q4
     6 P×P
     6 B–N2?! P×P! 7 N–B2 N–R3 (or
7 . . . B–KB4 8 N–K3 B–N3 9
N×BP QN–Q2 10 P–QR4 B–K2 11
0–0 0–0 12 P–N3 P–QR4 13 B–QR3
B×B 14 R×B R–K1 Goldberg-

Bronstein, Moscow 1961. With the KP so efficiently overprotected, Black is at least equal.) 8 N×P N×N 9 B×N N–B4 ($\mp$) 10 B–N2 B–K3 11 0–0 P–KR4! 12 N–K3 P–R5 13 Q–B2 P×P 14 BP×P Q–N4 15 R–B2 Q–R4 16 B–B3 Q–R2! 17 Q×Q R×Q 18 B–N4 B×B 19 N×B R–R4 20 R–N1 R–Q1 $\mp$ Hartoch-Vasiukov, Amsterdam 1969. After 6 P×P:

C31 6 . . . P×P
C32 6 . . . Q–N3

C31

6 . . .   P×P

The most direct move, but theory favours White, who will undermine the advanced Black pawns. He can do this by:

C311 7 B–N2
C312 7 P–Q3

C311

7 B–N2   N–B3

7 . . . B–QB4 8 N–N3 B–N3 **9 0–0!** is best, since **9 . . . P–KR4?** 10 P–Q3 is too slow for Black, and **9 . . . Q–K2** 10 P–Q3 P–K6? 11 P×P B×Pch 12 B×B Q×Bch 13 K–R1 is $\pm$. **9 . . . B–KB4** 10 P–Q3 P×P (10 . . . 0–0 11 B–N5) 11 P×P 0–0 12 B–N5 also gives White the initiative. In every case, Black will be forced to exchange his KP and be tied to protecting his isolated QP. Weaker in this line was **9 P–Q3?!** in Neikirch-Florian, 1959: 9 . . . N–N5! 10 P–K3 P–B4 11 P×P QP×P 12 0–0 N–QB3 13 N–Q5 B–K3 14 N×B and **14 . . . P×N!** was fine for Black (instead of **14 . . . Q×N?** 15 Q–Q6! $\pm$, as played),

since White's central squares are weak and his bishops are inactive ($\mp$).

8 N×N   P×N
9 P–Q3   P×P
10 Q×P (*25*)   *)*

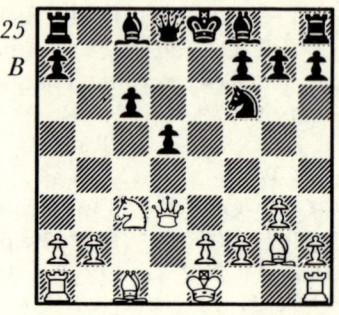

25
B

10 . . .   B–K2
Also **10 . . . B–QN5(!)** may be played. Then 11 0–0 0–0 **12 N–R4?** (It is very dangerous to decentralize this knight before completing development. **12 R–Q1** has been recommended, although 12 . . . R–K1 13 B–N5 P–KR3 14 B×N Q×B 15 QR–B1 P–QR4 appears level, or here **13 P–K4** B–N5! 14 P–B3 B–K3 etc.; 12 B–N5 R–K1 is similar. So perhaps 10 . . . B–QN5 equalizes!?) 12 . . . R–K1 13 P–QR3 B–Q3 14 B–K3 P–QR4! 15 KR–K1 B–R3 16 Q–B3 QR–N1 Δ . . . B–N4 $\mp$ Portisch-Spassky, Leningrad-Budapest 1961.

11 0–0   0–0
12 R–Q1

Other moves haven't succeeded in tying down Black's queenside pawns:
a) **12 B–K3** R–K1 (**12 . . . . B–K3** and if 13 KR–Q1?! N–N5! Δ 14 B–Q2 Q–N3 looks interesting.) **13**

KR–Q1?! B–K3 14 QR–B1 N–N5 15 B–Q2 Q–N3 16 B–K1 Q×P ∓ Panno-Keres, Mar del Plata 1957. Better **13 QR–B1**.

b) **12 P–QN3** (Schwarz) is not very assertive. 12 ... R–K1 13 B–N2 Q–R4! 14 KR–K1 B–R3 15 Q–B2 QR–Q1 16 N–R4 P–B4 etc..

c) **12 P–K4?!** P–QR4! (Schwarz) ∓.

12 ...	Q–N3
13 P–N3	N–N5

Black is almost committed to this, now that B–K3 is threatened, which with N–R4 and QR–B1 would blockade the central pawns. We are following Portisch-Olaffson, Moscow 1959: 14 Q–B3 B–K3 15 N–R4 Q–N4 16 B–N2 N–B3 17 Q–Q3 P–QR3 18 QR–B1. White is better, due to Black's weak queenside pawns, although the game ended in a quick draw when White unnecessarily exchanged queens on b5 and repaired Black's structure.

C312

7 P–Q3 (26)

Probably best, since in C311 10 ... B–QN5(!) apparently rid Black of his major problems.

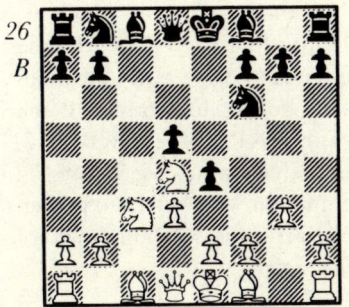

26
B

7 ... B–QB4

The usual move. Alternatives:

a) **7 ... P×P?!** 8 Q×P N–B3 9 B–N2 ±. White is not compelled to exchange on QB6, as in C311, e.g. 9 ... B–K2 10 0–0 0–0 11 B–B4 B–KN5 12 QR–B1 Q–Q2 13 N×N (only now!) 13 ... P×N 14 N–R4 KR–K1 15 KR–K1 B–KB4 16 Q–R6 B–QN5 17 R(K)–Q1 ± Fitzgerald-Massana, USA 1972.

b) **7 ... Q–N3** 8 N–N3 N–N5 9 P–Q4 (or 9 P–K3!?-Shatskes) 9 ... B–K3 (or 9 ... B–QN5!?) 10 P–B3 P×P 11 P×P N–KB3 12 B–K3 N–B3 13 K–B2 ('with the better chances',-Shatkes and Taimanov, but:) 13 ... B–Q3 **14 N–N5?!** B–N1 15 Q–Q2 0–0 16 B–N5 N–Q2 and Black was a little better in Korchnoi-Keres, Moscow 1962 (½–½, 38). **14 K–N2** or **14 R–B1** is more logical; but the position is unclear, not ±. Also the move 9 ... B–QN5 must be considered a problem for White. So **9 P–K3!?** may be best e.g. 9 ... B–QN5 10 P×P P×P 11 B–Q2 ±.

8 N–N3

a) **8 P×P** P×P 9 N–N3 Q×Qch 10 N×Q B–N5ch Seoev-Holmov, Moscow 1967.

b) **8 N–B2** B–B4 (**8 ... 0–0** 9 B–N2 Q–K2 10 0–0 N–B3 11 B–N5! ± Rabar-Suvalic, 16th Yugoslav Ch 1961) 9 P×P N×P! is better for Black (Taimanov). Also 9 P–Q4 B–QN3 10 B–N5 B–K3 is harmless.

8 ... B–QN5

8 ... B–N3? is an error after **9 P×P!** N×P 10 N×N P×N 11 Q×Qch B×Q 12 B–N2 P–B4 13 P N4! ± Taimanov-Gavlikovsky,

Sczvavno Zdroj 1955. Instead, **9 B–N2?!** B–KB4? 10 P×P (or **10 0–0** P–K6?! 11 B×KP B×B 12 P×B B–N3 13 R×N! P×R 14 N×P N–Q2 15 Q–KB1 0–0 16 Q–B4 ± Karpov-Karasev, 39th USSR Ch SF 1971) 10 . . . N×P 11 0–0 N×N 12 P×N B–K5 13 B–QR3! yielded an attack in B. Kogan-Chesnauskas, Palanga 1968. But here **9 . . . N–N5!** 10 P–K3 P–B4 transposes into Neikirch-Florian (C311, note to 7 . . . N–B3).

9 P×P

In other lines, Black gets time to bastion e4, although White may get some piece pressure in (b) notwithstanding:

a) **9 P–QR3?!** B×Nch 10 P×B N–B3 11 B–KN2 B–B4 12 0–0 0–0 13 B–B4 R–K1 (or **13 . . . R–B1** 14 Q–Q2 R–K1 15 KR–K1 P–KR3! 16 P–QR4?! P×P 17 P×P R×Rch 18 R×R Q–N3! ∓ Taimanov-Mikenas, 24th USSR Ch 1957) 14 Q–Q2 Q–K2 15 KR–K1 QR–Q1 = Uhlmann-Golz, E. Germany Ch 1968.

b) **9 B–N2!?** 0–0 (**9 . . . N–B3** 10 0–0 B–KB4 11 B–N5 B×N 12 P×B P–KR3 13 P×P B×P 14 B×N Q×B Ivkov-Keres, Leningrad 1957, and now 15 P–B3 B–N3 16 Q×P Q×QBP 17 P–K4 would be slightly ±-Shatskes) 10 0–0 B–KB4 11 P×P (**11 B–N5!?** may transpose into the last note e.g. 11 . . . B×N 12 P×B P–KR3 13 P×P etc.) 11 . . . P×P 12 B–N5 B×N **13 P×B** N(1)–Q2 14 N–Q4 B–N3 15 Q–N3! Korchnoi-Keres, USSR Ch 1957. This still seems a shade better for the first player. Also to be considered here

was **13 Q×Q** R×Q 14 P×B △ 14 . . . N(1)–Q2 15 N–Q4 B–N3 16 B–R3! when Black will be pressed to defend his centre and queenside.

9 . . .   N×P
10 B–Q2   Q–N3

a) **10 . . . B×N** 11 B×B N×B 12 P×N and White is better; Shatskes and Taimanov point out that the weakness of Black's QP is more important than that of White's QBP.

b) **10 . . . N×B** 11 Q×N △ B–N2, 0–0, and a rook to d1. The Black QP is a problem.

11 N×N   P×N
12 B×B Q×Bch 13 Q–Q2 (±) N–B3 14 B–N2 P–B4 15 Q×Q N×Q 16 0–0 B–K3(?!) 17 N–Q4 B–Q2 18 P–B3 P×P 19 R×P! ± Ivkov-Kozomara, Sarajevo 1967. 20 N×P and 20 R–N3 are threats (1–0, 62).

CONCLUSION:

After 4 N–B3 P–K5 5 N–Q4 P–Q4 6 P×P, the move 6 . . . P×P leaves Black with some difficulties in the lines with **7 P–Q3(!)** while **7 B–N2** gives him time enough to stabilize the centre and equalize.

C32
6 . . .   **Q–N3** (27)
The modern move, which was evidently first played by Mikenas. It intends to drive away the knight on d4 so as to protect Black's advanced KP by . . . B–KB4; 6 . . . Q–N3 has also been used in conjunction with a plan to pressure White's queenside, though without much success.

7 N–N3

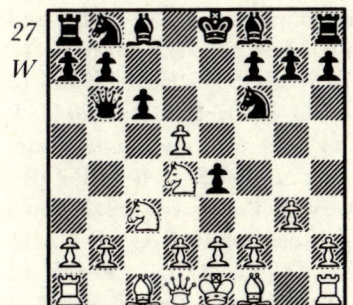

27
W

Lesser tried moves are not without point:

a) **7 N–B2** B–QB4 (**7 ... P×P** 8 B–N2 Δ P–Q3-Schwarz, or **8 P–Q3** B–QB4 9 P–Q4 B–K2 10 B–N5-Shatskes) 8 N–K3 P×P 9 N–R4 Q–B3 10 N×B Q×N 11 Q–B2 (**11 P–Q4** P×Pe.p. 12 Q×P P–Q5 Δ ... B–B4) 11 ... Q×Q 12 N×Q N–B3 13 P–N3 N–KN5! 14 B–QN2 N(5)–K4 Taimanov-Mikenas, Leningrad 1960, which Taimanov himself thinks is satisfactory for Black, but Shatskes and Schwarz both assess it as a bit better for White. The game continued 15 B–N2 0–0 16 0–0 B–K3 **17 KR–B1** QR–Q1 18 N–K1 Δ P–B3. Also possible was the direct **17 QR–Q1** QR–Q1 18 KR–K1 Δ P–Q3. Both positions are interesting – probably ± – because, despite Black's solid centre White can hold back the pawns and eventually open the game when his bishops give him the better chances in even a simplified position.

b) **7 P–K3** P×P 8 P–Q3 (**8 P–B3** P×P 9 Q×P N–B3 10 N×P N×N(4) 11 Q×N N×N 12 Q×N Q×Q etc.-Shatskes. But not **8 ... N–B3** 9 N×N P×N 10 P×P N×P 11 N×N

P×N 12 Q–B2 ± Shatkes-Alekseev, Moscow 1967) 8 ... B–QN5 9 B–N2 **N–B3?!** 10 0–0 N×N 11 P×N. Schwarz calls this '±'. Rather than encourage the development of White's queen bishop, one might substitute **9 ... 0–0** 10 0–0 R–K1, e.g. 11 P–QR3(?!) B×N 12 P×B N–Q2! Δ ... N–B4 or ... N–K4.

c) **7 Q–R4?!** B–QB4 8 P×P 0–0 (or **8 ... N×P** 9 N×N B–Q2!-Evans) 9 P×P B×P 10 P–K3 B×N 11 Q×B Q×Q 12 P×Q N–B3 13 B–N2 N×P 14 0–0 B–R3 ∓ Evans-Keres, Amsterdam 1971.

7 ...   P×P

a) **7 ... N–N5?!** is a mistake: 8 P–Q4! BP×P (8 ... P×Pe.p. 9 P–K3) 9 N×QP! (not **9 B–N2** B–N5 10 0–0 B×N 11 P×B 0–0 = /∞ Hartston-Basman, Hastings 1967, which continued 12 P–KR3?! – 12 P–B3 – 12 ... N–KB3 13 R–N1 Q–B3 ∓) 9 ... Q–QB3 10 N–K3 B–N5ch 11 B–Q2 N×N 12 P×N B×Bch 13 Q×B with an excellent game (Shatskes). This is surely true, for even if Black can play ... P–B4 and ... 0–0, White has R–QB1–B3, Q–B2 and the White king strolls to the queenside in preparation for P–KN4!

b) **7 ... P–QR4** 8 P–Q4! (**8 P–Q3** P–R5 9 N–Q2 BP×P!? 10 P×P P×P 11 B–N2!? P–K6! ∞ Nikolaevsky-Chesnauskas, Minsk 1966) 8 ... P×P (**8 ... P–R5** 9 N–B5! B×N 10 P×B Q×BP 11 B–K3 Q–N5 12 P–QR3! ±, according to everybody) 9 B–N2 B–K2 10 0–0 0–0 11 B–N5 R–Q1 12 P–K3 N–R3 13 P–B3! P×P 14 Q×P B–K3 15

Q–K2 N–B2 16 N–B5! B×N 17
N–R4 Q–N5 18 N×B ± Botvinnik-
Alekseev, Moscow 1968.

8 B–N2

White can also try **8 P–Q3!?**,
which worked out well in Pribyl-
Petrik, Czechoslovakia 1974: **8 . . .
B–KB4?!** 9 B–K3 Q–R3 10 N–Q4
B–Q2 11 B–N2 B–QN5˙ 12 0–0
B×N 13 P×B 0–0 14 B–N5! R–K1
15 Q–N1! P×P 16 P×P N–B3 17
N–N5! Q–R4 18 N–Q6 R–K2 19
Q–N3 ± (1–0, 42). But 8 . . .
B–KB4?! can be improved on. For
one thing, **8 . . . N–N5!?** is C312,
note (b), which is not at all clear
after 9 P–Q4 B–QN5 (or 9 . . .
B–K3) or 9 P–K3!? Also, **8 . . .
B–QN5** is a better move than
Petrik's 8 . . . B–KB4; because if 9
B–N2 0–0 10 B–K3 Q–R3, White
cannot play N–Q4 with tempo, and
after 11 0–0 B×N 12 P×B R–K1 13
P×P P×P, Black has good
counterplay (He has the typical
compensation for White's bishops
in the possibility of overprotecting
e4 and occupying White's weakened queenside squares).

8 . . .   B–KB4

Keres' move. Inferior are:
a) **8 . . . P–QR4?!** 9 P–Q3 (also **9
P–Q4** P–R5?! 10 N–B5! P–R6 11
P–N3 Q–N5 12 B–Q2 Q×QP 13
N–N5 Q×N 14 R–QB1! Q×N 15
R×Bch K–K2 – *15 . . . K–Q2 16
B–R3ch* – 16 0–0 P–N4 17 Q–R1!
and White is winning, Kimmelfeld-
Gergel, Moscow 1968) 9 . . . P–R5
10 B–K3 Q–N5 11 N–Q4 P–R6 (11
. . . Q×P? 12 N(3)–N5 ±±) 12
N–B2! Q×P 13 B–Q4 B–QN5 14
N×B Q×N 15 B×N P×B 16 0–0!

B–K3 Botvinnik-Tal (9) 1961, and
White's best here is Bronstein's 17
Q–B1! (Δ N×QP) 17 . . . N–B3 18
R–N1 Q–K2 19 P×P P×P 20 N×P
(Δ R×NP!) with a winning game.
b) **8 . . . N–B3** 9 0–0 P–QR4
(otherwise P–Q3 will break down
Black's centre) 10 P–Q3 P–R5 11
B–K3 Q–N5 (**11 . . . P–Q5** 12
N×QP N×N 13 P×P B–QB4 14
P–K5 N–N5 15 N–Q5! N×B 16
P×N Q×NP 17 N–B7ch and 18
N×R) 12 P×P! P×N 13 P–QR3
Q–R4 14 P×P N–K4 15 Q×P
Polugaevsky-Rossetto, Lugano
1968. White has three pawns for the
piece and an attractive position.

9 P–Q3

Both Shatskes and Taimanov
recommend **9 0–0** (to forego the
difficulties of . . . B–QN5), but they
evidently underestimate the point
of 8 . . . B–KB4: 9 0–0 P–Q5! 10
N–N1 (10 N–R4? Q–N5 ∓∓) 10
. . . N–B3 and Black has a
comfortable game e.g. 11 P–Q3
B–K2 12 B–N5 P×P 13 P×P 0–0 ∓.

9 . . .   B–QN5

9 . . . P×P?! 10 0–0! N–B3?
(better **10 . . . B–K2** 11 P×P 0–0,
when 12 N×P is sound, but gives
Black some counterplay – ±) 11
B–N5! 0–0–0 12 P×P B–K3 13
R–B1 K–N1 14 P–Q4 B–K2 15
N–R4 Q–B2 16 N(3)–B5 P–KR3
17 B–K3 R–QB1? (but 17 . . .
K–R1 18 P–QN4 ±±) 18 B–B4
B–Q3 19 Q–N3! 1–0 Polugaevsky-
Jongsma, Amsterdam 1970.

10 0–0

10 B–K3 is interesting, although
Black should be all right. One line is
10 . . . Q–R3 (or 10 . . . B×Nch 11

P×P!? B×P (**11 ... N×P** 12 0–0!
B×N 13 Q×P ∞) 12 B×B P×B (**12
... N×B** 13 0–0 looks promising.)
13 Q–B2 or 13 0–0, unclear.

10 ...	B×N
11 P×B	0–0
12 B–K3	Q–B2
13 R–B1	N–B3
14 P–QB4	QR–Q1

This position, from Reshevsky-
Keres, Los Angeles 1963, is usually
given as equal. Black has a strong-
point at e4 and play on the central
files; White has two bishops and
pressure down the QB-file. We
continue:

15 N–Q4	N×N
16 B×N	Q–K2!

16 ... P×QP 17 BP×P Q–Q2 18
B×N P×P 19 Q×P P×B 20 Q–N2
K–N2 21 Q–Q4 B–R6 is the original Reshevsky-Keres game
(drawn); yet Minev gives 22
KR–Q1 B×B 23 K×B **P–QR3** 24
P–Q6 ±. Of course, 23 ... **P–N3!**
improves. But a recent cor-
respondence game, Prieditis-Kask,
with Black's king rook in place of
queen rook on d8 (irrelevant in this
case), casts doubt on 16 ... P×QP
altogether. Instead of **20 Q–N2**,
Prieditis played **20 R–B4!** QR–B1
21 R–B4 B–R6 22 B×B Q×B 23
Q–K4 R–K1(?) 24 R–N4ch

K–R1? (but ±± anyway) 25
Q–KB4 1–0.

16 ... Q–K2! comes from Jezek-
Sapundziev, corres 1972/73: 17
BP×P (17 B×N P×B! ∞) 17 ...
R×P 18 Q–R4 P–QN3 19 B×N
P×B 20 B×P?! ('**20 P×P** R–R4 21
Q–B2 R–B1 **22 Q–N1?!** R×R 23
B–K3 =; or **22 Q–N2** R×R 23
R×R B×P 24 B×B Q×B 25 Q×P
...'-Minev, who shows this last line
leading to some White advantage.
But he doesn't consider **23 ...
B–K3** as in the first variation, e.g.
24 R–R1 K–N2 Δ ... Q–R6
= /∞) 20 ... R–R4 21 Q–B2 B×B
22 P×B R–K1 23 KR–Q1 (23
P–B3? P–B4!-Minev) 23 ... Q×P
½–½.

CONCLUSION:

The Keres System continues to
demonstrate an essential soundness.
Against the positionally logical 4
N–B3 P–K5 5 N–Q4 P–Q4 6 P×P,
best is **6 ... Q–N3**, and White to
this date has not found a clear way
to advantage. If Black should
nevertheless feel that this line is too
forcing or gives too few winning
chances, he might try Bronstein's **5
... B–B4** or Tal's **5 ... Q–N3**, both
of which retain considerable
latitude in piece placement.

4 THE MODERN VARIATION:
3 P–KN3 B–N5

1 P–QB4	P–K4
2 N–QB3	N–KB3
3 P–KN3	B–N5 (28)

This bishop development introduces the most popular defensive system versus 3 P–KN3. Black's set-up bears a similarity to the 'Main Line' (3 N–B3 N–B3 4 P–KN3 B–N5; see Chapter 7, D), to which indeed it occasionally transposes. Yet 3 ... B–N5 is especially flexible, since Black's queen knight can go to d7 or c6, and ... P–QB3 remains an important possibility. Thus White's move N–Q5, so often effective in Chapter 7, seldom amounts to much of a threat here. Of course the first player has more options too (e.g. 4 B–N2 0–0 5 P–K4, intending to bring his knight to e2), but present-day theory deems the Black position sufficient for equality in all variations.

As the title indicates, Black's third has not always been the approved choice it is today. Of the proponents (now many) of 3 ... B–N5, I should mention Smyslov, who played many of the earliest, ground-breaking games; and the Soviet player-theoretician Kapengut, who has done important analytical work and clarified many of the problems of this line. I have quoted from (and examined) his opinions frequently throughout this chapter.

Alternatives to **3 ... B–N5** (besides **3 ... P–B3** – Chapter 3 – and **3 ... P–Q4** – Chapters 5 and 6) are not used much, but deserve a look:

a) **3 ... N–B3?** seems natural enough, but is apparently weak! After 4 B–N2 **P–KN3**, 5 P–K3 and 5 N–B3, both intending P–Q4, are variations from Chapters 1 and 2 which have been shown to favour White. Also uncomfortable are **4 ... B–B4** 5 P–K3 (transposing to (b) below), and **4 ... B–N5** 5 N–Q5!, analysed to a verdict of manifest White advantage in Chapter 11, A11. This leaves only slow moves like **4 ... B–K2**, when White plays either P–K3 or N–B3, again with the idea of P–Q4. So much for 'knights before bishops'! b) **3 ... B–B4?!** has not fared well: 4

B–N2 N–B3 (**4 . . . P–B3** 5 P–K3-
Shatskes likes 5 *N–B3 P–K5 6*
N–KN5 P–Q4 7 P×P P×P 8 P–Q3 –
5 . . . 0–0 6 KN–K2 B–N3 7 P–Q4
P–Q3 8 0–0 R–K1 9 P–N3 QN–Q2
10 B–QR3 N–B1 11 P–Q5! ±
Olafsson-Keller, Zurich 1959) 5
P–K3 0–0 (Characteristic of the
problems facing both players was **5
. . . P–Q3** 6 P–QR3 B–K3 7
P–QN4 B–N3 8 P–Q3 Q–Q2 9
P–R3 0–0 10 KN–K2 N–Q1 – Δ
. . . *P–B3* = – 11 N–R4! P–B3 12
N×B P×N 13 B–N2 N–K1 14 P–B4
P–B3 15 P–N4! K–R1?! 16 0–0
Q–K2 17 Q–K1 B–B2 18 N–N3
B–N3 19 R–Q1 N–QB2 20 Q–B2
P–N4 21 P–QB5! KP×P 22 KP×P
± Taimanov-Hort, Tallin 1975
(1–0, 33). Instructive use of White's
space advantage and two bishops.)
6 KN–K2 P–Q3 (Now Black will
lose a tempo after his opponent's
P–Q4, when we may expect White
to have the better game. Two
attempts to avoid this are **6 . . .
R–K1** 7 0–0 P–K5? 8 Q–B2 Q–K2
9 P–QR3 P–Q3 10 N–B4 B–B4 11
P–QN4 ± and **6 . . . P–Q4?!** 7
N×P! N×N 8 P×N N–N5 9 P–Q4
P×P 10 P×P B–N3 11 Q–N3 –
analysis by Shatskes) 7 0–0 (or **7
P–QR3** P–QR4 8 0–0 B–R2 9
P–Q4 B–N5 10 P–Q5 N–K2 11
P–R3 B–R4 12 P–KN4 B–KN3 13
K–R2 P–KR4 14 N–N3 ±
Kolarov-Tsvetkov, Bulgaria 1964)
7 . . . R–K1 8 P–Q4 B–N3 9
P–KR3 B–KB4 (Better **9 . . .
N–Q2**, according to Schwarz; but if
that is so, White must be well off
indeed.) 10 P–Q5! N–N1 11
P–KN4 B–Q2 12 N–N3 P–KR3 13

K–R2 P–QR4 14 P–B4 P×P 15
P×P N–R2 16 P–N5! with a huge
advantage, Korchnoi-Szabo, Buch-
arest 1955, since 16 . . . P×P 17
P×P N×P? 18 Q–R5 P–KB3 19
B×N P×B 20 B–K4 wins.
c) **3 . . . P–KN3** 4 B–N2 B–N2 5
P–K3 (**5 N–B3** P–Q3 6 P–Q4
QN–Q2 7 0–0 is a King's Indian
Defence; 5 P–K4 is a Botvinnik
System, see Chapter 1, E and
English II, . . . N–KB3, Ch 7) 5 . . .
0–0 6 KN–K2 P–B3 (6 . . . P–Q3) 7
P–B4!? P–Q3 (**7 . . . P×P** 8 N×P
P–Q3 9 0–0 QN–Q2 10 P–QN4
N–N3 11 Q–N3 P–Q4 12 P–B5
P–Q5 ∞ Schwarz) 8 0–0 QN–Q2 9
R–N1 R–K1 10 P–QN4 N–N3 11
P–N5 B–Q2 12 Q–N3 Q–B1 13
BP×P QP×P 14 P×P B×P 15 N–Q5
N(B)×N 16 P×N? (16 B×N =) 16
. . . B–R5! 17 Q–R3 B–B7∓, a game
quoted as 'Goldberg-Geller.'
d) **3 . . . P–Q3** 4 B–N2 B–K2 5
N–B3 (or 5 P–K3) 5 . . . 0–0 6 0–0
N–B3 (6 . . . P–B3 7 P–Q4 is an Old
Indian) 7 P–Q3 P–KR3 8 R–N1
B–K3 9 P–QN4 Q–Q2 10 P–N5
N–Q1 11 R–K1 B–R6 12 B–R1. By
comparison with Chapter 1, Black's
king bishop is less agressively
posted, but is better for defence,
than its counterpart on g7 in that
chapter. Black does not stand badly
here.
After 3 . . . B–N5, White usually
chooses from:
A 4 N–B3
B 4 B–N2
Minor alternatives:
a) **4 Q–B2?!** 0–0 5 P–QR3 B×N 6
Q×B P–Q4! 7 B–N2 P–Q5 8 Q–B2
P–QR4 9 P–Q3 R–K1 (∓) 10

N–B3 P–B4 11 0–0 N–B3 12 B–Q2 P–KR3 (12 ... P–K5!?) 13 P–QN4! and White had just about equalized in Cuellar-Kuzmin, Leningrad 1973.

b) **4 Q–N3** is complex: 4 ... P–QR4 (**4 ... N–B3** 5 N–Q5 **B–Q3!?** 6 P–K3 N×N 7 P×N N–K2 8 N–K2 P–QB3 9 N–B3 P×P 10 N×P N×N 11 Q×N Q–K2 12 B–N2 = /∞ Korchnoi-Lein, Sochi 1966. As Taimanov puts it, the advantage of having won d5 can't be exploited in the absence of knights. In place of 5 ... B–Q3!?, Karpov played **5 ... B–B4(!)** against Korchnoi in the 25th game of their 1978 World Championship match: 6 P–K3 0–0 7 B–N2 N×N (7 ... P–Q3!) 8 P×N N–K2 9 N–K2 P–Q3 10 0–0 P–QB3!? with a complex game ($\frac{1}{2}$–$\frac{1}{2}$, 80). 5 P–QR3!? (5 B–N2—Pritchett) 5 ... B–B4!? (**5...B×N** 6 Q×B =; 6 NP×B!? – Pritchett) 6 B–N2 0–0 7 P–K3 R–K1 8 KN–K2 P–B3 9 0–0 B–B1! (Δ ... P–Q3) 10 P–B4!? P–K5 11 P–KN4? (11 Q–B2 ∞ – Pritchett) 11 ... N×P 12 N×P R×N! ∓ Speelman-Pritchett, British Ch 1975.

A

4 N–B3	P–K5
5 N–Q4	N–B3

5 ... 0–0 has its drawbacks after 6 B–N2 R–K1 7 Q–B2 (**7 N–B2** B×N 8 QP×B is B422): 7 ... B×N (Kapengut suggests **7...N–B3!?** Δ 8 N×N QP×N 9 N×P B–KB4 10 N×Nch Q×N 'with a very promising position.' But 11 Q–N3 P–QR4 12 P–QR3 B–B4 13 P–K3

QR–Q1!? 14 Q×NP is the logical follow-up, when Black has difficulty demonstrating compensation) 8 QP×B P–KR3 9 B–B4! P–Q3 10 0–0–0 N–B3?! (Better **10 ... QN–Q2**-Kapengut – although White would also have a nice position in that case) 11 N×N P×N 12 P–B5 with the advantage, Hübner-Jansson, Skopje 1972. If 12 ... P–Q4, 13 Q–R4 and 14 Q–R5 ties Black down.

6 N–B2

6 N×N? QP×N gives Black easy development and prospective pressure down the queen file.

6 ...   B×N

6 ... 0–0!? is an interesting possibility: 7 B–N2 R–K1 8 0–0 (**8 N×B** N×N 9 0–0 P–B3 Δ ... P–Q4 is reminiscent of Chapter 3 positions where Black's e4 pawn wedge combatted the White bishop pair's influence: **9 ... P–Q3** 10 P–QR3 N–B3 11 P–N3 is another typical configuration, hard to assess.) 8 ... B×N 9 QP×B. This was the order of Ribli-Browne, Manila 1976; it transposes to Chapter 7, D2242, but without giving White the option of an early B–KN5. Browne played 9 ... N–K4 10 P–N3 P–KR3 (see Chapter 7, note (b) to 8 ... P–KR3).

7 QP×B   P–KR3
8 B–K3

8 B–N2 0–0 9 0–0 is again Chapter 7, D2242.

8 ...   Q–K2
9 B–N2 (9 P–B5 P–QN3!- Petrosian) 9 ... P–Q3 10 N–N4!? N×N 11 P×N 0–0 12 Q–Q4 (**12**

P–B5!? R–Q1 13 P×P R×P 14 Q–B1 ± -Petrosian) 12 . . . R–K1 13 P–KR3 P–QN3 14 0–0–0 B–N2 15 K–N1 N–Q2 16 P–KN4 N–K4! 17 P–B5 Larsen-Petrosian, Milan 1975, and play was approximately equal (although 0–1, 39).

B

    4 B–N2   0–0 (*29*)

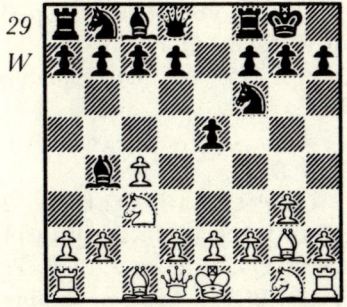

29
W

4 . . . N–B3? 5 N–Q5! is Chapter 11, A11 again. **4 . . . P–B3** 5 Q–N3! Q–K2 6 N–B3 (Shatskes, Δ N×P) 6 . . . P–K5 7 N–Q4 is attractive for White, e.g. **7 . . . 0–0?** 8 N–B5 Q–B4 9 N×KP! etc. or **7 . . . P–Q4** 8 P×P B×N 9 NP×B Δ 10 B–QR3. Best **7 . . . B×N** 8 Q×B P–Q3, but White has two strong bishops.

From the diagram, White has tried eight (!) moves, four of them with some frequency. We examine:
B1 5 Q–N3
B2 5 P–K4
B3 5 P–Q3
B4 5 N–B3

Ill-advised were:

a) **5 P–QR3** B×N 6 NP×B P–K5 (Better **6 . . . P–B3** Δ 7 P–K4 P–Q4 or 7 N–B3 P–K5-Kapengut) 7 N–R3 R–K1 8 0–0 P–Q3 9 N–B4

P–QN3 10 P–B3 (10 P–Q3-Shatskes) 10 . . . P–K6! 11 P–Q3 (11 P×P B–R3) 11 . . . B–N2 with a good game for Black, Botvinnik-Smyslov Moscow 1964. Botvinnik himself criticized 5 P–QR3.

b) **5 P–K3?!** B×N 6 NP×B R–K1 7 P–Q4 P–K5 8 N–K2 P–Q3 9 P–KR3 N–B3 10 P–KN4 N–QR4 11 Q–R4(?) P–QN3 ∓ Kubichek-Hort, Czechoslovakia 1972. 11 . . . B–R3 is coming.

c) **5 N–Q5** N×N 6 P×N P–QB3! (**6 . . . R–K1** 7 N–B3 P–QB3?! – 7 . . . P–Q3! – 8 Q–N3 B–B4 9 P–Q4 KP×P? – 9 . . . B×P! Pachman – 10 N–N5 P–KR3? 11 P×P! (±±) 11 . . . QP×P 12 Q×Pch K–R1 13 B–K4 B–N5ch 14 K–B1 with a winning game, Friedman-Pachman, Notanya 1973.) 7 Q–N3 (7 **P–QR3** B–K2 8 P–Q3? P×P 9 P–K3 P–Q3 10 N–K2 B–K3 ∓ Simagin-Polugaevsky, Moscow 1964) 7 . . . Q–K2 8 N–B3 B–B4! 9 P–Q3 P×P 10 Q×P N–B3 11 0–0?! (11 B–N5 B–N5ch ∓) 11 . . . P–Q3 12 B–N5 Q–K1 13 Q–N3 B–K3! 14 Q–Q1 Q–Q2 15 B–Q2 B–R6 16 B–B3 B×B 17 K×B KR–K1 ∓ Lekander-Pachman, Stockholm 1975.

d) **5 Q–B2** R–K1 6 P–QR3 (Maybe 6 P–N3!?, though that too seems slow) 6 . . . B×N 7 NP×B (7 **Q×B** P–Q4 'with initiative'-Kapengut. Or here **7 . . . N–B3!?** Δ 8 N–B3 P–Q4 or 8 P–K4 N–Q5) 7 . . . P–B3 8 P–K4 P–Q4 9 BP×P P×P 10 P×P N×P 11 N–K2 N–QB3 12 0–0 B–N5 13 R–K1 Q–Q2 14 P–Q3 QR–Q1 15 B–N2 B–R6 and White just hadn't developed quickly or actively enough. Quinteros-Bronstein, Vinkovci 1970.

B1

5 Q–N3

and now Black can exchange or defend his bishop.

B11 5 ... B×N
B12 5 ... N–B3

B11

5 ...   B×N

6 Q×B

Kapengut recommends 6 NP×B P–B3 (6 ... P–K5 7 P–B3) 7 P–K4, a position from B232, but one which hardly favours White, as we shall see.

6 ...   R–K1
7 P–Q3

7 N–B3?! N–B3 (or 7 ... P–Q4!-Kapengut) 8 0–0 P–Q4 9 P×P N×P 10 Q–B5 P–K5 11 N–Q4 (or 11 N–K1 B–N5!-Shatskes) 11 ... N–B5! 12 N×N N×Pch 13 K–R1 P×N 14 Q×BP R–N1 ∓ Blexin-Karasev, Leningrad 1966.

7 ...   P–Q4
8 P×P   N×P

9 Q–N3 N–N3 ·10 Q–B2? (10 N–B3) 10 ... N–B3 11 B×N P×B 12 Q×P?! R–N1 13 Q–B2 B–N2 14 P–B3 Q–Q2 ∓ Korchnoi-Filip, Curacao 1972.

B12

5 ...   N–B3!

6 N–Q5

a) **6 B×N** B×N 7 B–N2 B–Q5 =. According to Kapengut, 7 ... B–R4 8 P–K4 is not as strong, but 8 ... P–Q3 9 KN–K2 B–N3 looks fine.

b) **6 P–K3** B×N 7 QP×B P–K5 8 N–K2 N–K4 9 0–0 P–Q3 and Black stood well, Tal-K. Richter, Germany 1962.

6 ...   B–B4
7 P–K3   P–K5!

A spirited offer. **7 ... R–K1** or **7 ... P–Q3** were also plausible moves.

8 N×Nch

Declining by **8 N–K2** runs into 8 ... N–K4, and **8 P–Q4** P×Pe.p. 9 Q×P N–K4 10 Q–B3? N×N – 11 P×N?? B–N5 – is not enticing either.

8 ...   Q×N
9 B×P   R–K1

10 P–Q3 P–Q3 11 B–Q2 B–B4 12 B–QB3 Q–N3 13 B×B Q×B 14 R–Q1 P–Q4! Intending 15 P×P? R×Pch! Black had a lasting initiative in Korchnoi-Tseitlin, Leningrad 1973 (0–1, 30).

CONCLUSION:

Both **5 ... B×N** and **5 ... N–B3!** appear perfectly satisfactory against 5 Q–N3. The lack of any recent games with this early queen sortie tends to confirm that judgement.

B2

5 P–K4 *(30)*

This attempt to clamp down on

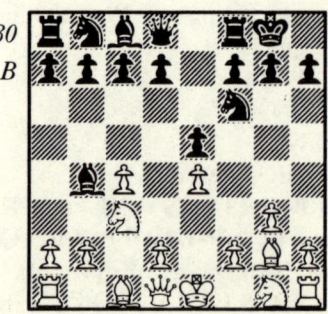

d5 is the way Black often defends against 3 B–N5 in the 2 ... N–QB3 Sicilian Defence. There are three main continuations and an outlandish recent one:

B21 5 ... P–B3
B22 5 ... N–B3
B23 5 ... B×N
B24 5 ... P–QN4

B21

 5 ...   **P–B3(?)**
 6 KN–K2 P–Q4!?

The radical continuation, though this pawn offer is unclear even when White plays it (a tempo up) versus the Sicilian! Alternatively, Black has **6 ... P–Q3** 7 0–0 B–K3 8 P–Q3 Q–Q2 (**8 ... P–Q4** 9 KP×P P×P 10 B–N5-Kapengut- ±) 9 P–QR3 B×N (Better 9 ... B–R4) 10 N×B B–R6 (**10 ... P–Q4** 11 BP×P P×P 12 B–N5! P–Q5 13 B×N P×B 14 N–Q5 Zhurakov-Alburt, Kiev, 1967) 11 P–Q4! B×B 12 K×B ± (Minev). This is hardly desirable for the second player.

 7 BP×P   P×P
 8 P×P

Also **8 N×P** N×N 9 P×N B–KB4 10 0–0 N–Q2 (**10 ... B–Q6** 11 Q–N3! B×N 12 R–K1-Kapengut) 11 P–Q3? (Best is **11 P–Q4!** P–K5 12 Q–N3 Q–N3 13 N–B3 N–B3 14 B–N5!-Kapengut) 11 ... R–K1 12 B–K3 N–B3 13 Q–N3 P–QR4 14 P–KR3 Q–Q2 15 K–R2 B–K2 16 P–QR4 P–KR4 17 QR–Q1 B–QN5 and Black had compensation, Ivkov-Ree, Amsterdam 1968 (0–1, 45).

 8 ...   B–KB4

 9 P–Q4   P–K5
9 ... B×Nch 10 N×B P×P 11 Q×P N–B3 12 Q–KB4 ±±; 9 ... N×P 10 0–0 B×N 11 N×B N×N 12 P×N ± (Korchnoi).

 10 B–N5   QN–Q2
 11 Q–N3   Q–N3

12 0–0 P–KR3 13 B–B4 KR–K1 14 N–R4 Q–R4 15 P–QR3 B–B1 (15 ... B–Q7!?-Korchnoi) 16 N(2)–B3 P–KN4 17 B–K3 ± Korchnoi-Taimanov, Leningrad 1973.

B22

 5 ...   N–B3
Simply watching over d4. **5 ... P–Q3** 6 KN–K2 N–B3 will transpose, and **5 ... R–K1** 6 KN–K2 N–B3 is common method of entering B221.

 6 KN–K2
Now Black has two strategies:

B221

 6 ...   **R–K1**
 7 P–QR3
7 0–0 allows 7 ... N–Q5 8 P–Q3 N×Nch 9 N×N P–B3. Then 10 P–QR3 B–B1 11 N–B3 B–B4 12 P–KR3 B–Q5 13 N–K2 B–N3 14 P–KN4?! P–Q4! ceded the initiative to Black in Prischbyl-Karasev, Leningrad 1970.

 7 ...   B–B1
 8 P–Q3!

Definitely more accurate than **8 0–0**, which allows the simplifying rejoinder 8 ... N–Q5 9 P–Q3 N×Nch 10 Q×N P–B3 11 B–K3 P–Q3 12 P–R3 P–Q4!? (Or **12 ... P–KN3** 13 P–KN4 P–KR4 14 P–B3 B–K3 = Tukmakov-Karasev, USSR Ch, 1971) 13

KP×P P×P 14 B–N5 P–Q5 15 N–Q5 B–K3 16 KR–K1 B×N 17 B×B R–QN1 = Karpov-Karasev, USSR Ch 1971.

8 ...   N–Q5?!

Now this move is weaker, as White can capture on d4 without losing his KP. Kapengut suggests **8 ... P–QR4** ($\pm$). We are following Smyslov-Karasev, USSR Ch 1971: 9 N×N P×N 10 N–K2 P–B4 (In the terminology of *Flank Openings*, Black now has a 'dead point' in the centre.) 11 P–QN4 P–Q3 12 0–0 B–Q2 13 P×P P×P 14 P–QR4 B–B3 15 B–N5; White's mobile kingside pawn preponderance gives him excellent chances.

B222

6 ...   **B–B4**

Perhaps more consistent than ... R–K1 and ... B–B1, since Black emphasizes his control over d4.

7 0–0

In Dubinin-Kryszton, corres 1975, White tried another idea: **7 P–KR3** P–Q3 8 P–Q3 N–K1 9 B–K3 B×B 10 P×B P–QR3 11 Q–Q2 R–N1 12 0–0–0? (Black has too specifically prepared for this; better is **12 0–0** or **12 P–QR4**.) 12 ... P–QN4 13 P×P P×P 14 N–Q5 N–K2! 15 P–Q4 P–QB3 16 N–N4 Q–N3 ∓ (0–1, 54).

7 ...   P–Q3

Kapengut suggests **7 ... P–QR3** 8 P–Q3 P–QN4!? e.g. 9 P×P P×P 10 N×P B–R3 11 N(2)–B3 N–QN5 12 P–QR3 N×QP 13 Q×N P–B3. White should probably try **8 P–QR3** ∆ 8 ... P–QN4 9 P–QN4 and 10 P×P.

8 P–KR3

Or **8 P–Q3** P–KR3 9 P–QR3 P–QR4(?) 10 R–N1 B–Q2 11 P–R3 N–KR2 12 K–R2 P–B4 13 B–K3 (13 P×P is a natural move.) 13 ... B×B 14 P×B P×P (14 ... N–K2!-Kotov) 15 N×P R×R 16 Q×R Q–K2 17 N(2)–B3 R–KB1 18 Q–K2 B–K3 19 P–QN4 Stein-Smyslov, Moscow 1971. White seemed to have the edge throughout; **9 ... P–QR3** ∆ ... N–Q5, ... P–B3 was less rigid.

8 ...   P–QR3

9 P–Q3

9 K–R2?! R–N1 10 P–QR3 P–QN4 11 P–QN4 B–R2 and White had to stop to protect his QBP: 12 P–Q3 N–Q5 13 P–B4?! KP×P 14 B×P N–Q2 ∓ Hartoch-Portisch, Amsterdam 1971. Compare what follows:

9 ...   R–QN1?

White is better prepared in the centre than after 9 K–R2, so Black should change course with the sober **9 ... N–Q5** (∆ ... P–B3, ... P–QN4) 10 N×N B×N 11 N–K2 B–R2, and if 12 P–Q4, 12 ... P×P 13 N×P R–K1 14 R–K1 P–B3, intending ... P–Q4.

10 P–QR3   P–QN4

11 P–QN4   B–R2

12 N–Q5!

Threatening B–N5; now on **12 ... P–KR3**, 13 B–N2 ∆ R–B1, K–R2, P–B4 etc. is strong. The text is D. Byrne-Portisch, San Antonio 1972, from which play continued **12 ... N×N** 13 BP×N N–K2 (or 13 ... N–Q5 $\pm$) 14 P–Q4 P–KB4 15 QP×P QP×P 16 Q–N3 K–R1 17

B–K3 B×B 18 P×B P×P 19 N–B3 ± White has excellent squares for his knight (e4 and c5) and active posts for his rooks (f1 and c1).

B23

5 ...   B×N

The most popular continuation. Both recaptures are interesting:

B231

6 QP×B   P–Q3
7 Q–K2

Planning to bring the king's knight to KB3, and from there to either K1 or Q2 (the latter idea preliminary to a further N–KB1–K3!). **7 N–K2** is thought to be weaker because White's knight has 'no future,' but then again, that move wastes no time! e.g. **7 N–K2** QN–Q2 (7 ... P–QR3!?) 8 0–0 P–QN3 9 P–B3 P–QR4 (Now Black has forfeited the possibility of ... P–QN4 which comes up in the text.) 10 B–K3 B–N2 11 Q–B2 Q–K2 12 N–B1 N–R4 13 N–Q3 (Rags to riches!) 13 ... P–N3 14 B–R6 N–N2 15 P–B4 P–KB3 16 P–KB5 P–KN4? (16 ... N–B4 = Minev) 17 P–KR4 P×P 18 P–KN4! ± Radulov–Radev, Bulgaria Ch 1974 (1–0, 55).

7 ...   QN–Q2

7 ... P–QR3 8 N–B3 P–QN4!? 9 P–B5! B–N2 10 P×P P×P 11 N–R4 (11 B–N5!-Rosenburg) 11 ... P–Q4!? 12 B–N5 P–R3 13 B×N Q×B 14 P×P N–Q2 15 0–0 KR–K1 16 P–QR4! P×P 17 R×P N–N3 18 R–R5 P–K5! 19 P–Q6! (**19 P–B3** P–K6! 20 P–KB4 QR–B1

‡ Rosenberg) 19 ... QR–Q1 and Black was very close to equality, Korchnoi–Kuzmin, USSR Ch 1973 (½–½, 38).

8 N–B3   N–B4

A different concept was **8 ... P–QR4** 9 0–0 N–B4 10 N–K1 P–R5 11 N–B2 P–B3 12 R–Q1 Q–K2 13 P–B3 (Kapengut recommends **13 B–N5** P–R3 14 B×N Q×B 15 R–Q2 and R(1)–Q1, but then Black should be able to defend ... d6 and his bishop is the better one. Nor are White's queenside pawns a long-term asset.) 13 ... B–K3 14 N–K3 KR–Q1 15 P–KN4? P–KN3 16 Q–KB2 N–K1 ‡ Martz–Browne, U.S.A. 1972. Black intends ... N–KN2, ... K–R1 and ... P–B4.

9 N–R4   P–QR3!

A paradoxical idea on the face of it: Black wants to liquidate White's doubled pawns. But in the process he either wins influence over the centre or opens lines for his pieces.

10 P–N3   P–QN4 (*31*)

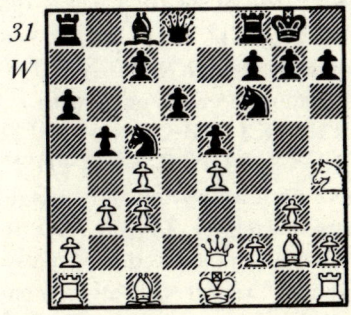

11 B–QR3	N(3)–Q2
12 0–0	B–N2
13 P–B3	B–B3!

Korchnoi-Mecking (1), 1974. Now **14 KR–Q1!** (Judović) was probably best ($\mp$); after **14 N–B5** P×P, as in the game, White had to reply 15 P×P (15 Q×P? B–N4), when 15 ... N–R5 16 Q–Q2 N(2)–B4 was excellent for the second player.

Kapengut's assertion that 7 N–K2 is bad appears inaccurate, but on the whole Black is reasonably well off after 6 QP×B.

B232
6 NP×B   P–B3!

a) **6 ... P–Q3** is slow: 7 P–Q3 QN–Q2 8 P–KR3 (Kapengut likes 8 P–B4! here.) 8 ... N–B4 9 N–K2 (White's 'dream plan' in this variation is to play P–Q3, 0–0 and P–B4. In the game before us Black does nothing to prevent this.) 9 ... B–Q2 10 B–K3 B–R5 11 Q–Q2 R–K1 12 0–0 N(3)–Q2 13 P–B4 P–QR3 (13 ... P×P might ease Black's woes a bit.) 14 P–B5 P–KB3 15 P–N4 ± Tukmakov-Vasiukov, USSR Ch 1969.

b) **6 ... P–QR3!?** 7 P–QR4 P–Q3 8 N–K2 Q–K1?! (8 ... P–QR4 was suggested, though 9 0–0 N–R3 10 P–Q4 must be contended with.) 9 P–R5! B–K3 10 P–Q3 N(3)–Q2 11 P–R3 N–QB3 12 P–N4 Q–Q1 13 N–N3 with an obvious advantage, Bertok-Korchnoi, Zagreb 1970. In this variation, a c4, d3, e4 pawn structure requires pawn confrontation (i.e. by ... P–QN4 and/or ... P–Q4), since Black cannot occupy the d4 square (as he did in, e.g. B22).

7 N–K2

a) **7 B–QR3** R–K1 8 Q–N3 P–QN3 9 R–Q1 B–N2 10 P–Q3 P–Q4 11 N–K2 P×KP 12 P×P Q–B1 13 P–B5 B–R3 14 P–B3 QN–Q2 15 B–R3 Q–N2 16 N–B1 QR–N1 17 P×P N×P 18 B–Q6 R̂(N)–Q1 $\mp$ Portisch-Mecking, Petropolis 1973 ($\frac{1}{2}$–$\frac{1}{2}$, 62). **9 R–Q1** seems wrong, since P–Q4 could not be prepared. Better was **9 N–K2** and castling.

b) Hort's **7 Q–N3!?** was rendered suspect in Forintos-Browne, Lone Pine 1975, where Black played 7 ... **N–R3!** 8 B–R3 P–Q3! (improving on Kapengut's **8 ... R–K1**, which, however, illustrates the themes of this position: 9 N–K2 P–Q3 10 0–0? N–B4 11 Q–B2 B–K3 12 P–Q4 – or **12 P–Q3** Q–R4 13 B–N4 Q–R3 14 KR–K1 N×QP! 15 Q×N P–QB4 etc. – 12 ... P×P 13 P×P N(4)×P! etc.. Better **10 P–Q3!** =) 9 N–K2 (Or **9 P–Q3** N–B4 10 Q–B2 Q–R4 $\mp$) 9 ... B–K3! 10 P–B4 (**10 P–Q4** P×P 11 P×P P–QN4 12 P–Q5 Q–R4ch) 10 ... P–QN4 11 Q–B2 B×P 12 P–Q3 P–N5 13 P×NP B–N4 14 N–B3? P×P 15 P×P N–N5 $\mp$. Acceptance of the pawn offer on move ten may offer White's best chance here e.g. **10 Q×P** B×P 11 Q×BP R–B1 12 Q–R4! (12 Q×P? Q–R4!) 12 ... Q–N3 13 Q–Q1 B–Q6 14 P–B3 (14 ... N(3)–Q2!?), but this remains to be tested. A solider defence is **7 ... P–QN3** 8 N–K2 B–N2 9 P–Q4 R–K1! (the stem game of 7 Q–N3 went **9 ... P–Q4?** 10 BP×P BP×P 11 QP×P N×P 12 B–QR3 R–K1 13 P–B3 N–N4 14 P–KB4 N–K5 15 R–Q1 ± Hort-Kozulichem, Venice 1971) 10 P×P R×P 11

P–B4? (11 B–B4 ∞) 11 . . . R×P! 12
B×R N×B with a pawn, the light
squares, and an airy White
structure to compensate Black for
the exchange (∓), Karasev-
Podgaets, Leningrad 1977.

7 . . .	P–Q4
8 BP×P	P×P
9 P×P	N×P
10 0–0	N–B3 *(32)*

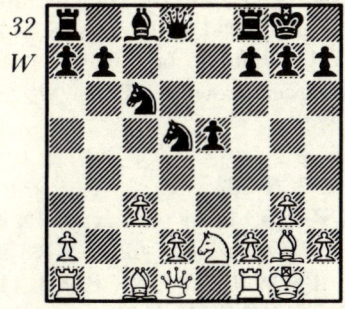

Black's central advantage, particularly on the light squares,
restricts the potential of White's
bishop pair.

11 R–N1

11 P–KR3 (Forestalling possibilities such as **11 P–Q4** P×P 12 P×P
B–N5!) 11 . . . B–K3 12 P–Q4
Q–R4 13 B–Q2 P×P 14 P×P Q–R3
(or 14 . . . Q–R6 =) 15 N–B4 N×N
16 B×N KR–Q1 17 P–Q5!?
Saharov–Krzyston, corres 1974,
and now **17 . . . N–K2!** was the
move. Instead, **17 . . . N–N5?** 18
P×B! R×Q 19 P×Pch K×P 20
KR×Q R–K1 21 QR–N1! ± was
the game continuation. 11 R–N1
has been a popular move, but it
does not help prepare the
positionally necessary P–Q4, and

leaves the QRP subject to tempo-
winning harassment:

11 . . .	N–N3

Also effective was **11 . . . R–K1**
12 B–QR3 N–N3 13 Q–B2 B–N5
14 P–Q3 Q–Q2 15 B–B5 B×N 16
Q×B N–R5 17 Q–K3 N×P 18
R–N3 N–Q4 ∓ Stein-Gheorghiu,
Las Palmas 1973, though the game
was drawn shortly thereafter.
Kapengut's **11 . . . R–QN1** looks
good too.

12 P–Q4

After **12 Q–B2** B–K3 13 P–Q3
Q–Q2 Black . was able to exert
pressure on White's weak central
pawns, Benko-Hecht, Olot 1971.

12 . . .	B–K3
13 P–QR4	

Also unsatisfactory was **13 Q–Q2**
B–Q4! 14 P×P N×P 15 B×B N×B
16 K–R1 Q–R4 ∓ Ivkov-Olaff-
sson, Wijk an Zee 1971 (although
½–½, 20).

13 . . .	B–B5!
14 R–K1	Q–Q2
15 B–QR3	KR–Q1
16 B–B5	N–Q4 ∓

Pribyl-Hecht, Luhacovice 1972.

B24

5 . . .	P–QN4?!

which had success in Karasev-
Kapengut, Beltsi 1977: 6 N×NP
B–N2 **7 P–QR3?!** P–QR3! 8 N×P?
(8 P×B =) 8 . . . Q×N 9 P×B Q×P
10 P–Q3 Q×Pch ∓.

As in the corresponding Sicilian
Defence position, White should
play **7 Q–B2!** e.g. 7 . . . P–B3 8
N–QB3 P–Q4 9 P–Q3! Δ 9 . . .
P–Q5 10 P–QR3 ± or 9 . . . P×BP
10 P×P Q–Q5 11 KN–K2! ±.

CONCLUSION:

5 P–K4 has to be considered one of the most important tries to deal with 3 . . . B–N5; but White has yet to find a promising method of meeting 5 . . . B×N(!): **6 QP×B** P–Q3 is comfortable for Black; and after **6 NP×B** P–B3!, the first player has had more than his share of problems. Hence the diminishing frequency of 5 P–K4 in recent years.

B3
5 P–Q3

Solid, but not very energetic in the centre. Black usually replies:
B31 5 . . . R–K1
B32 5 . . . P B3(!)

Less effective was **5 . . . B×Nch** (often queried) 6 P×B P–Q3? (The real culprit, **6 . . . P–B3** is playable.) 7 P–K4 QN–Q2 8 P–B4 ('!', according to several commentators, but **8 N–K2** with a slow build-up to follow may be better and ±) 8 . . . N–B4?! (**8 . . . P×P** should be tried) 9 N–B3 B–N5?! (Ditto) 10 P–KR3 B×N 11 Q×B N(3)–Q2 12 0–0 P–QB3 13 B–QR3! Q–R4 14 B–N4 Q–R5 15 Q–Q1 Q×Q 16 QR×Q P–QR4 17 B–QR3 KR–K1 18 KR–K1 ± Uhlmann–Schöneberg, Weimar 1968. P–Q4 is in the air, liberating White's bishops (1–0, 36).

B31
5 . . .   R–K1
6 B–Q2
6 P–K4 B×Nch! (**6 . . . P–B3** 7 KN–K2 P–Q4 8 BP×P P×P 9 P×P N×P 10 0–0 N–N3 – *or 10 . . .*

N–K2 11 P–Q4 P×P 12 N×P ± – 11 P–Q4 B×N 12 P×B N–B3 13 P–QR4 Korchnoi–Ree, Beverwijk 1968. White is clearly doing better here than in B232 above, but it's still complicated.) 7 P×B P–B3 8 N–K2 P–Q4 9 BP×P P×P 10 P×P N×P 11 0–0 B–N5! (Here's the difference: 12 . . . N×P is threatened.) 12 B–N2 (12 Q–N3 N–N3!-Browne) 12 . . . N–QB3 13 P–KR3 B–R4 14 Q–Q2 Q–Q2 15 QR–K1 QR–Q1 16 N–B1 B–N3 with pressure (17 R–Q1 should be tried), R. Rodriguez–Browne. USA 1973 (0–1, 61).

6 . . .   P–B3
7 N–B3
7 P–QR3 B–B1 (or **7 . . . B×N** 8 B×B P–Q4 =) 8 N–B3 P–KR3 9 0–0 P–Q3 10 P–QN4 B–K3 11 P–N5 (**11 R–B1!?** Δ 11 . . . P–Q4 12 P×P P×P 13 P–Q4 ±) 11 . . . Q–B1 12 P×P N×P 13 R–N1? (13 R–B1 ∞) 13 . . . P–K5! ∓ Bobekov–Tarasov, 1961.

7 . . .   P–Q4!

Not **7 . . . P–KR3?** 8 0–0 B–B1 9 P–K4 P–Q3 10 P–Q4 B–N5 11 P–Q5 P×P 12 BP×P (±) 12 . . . P–QN4? 13 R–K1 P–QR3 14 P–KR3 B×N 15 Q×B QN–Q2 16 B–KB1 Q–N1 17 P–QN4 ± (Δ P–QR4) Ivkov–Zuidema, Amsterdam 1968 (1–0, 23!).

8 P×P   P×P
9 0–0 (**9 P–Q4** P×P! 10 N×P N–B3 gives easy play) 9 . . . N–B3 10 P–QR3 B×N 11 B×B P–Q5 12 B–Q2? (**12 B–K1!**, to parry immediate threats, improves, e.g. **12 . . . Q–N3** 13 N–Q2 Q×P? 14 N–B4; but **12 . . . P–K5** 13 P×P

N×P is still equal.) 12 . . . Q–N3 13 P–QN4 P–K5 ∓ Blom-Perez, 1961.

B32

5 . . .   **P–B3(!)**
6 Q–N3!?
6 B–Q2? invites 6 . . . P–Q4! 7 Q–N3 N–R3 ⑧ P×P P×P 9 P–QR3 (**9 N×P** B×Bch 10 K×B N–B4 11 Q–B4 N×N 12 B×N Q–N3 with attack) 9 . . . B–R4 10 R–B1 B–K3 11 Q–Q1 P–Q5 12 N–N1 B×Bch 13 N×B Q–N3 14 R–B2 QR–B1 15 N(1)–B3 R×R 16 Q×R R–B1 17 Q–N1 B–R7! 18 Q–R1 R–B7 19 P–QN4 N–Q4 ∓ Brasket-Timman, Lone Pine 1978.

This illustrates a common fallacy about the English: that, as a 'slow' opening, it gives White leeway to play any sequence of consistent developing moves. Impressive games won by someone like Petrosian or Smyslov can fortify this belief: White undertakes nothing for the first dozen moves, his pieces confined to the first three ranks, and suddenly Black has to deal with unstoppable positional threats! But a careful examination of such games (there are many in this book) reveals that much of the thought behind White's 'slow' moves has been concerned with prevention, i.e. not only does White develop and aim at the centre with his pieces, but he also does so with an eye on specific Black threats like pawn expansion in the centre or aggressive piece development. In many systems, the preventive aspect even takes priority, and it certainly should do so after 5 P–Q3.

Although the first six moves by White in Brasket-Timman were consistent (i.e. even 6 B–Q2 indirectly aims at the light squares), the combination of them allowed Black's pawns to occupy e5 and d5 without having prepared a *specific method* of confronting them (e.g. by d4), *or* of restraining them, *or* of provoking their overextension. So Black's centre was really powerful and not just seemingly so.

Incidentally, the text move (6 Q–N3) can be faulted on the same count (see e.g. the next note). White's best is probably **6 N–B3** (=), so that even if Black achieves . . . P–Q4, White can exchange on d5 and play P–Q4 himself.

6 . . .   B–R4!?
More ambitious is Kapengut's **6 . . . N–R3! 7 N–B3** (7 P–K4 N–B4!) 7 . . . P–K5 8 N–Q4 P×P 9 P×P N–B4 10 Q–B2 P–Q4 ∓ or **7 P–QR3** B–R4! (7 . . . B×Nch 8 Q×B R–K1 is equal) and White has some difficulty developing e.g. **8 Q–B2** P–Q4 9 P–QN4 B–N3 (Kapengut), or **8 B–N5** N–B4 9 Q–B2 N–K3! ∓, or **8 B–Q2** P–Q4! as in the last note.

7 N–B3   P–Q4
7 . . . R–K1 8 0–0 P–KR3 9 B–Q2 P–Q4 10 QR–Q1 P–Q5 = Dorosh-kevich–Kärner, Moscow 1967.

8 0–0   P–Q5
8 . . . P×P 9 Q×BP or 8 . . . P–K5 9 P×KP P×KP 10 N–KN5 B×N 11 Q×B are worse.

9 N–QR4   P–QN4! (*33*)
An improvement on **9 . . . QN–Q2** 10 P–K3! P×P 11 B×KP R–K1 12 P–QR3 (or 12 P–Q4!) 12

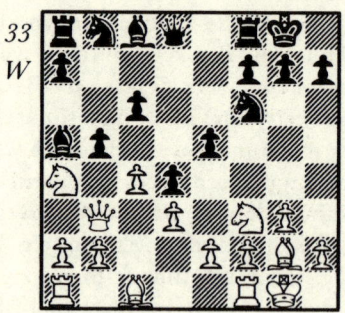

33
W

... B–B2 13 QR–Q1 B–Q3 14 P–Q4 with advantage to White, Karpov-Rogoff, Puerto Rico, 1971.

After **9 ... P–QN4!**, Kapengut gives 10 P×P B–K3 11 Q–B2 P×P 12 N–B5 (**12 N×KP?** B–Q4 13 N–B5 B×B 14 K×B Q–Q4ch and 15 ... R–QB1) 12 ... B–Q4 13 P–QR3 N–B3 14 P–QN4 B–N3.

CONCLUSION:

Both 5 ... R–K1 and 5 ... P–B3 are satisfactory replies to 5 P–Q3; indeed, the first player must be vigilant not to lose the battle for the centre altogether.

B4

5 N–B3   R–K1

5 ... N–B3 is Chapter 7, D2. 5 ... **P–K5** 6 N–Q4 is A above, unless an early ... R–K1 follows (see B42).

6 0–0 and:
B41 6 ... P–B3
B42 6 ... P–K5

One of the main ideas behind 5 N–B3 (currently White's most popular move) is to aim for a position from, or at least similar to, Chapter 7, D22. I have frequently drawn a comparison between the two lines below, and suggest their simultaneous study for fun and profit.

B41

6 ...   **P–B3**

6 ... B×N 7 NP×B˙P–K5 8 N–Q4 will transpose to B423. Here **7...N–B3** 8 P–Q3 P–Q3?! 9 P–K4 N–K2 10 N–R4 N–N3 11 N–B5 P–B3 12 R–N1 P–Q4 13 BP×P P×P 14 P–QB4! was clearly going White's way in Botvinnik-Langeweg, Hamburg 1965.

7 Q–N3

a) **7 P–K4!?** P–Q4! (**7 ... B×N** 8 QP×B N×P 9 R–K1 P–KB4 – **9... P–Q4?** *10 P×P P×P 11 N×P! R×N 12 R×N etc.* – 10´ N×P R×N 11 P–B3 Q–N3ch 12 B–K3 N–B4 13 P–QN4 P–Q3 14 R–N1 with the initiative.) 8 BP×P P×P 9 P×P P–K5 10 N–Q4 B–N5 11 Q–R4 (Q–N3 B–QB4) 11 ... B×N 12 QP×B Q×P =. All analysis by Kapengut.

b) **7 P–QR3** B×N! (**7 ... B–B1** 8 P–K4! – **8 P–Q4** *P–K5 9 N–K1 P–KR3 10 P–Q5 P–Q3 =* Steinberg-Belyavsky, Sukhumi 1971 – 8 ... P–Q4 9 KP×P P×P 10 P–Q4 – *or 10 P×P N×P 11 N×N Q×N 12 R–K1!* – 10 ... P–K5 11 N–K5 with advantage – Kapengut) 8 QP×B P–KR3 Δ ... P–Q4 (Kapengut) =.

c) **7 P–Q4!?** P–K5 8 N–KN5 P–Q4 9 Q–N3! B–B1?! (9 ... B×N) 10 P×P P×P 11 P–B3 P–KR3? (But **11 ...P×P** 12 B×P P–KR3 13 N×BP or 12 ... N–B3 13 N×BP!) 12 N×BP! K×N 13 P×P K–N1 14 P–K5 ±± Pribyl-Lutikov, Bucharest 1975. Note how this variation owes its success to a determined fight for the central squares, not characteristic of, say, 5 P–Q3 or the line (b) 7 P–QR3 just considered.

7 ...   B–B1?!

Perhaps better is **7 ... B–R4** 8 P–Q3 (**8 P–Q4** P–K5 9 N–Q2 P–Q4 10 P–K3 P–QR3 11 P–QR4 B–K3 with a good position – Kapengut; but **9 N–KN5!?** P–Q4 10 P×P P×P 11 P–B3 could be tried, as in Pribyl-Lutikov, note (c) above.) 8 ... P–KR3 9 B–Q2 P–Q4 =; this is B32, note to 7 ... P–Q4.

8 P–K4

Also **8 P–Q3** N–R3 9 N–KR4 P–KR3 10 P–K4 P–Q3 11 P–KR3 N–B4 12 Q–B2 P–QR4 13 B–K3 B–K3 14 K–R2 R–B1 15 QR–Q1 ± Geller-Bisguier, Italy 1971.

8 ...   P–Q3
9 P–Q4   QN–Q2
10 R–Q1

Szabo-Kuprianov, Zagreb 1964, which everyone agrees is better for White, but is just a standard Old Indian formation with White having played the dubious-looking Q–N3. This may be only equal after, say, 10 ... P–QR3 (10 ... Q–B2?! 11 P–B5! ∞) threatening ... P–QN4.

B42

6 ...   P–K5 and:
B421 7 N–KN5
B422 7 N–K1
B423 7 N–Q4

B421

7 N–KN5   B×N
7 ... P–Q4!? 8 P×P B–KB4 9

Q–N3!? B×N? 10 NP×B Q×P 11 P–B3! Q×Q 12 P×Q P×P 13 B×P P–B3 14 R–R5 B–N3 15 P–Q3 QN–Q2 16 N–R3 N–K4 17 N–B4 ± Hübner-Estevez, Graz 1972. Kapengut recommends instead **9 ... N–R3!** and if 10 P–B3, 10 ... P×P 11 R×P B–N5 12 R–B2 B–KR4! ∞. He then opines that 9 P–B3 is better.

8 QP×B   P–Q3

8 ... P–KR3 9 N–R3 P–Q3 10 N–B4 QN–Q2 (**10 ... N–B3** makes less sense as a White knight is headed for d5 and Black often has to play N–K4–Q2 thereafter. An example was Taimanov-Karasev, USSR Ch 1971: 10 ... N–B3 11 P–N3 B–B4 12 N–Q5 N×N 13 P×N N–K4 14 Q–Q4 N–N3 15 P–QB4 Q–Q2 16 B–N2 P–KB3 17 KR–Q1 P–QN3 18 P–QN4 ±; **10 ... P–QN3**, on the other hand, is logical and probably =, e.g. 11 N–Q5 B–N2 12 B–B4 QN–Q2 13 Q–Q2 N–K4, etc. – Kapengut.) 11 P–N3 P–QR4 (11 ... P–QN3) 12 P–KR3 P–R5 13 B–K3 ± Taimanov-Pytel, Bucharest 1973 (1–0, 53). Black's ... P–QR4–R5 usually doesn't even win the QR-file in such situations, and after ... P–QN3 and ... B–N2, he may well want to play ... P–QR3 instead (Δ ... P–QN4, to loosen White's hold on d5). Compare Chapter 7, D22.

9 P–B3

9 N–R3 P–QN3 10 N–B4 B–N2 11 N–Q5 R–K4 12 B–B4 R–KR4 (Kapengut).

9 ...   P–QN3!
Or **9 ... P×P** 10 P×P N–B3 11

Q–B2 P–KR3 12 N–R3 B–K3 13 P–N3 Q–Q2 14 N–B4 B–B4 = Holmov-Malich, Pech 1964.

10 B–K3   B–N2
11 B–Q4 QN–Q2 12 N–R3 P–QR4 13 N–B4 P–R5 and 'Black's position is preferable.' (Kapengut).

B422

7 N–K1   BxN

7 ... P–B3?! 8 N–B2 BxN 9 QPxB P–Q4 10 PxP PxP 11 B–N5 QN–Q2 12 P–KR3! P–KR3 13 B–K3 N–K4 14 B–Q4 Q–B2 15 N–K3 with a clear White advantage, Raicević-Ostojić. Vrnjacka Banja 1975 (but 0–1, 51).

8 QPxB

8 NPxB P–QN3 (Kapengut gives **8 ... P–Q3** 9 P–B3 Q–K2 10 PxP NxP 11 N–Q3 P–KB4 ∞ and 8 ... P–Q4 9 PxP QxP 10 Q–N3 Q–KB4) 9 N–B2 B–N2 10 N–K3 P–Q3 11 P–B3 PxP 12 BxP BxB 13 RxB QN–Q2 14 P–Q3 Q–K2 15 P–QR4 P–QR4 = Valvo-Vukić, New York 1976.

8 ...   P–Q3
9 N–B2   QN–Q2

'?!' (Kapengut), though it may well be the best move, since in Chapter 7, D2242 (now arrived at by **9 ... N–B3**), Black's knight often voluntarily loses two tempi to get to d7 (even via b8 if necessary!). And **9 ... B–K3** was unconvincing in Ivkov-Uhlmann, Skopje 1972: 10 P–N3 Q–B1 11 B–N5 QN–Q2 12 N–Q4 B–N5 13 P–B3 PxP 14 PxP B–R4 15 B–R3! Q–N1 16 Q–Q2 B–N3 17 QR–K1 and White later won.

Besides **9 ... QN–Q2**, Black may

choose the ever-reliable **9 ... P–QN3** and make a decision about his queen's knight later.

10 P–N3(?!)

Or **10 B–N5** P–QN3 11 N–K3 B–N2 = /∞, or **10 N–K3** P–QN3 11 N–Q5 B–N2 12 B–B4 (stopping ... R–K4), and instead of **12 ... N–R4** (?), given by Kapengut, 12 **... P–QR4** (or **12 ... P–QR3**) 13 P–N3 N–B4 is adequate (compare Chapter 7, D2).

10 ...   P–KR3
11 B–K3   P–QN3
12 Q–Q2?

12 B–Q4 Δ N–K3 covers some key squares. White never finds a plan.

12 ...   B–N2
13 QR–Q1   N–K4
14 Q–B1?

Better **14 N–N4!**; Black's next prepares ... Q–B4–R4 and:

14 ...   Q–B1
15 P–KR3   N–B6ch! (*34*)

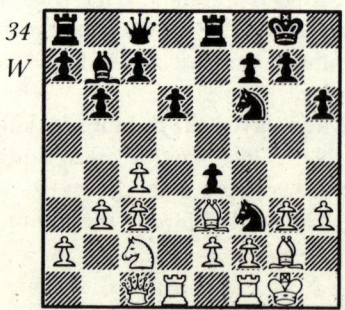

34
W

16 K–R1 (Acceptance would be fatal after **16 PxN** PxP 17 B–R1 QxP 18 R–Q4 N–K5! 19 BxP NxBP(6)! or 19 RxN BxR! 20 B–B4 P–KN4 etc. Uhlmann) 16 ... R–K4! 17 N–K1 R–KR4 18 P–KR4 Q–N5! 19 PxN PxP 20

N×P B×N 21 B×B Q×Bch 22 K–N1 P–KN4! (∓∓) 23 R–Q4 R–K1 24 Q–Q1? R×B! 25 P×R Q×NPch 26 K–R1 P–N5 0–1, Cuellar-Uhlmann, Leningrad 1973. A pretty illustration of how Black can work up an attack by sufficiently overprotecting e4 and using e5 as a base of operations. Of course White should have embarked on something more active in the centre (as in the notes to his 10th, 12th and 14th moves).

B423

7 N–Q4   B×N

a) Once again, **7 . . . N–B3 8 N–B2** leads to Chapter 7, D2242, and **8 N×N QP×N** is typically good for Black, who can support e4 easily and build up pressure on the queen file.

Unique after 7 . . . N–B3 was **8 N–N3!?** P–QR4! 9 P–Q4 P×Pe.p. 10 Q×P N–K4 11 Q–Q4?! (11 Q–B2! ∞-Uhlmann) 11 . . . P–R5 12 N–Q2 P–B4 13 Q–B4 B×N 14 P×B, S. Garcia-Uhlmann, Cienfuegos, 1973, and now 14 . . . P–Q4! 15 P×P N×P 16 B×N (forced) 16 . . . Q×B would have clarified the situation in Black's favour (Uhlmann).

b) Important is **7 . . . P–Q3**, trying to avoid transposition to Chapter 7, e.g. **8 N–B2** B×N 9 QP×B QN–Q2 is B422. If **8 Q–B2**, 8 . . . B–QB4!? 9 N–N3 B–B4 is far from clear. 7 . . . P–Q3 deserves a test.

8 NP×B

8 QP×B P–Q3 **9 N–B2** would be B422. White may also leave his knight on d4 with **9 P–KR3**

P–QN3 10 B–B4 B–N2 11 P–KN4!?, an interesting sequence proposed by (of course) Kapengut. After 9 P–KR3 P–QN3, one game continued instead: **10 P–N3** B–N2 11 N–B2 QN–Q2 12 N–K3 R–K4! 13 P–QR4 P–QR4 (or 13 . . . P–QR3) 14 Q–B2 (14 R–R2–Q2 could precede this move.) 14 . . . P–KR3 15 R–Q1 Q–K1 16 N–B1 N–B1 = Vukić-Korchnoi, Erevan, 1971.

8 . . .	N–B3
9 P–Q3	P×P
10 P×P	P–KR3
11 R–K1?	

Time-consuming. White should try **11 B–B4** , e.g. 11 . . . N×N(?!) 12 P×N P–Q4 13 B–K5 N–N5 14 P×P N×B 15 P×N R×P 16 Q–N3 ± (Kapengut).

11 . . .	R×Rch
12 Q×R	N×N
13 P×N	P–Q4

With a standard pawn blockade in the centre. This is Pfleger-Korchnoi, Hastings 1972/3; after 14 B–QR3?! (14 B–B4-Kapengut) 14 . . . B–K3 15 R–N1 P–QN3 16 R–B1 Q–Q2 17 Q–Q2 R–K1. Black was better. White's bishops don't have much to do, and pawn breaks which might increase their scope do not exist.

CONCLUSION:

5 N–B3 may be White's best, simply because it often transposes to Chapter 7. However, 5 . . . R–K1 6 0–0 P–K5 should be answered by 7 **N–Q4** for this purpose, since 7 **N–K1** B×N 8 QP×B P–Q3 9 N–B2 QN–Q2 seems to improve on

Black's formation in that chapter.

In general, 3 ... B–N5 has scored well for Black. Grandmasters hold the move in respect (evidenced by their propensity to play 3 N–B3), and a change in that attitude does not seem likely in the near future.

5 ACCELERATED FIANCHETTO REVERSED

1 P–QB4	P–K4
2 N–QB3	N–KB3
3 P–KN3	P–Q4
4 P×P	N×P
5 B–N2 (35)	

35
B

When White plays 1 P–K4 (!?) Black sometimes chooses 1 . . . P–QB4 2 N–KB3 N–QB3 3 P–Q4 P×P 4 N×P P–KN3, the Accelerated Fianchetto Sicilian. When facing 1 . . . P–K4 in the English, it is natural to aim for the diagrammed position, putting even quicker pressure on d5. Indeed, the main deterrent to the aforementioned Sicilian line is 5 P–QB4 (the Maroczy Bind), whereas here 5 ... P–QB4?? loses a piece.

In this chapter, we look at several Black responses to 5 B–N2, excluding therein two variations which transpose into Chapter 6 (5 ... **B–K3** 6 N–B3 N–B3 7 0–0 B–K2 and 5 ... **N–N3** 6 N–B3):

A 5 . . . N–K2
B 5 . . . P–QB3
C 5 . . . B–K3
D 5 . . . N×N
E 5 . . . N–N3

A

5 . . .   **N–K2**

Schwarz attributes this move to Opocensky. Black tries to control d4 via . . . N(1)–B3 and sometimes . . . N–B4.

6 N–B3

After Black's reply, White no longer has to worry about 6 . . . P–QB4. Considering all that follows, **6 P–QN4!?** is a thought. Then e.g. **6 . . . N(1)–B3** 7 P–N5 N–Q5 8 P–K3 N–K3 9 N–K2 ± or **6 . . . P–QR4** 7 P–N5 P–QB4 8 P×Pe.p. N(2)×P 9 R–N1 with excellent play, or 6 . . . N–B4 7 R–N1 B–K2 8 N–B3 etc. Maybe Black could try **6 . . . P–QB4!?** 7 P×P N–B4 8 N–B3 N–N3 9 0–0 B×P 10 B–N2 P–B3? Anyway, 5 . . . N–K2 is infrequent enough that the importance of such 'contributions' should not be exaggerated. Therefore, onto:

6 . . .   N(1)–B3

Now material divides:
A1 7 P–Q3
A2 7 P–QN4
A3 7 0–0

A1

7 P–Q3

Not very aggressive, yet still posing problems for Black. White seeks rapid development and posts for pieces on the queenside. Black has two ways to deploy his forces:
a) **7 . . . N–B4!?** 8 0–0 B–K2 9 P–K3! (Logical, taking d4 from Black's knights. **9 P–QR3** 0–0?! 10 P–QN4 B–K3 11 B–N2 P–B3 12 N–Q2! R–N1 13 Q–R4 P–QR3 14 QR–B1 N(4)–Q5 15 P–K3! N–N6? 16 N×N P–QN4 17 Q×RP R–N3 18 Q×R P×Q 19 B×N B×N 20 B×P(±) Q–R1 21 P–K4 R–Q1 22 N–Q5! Petrosian-Mikenas, ½F 25th USSR Ch, Kiev, 1957 (1–0, 47). Better was **9 . . . P–QR4!** 10 R N1 0–0 11 B–Q2 B–K3 12 P–QN4 P×P 13 P×P P–B3 =-Schwarz) 9 . . . 0–0 10 Q–K2 B–K3 11 P–N3 Q–Q2 12 B–N2 QR–Q1 13 KR–Q1 Δ QR÷B1, N–K4 etc. ± (analysis by Pachman and Mikenas).
b) **7 . . . P–KN3** 8 0–0 (8 P–N3!?) 8 . . . B–N2. This position can also arise via 1 P–QB4 N–KB3 2 N–QB3 P–Q4 3 P×P N×P 4 N–B3 P–KN3 5 P–KN3 B–N2 6 B–N2 P–K4 7 P–Q3 N–K2 8 0–0 N(1)–B3 (see Chapter 13, D1), so it is rather important for theory: 9 B–Q2 (perhaps 9 R–N1, Δ 10 P–QN4) 9 . . . 0–0 10 R–B1 (**10 P–QR3** P–KR3 11 P–QN4 N–B4?! 12 R–B1 P–QR4 13 P–N5 N(3)–Q5 14 N×N N×N 15 P–QR4 ± Evans-Mednis, USA 1954) 10 . . . N–Q5 11 N×N P×N 12 N–K4 P–KR3 13 Q–N3? (**13 R–B2!?** Δ Q–B1 looks better, or **13 P–QN4**)

13. . . P–N3! 14 Q–B4 (**14 B×P** B×B 15 N–B6ch K–N2 16 B×R K×N ∓) 14 . . . P–B3 15 B–N4 B–Q2 16 Q–R6 P–QB4 ∓ Hübner-Korchnoi (1), Solingen 1973 (0–1, 74).

A2

7 P–QN4

Schwarz and Shatskes say this transposes to **7 0–0**, but the move is usually played now and has some unique aspects:

7 . . .   P–QR3

7 . . . N×P?! 8 N×P cedes another central pawn.

8 B–N2

8 R–N1 N–B4 9 0–0 B–K2 10 P–QR4 P–B3 11 P–N5 P×P 12 P×P N(3)–Q5 13 P–K3 N×Nch 14 B×N 0–0 15 Q–B2 ± Stolyar-Pithart, Olomouc 1975 (1–0, 32).

8 . . .   N–B4

8 . . . P–KN3 is another strategy. Then 9 0–0 B–N2 transposes to A32.

9 P–QR3   B–K2

This is Pachman-Pietzch, Harrakov 1966: 10 R–B1 (For **10 0–0**, see A31) 10 . . . B–K3 (10 . . . N(4)–Q5-Taimanov-is like A31.) 11 P–Q3 0–0 12 N–QR4 P–B3 13 N–Q2 ±. White heads for c5.

A3

7 0–0

And Black has the usual choice of plans:
A31 7 . . . N–B4
A32 7 . . . P–KN3

A31

7 . . .   N–B4
8 P–QN4!

The most consequent; **8 P–Q3**
B–K2 9 P–QR3 P–QR4 = (Shatskes), or here 9 P–N3 B–K3 10 B–N2
0–0 11 R–B1 N(4)–Q5 $\mp$
(Schwarz).

8 ... P–QR3

8 ... B×P? 9 N×KP! etc.; **8 ...
P–B3** 9 P–N5 N(3)–Q5 10 N×N
(or 10 P–K3) 10 ... P×N 11 N–Q5
B–Q2 12 Q–N3 P–B3 13 N–B4
B–Q3 14 B–QR3! $\pm$ Zita-Gilg,
1937. If Black wants to play ...
P–KB3, he must be careful not to
forfeit castling.

9 B–N2

Again **9 R–N1** B–K2 10 P–QR4
is effective: 10 ... P–B3 11 P–N5
P×P 12 P×P N(3)–Q5 13 N×N
P×N 14 N–Q5 $\pm$ Aronson-
Korelov, Leningrad Ch 1963.

9 ... B–K2

The drawbacks of queenside
castling were made obvious in
Olafsson-Duckstein, Wageningeh
1957: **9 ... B–K3** 10 N–K4 P–B3 11
P–QR3 Q–Q2 12 Q–B2! 0–0–0 (**12
... N(4)–Q5** 13 N×N P×N 14
N–B5 B×N 15 Q×B $\pm$-Schwarz) 13
KR–Q1 N(4)–Q5 14 B×N P×B?!
15 Q–N2 P–Q6 16 P–K3 K–N1 17
QR–N1! N–R2 18 N–B5 B×N 19
P×B P–B3 20 N–Q4 B–B2 21 Q–N6
K–R1 22 B–R3 N–B1 23 B×Q
N×Q 24 B×P! 1–0.

10 P–QR3 (*36*)

10 N–K4 P–B3 (**10 ... N(4)–Q5**
11 N×N P×N 12 N–B5! 0–0 13
R–B1 R–N1 14 P–QR3 P–QR4?!
15 P–N5 N–R2 16 P–QR4 $\pm$
Botvinnik-Szabo, Tel Aviv 1964)
11 P–QR3 0–0 12 R–B1! (**12
Q–N3ch** K–R1 13 P–K3 P–QR4!
=, Δ 14 P–N5? P–R5 Simagin-

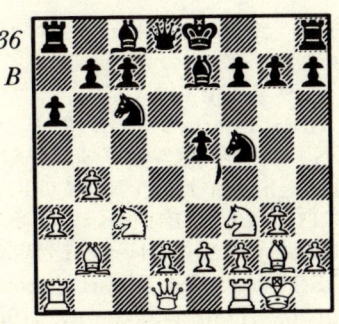

36
B

Flohr, 1953) 12 ... B–K3 13 N–B5
B×N 14 R×B N(3)–K2? (14 ...
N–N1!-Rellstab) 15 Q–B2 P–B3 16
P–K4 (Δ P–Q4) L. Schmid-
Rellstab, W. Germany 1948.

10 ... B–K3

11 P–Q3 0–0

12 R–B1 P–B3 13 N–QR4 Q–Q2
14 N–Q2! N–R3 15 N–K4 (White
threatens 16 N–B5, ×NP!.) 15 ...
Q–B1 16 N(K)–B5 B×N 17 N×B
B–R6 18 B–Q5ch K–R1 19 R–K1
(or 19 N×NP!) 19 ... N–Q1 20
P–Q4 Smyslov-Jimenez, Havana
1965. White has two strong bishops
and dominates the centre.

A32

7 ... P–KN3

8 P–QN4! P–QR3

8 ... B–N2 allows White to take
over on the queenside: 9 P–N5
N–Q5 10 P–QR4! (clearer than **10
B–N2** 0–0 11 P–Q3 P–QR3 12
P–QR4 B–K3 13 N×N P×N 14
N–K4 B–Q4 15 Q–B2 R–K1 16
KR–B1 P×P 17 P×P R×R 18 R×R
N–B4, slightly $\pm$, Schmidt-
Sigurjonsson, Nice 1974 ($\frac{1}{2}$–$\frac{1}{2}$, 39))
10 ... 0–0 11 B–QR3 R–K1 12
N–N5! R–N1 13 R–B1 P–KR3 14
N(5)–K4 P–KB4 15 N–B5 P–N3 16

N–R6 ± Taimanov-Wittkowski, 1959.

9 P–QR4

More assertive than **9 B–N2** B–N2 10 P–QR3 0–0 11 P–Q3, although after 11 . . . N–B4 (11 . . . P–N3!?) 12 R–B1 (or 12 P–K3-Schwarz) 12 . . . N(4)–Q5 13 P–K3 N–K3 14 N–QR4, White had some pull in Ilivitsky-Sakharov, 1967 (1–0, 26).

9 . . .   B–N2
10 B–QR3   0–0
11 P–N5 N–Q5 12 N–N5 (**12 P–K3** N×Nch 13 Q×N ± Zwaig-Romanishin, Hastings 1976/7, was not as convincing.) 12 . . . P×P 13 P×P B–Q2 14 B×P R–N1 15 B–N2 N×P 16 N×N B×N 17 R–N1 P–R3 18 N–K4 R–K1 19 P–Q3 Larsen-Lehman, Palma de Mallorca 1967. White's pieces are very active and Black's QBP is weak (1–0, 34).

B

5 . . .   **P–QB3?**

This is a legal move.

6 N–B3

6 N×N? P×N 7 Q–N3 B–K3! 8 Q×NP is not worth the effort: 8 . . . N–Q2 9 Q–N3 R–QN1 10 Q–Q1 B–QB4 with an attack (Taimanov).

6 . . .   Q–B2

6 . . . P–B3 7 0–0 and 8 P–Q4 confer White a big space advantage.

7 P–Q4   P×P

Or **7 . . . B–QN5** 8 B–Q2! P×P 9 N×N ± (Taimanov).

8 N×N!   Q–R4ch
9 N–Q2!   P×N
10 0–0 B–K3 11 N–N3 Q–N3 12

N×P N–B3 13 N×B P×N 14 B–R3 N–Q1 15 P–K4! ±± Euwe-Mulder, Amsterdam 1933.

C

5 . . .   **B–K3**

This can lead to Chapter 6; here we consider independent lines:

6 N–B3

a) **6 Q–R4ch** is not much use: 6 . . . N–B3 7 Q–N5? P–QR3 8 Q×P?? N–R4 ∓∓ (Shatskes).

b) **6 Q–N3!?** can cause Black considerable discomfort: 6 . . . N–N5 (practically forced, since 6 . . . N×N? 7 Q×N or 6 . . . N–N3?! 7 Q–N5ch loses material) 7 Q–R4ch N(5)–B3 8 Q–N5! Q–B1 9 N–B3 B–Q3 10 N–N5 Taimanov-Penrose, Hastings 1956/7. '±' according to all commentators, and that seems true after e.g. 10 . . . B–Q2 11 Q–B4 0–0 12 N–Q5! (Δ N–K4) or 11 . . . N–Q1 12 N–N5. So everyone traces the problem to **7 . . . N(5)–B3**, '?!', but **7 . . . B–Q2** 8 Q–Q1 B–B3 9 N–B3 N–Q2 10 0–0 ± was Pitschak-Foltys, 1933, when White's centre pawns are an asset, and **7 . . . P–B3** (Mikenas) allows simply 8 P–QR3 N(5)–R3 9 P–QN4± or 8 . . . N–Q4 9 N–B3 Δ P–Q4 ±. 6 Q–N3 is worth trying.

6 . . .   N–QB3

6 . . . P–KB3? 7 0–0 N–B3 8 P–Q4 P×P 9 N–QN5 B–QB4 10 N(5)×P N×N 11 N×N B–B2 12 Q–R4ch K–B1 (**12 . . . Q–Q2** 13 Q×Qch K×Q 14 R–Q1-Taimanov) 13 R–Q1 ± Alekhine-Duskhotimirski, Carlsbad 1911.

7 P–Q4?!

7 0–0! is Chapter 6. **7 N–KN5**

Q×N! (**7...N×N?!** 8 N×B N×Q 9 N×Q ±) 8 N×N Q–Q1 (**8 ... 0–0–0** 9 N–B3! ±) 9 N–B3 (Perhaps **9 N–K3** Δ P–QN3, B–N2, 0–0, P–B4) 9 ... Q–Q2 10 Q–R4 (**10 0–0?** B–KR6 Δ ... P–KR4– Schwarz) 10 ... B–KR6 11 B×B Q×B 12 P–Q3 B–B4 13 B–K3 B×B = /∞ Carls–Krause, 1928.

7 ...	P×P
8 N×P	N×N(6)!
9 P×N	N×N
10 P×N	B–N5ch

'=' (Schwarz). 11 K–B1 (11 B–Q2 Q×P) 11 ... B–B6 12 R–N1 0–0 may well be ∓ instead, so 7 P–Q4?! must be considered weak.

D

5 ...	N×N!?

An apparently anti-positional exchange, since it strengthens White's centre and opens his queen knight file. On the other hand, Black saves time for development and clears his own queen-file.

6 NP×N	N–B3

a) **6 ... P–QB4** 7 R–N1 N–B3 8 Q–R4 (or **8 P–Q3!** B–K2 9 N–B3 0–0 10 0–0 Q–B2 11 B–K3 B–B4 12 Q–R4 ± Kan–Ratner, 1945 8 ... Q–B2 9 N–B3 B–Q3 10 P–Q4! 0–0 11 0–0 BP×P 12 P×P Keres– Ekström, corres. 1935; 12 ... B–Q2! ±.

b) **6 ... B–QB4** 7 Q–R4ch! Q–Q2 8 Q×Qch N×Q 9 N–B3 P–QB3 10 0–0 0–0 11 P–Q4 P×P 12 P×P B–N3 13 P–QR4 R–K1 14 P–K3 N–B3 15 B–Q2! B–KB4 16 KR–B1 (Δ P–R5) ± Vondorffy–Rozinoz, corres. 1972–4. The advantages of White's centre pawns and his queenside pressure endured to the end (1–0, 34)!

7 P–Q3

A comical blunder is **7 R–N1** B–QB4 8 Q–R4 Q–Q2 9 Q–QB4? Q–B4! (Shatskes); 7 N–B3!? P–K5 8 N–Q4 N×N 9 P×N Q×P 10 R–QN1 is analyzed in Chapter 6, note to 6 B–N2.

7 ...	B–QB4!

7...B–K2 8 R–N1! 0–0 9 N–B3 R–N1 10 0–0 B–K3 11 Q–R4! (Shatskes and Taimanov) gives White good chances on the queenside and even possibilities of mobilizing his centre very quickly. After **7...B–QB4**, R–QN1 is met by a timely ... B–QN3; moreover, d4 has an extra guard.

8 N–B3	0–0
9 0–0	B–KN5
10 P–KR3	B–R4
11 Q–R4	R–K1

Shatskes says 'approximately equal' whereas Taimanov gives the nod to White. Interesting would be the double-edged 12 B–N5!? Q–Q2 (12 ... P–B3? 13 Q–B4ch) 13 Q–R4 B–KN3 14 N–Q2! B–N3 15 QR–N1 P–B3 16 B–K3.

E

5 ...	N–N3 (*37*)

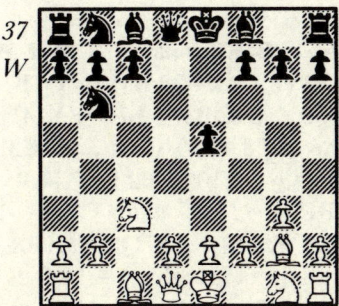

37
W

Now **6 N–B3** N–B3 (**6 ... P–KB3?** or **6 ... B–Q3?!** meets with 7 P–Q4!) transposes to Chapter 6. White also has

6 P–Q3

And these for your files:

a) **6 P–QR4** P–QR4 7 P–Q3 B–QN5! (The drawback to playing P–QR4 before ... B–K2) 8 N–B3 N–B3 9 0–0 0–0 10 B–K3 B–N5 (Black's bishops are aggressively placed. **11 P–R3** is now in order, but ...) **11 R–B1?!** P–B4! 12 N–KN5 P–B5 13 QB×N Q×N 14 B×BP Q–R4 15 B×N (Already there was no defence.) 15 ... P×B 16 R–B2 B×N! 17 R×B (17 P×B P–B6 ∓∓) 17 ... B×P 18 Q–N3ch K–R1 19 R–K1 Q–R6 20 B×KP P–B6 0–1 Leepin-Alekhine, 1941.

b) **6 N–R3** B–KB4! (**6 ... N–B3** 7 0–0 P–KR4!? 8 P–Q3 P–R5 9 N–KN5 B–K2 10 N–B3 P–N4 11 P–Q4! P×QP 12 N–N5 B–B3 13 P–K3! P–Q6 – 13 ... QP×P 14 Q–K2 – 14 N(5)–Q4 N×N 15 P×N P–N5?! 16 N×P! Q×P 17 R–K1ch ± Bilek-Benko, Hungary 1956) 7 0–0 (**7 P–B4!?** B×N 8 B×B P×P 9 0–0 P×P 10 Q–N3, or 9 ... B–Q3 10 P–K3-Schwarz; 7 ... Q–Q2!?) 7 ... Q–Q2 8 N–KN5 B–K2 9 P–Q3 N–B3 ∓.

6 ...　　　　N–B3

6 ... B–K2 is plausible: **7 N–R3** N–B3 (**7 ... B–Q2** 8 P–B4 Q–B1 9 N–B2 B–QB3 10 P–K4!±- Schwarz) 8 0–0 0–0 (**8 ... B–K3!** 9 P–B4 Q–Q2 10 N–B2 P×P 11 B×P P–B4? – *11 ... 0–0 = /∞* – 12 R–B1 P–N4 13 B–Q2 P–KR4 – delusions of grandeur! – 14 P–K4! P–R5 15 P×BP ± Uhlmann-

Häninen, 1957) 9 P–B4 B×N?! 10 B×B B–B4ch 11 K–R1 N–Q4 12 N×N Q×Nch 13 B–N2 Q–K3?! 14 P–B5 Q–Q2 15 Q–R4 QR–Q1 16 B–N5! ± Golombek-Scholtens, Leeuwarden 1947.

Despite the positions reached, 6 ... B–K2 doesn't lose its credibility in these examples. Perhaps White should really play **7 P–QR4**(!) now that the Black bishop would have to take two moves to reach b4. After 7 P–QR4 P–QR4, if White wants to do more than transpose to B22 of the next chapter, he might then try 8 B–K3!? and if **8 ... N–B3**, 9 B×Nch!; or on **8 ... 0–0**, 9 R–B1 P–KB4 10 N–N5 P–B3 11 Q–N3ch K–R1 12 N–R7! ± or 12 N–B7 ±.

7 N–R3　　　　B–KB4

7 ... B–K3 8 N–KN5 B–KB4 9 P–B4 B–K2 10 N–B3 ± (Schwarz). A well-known manoeuvre; maybe '=' is a better assessment.

8 P–B4　　　　Q–Q2
9 N–B2　　　　P×P
10 B×P　　　　B–K2

11 0–0 0–0 12 K–R1 (One doesn't often find grandmasters in such a position. White remains full of holes wherever he puts his king and queen pawns, yet his pieces are active. 12 P–QR3, preparing a general queenside advance, was another idea.) 12 ... QR–Q1 13 N–N5?! N–N5! 14 N–B3 (14 N×BP? P–KN4) 14 ... B–K3 15 B–Q2 P–KR3?! (Slow; **15 ... N–B3** and **15 ... P–QR4** were fine for Black.) 16 P–QR3 N–B3 17 P–QN4 P–B4? (**17 ... N–Q4** 18 P–K4?! N–B3) 18 P–N5 N–Q5?! 19 R–QN1 (Black has trapped his own

piece: ±) 19 ... B×P?! 20 P–K3 P–B5 21 P×N ±± Uhlmann-Duckstein, Munich 1958.

CONCLUSION:

Opocensky's **5 ... N–K2** is playable, but has not scored very well; Black should expect to suffer some pressure on the queenside. **5 ... N×N** opts for rapid development, but I prefer White's diagonal pressure and large centre. **5 ... P–QB3?** deserves its question mark. After **5 ... B–K3**, the irregular 6 Q–N3!? is a reasonable alternative to 6 N–B3; the line 6 N–B3 N–B3 7 P–Q4?!, however, is worse than the standard 7 0–0 of Chapter 6.

Most strong players would choose **5 ... N–N3** here, aiming for main lines. Then neither **6 P–QR4** nor **6 N–R3** leads to anything against straightforward play; **6 P–Q3** N–B3 7 N–R3 develops quickly, but tends to leave White's centre a bit airy. So, very likely correct is just **6 N–B3** N–B3 7 0–0, analyzed in the next chapter.

6 DRAGON REVERSED: 3 N–B3 N–B3 4 P–KN3 P–Q4

1 P–QB4	P–K4
2 N–QB3	N–KB3
3 N–B3	N–B3
4 P–KN3	P–Q4
5 P×P	N×P
6 B–N2 (38)	

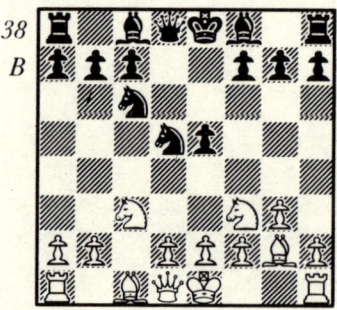

In 1973, Gligorić wrote: 'The Dragon Variation with a move up obviously favours White.' 4 ... P–Q4 introduces the set of positions he was referring to, in which White is playing the Black side of a Dragon (Sicilian Defence), and most grandmasters since 1960 have indeed shunned these systems. But the last few years have seen increasing dissatisfaction with Gligorić's view, partly due to the games of Soviet GM Romanishin. It seems wrong to assume that because the Dragon is a critical variation, an extra tempo should lead to decisive advantage. In many cases, White's extra move merely tips Black off to his proper defensive procedure; in others, the first player cannot make headway against simplifying play. Thus a variation which has lain fallow for some years is attracting renewed attention.

Actually, until White plays P–Q3, he hasn't completed a 'dragon-shape' with his pawns, and a few of the lines below are formally more related to the Accelerated Fianchetto Sicilian (see also Chapter 5). What is important, however, is that Black must cope with the fire-breathing power of White's KB. His first decision, in fact, is whether to support his knight in the centre, or retreat from the pressure:

A 6 ... B–K3
B 6 ... N–N3

The systems of A often come up when White chooses **6 P–Q3** instead of **6 B–N2**. Then Black needn't fear P–Q4 (see A1), and can keep his knight on the influential d5 square. For his part, White plays 6 P–Q3 to avoid 6 B–N2 N×N!? 7 NP×N P–K5, but that it is a real threat is not clear: a) **8 N–N1** P–B4 (8 ... B–B4 9 Q–R4! Q–K2 10 R–N1) 9 P–B3 (**9 N–R3** is a sound alternative,

although N–KB4 does not win a tempo, as in the analogous Sicilian position where White's bishop is on e3. **9 P–Q3** P×P 10 P×P B–K3 11 N–B3 B–K2 12 0–0 0–0 13 R–K1 B–B2 14 R–N1 was Tal-N.N., Radio game 1960. '±' seems fair.) 9 . . . P×P! (**9 . . . P–K6?!** 10 P–Q4! P–B5 11 Q–Q3 P–KN4 12 P–KR4! Δ Q–K4ch is good for White, whereas **9 . . . B–Q3?** 10 P×P P–B5 11 P–Q4 P×P 12 P–K5 P×P 13 N–B3 B–K2 14 R×P ± Arulaid-Heuer, Tallin 1964, is even better than the corresponding Accelerated Fianchetto line. Also weak is **9 . . . P–B5?** due to 10 Q–R4! ±) 10 N×P B–K2 11 0–0 0–0 and now both **12 R–N1!?** and **12 Q–N3ch** seem better than **12 P–Q4** B–K3! 13 B–B4 B–Q4 = /∞.
b) **8 N–Q4!?** N×N 9 P×N Q×P 10 R–N1 is plausible, the more so since Black's bishop is not on e6 attacking the QRP as White's does in the Sicilian. An example might be 10 . . . B–QB4 11 0–0 (or **11 P–K3** Q–B5 12 Q–N3!) 11 . . . 0–0 12 B–N2 Q–Q4 13 Q–R4 (13 Q–B2 B–B4 14 P–Q3 =) 13 . . . Q×QP 14 Q×KP Δ Q–K5 and White has attacking chances e.g. 14 . . . B–N3(?) 15 KR–Q1 Q–R3 16 B–QR3 P–QB4 17 Q–K7 etc.
Apparently, then, 6 P–Q3 is an unnecessary precaution. Returning to 6 B–N2:

A

6 . . .	**B–K3**
7 0–0	B–K2

Not 7 . . . B–QB4? 8 N×P N×N 9 P–Q4 ± or 7 . . . P–B3? 8 Q–N3, quelching the 'Yugoslav Attack in Reverse'! After 7 . . . B–K2:
A1 8 P–Q4
A2 8 P–Q3

A1

8 P–Q4 (*39*)

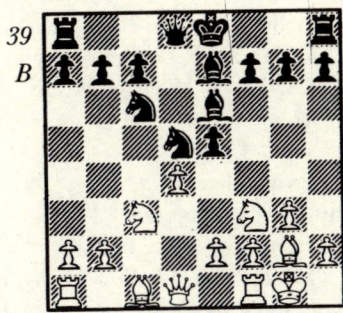

Perhaps the most important variation in this chapter. If White gains an advantage with 8 P–Q4, then Black must play the lines with . . . N–N3. If not, then this system is probably equal for the second player (see A2). Now Black has a choice:
A11 8 . . . N×N
A12 8 . . . P×P

A11

8 . . .	**N×N**
9 P×N	P–K5

9 . . . P×P 10 P×P (or 10 N×P ±) 10 . . . B–Q4 11 Q–Q3 ΔP–K4.
10 N–Q2
Usually played, but **10 N–K1** strikes me as a good option e.g. 10 . . . P–B4 11 N–B2 0–0 (11 . . . N–R4 12 P–B3 ± is comparable to later lines.) 12 N–K3 (or 12 P–B3) 12 . . . N–R4 13 P–Q5 B–Q2 14 P–QB4 (±?).

10 ...   P–B4
11 P–K3

a) **11 R–N1** (?!-Larsen) 11 ...
R–QN1 12 Q–R4 0–0 13 B–QR3
B×B 14 Q×B Q–Q4 15 R–N2
Q–R4 (=) 16 Q×Q N×Q 17
KR–N1 P–QN3 18 P–K3 N–B5?!
19 N×N B×N 20 B–B1 ± Larsen-
Bouteville, Lugano 1968 (1–0, 51).
b) **11 N–N3** (Δ 12 P–B3) 11 ...
P–QR4! 12 P–QR4 Q–Q4 etc.

11 ...   0–0
12 P–QB4

Schwarz leaves it here, liking
White. Ivkov suggests **12 P–B3.**

12 ...   N–R4
13 Q–B2 P–B3 14 B–N2 (Again
Ivkov gives **14 P–B3**, but after 14
... P×P, the play is balanced. **14
P–QR4?!** B–N5!) 14 ... P–QN4!
15 P–Q5 (positionally forced) 15
... BP×P 16 P×NP R–B1!? (16 ...
B–B3!?) 17 Q–R4 with a tiny edge,
Smejkal-Ivkov, Wijk an Zee 1972
(½–½, 44).

A12
8 ...   P×P
Also difficult to assess. White has:
A121 9 N×P
A122 9 N–QN5

A121
9 N×P   N×N(6)
Long thought to be best, but **9
... N×N(5)!?** is perhaps more
important: 10 Q×N N×N (**10 ...
B–B3?** 11 Q–R4ch P–B3 – *11 ...
B–Q2 12 Q–K4ch ±± –* 12 N×N
B×N 13 R–Q1 P–QN4 14 Q–B2
Q–N3 15 P–K4 B–B5 16 B–K3 – *or
16 P–K5 –* 16 ... Q–N2 17 B–B5

B–K2 18 B×B K×B 19 P–N3 B–K3
20 Q–B5ch etc. Müller-Palda,
1948. All forced!) 11 Q×N 0–0! (11
... B–B3 12 Q–N4!) 12 B×P (12
B–B4 may be barely ±.) 12 ...
R–N1. Cvetković assesses this
position as = /∞. After **13 B–N2**
Q–Q2!, White is tied down, but **13
Q–B6!?** is interesting, Δ 13 ...
B–R6 14 B–B4.

10 P×N   N×N
If **10 ... B–Q2**, 11 R–N1! Δ 11
... R–QN1? 12 R×P! R×R 13
N×N ±±. Possibly **10 ...
B–Q4!?**

11 P×N   P–QB3
12 R–N1

12 Q–R4 0–0 13 R–Q1 is
another, perhaps surer, method. In
Abramov-Kremenetsky, Moscow
1964, White followed up with
P–K4 and P–Q5, securing a
powerful passed QP.

12 ...   Q–Q2
13 Q–R4 0–0 14 P–Q5!? (pretty,
but not necessarily decisive) 14 ...
B×P 15 B×B Q×B 16 R×P B–B4 17
R–Q1 Q–K3 (17 ... Q–KB4) 18
Q–B2 B–N3 19 R–Q3!? Q–B4 20
B–B4 P–KN4!? 21 P–K4! Q–B1 (21
... Q×KP 22 B×P ± or 21 ...
Q–B3 22 R–Q6! ±) 22 R(3)–Q7
P×B 23 Q–B4 P×P?? (In this much-
analyzed game, I still wonder why
no one mentions moves like **23 ...
Q×R(N)!?** 24 R×Q P–B6! and by
the time White wins the pawn on f3,
Black has a rook on the seventh; or
23 ... Q–K1 24 R–K7 Q×R! 25
R×Q P–B6, so that after 26 Q–QB1
R(B)–Q1 27 Q–N5ch K–B1, the
White rook is attacked.) 24 R×BP
1–0 Carls-Antze, 1933.

A122

9 N–QN5 B–B3

a) **9 . . . P–Q6** 10 Q×P N(4)–N5, assessed by Cvetković as ∞, looks suspect after 11 Q–N1!. Compare A2, e.g. 11 . . . 0–0 12 P–QR3 N–Q4 13 R–Q1 ± or 11 . . . P–QR3 12 N–B3 0–0? 13 R–Q1 ±±.

b) **9 . . . Q–Q2?!** 10 N(3)×P N×N 11 N×N B–KR6 12 P–K4 B×B 13 K×B N–N3 14 N–B5 (! ±) 14 . . . B–B3 15 Q–B2 P–N3 16 N–R6 0–0–0 17 B–B4 R(R)–K1 18 QR–B1 P–B3 19 P–QN4 B–K4 20 KR–Q1! Q–B2 21 R×Rch K×R 22 B×B R×B 23 Q–B3 (Δ Q×R) 23 . . . K–K2 24 Q–B3 K–K1 25 R–Q1 Q–K2 26 Q–B4 K–B1 27 R–Q8ch 1–0 Larsen-Dückstein, 1974. A significant encounter, as Dückstein is an expert on the Black side of this variation.

10 N(3)×P	N×N
11 N×N	B×N
12 Q×B	0–0

13 P–N3 P–QB3 14 B–N2 P–KB3 15 KR–Q1 Q–K2 16 R–Q2 KR–Q1 17 QR–Q1 R–Q2 18 P–KR4! ± Fuderer-Aiken, Munich 1954. (Two strong bishops).

CONCLUSION:

Black may be better off answering 8 P–Q4 by 8 . . . N×N than by 8 . . . P×P, since in the latter case 9 N–QN5 looks excellent. Regardless of the reply, however, 8 P–Q4 causes enough difficulty that most players of Black have preferred systems with . . . N–N3.

A2

8 P–Q3

As we noted earlier, this is often played on the sixth move, or even the fourth (1 P–QB4 P–K4 2 N–QB3 N–KB3 3 N–B3 N–N3 4 P–Q3 P–Q4 etc.).

8 . . . 0–0 *(40)*

40
W

8 . . . Q–Q2 9 N–KN5 (9 P–Q4!?) 9 . . . B×N 10 B×B P–B3 11 B–K3! Uhlmann-Golz, E. Germany 1959, as in a Dragon; White is slightly better. After 8 . . . 0–0:

A21 9 P–Q4
A22 9 P–QR3
A23 9 B–Q2

A21

9 P–Q4!?

White still has this, a full tempo behind A1! Yet he is also a tempo *ahead* of certain Dragon lines, and both Taimanov and Shatskes approve of 9 P–Q4.

9 . . . P×P

9 . . . N×N 10 P×N P–K5 11 N–K1 P–B4 12 N–N2 N–R4 13 P–B3. Schwarz and Taimanov like this for White, which anyway reinforces our belief in 10 N–K1 in A11!

10 N–QN5

10 N×P N×N(5) (10 ...
N×N(6) 11 P×N B–B3! is good, or
even 11 ... B–Q4, although that
may be drawish.) 11 Q×N B–B3 (or
11 ... N×N =) 12 Q–QR4!?
(Miles).

   10 ...   P–Q6!?

10 ... N–B3 11 N(5)×P N×N 12
N×N B–Q4 (Miles) =; or 10 ...
B–B3.

   11 Q×P   N(4)–N5
   12 Q–N1!

Even a tempo down, White
preserves chances.

   12 ...   B–B3
13 N–B3 Q–K2 14 P–QR3 N–Q4
15 N–K4 P–KR3 16 N×Bch Q×N
17 P–K4?! (17 B–Q2 Δ P–K4 was
more foresighted) 17 ... N–N3 18
P–N3 KR–K1 19 B–N2 Q–N3 =
Miles-Romanishin, Hastings
1976/7.

A22

   9 P–QR3

An older move.

   9 ...   Q–Q2

Also feasible are:
a) **9 ... P–KR3** 10 B–Q2 Q–Q2 11
P–QN4 P–R3 12 R–B1 P–B4 (=?).
b) **9 ... K–R1** 10 B–Q2 P–B4 (10
... P–QR4-Schwarz) 11 P–QN4
B–B3 12 R–B1 Q–K2?? (12 ...
N–N3!?) 13 P–N5 P–K5 (If the
knight sidesteps, 14 N×N and 15
B–N4.) 14 P×N P×N 15 B×P ±±
Najdorf-Letelier, Viña del Mar
1945.

   10 B–Q2   QR–Q1
   11 P–QN4   N×N?!

Obliging; **11 ... P–QR3** was
better.

   12 B×N   B–B3

13 Q–B2 N–Q5 14 B×N P×B 15
N–Q2 B–K2 16 QR–N1 P–QB3 17
N–K4 ± Ragozin-Petrov,
Semmering-Baden 1937.

A23

   9 B–Q2 *(41)*

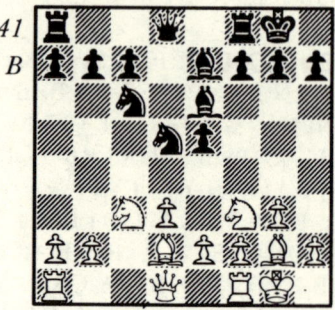

Popular in recent years, but not
very successful. Black has:
A231 9 ... N–N3
A232 9 ... Q–Q2
There are two promising
alternatives:
a) **9 ... P–KR3** 10 R–B1 Q–Q2 11
P–QR3 QR–Q1 12 P–QN4 P–R3
13 Q–B2 (**13 N–K4** may be more
accurate, before Black makes too
much progress on the kingside.
Then 13 ... P–B4?! 14 N–B5 B×N
15 R×B P–K5 16 N–K1 is attract-
ive for White.) 13 ... P–B4 14
N–QR4 P–B5 15 N–B5 B×N 16
Q×B B–R6 17 P–N5 N–Q5! 18
N×N B×B 19 K×B P×N 20 Q×QP
P–B6ch! 21 P×P N–B5ch 22 Q×N
R×Q 23 B×R Q×NP ∓ Karpov vs.
NDR Viewers, West German
Television, 1977. Perhaps the first
theoretically important game to be
played via television!
b) **9 ... P–B4** (why not?) 10
Q–N3!? Q–Q3! 11 Q–B2 (Of

course **11 N–KN5?** B×N 12 B×N as
in the Dragon, leaves the bishop on
d2 en prise after 12 . . . B×B(4))
11 . . . N–Q5? (11 . . . QR–Q1!)
12 N×N(4) N×N 13 P×N P×N
14 P×P P–B3 15 QR–N1 Q–Q2
16 B–B4 ± Watson-de la Cruz,
Mexico 1976.

A231

9 . . . **N–N3**

Similar to B below.

10 N–K4?!

10 R–B1 P–B4 11 P–QR3
P–QR4 12 B–K3 (tempo loss) 12
. . . N–Q4!? 13 N×N B×N 14 Q–R4
B–B3 15 R–B5 K–R1 16 N–R4
B×B 17 N×B B–K2 = /∞ Keene-
Dückstein, 1975.

10 . . . P–B3

Not **10 . . . Q–Q2?** 11 P–QN4!
P–B3 12 Q–N1 B–N5 13 R–K1
QR–N1 14 Q–N2 K–R1 15
QR–B1 N–R5 16 Q–N1 N–Q5 17
N×N P×N 18 Q–B2 ± Hort-Ree,
Wijk an Zee 1973, but **10 . . . P–B4!**
11 N(4)–N5 B–Q4 12 P–K4 P×P
13 P×P? (13 N×P =) 13 . . . B–B5
∓ (Sosonko).

11 Q–B2 N–N5?!
12 B×N B×B
13 KR–Q1

Liebert-Pithart, Olomouc 1975.
White achieved P–Q4 (±), but
½–½, 37. **11 . . . Q–K1!?** might have
led to greater turbulence.

A232

9 . . . **Q–Q2**

10 P–QR3

10 R–B1 QR–Q1 11 P–QR3
P–B3 12 Q–B2 N×N 13 Q×N
B–Q4 14 B–K3 Q–K3 15 P–QN4

P–QR3 16 B–B5 B×B 17 Q×B
R–B2! = Polugaevsky-Roman-
ishin, USSR Ch 1976 (0–1, 42).

10 . . . P–B4!

Natural, since moves like 9 B–Q2
and 10 P–QR3 do hot endanger
Black's centre. **10 . . . P–B3** 11
R–B1 R–B2 12 P–QN4 P–QR3 13
N–QR4 R–Q1 14 N–B5 B×N 15
R×B P–KN4!? 16 Q–N1 R–N2 17
KR–B1 K–R1 18 P–QR4 P–N5 19
P–N5! P×P 20 P×P N–R2 21 N×P!
P×N 22 Q–R1 led to some pull for
White in Andersson-Vasiukov,
Manila 1974, because both Q×N
and Q×KP are threats.

11 R–B1 N–N3
12 N–QR4?! (12 P–QN4) 12 . . .
QR–Q1 13 N–B5 B×N 14 R×B
P–K5! 15 N–N5 N–Q5 16 N×B
N×N 17 R–R5 P×P 18 B–QB3 (18
P–K3!?) 18 . . . P–Q7 19 B×QNP
P–B4 20 B–R6 P–B5 21 R–K5
R–B3 ∓ Panno-Shamkovich, Lone
Pine 1975.

CONCLUSION:

8 P–Q3 0–0 is probably quite
satisfactory for Black. If White
makes a move like **9 P–QR3** or **9
B–Q2,** an early . . . P–KB4 seems in
order, although solid central play
(. . . P–KB3, . . . Q–Q2, . . .
QR–Q1) may also be sufficient to
level the game.

B

6 . . . **N–N3** (*42*)

7 0–0

a) **7 P–QR3** (without castling;
otherwise see B1) 7 . . . B–K2 (**7 . . .
B–K3** 8 P–Q3 P–B3 9 P–QN4
P–QR4? 10 P–N5 N–Q5 11 N×N

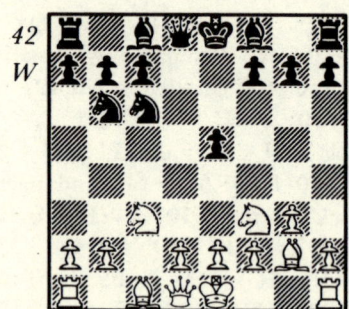

42
W

P×N 12 N–K4 P–R5 13 B–Q2 B–K2 14 Q–B1 B–Q4 15 O–O O–O 16 R–N1 with pressure on c7, Furman-Korchnoi, USSR 1964) 8 P–Q3 O–O 9 P–QN4 P–B4!? (9 . . . P–B3, see B131) 10 P–N5 N–Q5! 11 N×P!? (A daring pawn grab, which only works because White has not castled and allowed time for . . . B–K3.) 11 . . . B–B3 12 P–B4 B–K3 13 R–QN1 B×N 14 P×B P–B5! (persevering! now **15 B×P?** R×B 16 P×R Q–R5ch 17 K–Q2 Q×Pch 18 P–K3 Q–B7ch 19 N–K2 Q×B 20 P×N B–Q4! 21 R–N1 Q×P ∓∓- Schwarz) 15 O–O P–B6? (15 . . . P×P keeps the fire burning: 16 P×P *– 16 R×Rch? Q×R 17 P×P Q–QB4!* – 16 . . . R×Rch 17 Q×R and now either Botvinnik's 17 . . . N–Q4 or Schwarz's 17 . . . Q–Q2 Δ . . . R–KB1 gives good value for a pawn.) 16 P×P N×Pch 17 R×N Q–Q5ch? (17 . . . R×R) 18 R–K3! Q×N 19 P–Q4 Q–B5 20 R–N4 Q–R7 21 R–K2 Q–R8 22 P–Q5! QR–Q1 23 R–Q2 ±± Botvinnik-Dückstein, Munich 1958. A terrible drubbing for Black, but indicative of his attacking possibilities, too.
b) **7 P–QR4** P–QR4 **8 P–Q3** B–QN5! is a direct transposition to

Chapter 5, E, note (a) to 6 P–Q3. **8 O–O** improves, but at best transposes to B2, and may not even do that after 8 . . . B–KN5 (not 8 . . . B–QN5? 9 N–QN5) **9 N–QN5** Q–Q2, or here **9 P–KR3** B–R4 10 P–Q3 B–QN5 etc.

   7 . . .   B–K2
   7 . . . B–KN5 8 P–Q3 B–K2 is discussed in B4. **7 . . . B–K3** is seldom played; it can lead to these independent possibilities:
a) **8 P–Q3** P–B3 9 B–Q2?! (9 P–QR3; 9 B–K3) 9 . . . Q–Q2 10 Q–B1 B–R6 11 N–K4 O–O–O 12 N–B5 B×N 13 Q×B P–KR4 14 P–QN4 P–R5 Beni-Kovacs, 1955. By comparison with the . . . Q–B2 'Yugoslav Attack' Dragon, Black has gained two tempi by not moving his king's bishop, and White one by virtue of the first move. ∓?!
b) **8 P–QR4** N–Q5? (an instructive error. **8 . . . P–QR4** 9 P–Q3 B–K2 is B22, where Black might prefer not to have the move . . . B–K3 in so early. In this line 9 . . . B–QN5? can be answered by 10 N–KN5.) 9 N×N P×N 10 P–R5! P×N 11 P×N P×QP Kuppe-Rellstab, 1937. Now 12 R×P! P×B(Q) 13 Q×Q(1)! (Schwarz) would lead quickly to a win.
c) **8 P–N3!** looks appropriate once Black has committed himself to . . . B–K3. Then **8 . . . B–K2** 9 B–N2 is analyzed in B3, and **8 . . . P–B3** 9 B–N2 Q–Q2 10 P–Q4! grants an edge, e.g. 10 . . . P×P 11 N–QN5 P–Q6?! 12 N(3)–Q4 or 12 P×P.

   After 7 . . . B–K2, White can select from several logical paths:

B1 8 P–QR3
B2 8 P–QR4
B3 8 P–N3
B4 8 P–Q3

The Bizarre **8 P–QN4!?** was tried out in Tarjan-Yanofsky, Lone Pine 1975: 8 . . . B×P 9 B–N2 0–0 10 R–B1 R–K1 11 P–Q3 B–K3 12 P–QR3 B–KB1 13 N–K4 B–Q4 **14 N–B3** B–K3 15 N–K4 B–Q4 ½–½. White still might have tried **14 N–B5!?** B×N(4) 15 R×B P–K5 16 P×P B×P 17 Q–R1 with some compensation; but Black of course had a variety of reasonable defensive plans besides 10 . . . R–K1.

B1
8 P–QR3

A move with which Botvinnik won a number of games. White signals his intention to attack on the queenside, evoking one of these responses:
B11 8 . . . B–K3
B12 8 . . . P–QR4
B13 8 . . . 0–0

8 . . . P–B4 9 P–Q3 B–B3 **10 P–K4** 0–0 11 P–QN4 is B11, and in place of **10 P–K4**, White may choose **10 N–Q2!?** e.g. 10 . . . P–KR4!? (10 . . . 0–0) 11 P–B4 P–R5 12 P×RP B×P (12 . . . P×P!?) 13 N–B3 B–B3 14 P–K4! KP×P 15 P×P B×P 16 R–K1ch ± Reshevsky-Addison, USA 1964.

B11
8 . . .   B–K3

A position also arising from e.g. 6 . . . B–K3 7 0–0 N–N3 8 P–QR3 B–K2.

9 P–Q3
9 P–QN4 will usually transpose: 9 . . . P–B4 **10 P–Q3** B–B3. Not here **10 P–N5?!** N–Q5 11 N×P? B–N6 ∓∓.

9 . . .   P–B4
For **9 . . . P–QR4** and **9 . . . 0–0**, see B12 and B13.

10 P–QN4
10 B–K3 0–0 is B4 below. These transpositions may seem confusing at first, but are listed mainly so that the reader can track down specific games. Actually, there are not that many basic formations.

10 . . .   B–B3 (*43*)

11 P–K4
11 B–Q2 was Botvinnik's preference versus Lundin in Stockholm, 1962: **11 . . . 0–0** 12 R–B1 (discouraging . . . P–B5) 12 . . . K–R1 13 P–N5(?!) N–R4 (13 . . . N–K2 14 N–KN5 ±) 14 R–N1 P–K5(!) 15 N–K1 **N(4)–B5?** 16 P×N N×P 17 N×P! P×N 18 B–N4 R–K1 19 B×P B–R6 20 Q–B2! B×R 21 K×B N–Q3 22 B×N Q×B 23 B×RP(±) QR–Q1? (23 . . . P–QR3!-Schwarz) 24 N–B3 ±. White had two pawns and a nice attack for the exchange (1–0, 35). But **15 . . . P×P!** 16 P×P N(3)–B5!

17 P×N N×P improves considerably e.g. 18 N–K4 P×N 19 B–N4 Q×Q 20 R×Q P–K6 ∓ (Flohr).

A curious postscript to this was Lundin's choice, 15 years later, of **11 . . . P–KN4?!** against Kaiszauri in Gausdal, 1977: 12 P–N5 N–R4 13 P–K4! Q×P (13 . . . N–N6 14 P×P N×B 15 P×B N×R 16 N×NP! ±± or 13 . . . P–N5 14 N–K1 ± or 13 . . . P–B5 14 N–Q5!-Kaiszauri) 14 N×NP!? (But 14 B×NP ± was clearer-Kaiszauri) 14 . . . B×N 15 Q–R5ch B–B2 16 Q×B R–KN1 17 Q×P Q×B 18 Q×Pch with a deadly initiative (1–0, 35).

    11 . . .   0–0

11 . . . P–B5? is refuted by 12 P×P! P×P 13 P–K5 N×P (13 . . . B–K2 14 N–K4 ±) 14 N×N Q–Q5 (14 . . . B×N? 15 Q–R5ch) 15 R–K1 Q×N(6) 16 B–Q2 Q–Q5 17 Q–R5ch! P–N3 18 Q–K2 0–0 19 N×P KR–K1 20 N×P B–B2 21 B–K4 ±± Uhlmann-Tarnowski, 1959.

    12 P×P

12 B–N2 K–R1?! (**12 . . . P–B5!**, as in F Olafsson-Arnason, Reykjavik 1978, levels the play, as White has no tactical resolution that gets his pawns moving.) 13 P×P B×P 14 N–K4 ± Olafsson-Donner, 1961. White has a target in Black's KP plus control over e4 and c5.

    12 . . .   B×P

12 . . . P–K5? 13 N×P B×R 14 P×B with more than enough for an exchange.

    13 N–K4

Now White has eliminated the threat of . . . P–B5 and nearly transposed into the last note. 13 . . . B×N!? 14 P×B Q×Q 15 R×Q QR–Q1 looks odd, ceding White the two bishops and preserving a feeble one (on f6); but for the moment White will have to worry about invading Black cavalry on c4, d4, and/or a4. Unclear!

B12

    8 . . .   P–QR4

Sometimes played on the next move. The problem with . . . P–QR4 after P–QR3 is that Black weakens certain queenside squares without getting definite counterplay elsewhere.

    9 P–Q3   0–0

This may be the time for **9 . . . B–K3** 10 B–K3 N–Q4!? e.g. 11 N×N B×N 12 R–B1 0–0 13 Q–R4 R–K1 with White only a hair better in Botvinnik-Flohr, Wageningen 1958.

    10 B–K3

10 B–Q2 B–K3 is A231 above. After 10 B–K3, very interesting play results from:

B121 10 . . . B–K3
B122 10 . . . B–KN5

10 . . . P–B4 11 R–B1 K–R1 (11 . . . B–K3, see note to 11 N–QR4) 12 N–QN5 B–B3 13 B–B5 R–K1 14 N–Q2 B–K3 15 Q–B2 N–Q4 16 P–K4 (with initiative-Shatskes) Nikolaevsky-Lein, USSR 1967.

B121

    10 . . .   B–K3

    11 N–QR4

11 P–Q4 P×P 12 N×P N×N 13 B×N P–QB3 is harmless, but **11 R–B1** makes sense: **11 . . . P–B4?!**

12 N–QR4 (also 12 P–Q4! ±) 12
... N×N 13 Q×N B–B3 14 R–B5!
P–KN4 15 N–Q2! P–B5 16 R×N
P×R 17 B–B5 ± Zwaig-Pomar,
Costa Brava 1976. Better **11 ...
Q–Q2** 12 N–QR4 N×N 13 Q×N
KR–Q1 (Δ ... N–Q5) Clarke-
Penrose, England 1956.

    11 : ..   N×N

11 ... N–Q4 12 B–B5 ±
(Portisch). White could build up
via R–B1, P–K4, and P–Q4.

    12 Q×N   B–Q4
    13 KR–B1   R–K1
    14 R–B2! (*44*)

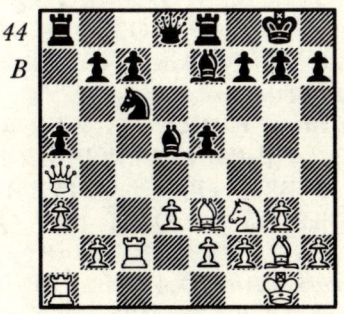

Unusual in this kind of position,
and excellently calculated.

    14 ...   B–B1

Not **14 ... P–QN4?** 15 Q×NP
R–N1 16 Q–R4 N–Q5 (16 ...
B–N6 17 Q×N) 17 N×N ±±
(Botvinnik). Portisch suggests **14
... B–Q3.**

15 R(1)–B1 **N–N1** (? **15 ... R–N1!**
±. **15 ... P–K5?** 16 P×P B×P 17
R–Q2 Q–B3 18 R–B4! ±-Portisch)
16 R×P! B–B3 17 R(1)×B! P×R 18
R×KBP! (the point of White's
elegant combination, winning two
pawns for the exchange and
exposing Black's king) 18 ...
P–KR3 (18 ... K×R 19 Q–B4ch

K–N3 20 Q–N4ch ±±) 19 R–N7
Q–B1 20 Q–B4ch K–R1 21 N–R4!
Q×R 22 N–N6ch K–R2 23 B–K4
B–Q3 24 N×Pch P–N3 25 B×Pch
K–N2 26 B×Pch! 1–0 Botvinnik-
Portisch, Monte Carlo 1968 (26 ...
K×B 27 Q–R4ch etc.).

B122
    10 ...   **B–KN5**

Our first encounter with this
logical move, which often has more
effect than ... B–K3 since it
supervises d4.

    11 R–B1

11 P–R3 B–K3 lets Black win a
tempo with ... Q–Q2 and provides
indirect protection for his QNP
(after, say, 12 P–Q4) by the
counterattack on White's KRP.

    11 ...   Q–Q2

11 ... R–K1 12 N–QR4 N–Q4
13 B–B5 B–B3 is too convoluted: 14
P–KR3 B–K3 15 K–R2 Q–Q2 16
Q–B2 P–KN3 17 KR–Q1 P–N3 18
P–K4! N(4)–K2 19 P–Q4! with
advantage Uhlmann-Korchnoi,
Moscow 1971.

    12 R–K1   KR–K1
13 N–Q2 B–K3 14 QB×N (An
exchange characteristic of these
positions, but usually unsuccessful.
White's QB was a useful piece.) 14
... P×B 15 N–B4 B–QB4
Taimanov-Kan, USSR 1954.
Schwarz hints that the normal
assessment of '=' is incorrect, but I
see no way for White to exploit the
weakened queen's wing, and
Black's pieces are quite active.

B13
    8 ...   **0–0** (*45*)

45
W

9 P–QN4

9 P–Q3 R–K1 10 P–QN4
N–Q5!? 11 N×P? (11 B–N2 ±) 11
. . . B–B3 12 P–B4 N–Q2! 13 P–K3
Polugaevsky-Wade, Skopje 1968,
and now 13 . . . B×N! 14 P×B N×P
∆ . . . B–N5 would have been ∓. 9
P–Q3 can also be answered by **9 . . .
P–B4** 10 P–QN4 B–KB3 and:
a) **11 B–K3** K–R1 (∆ . . . P–K5) 12
R–B1 B–K3 13 N–Q2 N–Q4?! 14
B–B5 R–B2 15 N×N B×N 16 P–K4
P×P 17 N×P (Again, control of e4
and c5 gives White the advantage.)
17 . . . N–Q5?! (17 . . . R–Q2 ±) 18
N–Q6! P×N 19 B×B R–B2 20 B×N
P×B 21 R×R Q×R 22 Q–B3
R–QN1 23 B–K4 Q–B2 24 R–QB1
P–KN3 25 P–KR4 and White's
superiority is clear, Pachman-
Altschul, 1961.
b) **11 P–N5** N–Q5 12 N×N P×N 13
Q–N3ch K–R1 14 N–R4 R–K1 15
N–B5 R–QN1 16 P–QR4 R–K4!
(praised by Botvinnik, who gives **16
. . . R×P** 17 B–B4 P–KN4 18
QR–K1! R×R 19 R×R P×B 20
Q–B7 B–Q2 21 P–R5 etc. ±±) 17
B–QR3 B–K2 18 KR–B1 Q–B1 19
Q–B2 N–Q4 and Black had rallied
his forces in Botvinnik-Olsson,
Stockholm 1962 (although 1–0, 28,
after mistakes).

9 . . .   B–K3
9 . . . P–B3 and **9 . . . P–QR3** will
transpose, but **9 . . . P–B4?** is
careless: 10 P–N5 N–Q5 11 N×P
B–B3 12 P–B4 B–K3, 13 P–K3
B–N6 14 Q–R5 (Shatskes).
  10 P–Q3
Another crossroads:
B131 10 . . . P–B3
B132 10 . . . P–B4
a) **10 . . . P–QR4?!** was unsuccess-
ful in Petrosian-Taimanov, Vin-
kovci 1970: 11 P–N5 N–Q5 12
N–Q2! (∆ B×P P–K3) 12 . . .
Q–Q2 13 B×P QR–N1 14 B–KN2
N×P 15 N×N Q×N 16 P–QR4
Q–K1 17 B–N2 B–Q3 18 B–QB3!
and the weakness of Black's
queenside was apparent.
b) **10 . . . P–QR3** 11 N–K4 P–R3
(11 . . . P–B3) 12 B–N2 P–B4?! 13
N–B5 B×N 14 P×B N–Q2 15 R–B1
Q–K2 (15 . . . Q–K1 16 P–Q4
P–K5 17 P–Q5 P×N 18 P×P etc.-
Shatskes) 16 N–R4 Q–B2 17 P–B4
Botvinnik-Benkner 1956. After 17
. . . P×P 18 P×P QR–Q1 19 Q–K1,
White had decisive pressure.
B131
  10 . . .   P–B3
Solid, but rather passive.
  11 B–N2
A creditable alternative is **11
B–K3**, as in Ragozin-Taimanov,
USSR Ch 1956: 11 . . . Q–Q2 12
N–K4 N–Q4 (12 . . . KR–Q1!?) 13
R–B1! (rather than the natural 13
B–B5 P–QN3 14 B×B N(4)×B 15
R–B1 P–QR4 16 P–N5 N–R2 17
P–QR4 P–B3 with counterplay-
Taimanov) 13 . . . KR–Q1 ('It is
hardly favourable for Black to
exchange on e3'—Shatskes. White

would control central squares, true, but 13 . . . N×B 14 P×N KR–Q1 Δ . . . B–Q4 or . . . B–R6 is as good as the text.) 14 B–B5 P–QN3 15 B×B N(4)×B 16 Q–B2 QR–B1 17 KR–Q1 P–QR4 (17 . . . P–KR3 18 Q–N2! Δ 18 . . . P–B4? 19 P–N5 ±-Taimanov) 18 P–N5 N–Q5 19 N×N P×N 20 Q–N2 ± (Δ R–Q2–B2).

    11 . . .   Q–Q2

    11 . . . Q–K1 (Δ . . . R–Q1) 12 R–B1 Q–B2 13 N–K4 P–QR3 14 N–B5 B×N **15 R×B?** P–K5! (15 . . . N–R5? 16 Q×N B–N6 17 N×KP!) 16 N–Q2 (16 P×P N–R5!) 16 . . . P×P 17 P×P QR–Q1 ∓ Dobias-Podgorny, **15 P×B** was correct, when White has two bishops, but Black is well-centralized.

    12 N–K4   QR–Q1
13 Q–B2 K–R1 14 N–B5 B×N 15 P×B N–B1 (15 . . . N–Q4!) 16 QR–N1 ± Johansson-Limbos, 1956.

B132

    10 . . .   P–B4 (*46*)

Generally considered best. As seen from B131, Black could use some activity! What follows differs from B11 because of the inclusion of . . . 0–0:

    11 B–K3

a) **11 P–N5** N–Q5 12 N×P B–B3 13 N–B4 (13 P–B4 N–N6 Δ . . . Q–Q5ch) 13 . . . N×N (13 . . . N×P? 14 N×N(5) B×R 15 B–B4! ±-Schwarz) 14 P×N B×P is supposed to be good for Black. 15 R–N1! seems equal.

b) **11 B–N2(!)** looks very logical, now that e5 lacks pawn support. I can adduce no examples here, but 11 . . . B–B3 12 N–Q2! (12 P–K4 P–B5! =) 12 . . . Q–Q2 13 N–N3! is strong, and other normal sequences for Black also seem to fall short of equality.

    11 . . .   B–B3
    12 R–B1

Ragozin's **12 N–K1** has been the subject of several discussions. The stem game, Ragozin-Balogh, corres 1956, continued **12 . . . P–K5** 13 R–B1 B×N 14 R×B N–Q4 15 R–B5 N×B 16 P×N Q–Q3 17 Q–B2 P–QR4 18 P–N5 N–K2 19 P×P P×P 20 R×Rch R×R 21 B×P N–Q4 22 N–N2 ±± The White KPs turned into powerful endgame threats.

Against 12 N–K1, Shatskes recommends **12 . . . R–N1** (Δ 13 . . . N–Q5) 13 KB×N P×B 14 R–B1 P–KR4. Perhaps not a line to play against Petrosian! Anyway, simplest is **12 . . . N–Q4!** 13 N×N B×N 14 B×B Q×B 15 R–B1 R–B2 = Keller-Burkhardt, corres 1977/78.

    12 . . .   N–Q5
Most other moves are met by P–Q4, but **12 . . . R–B2** merits a try.

    13 N–Q2
    13 B×N P×B 14 N–R4 N×N 15 Q×N P–B3 16 N–Q2 transposes.

13 . . .   P–B3
14 B×N P×B (14 . . . Q×B 15
N–N3!) 15 N–R4 N×N?! (Shatskes
gives **15 . . . B–B2!** 16 N–B5 R–N1
17 N(2)–N3 N–Q4 18 N–R5 Q–K2
19 R–K1 KR–B1 Δ . . . P–QN3. A
surprising defence!) 16 Q×N B–Q4
17 R–B5 B×B 18 K×B Q–K1?! (**18
. . . P–KN3**-Schwarz-improves,
but one still prefers White's better
minor piece and queenside
initiative.) 19 Q–N3ch K–R1 20
R×KBP Q×P 21 N–K4 Filip-
Barda, 1953. White is clearly better
(1–0, 51).

CONCLUSION:

8 P–QR3 makes a rather good
impression. Black has no 'easy
equalizer', but can try **8 . . . B–K3** 9
P–Q3 P–B4 10 P–QN4 B–B3 etc. or
8 . . P–QR4 9 P–Q3 0–0 10 B–K3
B–N5(!). The generally recognized
8 . . . 0–0 9 P–QN4 B–K3 10 P–Q3
P–B4 could run into 11 B–N2(!).

B2
8 P–QR4
Trading b4 for b5, a familiar
Dragon idea. Note that Black can
move his bishop to b4 only at the
cost of a tempo (compare note (b)
to B 7 0–0).

8 . . .   P–QR4
9 P–Q3 (*47*)
or **9 N–QN5** 0–0 10 P–Q4 P×P 11
N(3)×P N×N 12 Q×N?! Q×Q! 13
N×Q P–QB3 14 B–Q2? (but 14
B–K3 N–B5 ∓ or 14 B–B4 B–B3 ∓-
Florian) 14 . . . R–Q1 15 N–N3 (15
B–B3) 15 . . . B–K3 16 B×RP
R–R3 17 B×N R×B 18 N–B1 R×P
19 N–Q3 R×P ∓ Demeney-

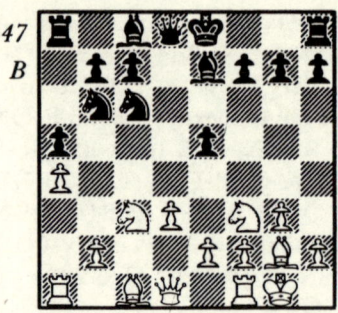

47
B

Florian, Hungary 1976 (0–1, 32).
9 . . .   0–0

9 . . . B–K3 is important because
White can force this position
against certain move orders with an
early . . . B–K3:
a) **10 B–K3** 0–0 (**10 . . . N–Q4** 11
N×N B×N 12 R–B1 0–0 =-
Pachman-but White usually has
some pressure in such positions) 11
R–B1 (**11 P–Q4** P×P 12 N×P N×N
13 Q×N Q×Q 14 B×Q P–QB4! 15
B–K3 N–B5 =-Schwarz. A well-
known trap is **11 N–K4** P–B4 12
N–B5 B–Q4!, since 13 N×NP??
Q–B1 14 N–B5 P–B5 is ∓∓.) 11 . . .
P–B4 12 N–QN5 B–B3 13 B×N
(seldom a productive idea) 13 . . .
P×B 14 N–Q2 R–B1 15 N–B4
B–K2 16 P–K3 B–B4 = Endzelins-
Ragozin, corres 1956.
b) **10 N–QN5** 0–0 (**10 . . . P–B4** 11
N–N5! B×N 12 B×B Q–Q2 – *12 . . .
Q×B 13 N×Pch K–B2 14 N×B
K×N 15 Q–N3ch* – 13 B–K3 N–Q4
14 B–B5 ± Stolyar-Berkman,
USSR 1961.) 11 P–K4! (Δ P–Q4)
11 . . . B–B3 12 B–K3 N–N5 13
B–B5 R–K1 14 R–R3! (Δ R–B3) 14
. . . N–Q2 15 B–K3 N–B1! 16 P–Q4
B–B5 17 R–K1 P×P 18 B×P B×B

19 N(5)×B P–QB4 20 R–B3 P×N 21 R×B P–Q6 = Geller-Flohr, 21st USSR Ch 1954. High calibre play, although Black later blundered and lost.

10 B–K3

10 N–QN5 P–B4?! (**10 ... N–Q4** 11 P–K4 N(4)–N5 12 P–Q4 P×P 13 N(3)×P N×N 14 N×N B–QB4 15 B–K3 R–R3! =-Shatskes) 11 Q–N3ch K–R1 12 B–Q2 P–B5 (White is a tempo up on Schwarz's suggestion in the note to 11 Q–B1 below!) **13 B–B3** B–Q3 Voronkov-Muchnik, Moscow 1957. Equal, according to Shatskes and Taimanov, but **13 QR–B1!** was probably better, and if 13 ... B–Q3, 14 KR–Q1 Δ B–K1 $\pm$.

10 ...   P–B4

Not necessarily best. **10 ... B–K3** transposes into the last variation, and **10 ... B–N5** 11 R–B1 Q–Q2 is logical, too.

11 Q–B1

Schwarz suggests **11 Q–N3ch** K–R1 12 N–QN5 Δ 13 N×BP. Then 12 ... P–B5 13 B–Q2 (13 N×BP? P×B 14 Q×N R–R3! $\mp\mp$) 13 ... B–N5 14 QR–B1 B–Q3 is double-edged.

11 ...   N–Q5
12 B×N   P×B
13 N–QN5   P–B4

' = ' (Pachman). At first sight, Black has too many weaknesses, but White will find it hard to make inroads and his KP can be vulnerable.

CONCLUSION:

8 P–QR4, though obviously sound, lacks the flexibility of, say, **8 P–QR3** or **8 P–Q3**.

B3

8 P–N3

Simagin's move.

8 ...   0–0

8 ... B–K3 9 B–N2 P–B3 10 R–B1 P–QR4?! 11 P–Q4 N×P 12 N×N P×N 13 N–K4 and White recovers his pawn with the better position (Shatskes).

9 B–N2   B–KN5

9 ... B–K3 10 R–B1 P–QR4? 11 N–QN5 P–B3 12 P–K4! Δ P–Q4 (Shatskes).

10 R–B1   P–B4

11 N–QR4! P–K5 (**11 ... N×N** 12 P×N P–K5 13 Q–N3ch K–R1 14 Q×P P×N 15 P×P $\pm\pm$-Shatskes) 12 N–K5 N×N 13 B×N P–B3 14 N×N Q×N (14 ... P×N may be better.) 15 P–Q4 QR–Q1 16 Q–B2 $\pm$ Simagin-Bebchuk, Moscow 1967. Of course both sides have many options, and 8 P–N3 could use more tests.

B4

8 P–Q3

The Dragon move. Black replies:
B41 8 ... B–K3
B42 8 ... 0–0

a) **8 ... P–KN4?!** is not so good as with colours reversed: 9 P–N3! (Other tries are less clear: **9 B–K3** P–B4 10 N–QR4 P–B5 11 B–B5 B–K3 12 R–B1 B–Q4 = or here 11 ... P–KR4!?; **9 P–QR4** P–QR4 10 B–K3 P–B4 11 R–B1 P–B5 12 B×N?! P×B 13 N–Q2 B–K3 14 N–B4 B–QB4 =. From analysis by Mercuri) 9 ... P–N5 (**9 ... P–B4** 10 B–N2 B–B3 11 P–QR4 P–QR4 12 N–N5 P–R4 13 P–Q4 P–K5 14 N×NP! $\pm\pm$ Δ 14 ... B×N 15

P–Q5-Schwarz) 10 N–Q2 P–KR4 (White was ready for B–N2 Δ N–B4 and/or P–B4.) 11 B–N2 P–R5 12 N–B4 ± Black cannot organize an attack and his centre is crumbling.

b) **8 . . . B–KN5** can transpose to 8 . . . 0–0 9 B–K3 B–N5 and indeed, 9 B–K3 may be best. Iskov-Romanishin, Dortmund 1976 continued instead: 9 P–QR3 P–QR4 10 B–Q2 0–0 11 N–QR4 R–R3! 12 P–QN4? (12 R–B1 or 12 N×N R×N 13 B–B3) 12 . . . P×P 13 P×P R×N 14 R×R N×R 15 Q×N P–K5! (∓∓) 16 P–N5 P×N 17 P×P B–Q2 18 P×N B×P with a winning advantage.

B41

8 . . .   B–K3
9 B–K3

9 P–QR4 P–QR4 is B2, which was okay for Black with exact play and **9 N–K4?** P–B4! 10 N(4)–N5 B–N1 was obviously good for him too, Stein-Kavalek, Sarajevo 1967.

9 . . .   0–0 (*48*)

a) **9 . . . Q–Q2?** 10 P–Q4! 0–0–0 (**10 . . . P×P?** 11 N×P N×N 12 Q×N Q×Q 13 B×Q loses a pawn!) 11 N×P N×N 12 P×N Q×Q 13 QR×Q N–B5 14 B–B4 P–KN4 15 B–B1 P–QB3 (15 . . . N×KP 16 N–Q5 ±) 16 N–K4 P–KR3 17 P–B4 P×P 18 P×P R(R)–N1 19 K–B2 N–N3 20 P–QR3 ± Savon-Romanishin, USSR 1974 (1–0, 43).

b) **9 . . . P–B4** 10 N–R4 (10 Q–B1 might transpose to the text) 10 . . . N–Q4?! (**10 . . . B–Q4** and if 11 N–B5, 11 . . . N–Q5 was recommended) 11 B–B5 B–B3 12 P–K4! N(4)–K2 13 P–Q4 BP×P 14

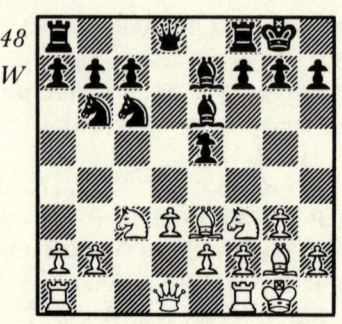

N×P B×N 15 P×B ± Barcza-Kovacs, 1966.

10 Q–B1

White has many moves, but his best has not been determined:

a) **10 P–Q4** P×P 11 N×P N×N 12 B×N (**12 Q×N** Q×Q 13 B×Q P–QB3 = Mikenas-Flohr, 17th USSR Ch 1949) 12 . . . P–QB3 13 N–K4 B–Q4 14 P–K3 Q–B1 15 Q–B2 Q–K3 16 N–B5 B×N 17 B(4)×B B×B 18 K×B KR–K1 Benko-Flohr, 1959 and Black should have had no serious worries.

b) **10 N–QR4** P–B4 (Obscure but not bad was **10 . . . P–K5!?** 11 N–K1 P×P 12 N×P B–Q4 13 B–R3! N–B5 14 B–B4 B–Q3 15 R–B1 ∞. Polugaevsky-Flohr, USSR 1960. Or **10 . . . B–Q4** 11 B–B5 B–Q3! 12 B×B? P×B 13 P–QR3 Q–Q2! 14 N–B3 B×N 15 B×B P–Q4 ∓ Kunsztavitz-Mihalchishin, 1976.) 11 B–B5 (11 N–B5? B–Q4! is 'the trick'.) 11 . . . N×N 12 B×B Q×B 13 Q×N B–Q4 Fridstein-Flohr, 1957; rather than 14 P–K4?!, 14 QR–B1 would have left a complex struggle ahead.

c) **10 R–B1** N–Q4?! (**10 . . . P–B3**-Schwarz, but then 11 P–Q4 could be tried; **10 . . . P–B4**) 11 N×N B×N 12 Q–R4 P–B3?! 13 B–B5

B×B 14 R×B N–K2 15 R(1)–B1
P–B3 16 P–K4 Δ P–Q4 ± Kan-
Chekover, Moscow 1936.

10 ... P–B4
11 R–Q1 K–R1
12 P–Q4 P–K5 13 N–K5 N–N5! 14
P–B3 P×P 15 P×P P–B3 16 B–B2
B–N1 17 P–QR3 N(5)–Q4 18
Q–B2 B–Q3 19 R–K1 = Ivkov-
Addison, Palma de Mallorca 1970
($\frac{1}{2}$–$\frac{1}{2}$, 42). White might have come
to the king file sooner.

B42

8 ... **0–0**
9 B–K3

9 P–QR3 is still possible,
transposing to B13, but **9 P–N3**
seems to have lost its effect, since the
White QP cannot jump to d4 in one
step: **9 ... B–KN5** (or **9 ... P–B4**
or **9 ... B–K3**) 10 P–KR3 B–K3 11
B–N2 P–B4 12 R–B1 B–B3 13
Q–B2?! N–Q5! 14 N×N P×N ±
Dobias-Keres, Prague 1937.

After 9 B–K3, material divides
for the last time:
B421 9 ... B–KN5
B422 9 ... P–B4
9 ... B–K3 is B41 again, and **9
... K–R1** may be met by 10 Q–B1!
Δ P–Q4 ±.

B421

9 ... **B–KN5** (*49*)
Alekhine's move as White in the
Classical Dragon. For one thing, it
discourages P–Q4 for some time.

10 P–KR3
The alternatives are certainly
interesting; I feel that attention
should come to 10 Q–B1 ('(c)'
below), which has not been

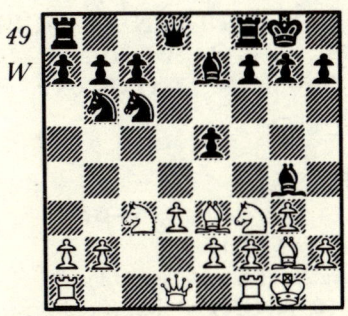

mentioned by any books I know of.
a) **10 P–QR4** P–QR4 is B2 above.
b) **10 R–B1** Q–Q2 (or **10 ... P–B4**
11 N–QR4 P–B5 12 B–B5 B–Q3 13
P–N4 Q–Q2 = Robatsch-Ree,
Karlovac 1977) 11 N–K4 (**11
N–QR4?** P–K5! 12 N×N RP×N 13
P×P? – *13 N–K1* ∓ – 13 ... Q×Q
14 KR×Q R×P ∓ Carls-Sämisch,
1937) 11 ... QR–Q1 12 N–B5
B×N 13 B×B KR–K1 =
c) **10 Q–B1** (! Logical. White clears
d1 for his rook and incidentally
avoids an exchange of bishops:) 10
... Q–Q2 11 R–Q1 B–R6 12 B–R1
ΔP–Q4. Black could try 10 ...
P–B4 11 R–Q1 B–B3, but then
either 12 P–Q4!? or 12 P–QR4 is
still worrisome.

10 ... B–K3
10 ... B–R4 11 P–KN4 B–N3 12
P–Q4 ±.

11 P–Q4
Now on **11 Q–B1**, 11 ... Q–Q2
12 K–R2 P–B4 Δ ... P–B5!. Also
inadequate was **11 N–K4** P–B4 12
N–B5 B–Q4 13 N–N3 (13 N×NP??
Q–B1 14 N–B5 P–B5 hasn't
changed.) 13 ... P–B5! ∓ in
Loverdos-Benko, Budapest 1956.

11 ... P×P
12 N×P N×N 13 B×N Q–B1!
(threatens the KRP and ... R–Q1)

14 B×N RP×B 15 N–Q5 B–QB4
(15 ... B–Q3 16 N×NP!) 16
P–QN4 B×N 17 Q×B B×P =
(Shatskes).

B422

9 ...   P–B4
10 Q–B1

Again the most sensible:

a) **10 N–QR4** P–B5 (or 10 ...
B–B3) 11 B–B5 B–N5 12 R–B1
B–Q3 13 R–K1 (**13 B×B?** P×B 14
Q–N3ch K–R1 15 N×N P×N 16
P–QR4 P–Q4 $\mp$) 13 ... Q–K2 14
N–Q2 K–R1 15 N–K4 B×B 16
N(R)×B N–Q5! $\mp$ Δ ... P–B6,
Czerniak-Alekhine, Buenos Aires
1939).

b) **10 P–QN4** B–B3 (10 ... B×P 11
Q–N3ch K–R1 12 N×P $\pm$; 10 ...
P–B5 11 B–Q2! $\pm$) 11 Q–N3ch
K–R1 12 QR–B1 N–Q5 13 B×N
P×B 14 N–QR4 = /∞ (Schwarz).

10 ...   K–R1
10 ... B–B3 can be countered by
11 R–Q1 or 11 B–N5 (Benko). **10
... P–KR3** 11 R–Q1 B–B3 (An
interesting note is **11 ... B–K3** 12
R–N1 P–QR4 13 P–N3 $\pm$-Panno.
White will play N–QR4 and/or
P–Q4.) 12 B–B5 R–B2 13 P–K3
B–K3 14 P–Q4 P–K5 (**14 ... P×P**
15 P×P! N–Q4 16 N–K5-Panno)
15 B×N! P×N 16 B×P(3) RP×B 17
P–Q5 B–Q2 18 P×N P×P 19
N–K2! R–R4 20 P–QN4! R–R2 21
N–Q4 $\pm$ Panno-Riemsdijk, For-
taleza 1975.

11 R–Q1
11 P–QR4 P–QR4 12 N–QN5
N Q4 13 B–B5 B–K3 14 R–Q1
P–B5 15 N–Q2 N(3)–N5 =
Kottnauer-Cortlever, 1945?

11 ...   B–B3
Better **11 ... B–K3** 12 P–Q4
P–K5 13 N–K5 N×N 14 P×N
Q–K1 15 P–B3 $\pm$ (Pribyl). Also **12
R–N1!?** might be tried♪
12 P–Q4
Or **12 B–B5**. This whole
variation looks good for White.
12 ...   P×P
13 N×P N×N 14 B×N B×B 15
P–K3 P–B4? (**15 ... Q–B3** 16 P×B
P–B3 $\pm$-Pribyl) 16 P×B P×P 17
Q–B4 Q–K2 18 R×P $\pm$ R–B3 19
P–QR4! P–QR4 20 R(1)–Q1
P–R3 21 R–Q8ch K–R2 22 P–R4!
Q–N5 23 Q×Q! P×Q 24 N–Q5 1–0
Pribyl-Kozlov, Stary Smokovec
1976.

CONCLUSION:

8 P–Q3 initiates a vigorous
discussion in which White banks on
his queenside pressure to counteract Black's temporary central
space advantage. **8 ... B–K3** is
better than its reputation, as 9
P–QR4 is not so strong (9 Q–B1
appears best). **8 ... B–N5** has its
good points too: after 9 B–K3 0–0,
10 Q–B1 may again be the way to
play it. Finally, **8 ... 0–0** 9 B–K3
P–B4, often seen, has the drawback
of loosening Black's centre
somewhat.

The Accelerated Fianchetto/
Dragon complex is fairly playable
and at least grants Black activity
with open lines. In practice, one
may expect White to win more
often than he loses, but the same
might be said of many sound
opening systems.

7 MAIN LINE: INTRODUCTION AND 4 P–KN3

1	P–QB4	P–K4
2	N–QB3	N–KB3
3	N–B3	

The analysis of 3 P–KN3 in Chapters 3 and 4 should give the reader some idea why modern masters have come to prefer 3 N–B3. By attacking the king pawn, White allows neither **3 . . . P–B3** nor **3 . . . B–N5**. Even after **3 . . . N–B3** 4 P–KN3 B–N5 (analyzed extensively below), Black has had to cede the option of an early . . . P–QB3, which was the key to his defence in most of the variations of Chapter 4. Hence he must be constantly on the watch for White's N–Q5 and, most important, cannot prepare a serious positional threat of . . . P–Q4 for many moves to come. Thus White gets time to organize his pieces effectively.

3 . . .	N–B3

In view of the preceding note, Black may wish to retain the elasticity of his formation by **3 . . . P–Q3**. That has, however, the drawbacks of blocking off his king's bishop and allowing White a leisurely build-up via P–KN3, B–N2, and P–Q4. Chapter 9, C33, analyzes the various methods of meeting 3 . . . P–Q3.

Are there any disadvantages of 3 N–B3 as opposed to 3 P–KN3? The main one, to which we continually return in this chapter and Chapter 8, is that Black now has the opportunity to play . . . P–K5 with tempo, thereby gaining space and perhaps disorganizing the White forces. Naturally, such a move can only succeed if the advanced KP is not overextended in the process; so we usually see Black castling first, and perhaps even eliminating the enemy knight on c3 (by . . . B–QN5, ×N) before he essays upon this strategy.

What about **3 . . . P–K5**, then? That would seem to contradict what we have just said, for after 4 N–KN5 (4 N–Q4 is Chapter 11, A2, and quite equal), the Black KP is already doubly attacked, and 4 . . . Q–K2 5 Q–B2 is no help. For years, in fact, players and theoreticians ignored this position, evidently assuming that the pawn falls without compensation. But in 1971, Bellon, who has many original and eccentric ideas, surprised Reshevsky at Palma de Mallorca with **3 . . . P–K5!? 4 N–KN5 P–N4!** (*50*).

The idea is an old one: sacrifice a flank pawn to establish a central majority; and in that game (after 5 N×NP P–KR3 6 N–KR3 P–B3). Black obtained reasonable counter-

play (see (a) below). Still, 3 ...
P–K5 did not catch on (perhaps
because Bellon lost) until the mid-
70s, when it received many tests,
and the best moves (particularly 5
P–Q3) were gradually unearthed.
Here is a summary of theory after 3
... P–K5 4 N–KN5 P–N4!:

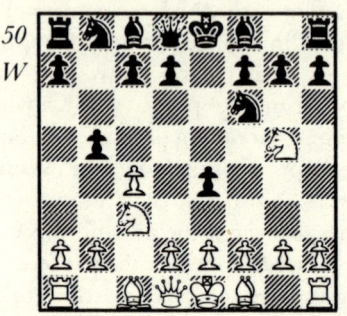

50
W

a) **5 N×NP** P–B3 (or **5 ... P–KR3**
6 N–KR3 P–B3 7 N–B3 P–Q4 8
P×P P×P 9 P–K3 B–Q3 10 B–N5ch
K–B1! 11 P–Q3 B–KN5 12 Q–Q2
Q–R4 13 P–QR3 N–R3 14 0–0
R–Q1 15 P–Q4 B–N1 – 15 ...
N–B2 ∞ – Ivkov – 16 B–K2 Q–B2
17 N–B4 P–N4?! – *Ivkov's 17 ...
B–B1 △ ... P–KN4 was much better –*
18 B×N P×N 19 P×P Reshevsky-
Bellon, Palma de Mallorca 1971.
White still has great defensive
problems, but was equal to them
and won in 46.) 6 N–QB3 P–Q4 7
P×P P×P 8 P–Q3 (**8 P–K3** B–Q3 9
B–N5ch K–B1 10 P–KR4 P–KR3
11 N–R3 P–N4 ∞ Biyiasis-Regan,
New York 1977) 8 ... P–KR3 9
N–R3 N–B3 10 P–KN3 (**10 P–K3**
B–QN5?! – *10 ... P×P 11 B×P
B×N 12 P×B B–Q3 ∞* – 11 P×P
N×P 12 B–N5 B–Q2 13 0–0 (±)
KB×N? 14 Q×P! N–B3 15 Q B4
0–0 16 P×B?! Adamski-Borkowski,
Poznan 1976; 16 Q×B! ±, but 1–0,

43, anyway) 10 ... B–KN5! 11
P×P (11 N–B4!?-Sokolov) 11 ...
P–Q5!? 12 N–QN1 Q–R4ch 13
B–Q2 Q–N3 14 P–B3 Q×P 15
Q–B1 Q×Qch 16 ฿×Q N–N5 17
N–R3 B–Q2 = /∞ Sznapik-
Bellon, Cienfuegos 1976.
b) **5 P–QN3?** P–N5 6 N–R4 (**6
N(3)×P?** P–KR3 ∓∓; 6 N–N1
P–KR3 7 N–KR3 B–B4 8 P–Q4
P×Pe.p. 9 Q×P 0–0 10 B–N2 B–N2
11 N–Q2 P–Q3 12 P–K3 QN–Q2
13 N–B4 N–K4! 14 Q–B2
N(3)–N5! 15 B–K2 B×KP! 16 P×B
N×KP 17 Q–B1 Q–N4 ∓∓
Uhlmann-Dobosz, East Germany-
Poland, 1974) 6 ... P–Q4 7 P–Q3
N–N5!? 8 N–R3 P–K6! 9 B×P!
N×B 10 P×N P×P 11 NP×P B×N
12 P×B Q–N4 13 K–Q2 N–R3 ∓
Lengyel-Perenyi, Hungary 1975
(½–½, 17).
c) **5 Q–B2?!** P×P (**5 ... P–K6!?** 6
BP×KP – *6 QP×P P×P 7 P–K4
looks* ± *–* 6 ... P×P 7 P–QN3 P×P 8
Q×P P–Q4 9 P–KN3 P–B3 – *9 ...
N–B3!?-Plachetka* – 10 B–QR3!
B–Q3 11 B–KN2 P–KR3 12 N–B3
0–0 13 0–0 N–R3 Adamski-
Plachetka, Rimavska Sobota 1975,
and now 14 N–Q4 ± would have
kept the advantage (½–½, 22)) 6
N(5)×P (**6 N(3)×P?** P–Q4 7
N×Nch Q×N 8 N×RP? R×N! 9
Q×R B–KB4 ∓-Plachetka) 6 ...
B–N2 7 N×Nch Q×N 8 Q–R4
N–R3! (**8 ... B–B4** 9 P–K3 0–0 10
Q×BP B–N3 11 N–Q5 Q–Q3
= /∞ Raicevic-Suba, Novi Sad
1974) 9 Q×BP 0–0–0 10 Q–QR4
B B4!? (10 ... N–B4!?) 11 P–K3
KR–K1 12 B×N! B×B 13 N–K4
R×N 14 Q×R P–Q4 15 Q–B2? (15

Q–B3 Q–K3! = /∞ Bednarski) 15
... Q–N4! 16 P–KN3 P–Q5 17
P–KR4 Q–R4! 18 P–Q3 P×P 19
B×P B×P 20 Q–Q1 B–N5ch 0–1
Kuligowski-Borkovski, Poland
1975.

d) **5 N(5)×P** N×N 6 N×N P×P 7
Q–R4 P–B3 (7 . . . B–N2? 8 N–B3)
8 N–N3 P–Q4 9 P–Q3 ∞.

e) **5 P×P** P–Q4 6 P–Q4 (**6 P–Q3**
P–KR3 7 N–R3 B–Q3 8 N–B4
B–N2 9 P×P P×P 10 P–K3 QN–Q2
11 B–Q2 N–K4 12 N–R5 N×N 13
Q×N P–N3 14 Q–Q1 Q–N4! 15
Q–B2 Q–B4 with a nice position for
the pawn, is a good example of the
central cramping influence Black
strives for, Szilágyi-Perenyi, Hun-
gary 1976.) 6 ... P–QR3!? (**6 ...
B–Q3** 7 P–KN3 P–KR3 8 N–R3
P–KN4! 9 N–KN1 P–R3 10
P–KR4 P–N5 11 P–K3 P×P 12
N×NP B–K2 13 N–K2 0–0 14
B–Q2 B–R3 Spassov-Ermenkov,
Bulgaria Ch 1975, and now 15
N–B4 looks good.) 7 P–KN3 P×P 8
N×NP B–N5 9 N–QB3 P–R3 10
N–R3 P–B4! 11 P–B3 P×QP 12
Q×P N–B3 13 Q–Q1 B–KB4 and
Black is not without compensation,
Malich-Nunn, Dečin 1976 (½–½,
67).

f) **5 P–Q3!** Now Black must release
the tension and White will develop .
rapidly. Sometimes 'the best way to
refute a gambit' is to *decline* it! We
examine three replies:

f1) **5 ... P×BP** 6 P×KP P–KR3
(White was threatening P–K5, △
P–K4 or Q–Q5; 6 ... N–B3 7
P–K3 B–N5 8 B×P 0–0 9 0–0 B×N?
10 P×B P–KR3 11 P–B4! ±±
Keene-Wockenfuss, Bad Lauter-

berg 1977.) 7 N×BP!? (This is
critical, and sometimes given as
'±', but the complications are
bewildering. Instead, **7 N–B3**
B–N2 8 P–K5 N–K5 **9 P–K3** B–N5
10 Q–B2 Q–K2 11 B×P N–N4!
gave Black good chances in
Polugaevsky-Estevez, Sochi 1976
(½–½, 33); better was **9 N×N!** B×N
10 N–Q2, and if 10 ... B–N5, 11
Q–R4 Q–K2 12 P–QR3 B×Nch 13
B×B Q×P 14 B–B3 with some
advantage.) 7 ... K×N 8 P–K5
P–Q4! (If the knight moves, 9
Q–Q5ch; **8 ... B–N2?** 9 P×N Q×P
10 P–K4 Q–K3 11 B–K2! B–B4 12
0–0 ± Cvetković-Nedeljkovic,
Yugoslavia 1976. **8 ... P–Q4** could
be critical if Black is to salvage 3 ...
P–K5!?. Since my analysis which
follows is not exhaustive, the
prospective gambiteer might spend
some profitable and entertaining
time here!) 9 P×N (**9 P–K4!?**
B–K3! – *9 ... N–N5 10 B×BP* – **10
P×N** will transpose, unless White
tries **10 B×BP** B–QN5!, which
looks worse, or **10 P–B4!?** N×KP 11
N×N P×N 12 Q×Q B–N5ch 13
Q–Q2 =.) 9 ... B–K3 10 P–K4
(**10 P–K3!?** N–B3 11 P×P – *11
B–K2 K×P!* – 11 ... B×P 12
Q–R5ch K–N1 13 B–K2 N–K4
with some play for a pawn: ±?) 10
... P–Q5 11 P–B4! (**11 P–K5**
B–QN5 ∓; 11 N–Q5!? B×N 12
Q–R5ch P–N3 13 Q×Bch Q×Q 14
P×Q B–N5ch ∞) 11 ... B–QN5
(**11 ... P–N3** 12 P–B5!; **11 ...
Q×P** 12 N–Q5!) 12 P–B5 and
White's attack is evidently the
stronger one, e.g. **12 ... B×P** 13
B×Pch! or **12 ... Q×P** 13 P×Bch

K–B1 (**13 . . . K–K2** 14 Q–R4! e.g.
14 . . . P–QR4 15 Q×Bch!, or **14
. . . Q–R5ch** 15 K–Q1) 14 P–QR3!
B–R4 (**14 . . . Q–R5ch** 15 P–N3
Q×KPch 16 K–B2 B×N 17 P×B
Q×R 18 Q–R5! ±±) 15 Q–R4
Q–R5ch 16 P–N3 B×Nch 17 P×B
Q×KPch 18 K–B2 Q×R 19
B–KN2 Q×P 20 Q–N4ch (simp-
lest) and 21 Q–N7 etc..

If this analysis is correct, then 5
. . . P×BP doesn't .work.

f2) **5 . . . B–N5** 6 B–Q2 P×QP 7
N×NP B×Bch 8 Q×B 0–0 (**8 . . .
P×P** 9 Q×Pch K–B1 10 0–0–0, or 9
Q–K3ch and 10 B×P) 9 P–K3 ±
Van der Sterren-Bellon, Wijk an
Zee 1977.

f3) **5 . . . P×QP** 6 P×NP P–KR3 7
N–B3 P×P 8 B×KP (Now White is
ahead in development, and Black
cannot touch his centre pawns
without creating weaknesses.) 8 . . .
B–N2 (**8 . . . P–R3?!** 9 0–0 B–B4 10
N–Q4 0–0 11 B–B3 R–R2 12 B–K3
(±) P×P? 13 N–B6! N×N 14 B×B
±± Stean-Regan, New York 1977;
8 . . . B–B4 9 0–0 0–0 10 N–K5
B–N2 11 B–B3 ± Alburt-Pribyl,
Dečin 1976) 9 0–0 B–B4 10 N–Q4
(Also good are **10 P–QN3** and **10
Q–B2** 0–0 11 N–QR4 B–Q3 12
N–B5 B×N 13 Q×B R–K1 14
N–Q4 P–R3 15 B–KB4 P–Q3 16
Q–B2 Watson-Whitehead, San
Francisco 1977.) 10 . . . 0–0 11
B–K3 (Δ N–B6) 11 . . . B–N3 12
B–B3 P–Q4 13 N–B5 ± Ghitescu-
Ermenkov, Moscow 1977. Black is
tied down and his queenside
squares and QP are weak.

f4, **5 . . . B–N2!?** 6 N(5)×KP P×P 7
P–KN3! P×P 8 P×P B–N5 9 B–N2

N×N 10 P×N Q–B3 11 0–0! B×N
12 P×B 0–0 13 B–B4! Q–B3 .14
R–N1 N–R3 15 Q–Q5! ±
Uhlmann-Bellon, Bucharest 1978.

Thus 3 . . . P–K5!? 4 N–KN5
P–N4 holds up fairly well against
all moves except 5 P–Q3 (!), after
which an equalizing method has
not been found. Perhaps the
variations of (f1) will prove tenable
for Black?!

We return (finally) to the
conventional 3 . . . N–B3:

4 P–KN3 (*51*)

51
B

The author once saw a (local
chess magazine) article where 4
P–KN3 was given a '?', and a game
quoted with 4 . . . P–K5 ('!') 5
N–KN5 P–Q4 ('!'). This was
substantiated by lots of analysis and
a nice victory for Black. Alas, what
the author had overlooked was
that, in his summary dismissal of
the line 6 P×P N×P 7 N(5)×P
P–B4, 8 N–KN5! stays a pawn up!

It would be strange indeed if 4
P–KN3 could be so easily refuted;
the variations stemming from it
have become practically the 'Ruy
Lopez' of the 1 . . . P–K4 English
Opening, in the sense that theory in
many lines is detailed and rather

definitive, while 'actual' play may even start on a move in the teens, a situation hardly typical (yet) of 1 P–QB4 in general! 4 P–KN3 is one of the basic English systems which world-class players employ to slug it out in Olympiads, Interzonals, and such. It also (therefore?) enjoys a persistent popularity among club players everywhere. I have devoted most of a chapter to its intricacies, and yet the variations below are far from being exhaustive; in fact, the reader can probably find new possibilities in even the best-known variants. Such is the vitality of an evolutionary opening!

Replies to 4 P–KN3:
A 4 . . . P–KN3
B 4 . . . N–Q5
C 4 . . . B–B4
D 4 . . . B–N5

And these in brief:

a) **4 . . . P–Q4** 5 P×P N×P 6 B–N2 or 6 P–Q3 is examined in Chapter 6.

b) **4 . . . P–Q3 5 P–Q4** is a position from Chapter 9, C31. Independent was 4 . . . P–Q3 **5 B–N2** B–K3 **6 P–N3** (perhaps 6 P–Q4!? Δ 6 . . . B×P 7 Q–R4!) 6 . . . P–KR3 7 P–Q4 B–N5 8 P–Q5 N–K2 9 P–KR3 B–Q2 10 P–K4 with a significant advantage, Portisch-Balashan, Lone Pine 1978 (but ½–½, 62).

c) Taimanov writes with some enthusiasm about **4 . . . B–K2** 5 B–N2 P–Q3 6 0–0 N–Q5!, but simply 6 P–Q4! (and if 6 . . . B–N5, 7 P–Q5) grants White a standard space advantage – see Chapter 9, C31.

A

4 . . .   P–KN3

This has a poor reputation. It strongly resembles Chapter 2, B2, from which move order (2 N–QB3 N–QB3 3 N–B3 P–KN3?!) it may arise.

5 P–Q4(!)

5 B–N2 B–N2 6 0–0 0–0 7 P–Q4(!) will make no difference.

5 . . .   P×P
6 N×P   B–N2
7 B–N2

If White feels that . . . N×N (or . . . N–K4) is a good idea for Black, he can immediately exchange by 7 **N×N** NP×N 8 B–N2, when one way for Black to avoid the main line is

a) **8 . . . N–N5?!** 9 Q–B2, see Chapter 2, B21 (but playing this is not recommended); and another is b) **8 . . . B–N2** 9 0–0 0–0 10 Q–B2 (or 10 Q–R4) 10 . . . P–Q3 11 R–Q1 N–Q2 12 B–K3?! (12 P–N3!) 12 . . . R–K1 13 Q–Q2 Q–B1! 14 QR–B1 N–N3 15 P–N3 P–QB4 = Ghitescu-Markland, European Team Ch 1973.

7 . . .   0–0
8 0–0   R–K1

8 . . . N×N 9 Q×N (This exchange could have taken place on Black's sixth or seventh moves, but with no essential difference. If Black moves his king's knight at any point, White just plays Q–Q2 Δ P–QN3 and Black has decentralized a piece for no good reason.) 9 . . . P–Q3 10 Q–R4! (Δ B–N5) 10 . . . N–N5 11 Q×Q R×Q 12 N–Q5 ± Filip-Averbach, Portoroz 1958.

9 N×N

Positionally clearest, since it makes long-term targets out of Black's central pawns. Apparently also good are:

a) **9 N–B2** P–Q3 (9 . . . N–KN5!?) 10 P–KR3 B–K3 11 N–K3 Q–Q2 12 K–R2, maintaining the bind, O'Kelly-Clarke, Hastings 1956/7.

b) **9 P–K3** N–K4 10 P–N3 P–Q3 11 B–N2 B–N5 12 P–B3 B–Q2 13 P–KR3 N–B3 14 N–B2 ± Rubinstein-Tarrasch, St. Petersburg 1914.

    9 . . .   NP×N

9 . . . QP×N does not lose tactically, but gives White an ending where his 4–3 king-side majority is a major factor.

    10 Q–R4!
    Δ Q–R5, B–B4 (Uhlmann)
    10 . . .   P–QR4
    11 R–Q1 (*52*)

    11 . . .   B–N2
    12 R–Q3   N–N5

13 N–K4! P–KB4 (**13 . . . N–K4** 14 R–Q1 threatens N–B5 – Bukić) 14 B–N5! (**14 N–B5** R×P 15 N×B R–K8ch 16 B–B1 Q–K1! – Rajković and Uhlmann) 14 . . . P×N 15 B×Q P×R 16 P×P! QR×B? (**16**

. . . B–Q5 17 P–B5 is only '±', according to Rajković and Uhlmann.) 17 P–B5! P–R4 18 P–KR3 R–K7 (If 18 . . . N–K4, 19 Q–N3ch picks up a bishop.) 19 P×N R–KB1 20 R–KB1! B–QR3 21 P×P R×NP 22 B–K4 ±± Uhlmann-Rajković, Hastings 1972/3.

B
    4 . . .   **N–Q5**

Attempting to regain the lost 'elasticity' referred to at the beginning of the chapter, but this costs Black two tempi (one of these he hopes to regain by the threat of . . . B–KR6 in a few moves), and condemns him to a passive if sometimes drawable position.

    5 B–N2

a) **5 N×P** (often seen with a '?' around its neck) 5 . . . Q–K2 6 P–B4 (6 N–Q3?? N–B6 Mate) 6 . . . P–Q3 7 N–Q3 B–B4 is usually dismissed as '∓' at this point, (e.g. 8 P–K3? B–N5!), yet there's no apparent refutation of 8 K–B2! when White's position is awkward but defendable.

b) **5 N–KR4!?** is of recent vintage: 5 . . . P–KN4!? (5 . . . P–B3! 6 P–K3 N–K3) 6 N–B3 N×Nch 7 P×N B–B4 8 Q–K2 Q–K2? 9 P–Q3 R–KN1 10 P–KR4 ± Botterill-Botto, England 1977.

    5 . . .   N×Nch
    6 B×N   B–N5

6 . . . B–K2 7 P–Q4 P–Q3 8 B–N5 0–0 9 0–0 P–B3 10 P–N3 B–B4 11 P–K4 ± Gheorghiu-Portisch, Skopje 1972.

    7 Q–N3

7 0–0 0–0 8 Q–N3 B–B4 (**8 . . .
P–QR4** is the next note) 9 P–Q3
P–Q3 (**9 . . . P–B3**-Hartson – gives
the bishop a route to retreat upon.)
10 N–R4 N–Q2 11 B–N2 P–QR4
12 N×B N×N 13 Q–B3 ±
Uhlmann-Korchnoi, Amsterdam
1972.

    7 . . .   B–K2!?

7 . . . P–QR4 8 0–0 0–0 9 P–Q3
P–KR3 10 B–K3 B×N 11 Q×B
P–Q3 12 P–B5 R–K1 13 P×P
Q×P?! (13 . . . P×P) 14 KR–B1 ±
Bronstein-Polugaevsky, Petropolis
1973 ($\frac{1}{2}$–$\frac{1}{2}$, 23).

    8 0–0   P–B3
    9 R–Q1

A quieter idea would be the
Botvinnik set-up with **9 P–Q3**
P–Q3 10 B–N2 Q–B2 11 P–K4,
meeting the straightforward 11 . . .
B–K3 (?!) by 12 P–QR4 e.g. 12 . . .
N–Q2 13 B–K3 N–B4 14 Q–B2
P–QR4 15 P–B4 or 12 . . . Q–Q2 13
P–B4 etc.

    9 . . .   P–Q3
    10 P–Q4   Q–B2

11 B–N2 (lest 11 . . . B–R6
inconvenience White) 11 . . . 0–0
12 Q–B2 B–K3 **13 P–N3** P×P! 14
R×P P–Q4 15 P×P P×P 16 B–B4
Q–N3 17 Q–Q2 QR–B1 18 N–R4
$\frac{1}{2}$–$\frac{1}{2}$ Gheorghiu-Hartston, Bath
1973. More play was offered by **13
P–Q5**, e.g. 13 . . . P×P 14 P×P
B–Q2 15 P–QR4, etc.

In general, 4 . . . N–Q5 tends to
limit things, particularly for Black.

C

    4 . . .   **B–B4**

An old move, now seldom
played; yet this neglect is almost
certainly unjustified. Of the few
practitioners of 4 . . . B–B4 in recent
years, Hort, Malich, and Knaak
deserve credit for their 're-
habilitation' work, which should
eventually receive more attention.
Not only have they helped clarify
the basic problems of the line, but
have also had fair success in the
process. The two important
answers are:

C1 5 N×P

C2 5 B–N2

C1

    5 N×P!?

This is the theoretical 'refutation,' but top-level masters very
rarely go in for 5 N×P, which is
perhaps an indication that Black is
not so badly off.

    5 . . .   B×Pch

5 . . . N×N is indeed unpromis-
ing: 6 P–Q4 B–N3 (**6 . . . B–N5?** 7
P×N N–K5 8 Q–Q4 with a pawn to
the good and space; **6 . . . Q–K2** 7
P×N Q×P 8 B–B4 – *or 8 B–N2-
Shatskes* – 8 . . . Q–B4 – *8 . . . N–K5
9 P–K3* – 9 P–K4! analysis by
Hasin) 7 P×N N–N5 8 P–K3 N×P
9 P–B4 (or **9 P–N3** P–Q3 10
B–KN2 0–0 11 B–QN2 ± –
Schwarz) 9 . . . N–B3 10 B–N2 0–0
11 0–0 R–K1 12 N–Q5 with
advantage (Taimanov and Shatskes).

    6 K×B   N×N
    7 P–K4

7 P–Q4!? N×P 8 P–K4 P–Q4
('∞' – Botvinnik) was tested in
Bergstrom-Wiedenkeller, Halls-
berg 1977/8: 9 B×N P×B 10
Q–R4ch P–B3 11 Q×P 0–0 12

R–K1 (12 K–N2!?) 12 . . . B–R6!
13 K–N1 N–N5 14 P–K5 Q–N3 (Δ
. . . QR–Q1) and Black had
excellent play (0–1, 57)⁻.

7 . . .   P–B4
Black sticks to the straight and
narrow, and so he should:
a) **7 . . . P–QN4?!** 8 P–Q4 N×BP 9
P–K5 N–N1 (**9 . . . B–N2** 10 B–N2
B×B 11 K×B N–N1 12 Q–N4
K–B1 13 P–N3 N–N3 14 B–R3ch
N–K2 15 KR–KB1-Shatskes) 10
N×P P–Q4 11 Q–B3 with a superb
position (Shatskes).
b) **7 . . . P–Q4?!** 8 KP×P
N(3)–N5ch 9 K–N2 Q–B3 10
Q–K2 N–B7 11 Q×N B–R6ch 12
K–N1 N–B6ch 13 Q×N Q×Q 14
B×B ∞ (Keres). But Taimanov's
11 P–Q4! refutes 7 . . . P–Q4.

8 P–Q3   P–Q3
9 P–KR3

9 B–K2 0–0 (9 . . . B–R6!) 10
K–N2 N–K1 11 B–K3 (**11 B–B4**
N–B2 12 Q–Q2 N–K3 13 QR–KB1
N–Q5 was at least equal in Jansson-
Malich, Skopje 1972) 11 . . . N–B2
12 P–KN4!? N–K3 13 P–KR4
N–B3 (or 13 . . . P–QR3 Δ . . .
P–QN4) 14 Q–Q2 N(K)–Q5 15
N–Q5 P–QN4? (**15 . . . B–K3!** and
if 16 P–R5, 16 . . . B×N 17 KP×B
N–K4 ∞. Black can easily assume
the attack in such situations.) 16
P×P N×P 17 P–R5 B–K3 18 P–R6
P–N3 19 B–N5 P–B3 20 N×Pch
R×N 21 KR–B1! R×R 22 B×Q
R–B2 (**22 . . . R×R** 23 Q–N5 R×B
24 Q–B6 R–Q2 25 Q×Bch R–B2
26 P–Q4 ±±) 23 B–R4 N(4)–Q5
24 R–KB1 ±± Pietzsch-Malich, E.
Germany 1974. Such play (i.e. 12
P–KN4!?) is critical, but uncon-

vincing. If White has to resort to
such a self-exposing attack, this
variation must be worth another
look. Compare what follows.

9 . . .   0–0!

9 . . . P–KR4?! 10 B–K2 N–R2
11 K–N2! P–R5 12 P–KN4 N–N4
(Black had fine outposts for this
piece on e5 and d4; he didn't need
to expend so much time securing
the less central g5!) 12 B–K3 B–Q2
14 Q–Q2 ('!'-Taimanov, but
Botvinnik himself called this
'routine play' and suggested **14
Q–KN!** Δ Q–B2.) 14 . . . N–K3 15
P–N4!? Botvinnik-Keres, Moscow
1966. White has a strong position,
although Black could have defended adequately to draw in the
play that followed. This famous
encounter – which White won – has
had the effect of deterring most
players of Black from 4 . . . B–B4 in
international play since. Such is the
influence of a widely-published
game between two immortals . . .

10 B–K2   N–K1
11 K–N2   N–B2
12 B–K3   N–K3
13 Q–Q2

13 N–Q5 transposes, but **13
P–KN4** is a tempo short of
Pietzsch-Malich above (note to 9
P–KR3). Garcia-Boey, Skopje
1972, continued 13 . . . P–QR3 14
Q–Q2 R–N1 15 N–Q5 P–QN4 16
P–N3 N–Q5 ∞.

13 . . .   N–B3
Here too **13 . . . P–QR3** merits
consideration. After the text, 14
B–N4!? (Estrin's idea) might at
least get rid of White's bad bishop.

14 QR–KB1   N(K)–Q5

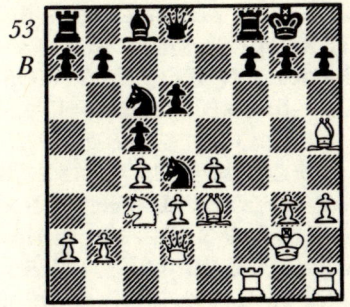

15 B–R5 (*53*)

Ulhmann's thought in a very similar position; it's not clear, however, what White can undertake here. The semi-locked centre limits his bishops, whereas Black's knights have found excellent posts from which to defend, and to assist in the coming queenside advance.

15 ...   B–K3
16 N–Q5   R–N1
17 R–B2   P–QN4

Hickman-Camaratta, US Corres Ch 1972–5. Black has a slight initiative (0–1, 39).

CONCLUSION:

Although 5 N×P!? is an enterprising continuation, it is hardly the refutation of 4 ... B–B4 and should by no means deter Black from playing that move.

C2

5 B–N2

Often White plays **5 P–Q3**, presumably fearing 5 ... P–K5 (see next note). 5 P–Q3 P–Q3 6 B–N2 will transpose into C21 below, where White has waived his opportunity to play for an early P–Q4.

5 ...   P–Q3

5 ... **P–K5** is held to be weak after 6 N–KN5 B×Pch 7 K×B N–N5ch 8 K–N1 Q×N and now **9 P–Q4** (Schwarz) or **9 N×P** (Shatskes and Taimanov). Neither of these moves is clearly advantageous for the first player: **9 P–Q4** Q–B3! ∞ or **9 N×P** Q–N3 10 P–Q3 0–0 11 P–KR3 N–R3! 12 K–R2 P–Q3 13 R–B1 B–K3, though in this last case White may stand minimally better.

After 5 ... P–Q3, White has two strategies, one involving 6 P–Q3 (C21) and one with 6 0–0, usually followed by P–K3 (C22):

C21

6 P–Q3

Now Black in turn chooses:
C211 6 ... P–QR4
C212 6 ... 0–0

a) **6 ... P–QR3** is the same idea (i.e. preservation of the king's bishop) as we see in C211, but in some ways more flexible: 7 0–0 0–0 8 P–QR3 P–R3 9 P–QN4 B–R2 10 R–N1 R–K1 11 P–K3 **B–K3** 12 Q–B2 Q–Q2 13 N–Q2 **B–R6?** 14 N–Q5! ± Kots-Mikenas, 30th USSR Ch 1962. Much better was **11 ... B–KB4** (∞) or **13 ... P–Q4** (±).
b) **6 ... N–Q5?** 7 N×N P×N 8 P–QN4! B–N3 9 N–R4 0–0 10 0–0 R–K1 11 B–N2 ± Roizman-Kärner, Baku 1966 (1–0, 35).

C211

6 ...   P–QR4

The attempt to safeguard Black's bishop from N–QR4 may be unnecessary (see the discussion in

C212); if so, the text move may be criticized for creating a weakness on the queenside.

    7 0–0   0–0
    8 P–QR3   R–K1

Gheorghiu opines that **8 ... P–KR3** is better. 9 P–K3 B–KN5?! 10 P–R3 B–B4 11 P–N3 R–K1 12 B–N2 (±) would be (by transposition) Benko-Rossolimo, Novi Sad 1972, exemplary of White's strategy: 12 ... N–KR2 13 N–Q5 N–N4 14 N×N P×N 15 K–R2 Q–Q2 16 Q–Q2 B–QR2 17 P–KN4 B–K3 18 P–N4 B–N1 19 P–N5 N–Q1 20 K–R1! B×N 21 P×B! Q×QNP 22 P–B4 (cracking open lines for the bishops) 22 ... NP×P 23 P×P P–KB3 24 QR–N1 Q–R5 25 P–N5! B–R2 26 QR–K1 B–Q5 27 B×B Q×B 28 R–K4 Q–B4 and now Benko gives 29 P–B5! P×P 30 R–QR4! leaving Black no answer to the attack via Q–K2–R5. Although a draw resulted, Benko's performance here was ingenious and worthy of study.

    9 B–N5   P–KR3
    10 B×N   Q×B
11 R–N1 B–K3 12 N–Q2 Q–Q1! 13 N(2)–K4 Q–Q2 14 N–Q5 (**14 N×B** ±-Gheorghiu, but that seems optimistic in view of Black's pressure down the queen-file; compare the comments of the next section.) 14 ... B×N 15 P×B N–K2 16 N×B P×N 17 Q–B2 N×P ½–½ Gheorghiu-Taimanov, Bucharest 1973.

C212

    6 ...   **0–0**
    7 0–0   P–KR3

Hort has experimented with **7 ... B–B4!?** and done well, e.g. **8 N–QR4** (**8 N–K1** Q–Q2 9 N–Q5?! N×N 10 P×N N–K2 11 P–K4?! B–N5 12 Q–B2 – *12 B–B3 P–B4!* ∓-Hort – 12 ... P–QB3 13 N–B3 P×P 14 N×KP B×Pch 15 R×B P×N 16 P×P N×P ∓ Barcza-Hort, Wijk an Zee 1973) 8 ... P–KR3 9 P–N3 R–K1 10 B–N2 Q–K2 11 N–R4 B–Q2 12 N×B P×N 13 Q–Q2 Q–Q3 14 KR–K1 QR–Q1 15 Q–B3 P–QN3 Saidy-Hort, Las Palmas 1973. Black is at least equal. In the game, he played his queen's bishop to ... a8, threatening ... N–Q5, and got the advantage (0–1, 41). This game is one of several illustrations of Benko's contention that taking the bishop on c5 is not to White's advantage, since he will not be able to move his KP or QP afterwards. Therefore measures to secure a retreat for that piece (e.g. 6 ... P–QR4) are probably unnecessary.

White very likely has superior methods of answering 7 ... B–B4 e.g. **8 P–QR3** (or **8 B–N5** P–KR3 9 B×N Q×B 10 N–Q2 ∞ as in C211.) 8 ... P–KR3 (**8 ... P–QR4** 9 P–K3 Q–Q2 10 R–K1 B–R6 11 B–R1 P–KR3 12 P–N3 N–KN5 13 N–Q5 is a sample treatment.) 9 P–QN4 B–QN3 10 B–N2 Q–Q2 11 P–K3 B–R6? (11 ... B–N5) 12 P–Q4, etc. Compare C22.

    8 N–QR4?!

A 'bluff', according to Benko. If this is the best White has, then the set-up with P–Q3 appears innocuous. To be considered is **8 P–K3** Q–K2 9 P–QR3, as in C22.

8 ...   Q–K2
9 P–K3   P–QR4

'!' (Knaak); but Benko thought that ... P–QR3, contemplating a later ... P–QN4, was better.

10 P–N3

10 P–Q4 B–R2 11 P–Q5 N–QN5 12 P–QR3 N–R3 13 B–Q2 P–K5 14 N–Q4 B–N5 15 Q–B2 N–B4 = Gheorghiu-Knaak, 1973.

10 ...   R–K1
11 B–N2   B–B4

12 P–QR3 B–QR2 13 N–B3 (Thus we see that 8 N–QR4 was a bit pointless; Benko claims that he never intended to take the bishop on c5!) 13 ... Q–Q2 14 R–K1 B–R6 15 B–R1 B–N5 16 Q–B2 N–R2 with approximately equal prospects, Benko-Malich, Skopje 1972.

C22

6 0–0 *(54)*

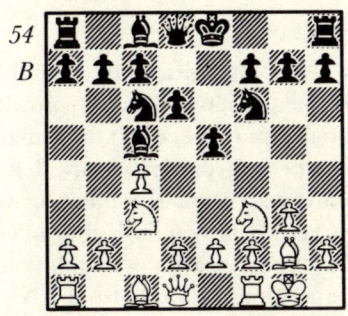

54
B

6 ...   0–0

At this point there are significant alternatives:

a) **6 ... P–QR3** 7 P–K3 0–0 8 P–Q4 B–R2 (**8 ... P×P** 9 P×P B–R2 10 P–KR3 B–KB4 11 B–K3 Q–Q2 12 K–R2 P–KR3 13 P–QR3 B–R2 14 P–QN4 N–K2 15 N–Q2

P–B3 16 N(2)–K4 Δ P–B5 ± Euwe-Colle, 1926.) 9 P–KR3 P–R3 10 P–N3 B–KB4 11 B–R3 and if 11 ... P–K5, 12 N–Q2 R–K1 13 Q–B2 Q–K2 14 N–Q5 ± Müller and Schwarz.

b) **6 ... B–K3** 7 P–Q3 (**7 P–N3!?** Δ P–K3, P–Q4 might be worth a try.) 7 ... 0–0 (And Black should consider **7 ... P–KR3** and ... Q–Q2.) 8 P–QR3 P–QR4 9 B–N5 (The 'normal' **9 P–N3** P–R3 10 P–K3 B–R2 11 B–N2 Q–Q2 12 R–K1 looks preferable.) 9 ... P–KR3 10 B–R4?! (costing a tempo; **10 B×N** Q×B 11 N–Q2 =) 10 ... N–Q5! 11 B×N (else ... N×N and ... P–KN4) 11 ... Q×B 12 N–K4?! Q–K2 13 N×B P×N ∓ Filip-Keres, Amsterdam 1956. Now 14 N×P? fails to 14 ... B–B4; but if Black is left alone, then he dominates the centre via the queen file. Again, White's KP won't be able to move because the QP will be so weak. But the play in this widely-quoted game was very poor by today's standards.

c) **6 ... B–KN5!?** 7 P–KR3 B–R4 may be one of the better plans e.g. 8 P–Q3 0–0 9 B–Q2 (**9 N–K4**, as in Carls-Bogoljubow, Breslau 1925, should be met by **9 ... N–Q2** or **9 ... P–KR3** rather than **9 ... N×N** 10 P×N as played. It was then *White* who had arranged pressure down the queen-file!) 9 ... P–QR4 10 P–KN4 B–KN3 11 B–N5?! Q–Q2! 12 B×N P×B 13 N–Q5 K–N2 14 N–R4 P–R4 ∓ Kotlerman-Sokolsky, Ukraine Ch 1949. Compare the text!

7 P–K3

Another 'non-P–Q3' strategy was 7 **P–QR3** P–QR3 8 P–QN4 B–R2 9 B–N2 R–K1 10 N–Q5?! (10 P–K3 is better, as in the text.) 10 ... N×N 11 P×N N–K2 12 P–K4 B–N5 13 P–Q4 P–KB3 14 P–R3 B–R4 15 P×P QP×P 16 Q–N3 N–B1 17 K–R2 N–Q3 = Sznapik-Martens, Lund 1973.

7 ...   B–KN5

7 ... R–K1 was successful in Uhlmann-Knaak, Halle 1974; 8 P–Q4 (**8 P–Q3** or even **8 P–KR3** – *and if 8 ... P–K5, 9 N–K1* – can be played here, although Uhlmann's move is more direct.) 8 ... B–N3 9 P–KR3 P–KR3 10 P–QR3 P–QR4 (?!) 11 P–N3 B–KB4 12 B–N2 Q–Q2 13 K–R2 QR–Q1 14 N–Q5?! (14 R–B1! ±) 14 ... N×N! 15 P×N N–K2 16 P×P B–K5 17 R–B1?! (17 P–K6 =) 17 ... B×QP 18 Q–B2 Q–K3 19 P×P R×P 20 P–QN4 P×P 21 P×P B–K5 22 Q–B3 P–B3 23 KR–Q1 KR–Q1 ∓ (0–1, 35).

	8 P–KR3	B–R4
	9 P–Q3	Q–Q2
	10 P–KN4	B–KN3
	11 N–KR4	QR–K1
	12 P–N3	P–QR4?!

As usual, a dubious idea because it weakens the queenside and wastes time. The immediate 12 ... N–Q1 or 12 ... P–QR3 is more suitable, although White can still expand in the centre with good chances. We are following Uhlmann-Thormann, E. German Ch 1975, in which White's conceptions met with complete success: 13 B–N2 N–Q1 14 P–Q4 P×P 15 P×P B–R2 16 P–Q5 B–K5?

(**16 ... B–QB4** is Uhlmann's recommendation, since **16 ... N–K5** may be answered by 17 N–N5! B–QB4 18 N–Q4 Δ N(R)–B5. The rest of the game is excruciatingly clear:) 17 N–N5 B–QN3 18 B×N P×B 19 B×B R×B 20 Q–B3 R(1)–K1 21 N–B5 B–B4 22 N–B3 R(5)–K4 23 Q–B4 K–R1 24 N–K4! R–KN1 25 K–R1 1–0 (If 25 ... R–N3, 26 N–R4).

Black's play was uninspired, yet White seemed better throughout. It is probable that Hort's plan of ... P–KR3 and ... B–KB4 was more appropriate than ... B–KN5, e.g. 7 ... P–KR3 8 P–Q4 B–N3 9 P–KR3 B–KB4 etc. Or, if Black wishes to preserve his dark-squared bishop from exchange on b6, 7 ... P–QR3 could precede ... P–KR3; positions with both black bishops on R2 are not easy for White to make progress in.

CONCLUSION:

4 ... B–B4 is logical and reasonably forceful. I have devoted proportionally more space to it than might be expected, partly because I feel that it may become popular again. Apart from Botvinnik-Keres, where Black was clearly overambitious, the positions resulting from 5 N×P are not impressive for White. Yet allowing ... P–Q3 has the drawback that all of Black's minor pieces can be brought into active play without his centre dissolving. White's best strategy then seems to lie in 6 0–0 0–0 (6 ... B–KN5!?) 7 P–K3, aiming for the earliest possible P–Q4 with a slight advantage in

space. But if White is better in such a line, his edge is likely no greater than that he commonly gets versus 4 ... B–N5, to which we now turn:

D

    4 ...   **B–N5** (*55*)

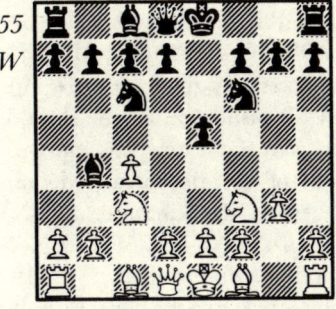

55
W

A clear majority of today's leading players have experienced at least one side of this position. **4 ... B–N5** is a logical developing move which prepares for immediate castling without being passive (e.g. **4 ... B–K2**) or subject to sudden tactics (e.g. **4 ... B–B4** 5 N×P). In many cases, Black will exchange on c3 and operate in the centre, often with ... R–K1, ... P–K5, ... P–Q3 and either ... B–KB4 or ... P–QN3 and ... B–N2.

White has tried many ideas against 4 ... B–N5. Already he has a choice:

D1 5 N–Q5
D2 5 B–N2

D1

    5 N–Q5

A fairly popular alternative to 5 B–N2. Now on **5 ... 0–0** 6 N×B N×N 7 N×P, Black doesn't get enough for a pawn e.g. 7 ... R–K1

8 P–Q4 P–Q3 9 N–Q3 N–B3 10 N–B4. But four other moves have been tried:

D11 5 ... B–Q3
D12 5 ... B–B4
D13 5 ... N×N
D14 5 ... P–K5

D11

    5 ...   **B–Q3!?**
    6 B–N2   N×N(?)

6 ... 0–0 7 0–0 R–K1 could be played. Now White achieves a distinct central superiority.

    7 P×N   N–K2
    8 P–K4   P–QB3
    9 0–0!   P×P
    10 P–Q4 ±

10 ... P×KP 11 N×P N–N3 12 N×N RP×N 13 B×P R–QN1?! 14 R–K1 K–B1? (If Black's 13th was slow, this is awful; he has no realistic use for the KR-file, so **14 ... 0–0** was called for, with some defensive chances.) 15 P–KR4! P–QN4 16 B–N5 Q–N3 17 Q–B3 B–N2 18 QR–B1 B×B 19 Q×B K–N1 20 Q–Q5 B–N5 21 R–K5 K–R2 22 Q×BP R(R)–KB1 23 Q×QP R–N2 24 Q–Q5 1–0 Petrosian-Vaganian, 43rd USSR Ch. Top L 1975.

D12

    5 ...   **B–B4**
    6 P–Q3   P–KR3
    7 B–N2   P–Q3
    8 0–0   0–0
    9 P–K3

A suggestion of Gheorghiu's. This is a position from C 4 ... B–B4, except that White's knight is on d5 instead of c3 (probably no

improvement). Worth noting are:
a) **9 P–QR3 N×N** 10 P×N N–K2
11 P–Q4 P×P 12 N×P N–B4 13
N×N̄ B×N 14 P–K4 **B–Q2?** 15
P–QN4 B–N3 16 P–QR4 P–QR4
17 P–N5 P–KB4?! 18 P×P R×P 19
B–N2 ± Naranja-Wotulo, Manila
1973. But **9 ... P–QR4** was
perfectly okay (White cannot
exploit the queenside holes here),
and **14 ... B–KN3,** giving Black
breathing room and maintaining
pressure on the White KP, was
still equal. As the game went,
Black's central squares were
weak and his QBP was a constant
worry.
b) 9 B–Q2 P–QR4 (**9 ... N×N** is
worse here: 10 P×N N–K2 – *10 ...
N–Q5!-Gheorghiu* – 11 P–QN4!
B–N3 12 P–QR4 P–QR3 13 Q–N3
B–Q2 14 B–B3 N–B4 15 P–K4
N–K2 16 P–Q4 P–KB3! 17 N–Q2 –
*17 P×P BP×P 18 N×P P×N 19
P–Q6ch K–R1 = – 17 ... P×P 18
B–N2 N–N3! 19 N–B3 P–Q6 20
Q×P ± Gheorghiu-Portisch,
Petropolis 1973 ($\frac{1}{2}$-$\frac{1}{2}$, 26)) 10 B–B3
B–KN5 11 Q–Q2 (**11 P–KR3** looks
better.) 11 ... N×N 12 P×N
N–N5!? 13 P–KR3 B–Q2 14 P–Q4
P×P 15 N×P Q–N4! = de Castro-
Larsen, Manila 1973.
    9 ...   P–QR4
    10 N–B3!?
By this widely applauded move
White avoids the exchange of
knights and plans to build up the
centre; yet the position before us
comes almost directly out of C2
above, Black having lost one tempo
and White two! Commentators on
this game seem to have missed this

analogy, for they unjustly award
White the advantage here and fail
to criticize Black's next two moves.
In accordance with our analysis in
that section, **10 ... B–B4!** or **10 ...
B–KN5** are undoubtedly best now.
    10 ...   B–R2?
    11 P–QR3   N–R2?
12 K–R1! B–N5 13 Q–B2 P–B4 14
N–QN5 Q–Q2?! (Since Black has
unnecessarily given up two tempi to
put his bishop on a7, he should at
least salvage it now, the more so in
view of his decentralized minor
pieces on the kingside.) 15 N×B
R×N 16 P–N3 R(2)–R1 17 N–N1!
Korchnoi-Petrosian (5), 1977.
White has two bishops in a fluid
position with several potential
pawn breaks (at least ±).
Nevertheless, Petrosian was in
unrecognizable form, and the move
5 ... B–B4 looks quite satisfactory.

D13
    5 ...   **N×N**
    6 P×N   N–Q5
An oft-quoted blunder is **6 ...
P–K5??** 7 P×N P×N 8 Q–N3 1–0
Petrosian-Ree, Wijk an Zee, 1971.
White wins a piece.
    7 N×N
a) **7 N×P?** Q–K2 8 P–B4 P–B3 (8
... Q–B4 9 K–B2–Georgadze) 9
N–Q3 Q–K5 (Georgadze).
b) **7 B–N2** N×Nch 8 B×N 0–0 9 0–0
P–Q3 10 B–N2 B–QB4 11 P–N3
B–Q5 12 R–N1 B–KB4 13 P–Q3
Q–Q2 = Saidy-Kapengut, Lublin
1973.
    7 ...   P×N
    8 B–N2
    8 Q–B2 (**8 Q–R4!?**-Georgadze)

8 ... Q–K2 9 B–N2 B–B4 10 0–0 0–0 11 P–K3 B–N3 12 P–QR4 Korchnoi-Karpov (27), 1978. Very slightly ±, though 0–1, 41.

8 ...   B–K2
9 0–0   P–QB4 =

Suba-Georgadze, Lublin 1974. After 10 P–QN4?! P×P 11 P–QR3 0–0 12 P×P? B×P (∓). Black won in 32 moves.

D14
5 ...   P–K5

The reply most often seen.

6 N–R4

6 N×B N×N (or **6 ... P×N** 7 N×N QP×N = Barcza-Bisguier, Tallin 1971) 7 N–Q4 0–0 8 N–B2?! N×Nch 9 Q×N P–Q4 ∓ Smyslov-Benko, Wijk an Zee 1972.

6 ...   B–B4

a) **6 ... P–Q3** is playable: 7 N×B N×N 8 P–QR3 N–B3 9 P–Q3 0–0 10 B–N2 R–K1 11 0–0 P–KR3 12 P×P N×P 13 B–K3?! P–QR4 14 Q–B2 Q–K2 = Saidy-Browne, San Antonio 1972; 13 P–B3!?.

b) **6 ... 0–0** 7 B–N2 R–K1 **8 0–0** B–B1 (?) 9 P–Q3 P×P (9 ... N×N 10 P×N P×P 11 Q×P N–K4 12 Q–B2 P–QB4 13 P–N3 ± Ghitescu-Tringov, Skopje 1972) 10 Q×P N–K4 11 Q–B2 P–B3 12 N×Nch Q×N 13 P–N3! P–Q3 14 B–N2 Q–R3 15 QR–Q1 ± Petrosian-Liebert, Siegen 1972. In both cases, **8 ... B–B1** resulted in the domination of the centre by White's bishops. For **8 ... P–Q3** (!), see D21, note to 7 ... B–B4.

7 B–N2

7 P–Q3!? makes a world of difference: 7 ... N×N 8 P×N

Q–B3! 9 P–K3 (**9 P×N?** B×Pch 10 K–Q2 P–K6ch and 11 ... Q×Pch, snaring the rook) 9 ... B–N5ch?! (**9 ... P–KN4!** 10 P×N B–N5ch ∞-Saidy) 10 B–Q2 Q×NP 11 R–B1 N–K4 12 P×P P–KN4 13 R–B2 B×Bch 14 R×B Q–N5 15 N–B3 Q×P 16 N×N! Q×R? (16 ... Q×N 17 P–Q6! ∞) 17 Q–R5 R–B1 18 P–Q6! with a strong attack, Gheorghiu-Joita, Bucharest 1972.

7 ...   P–Q3

7 ... 0–0 is D2 below.

8 0–0

8 P–Q3?! P×P?! 9 Q×P N–K4 10 Q–QB3! (**10 Q–B2** P–B3 11 N×Nch?! Q×N 12 0–0 B–K3 ∓ Timman-Bisguier, Malaga 1970) 10 ... P–B3 11 N–K3 (or 11 B–K3!-Korchnoi) 11 ... B–K3 (**11 ... Q–N3!** 12 0–0 0–0 13 N–B2 P–QR4 = Korchnoi-Ree, Amsterdam 1972) 12 N(4)–B5 0–0 13 P–QN4 ± Wirtensohn-Keene, Skopje 1972.

This is informative enough, particularly as an introduction to D21 below, but 8 P–Q3?! looks practically refuted by 8 ... N–KN5! 9 0–0 P–KN4 10 B×NP Q×B 11 N×Pch K–Q1 12 N×R N×BP, which plainly favours Black after 13 R×N Q–K6 14 Q–K1 N–K4.

8 ...   B–K3

8 ... P–KN4?! 9 P–Q4! N×N 10 P×N (or here **10 P×B!?** N(4)–N5 11 P–QR3 N–R3 12 P–QN4 P×N **13 P×QP!**, but not **13 P–N5?** N×P 14 P×N Q–K2! ∓ Kushnir-Hecht, Wijk an Zee II, 1973) 10 ... N×P 11 P–K3 N–N4 12 P–QR4 P×N 13 B×P ± (Antunac).

9 P–Q3

a) **9 N×Nch** Q×N 10 B×P B×P 11 Q–R4! P–Q4 12 B–B3 0–0 13 P–Q3 B–R3 14 B×P N–Q5 15 Q–Q1 ½–½ Antunac-Hecht, Wijk an Zee II 1973.

b) **9 N–QB3?!** B×P 10 N×P N×N 11 B×N B–K3 12 B–N2 P–Q4 13 Q–B2 B–K2 14 N–B3 P–Q5! $\overline{\overline{\mp}}$ Ghitescu-Browne, Wijk an Zee 1974.

9 ...   N×N

10 P×N B×P 11 P×P B–K3 12 N–B5 0–0 13 B–Q2 Q–Q2 14 Q–B2 N–Q5 = Gheorghiu-Savon, Petropolis 1973.

CONCLUSION:

5 N–Q5 appears to be a rather premature foray, as Black can guarantee himself rather dull equality by playing **5 . . . N×N** or even **5 . . . P–K5**, if he knows it. **5 . . . B–B4** probably also levels things, and does not limit the play so much. A safe line for players who trust their endgame abilities.

D2

5 **B–N2**   0–0

5 . . . P–Q3 has no particular advantages and, as we shall see, Black would sometimes like to play without that move for a while. Now:

D21 6 N–Q5

D22 6 0–0

D21

6 **N–Q5**   P–K5

The main idea, but **6 . . . N×N(!)** 7 P×N N–Q5 is probably equal too: 8 N×N P×N 9 0–0 (**9 P–N3** B–K2

10 B–N2 P–QB4! 11 0–0 P–Q3 12 P–K3 P×P 13 BP×P P–B4 14 P–K4 B–B3 = Polugaevsky-Kuzmin, USSR Ch 1973) 9 . . . B–Q3 10 P–K4 P×Pe.p. 11 QP×P P–QB4 12 Q–B2 B–K2 13 B–Q2 P–Q3 14 P–QR4 B–B3 = Smejkal-Korchnoi, Leningrad 1973.

Note that **6 . . . R–K1** 7 0–0 B–B4 (**7 . . . B–B1** 8 P–Q3 is D14, note (b) to 6 . . . B–B4) transposes to Gheorghiu-Benko-D22313 below.

7 N–R4   B–B4

7 . . . R–K1 8 0–0 P–Q3 (**8 . . . B–B1** is again D14, note (b) to 6 . . . B–B4.) 9 P–Q3 N×N 10 P×N P×P 11 Q×P N–K4 12 Q–B2 B–QB4 ½–½ Szabo-Andersson, AVRO 1973. In this sort of position, Black's dark-squared bishop stands much better *outside* the pawn chain, where it can influence the centre and protect the queenside.

8 0–0   R–K1

9 P–Q3   P×P

10 Q×P   N–K4

11 Q–B2

Perhaps **11 Q–B3**, to answer 11 . . . P–QB3 with **12 B–K3!** ∞, but not with **12 N–K3** Q–N3!, when 13 P–KR3, 13 N(4)–B5 and 13 R–Q1 are all met by 13 . . . P–Q4!

11 . . .   P–B3

12 N–QB3?

Mecking suggests **12 N×Nch**, and Gligorić prefers **12 N–K3**. Actually, **12 N×Nch** Q×N gives Black very free play, and **12 N–K3** Q–N3! is like the last note ($\overline{\overline{\mp}}$).

The right move may well be **12 B–K3**, as in Gheorghiu-Szmetan, Torremolinos 1976: 12 . . . P×N (**12 . . . B–B1?!** 13 N×Nch Q×N 14

B–Q4 ±-Szmetan) 13 B×B **P–Q3**
14 B–Q4 P×P 15 KR–Q1! N–B3 16
Q×P N×B 17 R×N ± (½–½, 32).
But **13 ... Q–B2(!)** was also
possible, and on 14 B–Q4, 14 ...
P×P (not **14 ... Q×P** 15 Q×Q
P×Q 16 N–B5 P–Q4 17 N–K3! ±),
White might have nicely-placed
pieces, but is a pawn down. This
needs testing.

    12 ...   N×P!
    13 N–R4   B–B1
    14 Q×N   P–QN4
15 Q–Q4 P×N 16 P–K4 B–R3 17
R–K1 Q–N3! 18 B–K3 B–N5! 19
Q×Q P×Q 20 KR–Q1 B–K7 ∓∓
Smyslov-Mecking, Petropolis 1973.

The early N–Q5 sortie again
gave few prospects after the
simplest of developing moves by
Black. Hence our attention turns to:
D22

      6 0–0 (*56*)

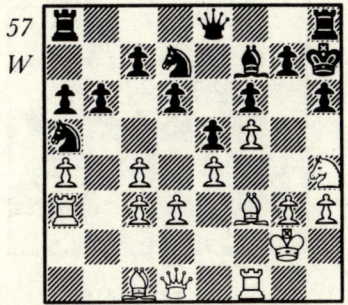

56
B

The basic position of 4 ... B–N5,
crucial for the theory of 1 ... P–K4.
Multitudes of games have been
played from the diagram and,
rather than plunge into a
bewildering mass of material, we
will begin by taking a theoretical
overview of the variation's salient
features.

One of Black's main ideas is to
capture White's knight on c3,
either immediately or after
preparation (e.g. 6 ... R–K1 7
N–K1 P–Q3 8 N–B2 B×N). White
can retake the bishop with his NP or
QP, a decision which radically
defines the play to follow.

If White takes with the NP
(sometimes compulsory, if he has
already played P–Q3), Black in
turn must choose whether or not to
push ... P–K5. The advantage of
this move are (a) that it gains space
and (b) that it prevents White from
using his central pawn mass with
P–Q3 and P–K4, the ideas behind
which we examine shortly. On the
debit side, ... P–K5 will sometimes
tend to open the game for White's
bishops.

Let us compare two (rather
ideal) positions after NP×N, both
from games referred to in the main
text below:

The first diagram (*57*), from
Pfleger-Vasiukov, of D2221, illustrates what can happen if Black
allows P–K4 and can't accomplish
anything active soon thereafter.

57
W

White has played P–KB4–B5 and
has an excellent position on the
kingside, while his four central
pawns have denied Black effective

counterplay in that sector. Such games often end by White simply advancing his kingside pawns (P–KR4, P–KN4–N5), and using his two bishops and newly opened kingside files to track down the exposed Black king. In the diagram, Black has elaborately prepared for that advance, but weakened himself by doing so; White played 20 N–N6!, invading on the light squares (±).

Usually, therefore, Black will try to prevent P–K4 by . . . P–K5 at some point, or else prepare an immediate counterattack by . . . P–KB4 or . . . P–QN4. The second diagram (*58*), from Bobotsov–Fuchs of D2242, note (c), typifies the variations where Black advances . . . P–K5 and White does not challenge the e4 pawn. In this case, the second player's forces are perfectly centralized and he can use his pawn wedge to support a reorganization such as . . . Q–KR4, . . . B–R6, . . . QR–Q1, and . . . N–K4.

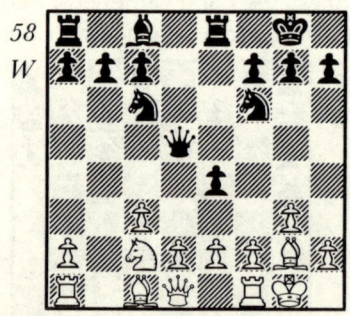

If White plays **11 P–Q3**, 11 . . . Q–QB4! 12 Q–Q2 (or **12 B–N2** P×P 13 P×P B–N5) 12 . . . B–B4 prevents White from disturbing the central tension without creating

weaknesses in his own camp. **11 P–B3** would be better, but again White's lack of development shows: 11 . . . Q–B4ch (or 11 . . . B–B4 =) 12 K–R1 P×P 13 B×P B–R6 Δ . . . QR–Q1. The game itself saw **11 P–Q4?!** Q–KR4 (11 . . . Q–B5 was also good) 12 P–QB4 P–QR3! 13 B–B4 P–QN4! and the light squares were collapsing (∓).

In general, White will not let Black play . . . P–K5 and . . . P–Q4 as easily as he did in this example; instead he anticipates or immediately challenges . . . P–K5 with P–Q3 or P–B3. Then neither side has an easy time of it, White's two bishops being pitted against Black's space advantage (see e.g. D2222 and D2241).

Now we turn to positions where White answers . . . B×N with QP×B. Diagram (*59*) comes from analysis in D222.

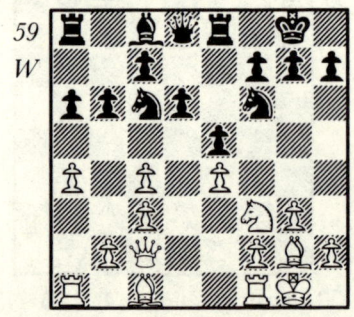

White's bishops are temporarily inactive and Black's has a nice view. Therefore we cannot talk of a two bishop advantage unless White can break down Black's solid centre and open some diagonals. To achieve this, however, the first player would usually need a phalanx of centre pawns. Here, White lacks a QP for P–Q4, and P–KB4 will allow simply . . . P×P, after which White gets either a weak isolated KP (after B×P) or hanging central pawns (after P×P). The latter would hardly be mobile in view of Black's restraint on e5. These problems too arise from the lack of a QP. Note that the same basic problem of destroying Black's centre exists with White's king pawn back on e2.

But is QP×B therefore always a bad move? In diagram (60), from

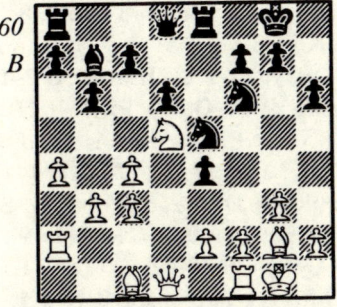

60
B

Korchnoi–Karpov of D2242, note (b) to 9 . . . R–K1, White has d4 as a base of operations and the pawn on e4 is subject to attack. Often White pushes his BP to f4 in such situations, threatening to advance on the kingside (i.e. by P–KR3, P–KB5, P–KN4–5). If Black captures en passant, the cramping e4 pawn disappears with the effect that central files and diagonals are opened for White's pieces. (i.e. he recaptures on f3 with the pawn and again plays P–KB4). On the other hand, Black's pieces are nicely posted and he has e5 as a transfer point for his knights, rooks, and queen. Other features of the position are White's rook on a2, ready to swing to the centre files,

and Black's option of . . . P–QR3 . . . P–QN4 or . . . P–QR4 (starting counterplay on the queenside or securing c5 for a knight). Although one may speak of some White advantage, both sides have play (see examples in D224). What these two diagrams do indicate is that QP×B is generally more appropriate when Black has already committed himself to . . . P–K5.

With these ideas in mind, we move on to specifics. After 6 0–0:
D221 6 . . . P–Q3
D222 6 . . . B×N
D223 6 . . . R–K1
D224 6 . . . P–K5

D221
      6 . . .   P–Q3
Not very popular, but certainly playable. 6 . . . P–Q3 does have the disadvantage that Black cannot play . . . P–Q4 in one move.
      7 P–Q3
There are few examples; this move will usually transpose into D222. Independent would be **7 Q–B2** P–QR4 (**7 . . . N–Q5** 8 N×N P×N 9 P–QR3! ±; **7 . . . P–KR3** 8 P–QR3 B–R4 9 P–QN4 B–N3 10 P–K3 would be similar to Section C above; **7 . . . Q–K2** 8 P–Q3 P–KR3 9 P–N3! B–KB4 10 P–QR3 B×N 11 Q×B ±) 8 P–Q3 P–KR3 9 P–QR3 B–QB4 10 P–K3, a position akin to Korchnoi–Petrosian of D12 above.
      7 . . .   P–KR3
a) **7 . . . B×N** (best?!) 8 P×B is D222 below.
b) Suetin's suggestion of **7 . . . N–K2!?** is intriguing. White might try **8 B–N5** B×N 9 P×B (9 B×N

B×P) 9 ... N–N3 10 N–Q2 (10
N–R4!?) 10 ... P–KR3 11 B×N
Q×B 12 R–N1 with a structure
closely resembling C22 of Chapter
8, or he could take the rare
opportunity to avoid doubled QBPs
by **8 B–Q2** P–QR4 (8 ... P–B3 9
N–K4! ±) 9 P–QR3 B–QB4 10
R–N1 or 10 N–QR4.
      8 N–Q2!?   B×N?!
    8 ... B–KB4! is only slightly
better for White, in Suetin's
opinion.
      9 P×B   B–Q2?!
    Offhand, **9 ... K–R1!** Δ 10
P–K4 N–KN1 and 11 ... P–B4
looks more accurate. We are
following Suetin-Zilberstein, Kislovodsk 1972: 10 P–K4! K–R1 11
N–N3 P–QN3 12 P–B4 N–KN1 13
P–KB5 P–KN4 14 B–K3 P–B3 15
P–KR4 ±. Once P–KB5 is in, this
e4, d3, c3, c4 pawn formation is
ideal for White.
D222
      6 ...   **B×N**
      7 NP×B
    7 QP×B has the drawbacks
outlined in the introduction
(theoretical overview) to D22 (6
0–0). A sample line would be 7
QP×B P–Q3 8 Q–B2 (8 N–K1
B–K3 9 P–N3 Q–Q2 10 N–B2
B–R6 11 N–K3 N–Q1 12 N–Q5
N–K1! Δ ... P–QB3, ... P–QN4)
8 ... R–K1 9 P–K4 P–QR3(!) 10
P–QR4 P–QN3, reaching the
diagrammed position discussed
there. Since Black's main problems
after 6 ... P–K5 (and often after 6
... R–K1) stem from variations
with QP×B rather than NP×B (see
D224 and D223), 6 ... B×N

appears to be a handy transpositional device (A fact escaping
general notice; indeed, 6 ... P–K5
has been none too successfully
replacing 6 ... B×N in international chess).
      7 ...   P–Q3
    There are important alter-
natives, which may very well be
better, since they reserve the
possibility of playing ... P–Q4 in
one step:
    a) **7 ... R–K1**(!) is mentioned by
Archives, so that on **8 Q–B2**, 8 ...
P–K5 can cross White's intentions
(9 N–N5 Q–K2). Instead, **8 P–Q3**
P–K5 **9 N–Q4**(?) P×P 10 P×P
N×N 11 P×N P–Q4 is good for
Black, and here **9 N–K1** P–Q3
would be D2222, '(b)' below, but
Black also has **9 ... N–K4** or **9 ...
P–Q4**(!). **9 N–N5** is D2241. If
White regroups with **8 N–K1**, in
order to play P–K4, 8 ... P–K5 9
P–B3 P×P 10 N×P P–Q4! is
D22412 below (= or ∓).
    b) **7 ... P–K5** 8 N–N5 and 8 N–K1
are D2241 and D2242 respectively
(Illustrating the advantage of 6 ...
B×N before ... P–K5: White is
committed to recapturing with one
pawn or the other, and Black can
adjust his strategy accordingly.)
    c) **7 ... P–KR3** 8 P–B5?! P–Q4
9 P×Pe.p. Q×P 10 P–Q3 P–K5! 11
N–Q4 P×P 12 N×N P×P 13 Q×P
P×N 14 B–B4 Q–B4 15 KR–B1
B–N5! 16 Q–K5 N–Q4 17 P–B4
P–B3! ∓ Uhlmann-Hecht, Solin-
gen 1974.
      8 P–Q3
    a) **8 N–K1** B–B4 9 N–B2 Q–Q2 10
P–Q3 P–K5 11 N–K3?! (11 B–N5!

and on 11 ... P×P 12 P×P N–KN5, 13 N–Q4 ±) 11 ... P×P 12 N×B Q×N 13 P×P N–K4 14 P–Q4 N×P 15 B×P QR–N1 ∓. Neckart-Podgaets, USSR 1974 (0–1, 41).

b) If White is dissatisfied with the prospect of ... P–K5, he might try Archives' suggestion **8 Q–B2,** which dissuades Black from that move (**8 ... P–K5** 9 N–N5 N–K4 10 N×P ±). **8 ... R–K1** 9 P–K4 P–KR3 10 P–Q3 N–R2 11 N–R4 Δ P–B4 is also ±, so Black does better to respond with **8 ... B–Q2** 9 P–Q3 K–R1, and if 10 P–K4, 10 ... N–KN1 Δ ... P–B4.

After 8 P–Q3, Black decides whether or not to allow 9 P–K4:

D2221 8 ... P–KR3
D2222 8 ... P–K5

There are other ways to forego ... P–K5; in particular, '(a)' illustrates a better-defined Black counterplan than he gets in D221:

a) **8 ... B–Q2** 9 P–K4 (Thematic, but Uhlmann chose **9 N–Q2** in a more successful game versus Zinn in Leipzig, 1973: 9 ... Q–K2 10 N–N3 **B–K3?!** 11 R–N1 QR–N1 12 P–K4! N–Q2 13 Q–K2 – Δ *P–Q4* – 13 ... N–N3 14 B–QR3 P–B4 15 P×P B×P 16 P–B5! (±) N–Q2 17 P×P P×P 18 N–Q2 R–B3? 19 N–B4 N–B4? 20 B×N(6) B×P 21 B–Q5ch K–R1 22 Q–Q2 1–0. Confining analysis to the opening, **10 ... QR–K1** Δ ... P–KR3, ... N–R2 etc. was more pointed.) 9 ... K–R1! (**9 ... P–QR3** 10 P–QR4 N–QR4 11 N–R4 N–K1 12 P–B4 P×P 13 B×P N–QB3 14 N–B3 Q–B1 15 P–Q4 ± Smejkal-Hecht,

Siegen 1970) 10 N–R4 (10 N–K1!? Δ N–B2–K3) 10 ... N–KN1 11 B–K3 B–K3 12 Q–Q2?! (**12 R–N1** P–QN3 13 R–N2! N–K2 14 P–B4 seems a more efficient deployment of White's forces.) 12 ... KN–K2 13 P–B4 P×P 14 B×P P–B3 ∓ Uhlmann-Korchnoi, Leningrad 1973 (½–½, 27).

b) **8 ... K–R1** (trying to save a tempo on (a), but White isn't committed to an early P–K4:) 9 R–N1 N–KN1 10 N–K1 KN–K2 11 N–B2 P–B4? (Black merely cuts off his own bishop here.) 12 P–B4! Q–K1 13 P–K3 R–QN1 14 N–N4 B–Q2 15 N–Q5 N×N 16 P×N N–K2 17 P×P P×P 18 P–B4 P–QN3 19 R–N2! N–N3 20 R(2)–KB2 Q–K2 21 Q–N3 P–N4 22 P×P R×P 23 Q–B3 R–B1 24 P–K4 P×P 25 B–QR3 Q–K1 26 B×P R(4)–N1 27 B×N 1–0 Portisch-Kuijpers, Wyk an Zee 1975 (27 ... Q×B 28 Q×BP!). An irreproachable performance by White.

D2221

8 ... P–KR3

Apparently too casual. Once White plays P–K4, the KRP provides a target for P–KN4–N5, while a counterthrust with ... P–KB4 will be too weakening of the light squares around Black's king.

9 P–K4

9 N–K1 is also logical, since the knight will have to be moved before P–KB4 can be played. Then 9 ... B–K3 **10 P–K4** maintains White's advantage, but **10 P–KB4?** P–K5! 11 P–KB5 B–Q2 is good for Black, since **12 P×P** is met by **12 . . . N–K4** or **12 . . . R–K1**. Balashov-Makarichev, USSR 1973, continued **12 N–B2** N–K4!? 13 N–K3 P×P 14 P×P B–B3 with fine play (0–1, 46).

      9 . . .   P–QR3

  Or **9 . . . N–K2** 10 N–R4 P–KN4 11 N–B3 N–N3? (11 . . . N–R2 12 P–B5-Jansa) 12 N×NP! P×N 13 B×P K–R2 14 P–B4 P×P 15 P×P R–KN1 16 Q–K1! ± Jansa-Bisguier, Skopje 1972.

     10 P–QR4   P–QN3

  10 . . . R–N1 was pointed out by Ljubojević; . . . P–QN4 tends to loosen White's central bind, so this was preferable to the text.

     11 N–R4   B–N5

12 Q–K1 N–QR4 13 R–R3 N–Q2 14 P–R3 B–K3 15 P–B4 P–KB3 (15 . . . P×P 16 P×P – *the point of 12 Q–K1* – 16 . . . N–B4 17 R–B3-Ljubojević. Black's kingside would be in trouble.) 16 Q–Q1 K–R2 17 B–B3!? (Better 17 P–B5) 17 . . . Q–K1?! (17 . . . P×P 18 P×P B×RP 19 R–B2 P–KB4!-Ljubojević) 18 P–B5 B–B2 19 K–N2 R–R1 20 N–N6! B×N 21 P×Bch K–N1 22 B–N4 with a very strong attack, Pfleger-Vasiukov, Manila 1974 (1–0, 42).

D2222

   8 . . .   **P–K5** (*61*)

  As we have seen, White can work up dangerous kingside threats once he achieves P–K4, so this pawn push is the critical continuation.

     9 N–Q4

  The game has become very fluid, and White's best is not at all certain. Important are:

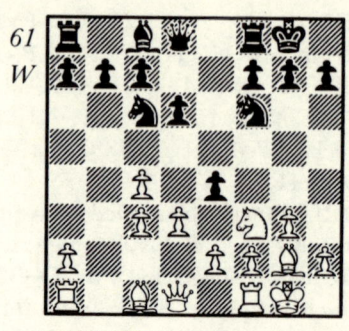

a) **9 N–N5**, which is often suggested, but not often played! Archives gives: 9 . . . P×P 10 P×P B–N5 (**10 . . . P–KR3** 11 N–K4 is similar to, and **10 . . . R–K1** 11 R–N1 transposes to, D22411 below.) 11 Q–B2 R–K1 12 P–KR3 'and Black is not yet rid of his worries.'

b) **9 N–K1(!)** R–K1 10 R–N1 P–QN3?! (**10 . . . P–KR3** looks better. **10 . . . P×P** 11 P×P B–N5 12 N–B3 R–N1 13 P–KR3-Soltis) 11 B–N5 P×P 12 N×P B–N2 13 N–N4 (**13 P–B4!?**, covering e5 and maintaining the bishop on the KR4–Q8 diagonal, is extremely double-edged but promising.) 13 . . . N×N 14 B×B R–N1 15 B–B3 Rogoff-Bisguier, Norristown 1973. White's bishops are very strong. 9 N–K1 needs further tests; evidently Black should improve on his tenth move.

     9 . . .   P×P

  A nice game resulted from **9 . . . N–K4?!** (often recommended) 10 P×P! N×BP 11 R–N1 (±) R–K1?! 12 B–N5! N–N3 (**12 . . . P–KR3?** 13 B×N Q×B?? 14 Q–R4 ± ±) 13 P–B4 P–KR3 14 B–R4 N(N)–Q2 15 N–B5 R–K3 16 P–K5! P×P 17 P×P Q–B1 (**17 . . . R×P** 18 N×Pch P×N 19 B×N) 18 P×N P–KN4 19

N–K7ch K–R1 20 N×B ±±
Christiansen-Shamkovich, USA
1975 (1–0, 27).

10 N×N

10 P×P N×N 11 P×N P–Q4 (as
in the note to 7 . . . P–Q3, where
Black had an extra tempo!) 12
B–N5 **P–B3** = (Archives). 13
R–N1 would keep some play in the
position, but conversion to a win is
unlikely. Here **12 . . . P–KR3?!** is
somewhat worse than 12 . . . P–B3
after 13 B×N Q×B 14 P×P Q×P 15
R–B1.

10 . . .   P×P
11 Q×KP   P×N

12 B×P R–N1 13 B–K3 B–N2 14
B×B R×B 15 P–B5 P×P 16 B×P
R–K1 17 QR–Q1 Q–R1 = Meck-
ing-Korchnoi (8), 1974.

CONCLUSION:

6 . . . B×N 7 NP×B **P–Q3** has
various drawbacks. After **8 P–Q3** (**8
Q–B2** should be considered too), **8
. . . P–KR3**, **8 . . . B–Q2** and other
slow moves give White time to play
P–K4, break open lines, and activate
the dormant bishops. **8 . . . P–K5** is
likely best, but even then White
achieves some pull (e.g. 9 N–K1).
Quite possibly 7 . . . P–Q3 is itself an
inaccuracy, and ought to be replaced
by **7 . . . R–K1(!)** or **7 . . . P–K5**,
which transposes to D224. Again,
the idea would be to eliminate
White's option of QP×B which
causes difficulty in the lines below.

D223

6 . . .   **R–K1**

Rather uncommittal. Black is
willing to face:

D2231 7 N–Q5
D2232 7 P–Q3
D2233 7 N–K1

An obscure attempt was

a) **7 Q–N3 P–K5** 8 N–K1 B×N? 9
NP×B P–Q3 10 N–B2 B–N5 11
R–K1 N–K4?! 12 N–K3 B–K3 13
Q×P N×P 14 P–Q3 ± Fitzgerald-
Krystall; Lone Pine 1974.

Actually, White's queen is
misplaced on b3; **7 . . . P–QR4!** is a
good reply, or 7 . . . P–K5 8 N–K1
P–Q3 (or here 8 . . . B–B4 Δ 9
N–R4 B–B1) 9 N–Q5 B–B4 etc.

b) **7 P–QR3?!** urges Black to
exchange with a gain of tempo: 7
. . . B×N 8 NP×B P–K5 9 N–Q4
N×N 10 P×N P–Q4 11 P–Q3 P–B3
= Lehmann-Ulvestad, Malaga
1964.

D2231

7 N–Q5 (*62*)

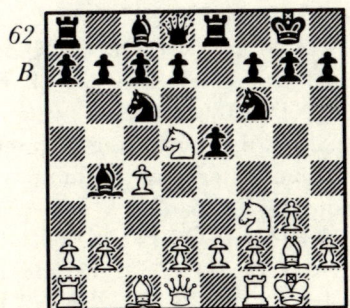

62
B

The standard move in this
position for many years. Now
Black has a whole row of defences:

D22311 7 . . . B–B1
D22312 7 . . . P–K5
D22313 7 . . . B–B4
D22314 7 . . . N×N

D22311

7 ...   B–B1

The original idea behind 6 ... R–K1, but it is too passive.

8 P–Q3   P–KR3

To stop 9 B–KN5. Other moves do not provide relief:

a) **8 ... N–QN5?!** 9 N×Nch Q×N 10 N–N5! P–B3 11 N–K4 Q–Q1 12 B–N5 P–B3 13 B–Q2 N–R3 14 N–B3 P–Q3 15 R–N1 B–K3 16 P–QN4 ± Malich-Golz, East Germany 1971 (1–0, 46).

b) **8 ... N×N** 9 P×N N–N5 10 P–K4 P–QB3 11 P–QR3 N–R3 12 P–Q4 ± Gheorghiu-Jakobsen, Helsinki 1972.

9 B–Q2

White has many moves; all (!) of them appear quite good:

a) **9 N×Nch** Q×N 10 N–Q2 is Petrosian-Gheorghiu of D2232.

b) **9 P–K4** P–Q3 10 P–KR3 P–QR4 11 B–K3 B–Q2? (11 ... N×N) 12 N–B3! N–K2 13 P–Q4 N–N3 14 P–N3 Q–N1 15 Q–B2 P–B3 16 P×P! P×P 17 P–B5 P–QN4?! 18 P×Pe.p. with a positionally crushing game, Furman-Osterman, Ljubljana. (notes by Furman).

c) **9 P–N3** P–Q3 (**9 ... N×N** 10 P×N N–Q5 11 N–Q2 P–QB3 12 N–B4 P–QN4 13 N–Q2! B–N2 14 P–K3 N–B4 15 P×P B×P 16 B–N2 B×B 17 K×B P–Q4 18 Q–B3 Q–Q2 19 QR–B1 and Black cannot challenge the file, Portisch-Filip, Varna, 1962) 10 B–N2 N×N 11 P×N N–K2 12 P–K4 P–QB4 13 P×Pe.p. N×P 14 P–Q4 B–N5 15 P–Q5 N–K2 16 Q–Q3 Q–Q2 17 N–Q2! B–R6 18 P–R4! ±

Rubinstein-Duras, Carlsbad 1911 (!).

d) **9 P–KR3** P–Q3 10 P–K4 N–Q5 11 N×Nch Q×N 12 N×N P×N 13 P–B4 ± Petrosian-Keres, Bled 1950. Compare the mobility of each side's pawns.

9 ...   P–QR4

9 ... P–Q3 10 B–B3 N×N?! 11 P×N N–K2 12 P–K4 P–QB3 13 P×P N×P 14 P–Q4 ± Stein-Barcza, Zagreb 1972.

10 B–B3   P–Q3

11 N–Q2!   N×N!?

White was about to play P–B4, but **11 ... B–Q2** (Gufeld) was nevertheless plausible, to avoid surrender of the centre.

12 P×N   N–K2

13 P–Q4   P×P

14 B×P P–QB4 15 B–QB3 P–QN4 16 P–N3 B–R3 17 P–QR4! P–N5 18 B–N2 (Now White has a significant space advantage and control over c4.) 18 ... N–B1 19 R–K1 N–N3 20 P–K4 Q–Q2 21 R–B1 ± Polugaevsky-Podgaets, Moscow 1973 (1–0, 43).

When all is said and done, 7 ... B–B1 does not inspire confidence!

D22312

7 ...   P–K5

Now **8 N–R4** B–B4 would transpose into D21, but White has another retreat available:

8 N–K1   P–Q3

Usually queried, but **8 ... B–B1** 9 P–Q3 P×P 10 N×P ± is about as promising as **8 ... P–QR4** 9 P–Q3 P×P 10 N×P P–R3 11 B–B4! N×N 12 P×N N–Q5 13 P–K4 B–B1 14 R–B1 P–Q3 15 B–K3 P–QB4 16

P×Pe.p. N×P 17 N–B4 ±
Ermenkov-Grabczewski, Polanica
Zdroj 1973.

9 P–Q3

9 P–Q4!? B×N!? 10 R×B P–KR3
11 P–QR3 B–B4 12 N–K3 B–N3 13
P–QN4 P–Q4 Janosević-Vukic,
Yugoslavia 1973. White doesn't
have much.

9 . . .   B×N

9 . . . B–N5 10 N×Nch Q×N 11
B×P N–Q5 12 P–B3 ± (Mestel).

10 R×B   P×P
11 B–N5! (63)

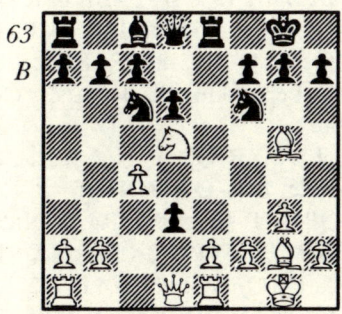

For only a pawn, White gets to
shatter his opponent's kingside.

11 . . .   P×P
12 R×P   R×R
13 Q×R   B–K3
14 N×Nch   P×N
15 B–R4 N–K4 16 B×NP B×P 17
Q–R5 R–N1 18 B–K4 N–N3 19
P–N3 B–R3?! (According to
Mestel, Black had **19 . . . B–K3!**
and if **20 P–B4**, 20 . . . B–Q2 with a
good game. Bukić gives 19 . . .
B–K3 **20 R–K1** ± – presumably
intending R–K3–B3. At any rate,
things now deteriorate past repair:)
20 R–K1 R–N4 21 B–Q5! K–N2
(21 . . . P–B3? 22 Q–R6! R×B 23
B×P etc.) 22 P–R4 R–N5 23 B×P!

Q–Q2 24 B×N P×B 25 B×Pch!
K×B 26 Q–R8ch K–N4 27 P–B4ch
K–N5 28 R–K3 P–N4 29 Q–R6
and White won in a few moves,
Smyslov-Mestel, Hastings 1972/3.

D22313

7 . . .   **B–B4**

Obscure, but not bad.

8 P–Q3   N×N

8 . . . P–KR3 9 N×Nch Q×N 10
N–Q2, as in D2232, or here 9
B–Q2.

9 P×N   N–Q5
10 N–Q2!   P–Q3

11 P–K3 N–B4 12 N–B4 N–K2 13
B–Q2 (13 K–R1!? Δ P–B4) 13 . . .
P–QB3 14 P–QN4 B–N3 15 P×P
P×P 16 P–N5 B–B2! 17 P×P P–Q4
18 N–R3 B–Q3 ½–½ Gheorghiu-
Benko, Las Palmas 1972.

D22314

7 . . .   **N×N**
8 P×N   N–Q5

This and the preceding are the
variations which seem closest to
equality.

9 N–K1

White's best at this point has not
yet been determined:

a) **9 N×N** P×N 10 P–N3 P–QN3
(10 . . . P–Q3!?) 11 B–N2 B–B4 12
P–K3 B–R3 13 R–K1 Q–B3!
Uhlmann-Portisch, Skopje 1972,
and 14 Q–B1 (Δ P–QN4) is
recommended (∞). Instead, 14
Q–B2 P×P! 15 QP×P Q–N3 was
about equal.

b) **9 P–Q3** N×Nch 10 B×N B–B4
11 B–Q2 P–Q3 12 Q–B2?! (12
B–B3; 12 Q–B1!?-Krnić) 12 . . .
B–Q2 13 P–QN4 B–Q5 14 B–B3
B–N3 15 P–QR4 P–QR3 16 P–R5

B–R2 17 QR–B1 R–QB1 18 P–K3
P–KN4 $\mp$ Rogoff-Portisch, Biel
1976.

9 ... P–QB3

Trying to eliminate the cramping d5 pawn; as a side benefit, this
leaves a retreat for the bishop
(perhaps not so vital; see (b)).

a) 9 ... **B–B1** 10 P–K3 N–B4 11
P–N3 P–B4 12 P–B4 P–Q3 13
B–N2 P–QN3 14 B–K4 P×P 15
R×P with only a small advantage,
Uhlmann-Osnos, Zinnowitz 1971.

b) 9 ... **P–Q3** 10 P–K3 N–B4 11
N–B2 (As this knight is flexibly
placed, **11 P–B4!?** – waiting to see
what Black is up to – is probably
somewhat better, e.g. 11 ... P×P
12 R×P B–B4 **13 P–Q4** B–N3 14
N–B2 or here **13 P–QN4** B–N3 14
K–R1 Δ B–N2, Q–B2 etc.) 11 ...
B–B4 12 P–QN4 B–N3 13 B–N2
B–Q2 14 P–QR4 (else ... B–QR5)
14 ... P–QR3 15 P–Q4 (15
K–R1!? Δ P–B4) 15 ... R–QB1 16
Q–Q3 Q–K2 17 P–N5!? P×P 18
P–R5 B–R2 19 P–R6 P×P 20 R×P
B–N3 ∞ Smyslov-Léin, Moscow
1973 ($\frac{1}{2}$–$\frac{1}{2}$, 33).

10 P–K3

10 N–Q3 B–B1 11 P–N3! would
be nice, but 10 ... B–Q3! is better.
Perhaps **10 P–N3!?** Δ 10 ... N–N4
11 N–B2 B–Q3 12 N–K3.

10 ... N–N4!

11 P–Q3 N–B2 12 N–B2 B–B1 13
P×P QP×P 14 Q–K2 B–K3 15
R–Q1 Q–Q2 = Petrosian-Kuzmin,
USSR Ch 1974. Kotov claims a '$\pm$'
after 16 P–N3 B–KN5 17 B–B3 B×B
18 Q×B, but 18 ... QR–Q1 19
B–N2 Q–Q4 20 Q–K2 (20 P–K4?!
Q–K3) 20 ... N–K3 =.

D2232

7 **P–Q3** P–KR3

This (preventing B–KN5) will
usually transpose to D22311, to
which an instructive game is
appended here. Soundest is 7 ...
B×N 8 P×B P–K5, when **9 N–N5** is
D224, **9 N–Q4** is a poor version
of D222 and **9 N–K1** P–Q4!?
appears to give Black the initiative.
Otherwise:

a) **7 ... P–QR4?!** 8 N–Q5 N×N 9
P×N N–Q5 10 N–K1 P–QB3 11
P–K3 N–B4 (11 ... N–N4! $\pm$) 12
N–B2 B–B1 13 P–B4 P×BP 14 R×P
N–K2 15 B–Q2! N×P 16 B×N P×B
17 Q–R5 Q–K2 18 QR–KB1 $\pm\pm$
Stein-Lepeshkin, 33rd USSR Ch
1965.

b) **7 ... P–Q3** 8 N–QR4?! (**8
B–N5!?**; **8 B–Q2**; **8 N–Q5**) 8 ...
B–QB4 9 P–QR3 P–QR4 10 N×B
P×N 11 B–N5 P–R3 12 B×N Q×B
13 N–Q2 Q–K2 14 N–K4 B–N5! 15
N–B3 N–Q5 16 P–N3 P–QB3 $\mp$
Larsen-Ochoa, Spanish Team Ch
1975. Further support for our
argument in C above that N×B after
... B–QB4 is usually bad for White.

8 N–Q5 B–B1
9 N×Nch

For other ninth moves, all
promising, see D22311.

9 ... Q×N
10 N–Q2 P–Q3
11 N–K4 Q–Q1
12 N–B3!

White's manoeuvre has given
him domination of the central light
squares. We are following
Petrosian-Gheorghiu, Moscow
1966, exemplary of the kind of
game many players aim for when

they open 1 P–QB4: 12 . . . B–Q2 13 P–QN4! Q–B1 14 R–N1 B–R6 15 P–K4! (With the light-squared bishops going off, watch where Petrosian puts his pawns . . .) 15 . . . B×B 16 K×B P–KN3 17 P–KR4! B–N2 (?! 17 . . . P–KR4) 18 P–R5 P–KN4 19 N–Q5 (Now Black's bishop is hemmed in by his own pawns, so he works to free it:) 19 . . . N–Q5 20 N–K3 P–KB4 21 B–N2! P×P (21 . . . P–B5? 22 B×N P×B 23 N–B5 would be excruciating!) 22 P×P Q–K3 23 B–B3 P–QN4(?) 24 P×P Q×P 25 Q–Q3 Q–K7 26 Q×Q N×Q 27 N–Q5 QR–N1 28 KR–K1! Perfectly timed! White is winning the endgame handily now (1–0, 41). Petrosian's play set the precedent for a slew of English games involving just his N–Q2–K4–QB3 manoeuvre.

D2233
7 N–K1!?

This knight retreat, planning N–B2, reveals White's intentions rather early; yet one should investigate 7 N–K1 if one is convinced that, say, **7 N–Q5** N×N 8 P×N N–Q5 is prospectless.

    7 . . .   B×N

Black can play a number of useful moves here, e.g. **7 . . . P–KR3** and **7 . . . P–Q3**, but after 8 N–B2 he will probably exchange anyway.

    8 QP×B   P–K5?!

Better **8 . . . P–KR3** Δ . . . P–Q3 (Uhlmann). Or just **8 . . . P–Q3**; the resulting positions would be crucial for the assessment of 7 N–K1; it's a pity we didn't get to see

Uhlmann on the White side of this situation.

The text, by putting pawns on d6 and e4 after QP×B, improves White's game a la the introduction to 6 0–0. His next move explains Black's move order of D224 below:

  9 B–N5!   • P–KR3
  10 B×N   Q×B
  11 N–B2   P–Q3
  12 N–K3   R–K4
12 . . . B–B4 13 P–B4! ± (Uhlmann). We shall see concrete examples of this is D224.

  13 Q–N3!

An instructive comparison with the text was Portisch-Uhlmann, Madrid 1973: **13 Q–B2** B–B4 14 QR–Q1 QR–K1 15 R–Q5 (the same idea as follows 13 Q–N3, but White has a tempo less in the centre, giving Black time for:) 15 . . . N–K2! 16 R×R Q×R 17 Q–R4 N–B3 18 Q–N5 (18 R–Q1!?) 18 . . . Q×Q 19 P×Q N–K2 20 R–Q1 B–Q2 21 P–QB4 P–KB4 = /∞ (½–½, 42).

  13 . . .   R–N1
  14 QR–Q1   P–QN3
  15 Q–B2   B–B4
  16 R–Q5   R(1)–K1
  17 R(1)–Q1

and now Black decided to give up his KP by 17 . . . B–Q2 18 R×R N×R 19 Q×P P–KR4! 20 Q–Q4 N–N5 in Uhlmann-Reshevsky, Skopje 1976. The ending thereafter, very difficult because of White's doubled pawns, is unfortunately not within the scope of this book (but well worth playing over – Informant #21, game 40). White won (deservedly) in 76 moves.

    Instead of **17 . . . B–Q2,**

Uhlmann gives **17 ... R×R?** 18 P×R N–K2 18 N×B ±±, or here 18 ... N–Q1 19 Q–R4 ±±. We should also compare **17 ... N–K2**, as in the Portisch-Uhlmann encounter: 18 R×R Q×R 19 N×B N×N 20 R–Q5 Q–K3 21 Q–R4! (Δ R×N, Q×RP) ±.

CONCLUSION:

6 ... R–K1 almost, but not quite, solves Black's problems. 7 N–Q5 ekes out the edge in every variation (but only does so barely after 7 ... B–B4 or 7 ... N×N); Nor are 7 P–Q3 and 7 N–K1 without bite; in both cases 7 ... B×N is Black's best bet.

D224
   6 ...   **P–K5**
Very much in vogue. White has two replies:
D2241 7 N–KN5
D2242 7 N–K1

D2241
   7 N–KN5   B×N
   8 NP×B
According to our 'rule' above, **8 QP×B** has some logic now that Black's pawn is on e4. In this instance, however, White's knight is a long way from the ideal e3 and d4 squares. 8 ... R–K1 and:
a) **9 N–R3** (Δ N–B4) 9 ... N–K4 10 P–N3 N–N3?! (10 ... P–KR3 or 10 ... P–QN3!) 11 Q–Q4 P–KR3 12 P–B5! P–QN3 13 N–B4 P×P 14 Q×P P–Q3 15 Q–B6 B–Q2 16 Q–B4 N×N 17 B×N Q–B1 18 Q–Q4 (18 KR–Q1!) 18 ... B–R6! 19 P–QB4 B×B 20 K×B R–K3 and

White had a tiny edge in Tal-Liebert, Halle 1974.
b) **9 P–B3** P–Q3! (9 .. P×P and 9 ... P–QN3 are also fine) 10 P–N3 (**10 N×P** N×N 11 P×N N–K4 ∓-Smyslov, or 11 ... B–N5 ∓-Haag) 10 ... B–Q2?! (But here Black should try **10 ... P–QR4!** Δ 11 P–QR4 P×P 12 P×P P–R3 13 N–R3 P–Q4 =) 11 N–R3 P×P 12 P×P N–K2?! (Again **12 ... P–QR4!** and if 13 P–R4, 13 ... N–K4 14 P–B4 N(4)–N5 ∞) 13 B–N5 N–B4 14 Q–Q3! P–KR3 15 B–Q2 N–K2 16 KR–K1 (or **16 P–KN4!** N–N3 17 P–N5 ±) 16 ... B–B4 17 Q–B1 Q–Q2 = Smyslov-Portisch, Petropolis 1973 ($\frac{1}{2}$–$\frac{1}{2}$, 41). Notes based on ones by Haag.

   8 ...   R–K1 (*64*)

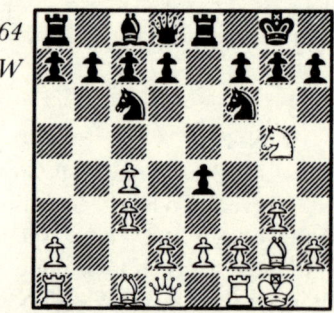

64
W

Now for a major decision:
D22411 9 P–Q3
D22412 9 P–B3
   9 Q–B2?! was effective in Gheorghiu-Bisguier, Buenos Aires 1970: 9 ... Q–K2?! 10 P–Q3 P×P 11 P×P P–QN3 12 N–K4 N×N 13 B×N B–N2 14 R–K1 K–R1 15 B–B4! N–R4 16 B×B ±. But the correct answer is obviously 9 ... P–Q4! e.g. 10 P×P Q×P 11 P–Q3 B–B4! ∓ Padevsky-Ciocaltea, Vrnjacka Banja 1974.

D22411

9 P–Q3	P×P
10 P×P	P–Q3

a) The main alternative is Bronstein's **10 ... P–KR3** 11 N–K4 P–QN3!? Then 12 B–B4 (**12 P–B5!?** N×N 13 B×N **P×P** 14 B–R3 Q–K2 15 Q–R4 has been recommended; perhaps **13 ... Q–B3** or **13 ... R–N1!?**) 12 ... B–N2 and:

a1) **13 Q–Q2** (eyeing h6) 13 ... N–QR4? (Better is 13 ... N×N 14 B×N N–QR4-Sofresky; but 15 P–B3! still leaves Black a bit short of equality.) 14 P–B3! P–Q3 15 QR–K1 N–Q2 16 B–R3! N–K4 17 B×RP! P–Q4 18 P×P Q×P 19 R–Q1 ±± Sofresky-Hadzimanev, Yugoslavia 1975;

a2) **13 R–K1** N–QR4 14 P–B3 (A recent attempt was 14 P–B5!?, when 14 ... N×N 15 B×N B–B3! Δ ... N–N2 ∞ is Taimanov's suggestion. Much worse was 14 ... P×P? 15 Q–R4! B×N 16 P×B N–B3 17 P–K5 N–R2 18 QR–Q1 ± Romanishin-Taimanov, Leningrad 1977.) 14 ... P–Q4! 15 N×Nch Q×N 16 Q–Q2 P–B4 17 P×P B×P 18 P–Q4 Q–B3! and Black had a beautiful game in Taimanov-Bronstein, Tallin 1975.

b) The immediate **10 ... P–QN3** is possible: 11 R–N1 R–N1 12 B–QR3!? B–N2 13 P–Q4 Hendrickson-Kull, Colorado 1975, and 13 ... N–K2! would level the game.

11 R–N1	P–KR3

Too meandering was **11 ... N–K4?** 12 P–B4 N(4)–Q2 (**12 ... N(4)–N5** 13 B×P R–N1 14 B×B!-Pachman) 13 R–N2! P–KR3 14

N–R3! N–B4 15 P–B5! B–Q2 16 P–KN4 B–R5?! 17 Q–B3 N(3)–Q2 18 Q–N3 B–B3 19 P–N5 P×P 20 P–B6! P–N5 21 P×P! N–K3 22 Q×NP N–K4 23 Q–N3 N–N3 24 N–N5 N×N 25 B×N Q–B1 26 R(2)–B2 Q–K3 27 B–R3 Q–K4 28 R×P Q×Qch 29 P×Q R–K4 30 B–R6 1–0 Dueball-Reichenbach, Mannheim 1975.

12 N–K4

12 N–R3 N–K4 13 P–B4 N(4)–N5 14 N–B2!? (Supposedly Black gets compensation for his pawn after **14 B×P** B×B 15 R×B N–K6 – *15 ... Q–B1!? 16 R–N2!* ± – 16 B×N R×B. With the White knight still on g5, this would have been answered by R–B3, and if ... Q–K1, N–K4. Yet 17 R–B3 is possible here, too: 17 ... Q–K1 18 R×R Q×Rch 19 N–B2. So is 14 B×P the move?!) 14 ... P–B3! 15 P–KR3 N–K6 16 B×N R×B 17 K–R2 P–Q4 18 Q–Q2 R–K2 19 P×P P×P = Bagirov-Vaganian, Tbilisi 1973.

12 ... N×N

12 ... N–K4 is also feasible, e.g. 13 P–B4 (**13 R–K1?** N×N 14 B×N B–N5!; 13 P–B3?! R–N1 14 N–B2 P–QN3 15 P–N4 P–Q4 ∓ Helmers-Littlewood, Kringsja 1978) 13 ... N(4)–N5 14 P–KR3 (14 P–B5!? would be more enterprising.) 14 ... N×N 15 P×N(K) N–B3 16 P–K5?! P×P 17 Q×Q R×Q 18 P×P N–Q2 19 B–Q5 N×P 20 B–B4 P–B3 etc.

13 B×N	N–K4
14 P–B4!	N×P
15 P–B5	

White has an attack for his pawn.

This is Mecking-Tan, Petropolis 1973, in which Black defended stoutly for a while and then strayed: 15 . . . P–Q4 16 B–KN2 N–K6 17 B×N R×B 18 P–B6 P–N3 19 Q–Q2 R–K3! 20 Q×P R×P 21 R×R Q×R 22 B×P B–B4! 23 R×P R–Q1 24 B–B4 Q×BP?? (24 . . . B×QP! = -Gheorghiu) 25 B×Pch! K×B 26 R×Pch Q×R 27 Q–R7ch ±±.

D22412
   9 P–B3(?!)
Smyslov's variation, from both sides of the board!
   9 . . .   P×P
   9 . . . P–K6? 10 P–Q3!
   10 N×P(3)
   10 P×P P–Q4!; 10 B×P N–K4.
   10 . . .   P–Q4
   10 . . . Q–K2 11 P–K3 P–Q3 12 P–Q3 (**12 R–N1** R–N1 13 Q–B2 N–K4 14 P–Q3 N×Nch 15 R×N P–QN3 16 P–K4 N–Q2! 17 P–KR3 N–K4 18 R–B2 B–K3 = Giardelli-Winston, World Junior Ch 1974) 12 . . . B–N5 13 P–KR3 B–Q2 14 P–K4 P–KR3 15 R–N1 QR–N1 (15 . . . P–QN3-Sokolov) 16 N–R4 N–K4 17 B–K3 P–QN3 18 N–B5 B×N 19 R×B ± N(3)–Q2 20 Q–KB1 N–B1 21 P–Q4 N(4)–Q2 22 Q–Q3 N–R2 23 R(1)–B1 with a crushing game, Smyslov-Peev, Cienfuegos 1973. An impressive demonstration of the power of two bishops and a central pawn mass!
   11 P×P   Q×P!
   11 . . . N×P?! 12 P–K4! (**12 P–B4** N–N3 13 P–Q3 B–N5 14 R–N1 Q–K2 = Sliwa-Smyslov,

Polanica Zdroj 1966) 12 . . . N–N3?! (**12 . . . R×P?** 13 N–N5 R–K2 14 Q–R5 ±±; **12 . . . N–B3** 13 P–K5! N×P 14 N×N R×N 15 P–Q4 **R–K1** 16 B–N5-Archives and Bukić; but **15 . . . R–K3!** would be better here, so 12 . . . N–B3 looks like Black's best bet.) 13 P–Q4 B–N5 14 P–KR3 (Even better seems to be **14 Q–N3!** N–R4 15 Q–B2 N(4)–B5?! 16 P–K5 P–KR3 17 N–R4! P–QB3? – *17 . . . B–K3 18 N–B5! ± -Sher* – 18 B×RP! P×B 19 R×P! K×R 20 Q–N6ch K–K2 21 Q–N7ch K–K3 22 Q×Bch ±± Sher-Zahartchenko, USSR 1973.) 14 . . . B–R4 15 P–K5 N–Q4 16 B–Q2 Q–Q2 17 P–N4 B–N3 18 N–N5! N–R4 19 P–KR4! P–KR3 20 P–R5! with a decisive attack, Uhlmann-Smyslov, Hastings 1972/3.
   12 N–Q4
A good move is hard to find e.g. **12 P–Q4?!** worked out poorly in Ribli-Vasiukov, Camaguey 1974: 12 . . . Q–KR4 13 R–N1 N–K5 (or **13 . . . Q–R4!** 14 P–K4!? N×KP 15 N–K5 R×N! ∓ Tasić-Ciocaltea, Nice 1974) 14 Q–Q3 N–Q3! 15 Q–Q1 B–B4 16 R–N2 B–K5 ∓ (0–1, 38).
   12 . . .   Q–KR4!
   13 N×N   P×N
   14 P–K3
Not **14 B×P??** Q–B4ch ∓∓.
   14 . . .   B–N5
From this position the action has been fierce:
a) **15 B–B3** Q–N3! (preventing 16 R–N1!) 16 B×B N×B 17 Q–K2 QR–Q1 18 B–R3 P–KR4 Uhlmann-Makarichev, Amster-

dam 1975. Black is somewhat better due to White's humdrum bishop and airy position.

b) **15 Q–R4!?** R–K3(?) (**15 ...
B–K7!**-Makarichev. Then if 16 R×N, 16 . . . B–N4! This appears to be the way to play it after 15 Q–R4, and may virtually refute 9 P–B3. Both 16 R–B2 and 16 R–B4 are well met by 16 . . . N–N5!) 16 B–QR3! (Completely turning the tables on **16 R–N1?** B–K7 17 R–K1 N–N5 18 P–KR3 Q–KB4! 19 R×B Q×R 20 R–K1 – 20 Q×N? **Q×Bch** 21 K–R2 R–Q1 ∓∓ Sigurjonsson-Smyslov, Reykjavik 1974 – **20 ...
N–K4** 21 B–K4 Malich-Peev, Varna 1974 and now 21 . . . Q–N3! would have kept the advantage.) 16 . . . B–K7 (**16 . . . R–Q1** 17 Q×RP! R×QP 18 R×N ±±-Ciocaltea) 17 R–B4 P–N4?! 18 R–B5 B–Q6 19 R×N! R×R 20 Q–Q4 Q–N3 21 P–K4 B–K7 22 P–B4 ± (Δ B–N2, R–K1, P–K5) Stefanov-Kertesz, Romanian Ch 1977.

So if you can just improve on 15 Q–R4 B–K7 for White, you might be interested in playing 9 P–B3!

CONCLUSION:

6 . . . P–K5 7 N–KN5 B×N 8 NP×B R–K1 9 P–Q3 should not frighten Black away from this line, although White seems to get a slight pull if he is careful. 9 P–B3, on the other hand, is probably just a mistake, unless a bright new idea appears around move 12 or 15.

D2242
7 N–K1

A sensible continuation, avoid-

ing the fireworks of D2241.

7 ...   B×N

Black usually exchanges now, since the coming N–B2 encourages this trade anyway; and he may fear N–Q5 in the meantime, e.g. **7 ...
R–K1** 8 N–Q5 B–B4 9 P–Q3.

8 QP×B (!)

As we have mentioned before, this capture makes sense once Black is committed to . . . P–K5. **8 NP×B** used to be more common, when 8 . . . R–K1 9 N–B2(*65*) (for **9 P–Q3**

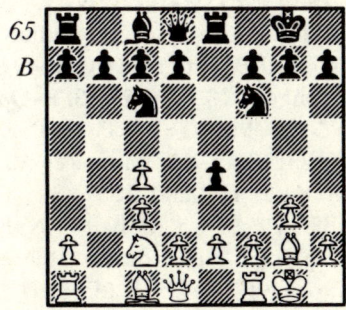

P–Q3, see D222; or 9 . . . P–Q4!? 10 P×KP ∞) gives a position that can also arise from Chapter 4, i.e. 3 P–KN3 B–N5 4 B–N2 0–0 5 N–B3 R–K1 6 0–0 P–K5 7 N–Q4 N–B3 8 N–B2 B×N 9 NP×B. White has more central pawns than after QP×B, but has not done much about Black's expansionist tendencies (see especially (c)):

a) **9 . . . N–K4** 10 P–B5! (**10 N–K3** P–QN3! 11 P–Q3 B–N2-Kapengut) 10 . . . P–QN3 11 P×P RP×P 12 P–Q3 P×P 13 P×P (13 B×R? B–R3!) 13 . . . P–Q4 (13 . . . R–R4-Kapengut) 14 B–N5 B–N5 15 P–B3 B–B4 16 N–N4 P–QB3 17 Q–Q2 B–Q2 18 P–KB4 N–N3 19 P–B4 ± Tseitlin-Grigorian, USSR Ch

1972. Black's centre is rotting away.

b) **9 . . . P–Q3** 10 N–K3 N–K4 (**10 . . . N–KN5** 11 N–Q5 N(5)–K4 12 P–Q3 P×P 13 P×P B–N5 14 P–B3 B–B4 15 P–B4!? N×QP 16 P–N4 N×B 17 P×B N–K7ch 18 K–R1 N–R4 – *18 . . . Q–R5 19 Q–K1 ±* – 19 R–K1 P–QB3 20 R×N R×R 21 Q×R P×N 22 B×P Q–B3 23 R–K1 R–KB1 ∞!-Kapengut) 11 P–Q3 P×P 12 P×P N(3)–N5 (**12 . . . P–B3** 13 R–N1 Q–R4 14 Q–B2 N(4)–Q2 **15 R–K1?!** N–N3 16 B–Q2 B–K3 = Tal-Holmov, Tbilisi 1969; better was **15 P–Q4!**- Kapengut) 13 N–Q5 (**13 P–Q4?** N×N 14 P×N(3) N×P 15 P–K4 P–QB3 16 Q–R5 Langeweg-Van den Berg, Holland 1961; 16 . . . P–B3! ∓) 13 . . . B–B4 14 N–B4 'cramping the Black pieces' (Kapengut), e.g. 14 . . . P–KN4 15 N–R3!.

c) **9 . . . P–Q4(!)** 10 P×P Q×P **11 P–Q4?** Q–KR4 (or 11 . . . Q–B5- Kapengut) 12 P–QB4 P–QR3! 13 B–B4 P–QN4! with Black advantage (e.g. 14 P×P P×P 15 B×BP? N–Q4 and 16 . . . N–B6 etc.) Bobotsov-Fuchs, Sochi 1966. Somewhat better is **11 N–K3** Q–KR4 12 P–B3, but Black stands well in any case. See the discussion in the 'theoretical overview' (note to 6 0–0).

    8 . . .   P–KR3

Usually played here, to prevent B–N5 e.g. **8 . . . R–K1 9 B–N5!** is D2233 above (Uhlmann-Resh- evsky), where Black fails to equalize. Here are some other examples with 8 . . . R–K1 **9 N–B2**, important

because of the move order 7 . . . R–K1 8 N–B2 B×N 9 QP×B:

a) **9 . . . P–Q3** (8 . . . P–Q3 9 N–B2 R–K1 is the same) 10 B–N5 (**10 N–K3** P–KR3 transposes to the main line; this was the order of Korchnoi-Necking, (9), 1974, discussed below) 10 . . . P–KR3 11 B×N Q×B 12 N–K3 B–B4?! (**12 . . . R–K4** is D2233) 13 P–B4! Q–N3 14 Q–Q5 B–K3 15 P–KB5! B×Q 16 P×Q B–K3 17 B×P B×P 18 B–Q5! R×N 19 B×B N–K4 20 B×Pch K–R1 21 R–B4 ± Averbach- Chavksy, Riga 1961.

b) **9 . . . N–K4** 10 P–N3 P–KR3 (an improvement on **10 . . . P–Q3** 11 B–N5 – *11 P–KR3?! P–KR3 12 K–R2 P–QN3 13 N–K3 B–N2 was rather pointless for White in Schmidt-Lewi, Lublin 1969* – 11 . . . N(4)–Q2 12 Q–Q4 P–KR3 13 B×N N×B 14 N–K3 Q–K2 15 QR–K1 B–Q2 16 P–B4 P×Pe.p. 17 P×P ± Olafsson-Smyslov, Bled 1959; or here 15 N–Q5 ±) 11 P–B4! P×Pe.p. 12 P×P P–Q3 13 N–K3 B–Q2 14 P–QR4 Q–B1 15 R–R2 B–R6 16 R–K1 B×B Ribli-Browne, Manila 1976. Now 17 R×B Δ P–KN4, N–B5 ± (Ribli) or 17 K×B as played leaves White on top, but in both cases only very slightly.

    9 N–B2   R–K1

Again reaching a position which could have arisen from Chapter 4, i.e. 3 P–KN3 B–N5 4 B–N2 0–0 5 N–B3 R–K1 6 0–0 P–K5 7 N–Q4 N–B3 8 N–B2 B×N 9 QP×B P–KR3.

a) **9 . . . P–Q3 10 N–K3** transposes, but independent was **10 B–K3!?** R–K1 11 P–B5! P–Q4?! (11 . . . P×P ±) 12 B–Q4 N×B 13 Q×N with a clearcut positional edge, Sokolov-Mapanyiuk, 1977.

b) **9 ... P–QN3** is typical of this variation, and informative: 10 N–K3 B–N2 11 N–Q5 (**11 P–N3** Δ 12 P–QR4, 13 R–R2, and 14 P–B4!-Botvinnik) 11 ... N–K4 12 P–N3 R–K1 13 P–QR4 P–Q3 14 R–R2 (**14 P–B4! P×Pe.p.** 15 P×P ± or **14...N(4)–Q2** 15 N–K3± or **14 ... N×N** 15 P×N N–Q2 16 P–B4 ±-Botvinnik) 14 ... N(4)–Q2 15 P–KR3 P–QR4 (**15 ... P–QR3!**-Botvinnik; see note below) 16 B–K3 N×N 17 P×N Q–B3 18 P–QB4 Q–N3 19 Q–N1 B–B1 20 B–Q4 (**20 P–QN4!** P×P 21 Q×P R–R4 22 Q–N3 N–B4 23 Q–B2 B–Q2 24 R(1)–R1 ± Δ B–Q2 and P–R5 is a fantastic suggestion by Botvinnik.) 20 ... N–B4 21 K–R2 B–Q2 22 R–N1 P–KR4 = Korchnoi-Karpov (9), 1974.

One gets the impression that '±'s such as those in the notes to moves 14 and 20 are not convertible to wins against careful defence. Another feature of this game is the move ... P–QR4, which in several later contests was replaced by ... P–QR3 Δ ... P–QN4; this latter idea is more flexible and denies White too leisurely a build-up.

10 N–K3

10 P–KR3 P–Q3 is (by transposition) Etruk-Tal, Parnau 1971: 11 P–N3 B–Q2 12 B–K3 **Q–B1?!** 13 P–KN4! and White got attacking chances. The idea of P–KR3 and P–KN4 should not be dangerous, however; **12 ... N–K2** was easier, intending ... N–B4, e.g. 13

P–KN4 N–N3 14 P–N5? (but otherwise ... N–R5 and ... Q–K2) 14 ... N–R4! 15 P×P Q–R5 etc.; or simply **11 ... N–K4** Δ ... P–QN3, ... B–N2.

10 ...   P–Q3 (*66*)

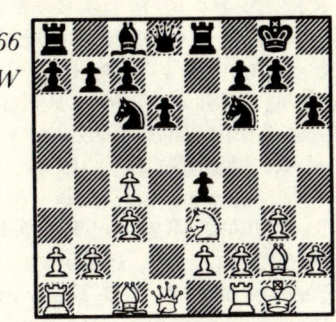

10 ... P–QN3 is again possible: 11 Q–B2?! (**11 P–N3!**-Keres; **11 P–B4!?** P×Pe.p. 12 P×P B–N2 13 N–Q5! ± N×N 14 P×N N–K2 15 P–QB4 N–B4 16 Q–Q3 Q–B3 Ungureanu-Ogaard, Bucharest 1976 and now 17 B–R3! – Gheorghiu – would emphasize the strength of White's bishops.) 11 ... B–N2 12 B–Q2 (12 P–N3) 12 ... N–K4 13 QR–Q1 Q–K2 14 P–KR3? Q–K3 15 P–N3 N–B6ch! 16 K–R1 (Taking would be fatal.) 16 ... Q–K4 17 B–B1 Q–KR4 with an ongoing attack, Hernandez-Olafsson, Tallin 1975 (but ½–½, 28).

The diagrammed position has been seen often in international tournaments. White has an interesting choice of ideas:
D2241 11 P–N3
D2242 11 P–B4
D2243 11 Q–B2

D22421
   11 P–N3   P–QR4

Black can also reply with **11 . . . N–K4**, but he might not like 12 P–B4.

12 N–Q5

12 P–QR4 P–QN3 13 Q–B2!? (13 R–R2) 13 . . . B–N2 14 N–Q5 N–N1! 15 R–Q1 N(1)–Q2 16 P–KR3 N–B4 17 B–K3 B–B3 18 B–Q4 N×N 19 P×N B–Q2 20 QR–N1 Q–N4 ½–½ Polugaevsky-Holmov, Moscow 1969. Perhaps White should have played on, e.g. 21 K–R2 (Δ B×N) 21 . . . Q–N3 22 R–N2, preparing Botvinnik's plan of R–R1, R(2)–R2, and P–QN4.

12 . . .   P–R5!?

Perhaps just **12 . . . B–B4**, which is the usual response to an early N–Q5. We are following Portisch-Hecht. Teesside 1972: 13 B–K3 B–B4 14 Q–B2 B–R2 15 QR–Q1 N–KN5 16 P–B5 RP×P 17 P×P P×P 18 B×BP P–K6 19 Q–B1 P×Pch 20 K–R1 Q–B1 ∞.

D22422
11 P–B4

Directly denying Black's pieces access to e5. Now if **11 . . . P×Pe.p.** 12 P×P, White will play for P–B4 and central control. Compare **11 Q–B2** below.

11 . . .   N–K2!

Trying for a light-square blockade on the king's wing, where White is intending to expand. On **11 . . . N–KN5**, White can play 12 N–Q5!?

12 P–KR3   N–B4

12 . . . P–KR4? 13 P–KB5 ±.

13 P–KN4(?!)

13 N×N!? B×N 14 P–KN4 (Holmov). He gives no assessment, but Black's resources seem

adequate, e.g. 14 . . . B–Q2 15 B–K3 B–B3 **16 B–Q4** P–K6! 17 B×B P×B 18 R–B3 P–B4! 19 B×KP N–K5, an idea of Rogoff's. Here **16 Q–K1** would be met by 16 . . . P–QR3 Δ . . . P–QN4, eating away at White's bind on the centre, which is paradoxically the function of his doubled pawns.

13 . . .   N×N

14 B×N   P–KR4!

15 P–N5 N–R2 16 P–QB5 (16 P–KR4 P–KN3) 16 . . . P×P 17 B×P B–B4 18 Q–B2 Q–Q4 19 B–K3 Q–K3 20 K–R2 N–B1 21 QR–Q1 QR–Q1 Holmov-Vaganian, Moscow 1975. Black has achieved the desired blockade.

D22423
11 Q–B2

Most often seen. White ties Black to the defence of his KP and clears d1 for a rook.

11 . . . .   P–QN3

The best move has not been determined, and all of the following deserve consideration:

a) **11 . . . N–K4!?** (anyway!) 12 P–KR3 (Kavalek says the pawn on e4 cannot be touched, but 12 B×P!? N×P – *12 . . . N×B 13 Q×N B–R6 14 R–K1 ±* – 13 B–N2 appears minimally better for White.) 12 . . . B–K3?! (12 . . . P–QN3) 13 P–N3 P–QR4 14 P–QR4 N(4)–Q2 15 P–B4! P×P 16 P×P P–Q4? (But **16 . . . N–B4** 17 P–QN4! or **16 . . . N–B1** 17 P–B4 are ±.) 17 P–B4! P×P 18 P–B5 P×P 19 Q–B2 N–K4 20 P×B R×P (**20 . . . N–Q6** 21 P×Pch K×P 22 Q–B5 ±± - Kavalek) 21 N–Q5! with a decisive attack, Ftačnik-Vera, Groningen 1976.

b) **11 ... P–QR4** 12 R–Q1 (Here **12 P–B4** and **12 P–QR4** deserve a look.) 12 ... P–QN3 13 .P–N3 R–N1 14 P–QR4 N–K4 15 N–Q5 N×N 16 P×N P–KB4 17 P–QB4 B–Q2 18 B–N2 Q–N4 19 Q–B3 N–N5 20 R–K1 R–K2 21 P–B4! Q–N3 22 P–K3 P–R4 23 Q–Q2 K–B2 24 P–N4 ± Korchnoi-Mecking Match (9), 1974.

c) **11 ... R–K4** is often recommended, but not really too useful:

c1) **12 R–Q1** B–K3?! 13 P–B4! P×Pe.p. 14 P×P R–KR4 (else P–B4–B5) 15 Q–B2 B–Q2 16 P–B4 N–KN5 17 Q–B3 N×N 18 B×N R–R4 19 P–QB5! Q–QB1 20 Q–B2 P×P 21 B×P ± Hardicsay-Peev, Olomouc 1976;

c2) **12 B–Q2** B–Q2 (12 ... P–QN3!?) 13 P–B4 P×Pe.p. 14 P×P Q–QB1 (**14 ... R–K1** 15 QR–K1 N–K2? – *15 ... Q–B1-Minić* – 16 P–QN4! Q–B1 17 R–B2 P–QR4 18 R(B)–K2 ± Uhlmann-Jansa, Amsterdam 1975) 15 KR–K1 R–K1 16 N–Q5 N×N 17 R×Rch! Q×R 18 P×N N–K4 19 P–QB4 with a small advantage, Polugaevsky-Savon, Petropolis 1973 (½-½, 32).

d) **11 ... N–N1** (to get to d7 without sacrificing the KP as in (a)) 12 B–Q2 (**12 P–N3** Δ N–Q5) 12 ... P–QN3 13 P–B4 QN–Q2 14 QR–Q1 B–N2 15 B–K1 P–QR3! 16 P–KN4 P–QN4 17 P–KR3 R–N1 = Szilagyi-Cipslis.

12 B–Q2?!

As usual, White's best is probably

a) **12 P–B4!** and if **12 ... P×Pe.p.** 13 P×P B–N2, 14 P–B4 (14 ... N–QR4? 15 P–QN4!). Uhlmann-Tan, Manila 1976 continued: **12 ... B–Q2** 13 B–Q2 (? The immediate **13 P–KR3!** Δ P–KN4 seems preferable.) 13 ... N–K2! 14 P–KR3 N–B4 15 N×N B×N 16 P–KN4 B–Q2 17 B–K1 Q–K2 18 B–R4 P–KR4! 19 P×P (**19 P–B5** P×P 20 P×P Q–K4) 19 ... B–B4 20 P–R6? P×P 21 K–R2? N–N5ch! and Black was winning, since 22 K–N3 N–K6 is hopeless. White's play is clearly improvable.

b) **12 P–N3** P–QR4 13 B–N2?! (**13 P–B4**) 13 ... B–Q2 14 QR–Q1 P–R5!? 15 B–B1 P×P 16 P×P R–R4! 17 N–Q5 B–B4 18 B–K3 N–K4! = Savon-Vaganian, USSR Ch 1974.

12 ...   N–K4!

13 QR–Q1 (This time the KP really *is* mined: 13 B×P N×B 14 Q×N B–R3! 15 Q–Q5 – *15 Q–Q4 P–Q4!* – 15 ... P–QB3 16 Q–Q4 P–Q4!-Rogoff) 13 ... N(4)–N5! 14 P–KR3 N×N 15 B×N Q–K2 16 B–Q4 B–B4 17 Q–B1 Q–K3! 18 P–KN4 B–N3 19 P–N3 P–QB4! ½-½ Petrosian-Rogoff, Biel 1976. 20 B–K3 P–Q4 ∓ (Rogoff).

CONCLUSION:

The variations beginning with 6 ... P–K5 offer Black some of his best counterplay in this Main Line English, e.g. after **7 N–KN5** B×N 8 NP×B R–K1 9 P–B3?! But with accurate play, especially after **7 N–K1** B×N 8 QP×B, White retains the two bishops and excellent long-term chances. Thus far, no sure defensive plan has been found for Black, although systems involving ... P–QN3 seem closest to equalizing.

As for 4 P–KN3 B–N5 in general, the reader may be a bit overwhelmed by the sheer number of games I have quoted. For one thing, I wanted to be sure that he could trace a game he finds to a specific section where specific move orders are analyzed. That doesn't mean that one is obliged to memorize, say, note (b) to D2242. Whether one is Black or White, what is important in this instance is a careful study of the ideas and their timing, and the acquisition of over-the-board experience.

8 MAIN LINE: 4 'OTHERS'

1	P–QB4	P–K4
2	N–QB3	N–KB3
3	N–B3	N–B3

Not all English Opening players are satisfied with the kind of game produced by 4 P–KN3 (Chapter 7). Some feel that Black's resources are sufficient in these lines, and others that the body of theory is just too large to handle. Here we look at various fourth-move alternatives to 4 P–KN3.

The classical 4 P–Q4 is not often played these days, owing both to the difficulty of handling the White pieces and to several excellent Black defensive systems. 4 P–K4 is an outdated Nimzowitsch idea which is still playable but somewhat limited in scope. The other moves—4 P–Q3, 4 P–QR3 and 4 P–K3—are 'reversed Sicilian' attempts (for more on this topic, see Chapter 11), of which 4 P–K3 is the most often seen and currently the subject of much debate. Finally we speculate on 4 Q–R4, a completely new perception of the problem.

A 4 P–Q4
B 4 P–K4
C 4 P–Q3
D 4 P–QR3
E 4 P–K3
F 4 Q–R4

4 P–QN3 is a bit humdrum: 4 . . . P–Q4 (**4 . . . P–KN3** is not bad either.) 5 P×P N×P 6 P–B6 B–N2 N×N (or **6 . . . B–KN5**) 7 B×N B–Q3 8 P–Q3 0–0 9 P–K3 Q–K2 (**9 . . . P–B4** 10 P–Q4 ∞ -Gipslis) 10 B–K2 B–Q2 11 0–0 QR–Q1 12 N–Q2? (**12 Q–Q2** Δ Q–N2, P–QR3 is preferable.) 12 . . . P–B4 13 N–B4 P–B5 14 N×B Q×N! 15 P×P R×P 16 B–B3 R(1)–KB1 17 B–K4 N–Q5! 18 B–Q2 R(5)–B2 19 B×P P–B3 20 B–QR6 Q–N3 21 B–QB4 B–R6 ∓ Korchnoi-Gipslis, USSR 1976. At the least, Black will recover his pawn with a strong attack (but 1–0, 47 after severe errors).

A

4 P–Q4

Formerly the main line of the English! The defences to this move are so convincing, however, that P–Q4 has become one of the *least* popular of White's fourth moves! Reti, and later Botvinnik, did a lot of the groundwork on this variation; today, Raicević stands out as its most faithful practitioner.

Black has two main replies:

A1 4 . . . P–K5
A2 4 . . . P×P

4 . . . P–Q3 5 P–KN3 is discussed in Chapter 9, C31, and **5 P–Q5** (Taimanov) can't be bad either.

A1

$\qquad$ **4 . . .** $\qquad$ **P–K5** (67)

67
W

5 N–Q2

Innocuous or worse are:

a) **5 P–Q5** P×N 6 P×N P×KP (or 6 . . . P×NP =) 7 P×Pch Q×P 8 B×P Q×Qch 9 B×Q B–K3 10 B–K2 0–0–0 11 P–QR3 B–QB4 with slight Black initiative, Kramer-Seitz, 1930.

b) **5 N–K5** B–N5 6 B–N5 (6 N×N QP×N =) 6 . . . P–KR3 7 B×N Q×B 8 N×N P–K6! 9 P×P QP×N 10 Q–N3 Q–R5ch 11 K–Q2 P–QB4 12 P–N3 Q–N4 (Taimanov incorrectly gives Alekhine's move as **12 . . . Q–K5**, but that is also strong!) 13 P×P Q×BP 14 P–QR3 B×Nch 15 Q×B 0–0 ∓∓ Bigelov-Alekhine, Bredlay Beach 1929.

c) **5 N–KN5** P–KR3 (**5 . . . Q–K2?** 6 P–Q5 N–K4 7 P–K3 P–KR3 8 N(5)×P N×N 9 N×N N×P 10 N–B3! ±; **5 . . . B–N5 6 P–Q5!** - Shatskes, or **6 N–R3!** -Schwarz) 6 P–Q5 (6 N(5)×P N×N 7 N×N Q–R5 **8 N–B3** Q×QP 9 P–K3 Q×Qch 10 K×Q B–K2 = Gerstenfeld-Lilienthal, USSR Ch 1940; in this line **8 Q–Q3?** loses to 8 . . . P–Q4! 9 P×P N–N5 10 Q–N1 B–B4 11 N–Q6ch P×N! 12 Q×B P–KN3 13 Q–N1 R–B1 ∓∓ -

Sudnitsyn) 6 . . . P×N 7 P×N B–B4 8 P×NP B×P 9 P–K3 Q–K2 10 P–QR3 P–R4 11 B–K2 B–B3 12 P–R3?! P–R5 ∓ Kostic-Opocensky, Prague 1931.

After 5 N–Q2, then:
A11 5 . . . N×P
A12 5 . . . B–N5

5 . . . P–K6 6 P×P might be 'justified' by **6 . . . B–N5** 7 P–QR3 B×N 8 P×B **P–Q4** ∞, although here **8 . . . 0–0?!** 9 P–K4 P–Q3 10 P–K3 would be more picturesque! A game of Sokolsky's saw **6 . . . P–Q4 (?)** 7 P×P N×P(4) 8 N–B3 B–N5, and now 9 Q–Q3! ± is Shatskes' suggestion.

A11

$\qquad$ **5 . . .** $\qquad$ **N×P**

Direct and sufficient.

$\qquad$ 6 N(2)×P $\qquad$ N×N

6 . . . N–K3 7 P–KN3 N×N 8 N×N B–N5ch 9 B–Q2 B×Bch 10 Q×B 0–0 11 B–N2 P–Q3 12 0–0 B–Q2 13 N–B3 B–B3 14 N–Q5 P–QR4 15 P–K4 N–B4 = Botvinnik-Flohr (5), 1933. Botvinnik recommended **7 P–QR3** instead, but 7 . . . P–KN3 looks about equal. Probably **7 N×Nch** Q×N 8 N–Q5 Q–Q1 9 P–KN3 is as good as anything.

$\qquad$ 7 Q×N $\qquad$ N×N
$\qquad$ 8 Q×N

8 P×N (to prevent . . . P–Q4) 8 . . . P–Q3 (**8 . . . Q–B3** -Euwe; **8 . . . B–K2!?** 9 Q×NP B–B3 10 Q–N3 Q–K2 11 Q–Q3! and according to Taimanov, White plays P–K4 and P–B3 with a strong centre and extra pawn. But 11 . . . P–B3!? Δ . . . P–Q4 would expose both kings!) 9

P–K4 (**9 P–B3?** and **9 P–N3?** both allow 9 ... B–K2!.) 9 ... P–QB3! 10 B–K2 B–K2 11 Q×NP B–B3 12 Q–N3 Q–R4 13 B–Q2 B–K3 14 0–0 0–0–0 with plenty for a pawn (Pachman).

| 8 ... | P–Q4 |
| 9 P–K3 | |

9 B–K3 Q–R5! 10 Q–K5ch B–K3 11 P×P 0–0–0! ∓ (Taimanov).

9 ... B–K3
10 B–Q2 B–K2 11 B–K2 0–0 12 R–Q1 P–QB3 = Ragozin-Mikenas, Moscow 1944.

A12

| 5 ... | **B–N5!** |

'!' for enterprise!

| 6 P–K3 | 0–0 |
| 7 B–K2 | |

White has a wide choice:

a) **7 Q–B2** R–K1 8 P–QR3 B×N 9 Q×B P–Q4 10 P–QN3 B–B4 11 B–N2 N–K2 12 P–R3 P–B3 13 B–K2 P–QR4?! (**13 ... Q–Q2**; White's bishops would still lack activity.) 14 P–KN4! B–K3? 15 P–N5 N–Q2 16 N×KP! Riumin-Ragozin, Moscow 1942. Cheap but effective.

b) **7 N–Q5** N×N 8 P×N N–K2 9 Q–R5 P–QB3! 10 P–Q6 B×P 11 N×P B–B2 12 B–Q3 P–KB4 ∞ / = Bastrikov-Ragozin, Moscow 1942.

c) **7 P–B3** B×N 8 P×B is (by transposition) Lonoff-Frankle, Massachusetts 1977: 8 ... P×P 9 Q×P P–Q4 10 B–Q3 P×P 11 B×P B–N5 12 Q–B2 B–R4! 13 0–0 Q–K2 =.

d) **7 P–KN3(!)** R–K1 8 B–N2 P–Q3 9 Q–B2 B–KB4 10 0–0 Q–K2 11

P–QR3 B×N 12 Q×B ± Fine's idea.

| 7 ... | R–K1!? |

Quite unclear, as we shall see. Possible is **7 ... Q–K2** (when the KBP is protected), or **7 ... P–Q3** 8 0–0 B–KB4 9 N–Q5 N×N 10 P×N N–K2 11 Q–N3 B–R4 12 Q×P R–N1 = Gerstenfeld-Ragozin, USSR Ch 1940.

8 0–0	B×N
9 P×B	P–Q3
10 P–B3	P×P

Old analysis by Botvinnik runs **10 ... B–B4** 11 P×P B×P? 12 N×B N×N 13 B–Q3 and if 13 ... P–KN3, 14 B×N R×B 15 R×P!. This is always quoted to demonstrate that Black cannot hold e4 with his pieces. But in place of 11 ... B×P, Lonoff-Frankle, Massachusetts 1974 went **11 ... N×P!** 12 N×N (**12 R×B** N×BP 13 Q–B1 N×Bch 14 Q×N N×P 15 Q–Q3 N×R and Black stands well - Frankle) 12 ... B×N 13 B–Q2 Q–N4 14 B–B3 P–B4 15 B×B R×B 16 R–N1 P–QN3 17 R–N5 N–K2 ∓ Δ ... N–N3.

| 11 B×P!? | R×P |
| 12 N–N3 (68) | |

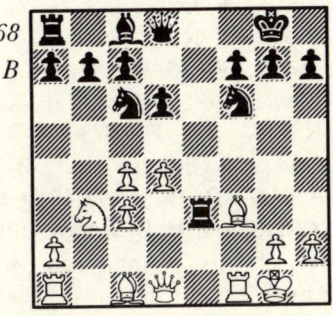

68
B

| 12 ... | R×BP! |

12 . . . R–K1? 13 B–N5 N–K2 14 Q–Q2 with a terific attack, Botvinnik-Ragozin, match game 1940. On this basis, Taimanov concludes that Black has 'difficult play' after 5 . . . B–N5, but:

13 B–N5   N–K2!
14 Q–Q2   R×P

15 B×N P×B 16 B–K2 R–B3 17 P–Q5!? (**17 R×P** or **17 N–R5** - Knaak) 17 . . . R–N3 18 R×P N×P! 19 R×BP!? (**19 R–R6?** Q–K2 ∓∓) 19 . . . K×R 20 Q×Nch B–K3 21 B–R5ch K–K2 22 R–K1 Q–N1 Adamski-Knaak, East Germany-Poland 1973. and White's attack was running out of steam, since 23 N–Q4? runs into 23 . . . R–N8! (0–1, 65).

A2

4 . . .   P×P
5 N×P

Black has 'surrendered the centre'; but he can develop rapidly, whereas White will have difficulty holding down . . . P–Q4 and getting his king into safety. Black has three interesting strategies:

A21 5 . . . N–K4
A22 5 . . . B–B4
A23 5 . . . B–N5

a) **5 . . . P–Q3?** 6 N×N (or 6 P–KN3 ±) 6 . . . P×N 7 P–KN3 B–K2 (**7 . . . P–KN3** at best transposes to Chapter 7, A.) 8 B–N2 B–N2 9 0–0 0–0 and now **10 Q–B2, 10 Q–N3,** and **10 Q–R4** are still at least ±. A comparison with Chapter 2 might be worthwhile.

b) **5 . . . N×N?** 6 Q×N (As in the Scotch Game or the Sicilian Defence, the early exchange of Black's QN develops White and strengthens his influence over d5.) 6 . . . B–K2 (**6 . . . B–N5** 7 B–N5) 7 P–K4 (or **7 P–KN3 ±**) 7 . . . P–Q3 8 P–QN3 B–K3 9 B–N2 N–N5!? 10 N–Q5! N–K4 11 N×B Q×N 12 B–K2 ± Zvetkov-O'Sullivan, Hilversum. 1947.

A21

5 . . .   N–K4
6 B–N5!

a) **6 P–K3** B–N5 7 Q–N3! ± (Schwarz), but that is far from clear after 7 . . . B–K2! (or even 7 . . . B×N and 8 . . . 0–0)

b) **6 P–K4** B–N5 7 P–B4 N–N3 (**7 . . . N×KP?** 8 Q–K2! 0–0 9 Q×N N–N5 10 Q–B3 ±± -Schwarz) 8 Q–B3 P–Q3 9 B–Q3 0–0 10 B–Q2 (**10 0–0** B–B4 11 B–K3 N–N5 - Shatskes; maybe **10 B–K3!?**) 10 . . . R–K1 11 P–KR3 B×N 12 B×B N×KP! (Shatskes).

6 . . .   B–N5

6 . . . N×P 7 P–K4 ±±; **6 . . . P–KR3?** 7 B×N Q×B 8 N–Q5 Δ 9 N–N5.

7 Q–N3

Simplest. **7 P–B4!?** N×P 8 P–K4, which Taimanov says transposes into Kottnauer-Fichtl of A2333, does not do so after 8 . . . N×NP! (in place of 8 . . . B×Nch?) 9 Q–N3 Q–K2! (Δ 9 . . . N–R5).

7 . . .   B×Nch

7 . . . B–B4 8 0–0–0; for similar play, see **7 . . . N–K4** of A2334 below.

8 Q×B   P–Q3
9 P–B3 ±

A22

5 . . .   B–B4

6 N×N

Ensuring a positional plus. Else:
a) **6 N–B2** 0–0 7 P–K3 (7 B–N5?
B×Pch) 7 . . . R–K1 8 B–K2
P–Q3 =.
b) **6 N–N3** B–N5 7 B–N5 P–KR3 8
B×N Q×B 9 R–B1 N–R4! 10 N–Q2
0–0 11 P–KN3 P–QN3 = Ojanen-
Keres, Estonia-Finland 1959.
c) **6 P–K3** 0–0 7 B–K2 P–Q3 (7 . . .
N–K2! 8 0–0 P–Q3 – or 8 . . . P–Q4
= – 9 N–R4 B×N 10 P×B R–K1 11
N–B3 N–N3 = Tartakower-
Bogoljubov, 1925; or 7 . . . P–Q4) 8
0–0 R–K1 9 N×N P×N 10 B–B3 ±
Nilsson-Malmgren, corres 1940.
d) **6 N–B3** B–N5 (or 6 . . . 0–0)
7 B–Q2 P–Q4 8 P×P N×P 9
N×N Q×N = Bronstein-Balashov,
Moscow 1974.

6 . . .   NP×N

7 P–KN3 (*69*)

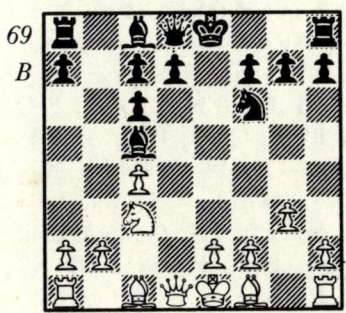

69
B

7 . . .   P–KR4?!

Alekhine's move. Black has had a
hard time of it from the diagram:
a) **7 . . . P–Q4?** 8 B–N2 B–K3 9 0–0
0–0 10 Q–R4 B–Q2 11 B–N5 B–K2
12 QR–Q1 ± Reti-Przepiorka,
Marienbad 1925.

b) **7 . . . 0–0** 8 B–N2 R–K1 9 0–0
R–N1 (**9 . . . B–B1** 10 B–B4 R–N1
11 Q–B2 B–N2 12 KR–Q1 P–QR3
13 R–Q2 P–B4 14 B×B R×B 15
B–N5 ± Reti-Grünfeld, Baden-
Baden 1925) 10 P–N3 (**10 Q–R4!?;
10 Q–B2!?**) 10 . . . B–N2? (Why not
10 . . . P–Q4?) 11 B–N2 Q–K2 12
P–K4! ± Reti-Janowski, Semmering 1926. Themes strikingly like
Chapter 2, B2.
c) **7 . . . R–QN1** 8 B–N2 B–R3 9
P–N3 (**9 Q–R4** Q–B1 10 P–QR3 –
stopping 10 . . . R–N5 – 10 . . . B–Q5
∞ -Raicević) 9 . . . N–N5?! (9 . . .
0–0 – Raicević. Then White may
find it hard to prove an advantage.)
10 N–K4 B–K2 11 0–0 0–0 12
B–N2 P–Q4 13 Q–Q4! ± Raicević-
Tal, Novi Sad 1974 (but 0–1, 56). 7
. . . R–QN1 deserves further tests.

8 B–N2

Carles-Alekhine, Prague 1943
illustrates the too timid **8 P–KR4:** 8
. . . N–N5 9 N–K4 Q–K2 10 B–N2
(**10 N×B** Q×N 11 P–K3 Q–B4 ∞ -
Pachman) 10 . . . B–N5ch 11 B–Q2
N–K4 12 0–0 B×B 13 N×B R–N1
14 P–N3 P–QB4! with good
chances.

8 . . .   P–R5

9 0–0   P×P

10 P×P   Q–K2

10 . . . P–Q4? 11 P×P N–N5 12
Q–R4 B–N3 13 P–Q6! K–B1 14
Q×BP R–QN1 15 B–B4 ±±
Lengyel-Barcza, Hungary 1964.

11 B–B4

Black threatened . . . Q–K4–R4.

11 . . .   B–N2

Padevsky-Ree, Bad Pyrmont
1970 ended in a fiasco for Black: **11
. . . N–R4?** 12 B(4)×P P–Q3 13

P–QN4! Q×B 14 P×B P×P 15 N–K4 R–R3 16 Q–Q2 B–K3 17 N×P ±±.

12 Q–Q3

12 P–QR3? N–R4 ∞ was Pachman-Keres, Bled 1961, but Cortlever's **12 P–K3!** is apparently strong e.g. **12...0–0–0** 13 P–QN4! B–Q3 (**13...B×P** 14 Q–N3) 14 P–N5! B–K4 15 P×P B×P 16 N–Q5! ±; on **12...N–R4**, both 13 N–K4 and 13 P–R3 do the trick.

12 ...   0–0–0

12 ... N–R4 13 B(4)×P P–Q3 14 B–R5 etc.; or 12 ... P–Q3 13 P–QN4! B×P 14 QR–N1 B×N 15 Q×B R–QN1 16 R×B ±±.

13 P–QN4!   B×P

14 KR–N1 B–B4 15 N–R4 B–N3 (**15 ...N–R4** 16 N×B Q×N 17 B–K3 Δ R×B) 16 P–B5 B×P 17 N×B Q×N 18 R–N3 'with the decisive threat R(1)–N1' (Shatskes).

CONCLUSION:

If Black wants to enter the line 5 ... B–B4 6 N×N NP×N, then he should answer 7 P–KN3 not with **7 ... 0–0** (cramped) or **7 ... P–KR4?!** (evidently unsound), but with **7 ... R–QN1**.

A23

5 ...   **B–N5**

The move that drove 4 P–Q4 out of business. White has two passive approaches and one ambitious one:
A231 6 P–KN3
A232 6 N×N
A233 6 B–N5

6 N–B2?! B×Nch 7 P×B P–Q4 8 P–K3 B–K3 9 P×P N×P (∓) 10 P–QB4? N(4)–N5 11 Q–Q2

(What else?) 11 ... Q–B3 12 R–QN1 P–QR4 13 N–Q4 0–0–0 14 B–N2 Q–N3 15 R–B1 N×N 16 P×N KR–K1 17 K–Q1 B–Q2! 18 R–B3 B–R5ch 19 K–B1 N×P MATE Schmitt-Michel, Germany 1937. Quick development took precedent over the containment of White's doubled pawns.

A231

6 P–KN3 (*70*)

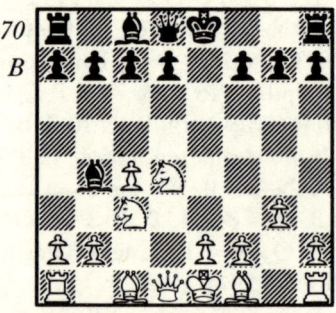

70
B

6 ...   N–K5

Black can hardly go wrong:

a) **6 ... B×Nch** 7 P×B N–K4 8 B–KN2 0–0 (**8...N×P!?** 9 Q–N3 N–N3 is also feasible.) 9 Q–N3 P–Q3 10 0–0 N(3)–Q2 11 P–QR4 N–B4 12 Q–R2 P–QR4 13 P–B4 N(K)–Q2 14 P–K4 R–K1 15 Q–K2 N–N3 = (Schwarz).

b) **6 ... N–K4** (the most tenuous move, but not bad) 7 Q–N3 (**7 Q–R4** B×Nch! 8 P×B Q–K2 – Δ ...*N–Q6ch* or ...*Q–B4* – 9 B–K3 N(3)–N5 10 N–B2 N×KBP! 11 K×N N–N5ch 12 K–B3 P–KB4 13 P–B5 P–QN4! ∓∓ -Grünfeld; **7 N–B5?** 0–0 N–K3 N–K5 ∓) 7 ... B×Nch! (**7 ... Q–K2?** 8 B–K3! N–K5 9 N(4)–N5! ± Purdy-Malmgren, corres 1947–53) 8 Q×B

P–Q4 9 N–N5 N–N3 (**9 . . . N×P?** 10 B–B4) 10 P×P 0–0 11 N×BP N×P 12 N×N Q×N 13 Q–B3 (a courageous defender might try **13 P–B3**.) 13 . . . Q×Q (**13 . . . Q–QN4** 14 B–N2 R–K1 15 0–0 ± Bernard-Koch, Berlin 1934) 14 P×Q R–K1ch 15 B–K3 N–K4. Taimanov and Shatskes say that Black has enough compensation here. 16 B–K2 is the obvious move, when neither **16 . . . B–R6?** 17 R–KN1! B–B4 18 P–KN4 Δ P–B4 nor **16 . . . B–B4** 17 R–Q1 QR–B1 18 P–KN4 B–Q2 19 R–KN1! is what Black wants. But **16 . . . B–Q2!** Δ . . . B–B3 will practically force a bishop of opposite colours ending.

    7 Q–Q3   Q–K2
    8 B–N2   N×N
    9 P×N   N–K4

10 Q–B2 B–B4 11 Q–N3 P–Q3 12 0–0 0–0 13 K–R1 B–K3! 14 P–B4 (**14 N×B** Q×N 15 Q×NP Q×BP is at least equal for Black.) 14 . . . B×P 15 Q–R4 P–QN4 16 Q–B2 N–N5 17 B×R R×B (Shatskes/Taimanov). Black has more than enough for the exchange.

A232

    6 N×N   B×Nch

Or **6 . . . NP×N** and:

a) **7 Q–B2** P–Q4 8 P–QR3 B–K2 9 P–KN3 0–0 = (Taimanov);

b) **7 P–KN3?** Q–K2! 8 B–N2 B–R3! 9 Q–Q3 P–Q4 10 P–N3 P–Q5! 11 B×Pch K–B1 12 Q×P R–Q1 13 B–Q5 R×B! ∓∓ (Müller);

c) **7 P–K3?!** B×Nch 8 P×B P–B4! 9 B–Q3 B–N2 10 0–0 0–0 11 P–B3

P–Q3 ∓ Tartakower-Sämisch, Manerbad 1925.

    7 P×B   QP×N

7 . . . NP×N? 8 P–KN3 P–Q3 9 B–N2 B–Q2 10 0–0 0–0 11 P–B5! P–Q4 12 B–K3 with a promising position (Taimanov).

    8 Q×Qch   K×Q
    9 B–N5

9 B–B4 B–K3 10 P–K3 N–Q2 ∓

    9 . . .   K–K2
    10 P–K3   B–K3 =

Analysis by Taimanov. The assessment seems fair because Black cannot get to the weak White pawns without concessions, whereas White can't make inroads.

CONCLUSION:

Neither **6 P–KN3** nor **6 N×N** creates serious difficulties for the second player.

A233

    6 B–N5

The most important move, continuing to fight for e4 and d5. Black has these rejoinders:

A2331 6 . . . P–Q4
A2332 6 . . . 0–0
A2333 6 . . . B×Nch
A2334 6 . . . P–KR3

A2331

    6 . . .   P–Q4

A radical attempt to free Black's game, not convincingly refuted!

    7 P–K3

a) **7 P×P** Q×P 8 B×N P×B 9 N×N B×Nch 10 P×B Q×N 11 Q–B2? (**11 Q–Q4** B–B4 12 P–K3 R–Q1 13 Q–QB4 =**)** 11 . . . B–B4 ∓∓ (decisive pressure) Losekoot-

Madsen, corres 1948.

b) **7 N×N P×N 8 Q–Q4 (8 P–K3** P–KR3 9 B×N Q×B 10 Q–Q4 = ; 8 Q–N3!?) 8 ... P–KR3 9 B–Q2 Q–K2! 10 P×P P×P 11 N×P B×Bch 12 Q×B N×N 13 Q×N 0–0! ∓ Keller-Smith, corres 1954.

          7 ...   P–KR3

Taimanov mentions **7 ... N×N** 8 Q×N P×P; maybe 7 ... B–K3!?

          8 B×N   B×Nch
9 P×B P×B 10 Q–R4 Q–Q2 11 P×P! (**11 N–QN5?** P×P = J. Benko-Desler, corres) 11 ... Q×P 12 N×N P×N 13 R–Q1 Q–B4 14 Q–Q4 ± (Rellstab).

A2332

          6 ...   0–0

Schwarz and Shatskes brand this with a '?', and Taimanov calls it 'disadvantageous'. Their point is that White now avoids doubled QBPs, but that should hardly seal Black's fate:

          7 R–B1   R–K1?

This is the mistake, I think. True, Black must eschew **7 ... P–Q4?** 8 P×P Q×P 9 B×N P×B 10 N×N Q×N 11 P–QR3 B–R4 12 P–K3 B–B4 13 Q–R5! ± Endzelins-Balogh, 2nd World Corres Ch. 1956-9; but **7 ... P–KR3! 8 B–R4** is A23342 (8 ... N–K4!), and neither **8 B×N** nor **8 N×N** NP×N is particularly useful.

          8 P–K3   P–Q3
          9 B–K2

Or **9 N×N** P×N 10 B–Q3! (Alekhine). **9 B–K2** follows Flohr-Johner, Zurich 1934: 9 ... N–K4 (**9 ... P–KR3** 10 B–R4 will not

change anything now.) 10 0–0 B×N (Both B×N and N–Q5 were threatened.) 11 R×B P–KR3 (**11 ... N–N3?** 12 N–N5! B–Q2 13 B×N P×B 14 B–Q3 K–R1 15 N–Q4 R–N1 16 Q–R5 ± Alekhine-Yates, Semmering 1962) 12 B–R4 N–N3 13 B×N Q×B 14 N–N5 Q–Q1 15 R–B1! ±. White has in mind N–B3–Q5, with continuing positional pressure.

A2333

          6 ...   B×Nch
          7 P×B   N–K4?

7 ... P–KR3 is certainly preferable. Then on **8 B–R4** one reaches A23343 unscathed; while **8 N×N** gets nowhere after 8 ... NP×N! (not **8 ... QP×N?** 9 Q×Qch K×Q 10 B×Nch P×B 11 0–0–0ch K–K2 12 R–Q4! ±) 9 B–K3?! Q–K2! 10 P–B5 0–0 11 Q–Q4 R–K1 (∓ -Kotov) 12 B–B4 (**12 P–KN4** Δ R–KN1 -Zaitsev; probably best!) 12 ... B–R3! 13 P–K3 B×B 14 K×B QR–N1 15 B×P R–N7 16 R–K1 Q–K3! ∓ Taimanov-Savon, USSR Ch 1974 (0–1, 34). Hard to meaningfully improve upon.

          8 P–B4!

8 P–K3 P–KR3 9 B–R4 P–Q3 is a poor variant (for White) of A23343 below.

          8 ...   N–N3

8 ... N×P? 9 P–K4 N–K6 10 Q–K2 N×B 11 P–K5 0–0 12 N–B5! is completely crushing, Kottnauer-Fichtl, Prague 1945.

          9 P–N3   P–KR3
          10 B×N   Q×B
          11 B–N2

White is a tempo ahead of A23343 below, because he wasn't required to make the move B–KR4! We follow Kottnauer-Euwe, Groningen 1946: 11 . . . 0–0 12 0–0 P–Q3 13 R–N1 P–B3 14 Q–Q2 R–K1 15 P–K4 N–B1 16 KR–K1 N–Q2? (16 . . . Q–Q1 ±) 17 N–B5 ±.

CONCLUSION:

6 . . . 0–0 and **6 . . . B×Nch** are plausible, but only worth it if Black follows up with 7 . . . P–KR3 anyway.

A2334
6 . . .   **P–KR3**
Black's most prudent course.
7 B–R4 (*71*)

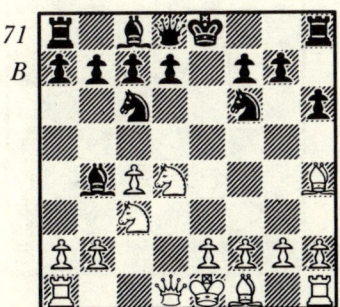

7 B×N is harmless and, again, **7 N×N** B×Nch 8 P×B NP×N 9 B–K3?! gives us Taimanov-Savon above (A2333, note to 7 . . . N–K4), a subvariant barely playable for White!

But with the bishop on h4, Black has had fine results:
A23341 7 . . . N–K4
A23342 7 . . . 0–0
A23343 7 . . . B×Nch

Not the brilliant **7 . . . N–K5??** 8 B×Q N×N 9 N×N ± ±, but these bear notice:

a) **7 . . . P–KN4** 8 B–N3 P–Q3 (8 . . . N–K5 9 R–B1 Q–B3?! – *9 . . . 0–0 must be better* – 10 N(4)–N5! B×Nch – *10 . . . B–R4 11 N×Pch!* – 11 P×B N×B 12 RP×N Q–Q1 13 P–B5! -Schwarz, and White holds the reins.) 9 R–B1 (9 N×N! P×N 10 Q–R4! B×Nch 11 P×B B–Q2 12 P–B5! P–Q4 13 P–R4 with advantage -Shatskes) 9 . . . N×N 10 Q×N B–KB4 11 P–KR4?! (11 P–B3) 11 . . . K–Q2!! 12 R–Q1 N–K5! 13 Q–K5 B×Nch 14 P×B N×B 15 P×N (15 Q×N P–N3) 15 . . . B–N3 16 P×P Keres-Richter, Munich 1942 and Black, who has played inspired chess thus far, should now simply recapture 16 . . . P×P with a winning endgame in sight.

b) **7 . . . P–Q3** 8 P–K3 (or 8 R–B1) 8 . . . Q–K2?! (**8 . . . P–KN4!**, and on **9 N×N** P×N 10 B–N3 B×Nch 11 P×B P–B4!, Black has done much better than in (a) e.g. 12 P–KR4 R–KN1! 13 P×P P×P 14 R–R6 Q–K2 etc.; or **9 B–N3** N–K5 10 R–B1 Q–B3! Δ . . . P–KR4.) 9 B–K2 P–KN4 10 B–N3 N–K5 11 N×N!? ('**11 R–B1!** 0–0 12 0–0 B×N 13 P×B N×B 14 RP×N ±' - Botvinnik; 11 . . . Q–B3!?) 11 . . . P×N 12 R–B1 0–0 13 0–0 B×N 14 P×B N×B 15 RP×N B–B4! = Botvinnik-Flohr, March (7) 1933.

A23341
7 . . .   **N–K4**
8 Q–N3!
8 P–K3 0–0 9 B–K2 N–N3 10

B–N3 N–K5 = (Schwarz); or here
8 . . . N–N3 9 B×N B×Nch! 10 P×B
Q×B =. 8 P–B4? N×P 9 P–K4 loses
perforce after 9 . . . N×NP 10
Q–N3 B×Nch (or 10 . . . P–B4) 11
Q×B N×P! ∓∓.

8 . . .   B×Nch

a) **8 . . . P–B4?** 9 N–B5 P–KN4 10
N–Q6ch! K–K2 11 B–N3 K×N 12
0–0–0ch K–K3 13 N–N5 N–K1 14
P–KR4 Q–B3? (14 . . . P–B3 ±) 15
R–Q6ch! ±± van Dork-
Struylaart, corres 1950 (1–0, 29).
b) **8 . . . P–QR4** 9 P–QR3 B–B4 (9
. . . B×Nch 10 Q×B N–N3 11
Q–K3ch! ± -Schwarz) 10 0–0–0 ±
Tolush-Kan, Leningrad 1952.

9 Q×B   P–Q3
10 P–B3   0–0

11 0–0–0 (**11 B–B2** -Schwarz,
allows the complex 11 . . . P–Q4!)
11 . . . N–K5! 12 Q–K1 P–KN4 13
B–N3 N×B 14 P×N Q–B3 15 P–K4
B–K3 = E. Richter-Tartakower,
Marianske Lazne-Karlovy Vary,
1948.

A23342

7 . . .   0–0
8 R–B1

8 P–K3 R–K1?! 9 B–K2 N–K4
10 Q–N3 B–R4 11 0–0 N–N3 12
B×N Q×B 13 N–Q5 Q–Q1 14
Q–R3! P–QB3 15 P–QN4 B–B2 16
N×B Q×N 17 P–N5 P–QB4 18
P–N6! ± Szabo-Smyslov, Budapest
1950. But **8 . . . P–Q4!?** seems
sound e.g. 9 P×P Q×P 10 B×N
P×B 11 N×N (What else? 11 Q–B3
Q–QB4 or 11 R–B1 N×N 12 Q×N
Q×Q ∓) 11 . . . B×Nch 12 P×B
Q×N 13 Q–Q4 B–K3! 14 Q×BP
KR–Q1 =. Moreover, **8 . . .**

N–K4! = is A23341 above, note to
8 Q–N3.

After the text (8 R–B1) the books
agree that White is better.
However:

8 . . .   N–K4!
9 P–QR3

9 P–K3 is recommended in
Informant #18, but then 9 . . .
N–N3 10 B–N3 N–K5 is
comfortable for Black. The point of
the . . . N–K4–KN3 manoeuvre
(seldom permitted by White) is to
trade off White's QB without the
debilitating . . . P–KN4.

9 . . .   B×Nch
10 R×B   N–N3
11 B×N   Q×B
12 P–KN3 (*72*)

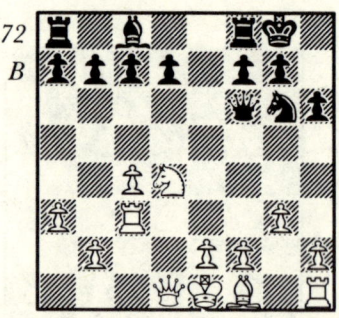

12 **N–N5!?** Q–Q1 13 R–B1 (Δ
N–B3) can still be tried, as in Flohr-
Johner (A2332 above), but White
has wasted P–QR3 and is still three
moves short of castling. Black might
continue 13 . . . P–QB3 14 N–B3
R–K1 15 P–K3 (**15 P–KN3?** N–K4)
15 . . . P–Q3 (or **15 . . . P–KB4!?**) 16
B–K2 Q–N4! 17 P–KN3 B–R6 18
Q×P QR–Q1 19 Q–N4 B–N7! 20
R–KN1 P–QB4 21 Q–N3 B–B3 Δ
. . . R×P! or . . . N–K4.

From the diagram, we look at two methods of combatting White's hold on d5.

a) **12 . . . P–QR3** 13 B–N2 P–Q3 (**13 . . . P–B4!?**) 14 0–0 P–B4 15 N–B2 R–N1 (The point of Black's strategy: while White catches up on development, a queenside pawn storm is in the works.) 16 N–K3 N–K2 17 Q–Q2 (**17 P–QR4!?**) 17 . . . P–QN4 18 R–Q3 B–K3 19 P×P R×P 20 P–QN4 P×P 21 P×P P–Q4 22 N×P B×N 23 B×B N×B 24 R×N R×R 25 Q×R R–N1 Alburt-Kuzmin, USSR Ch 1972. Although still suffering some disadvantage, Black managed to hold the draw ($\frac{1}{2}$–$\frac{1}{2}$, 84).

b) **12 . . . P–B4** (initiating the same strategy as in (a), but without loss of time) 13 **N–B3(?!)** R–N1 14 B–N2 P–N4 $\mp$ Raicević-Dukanović, Yugoslavia 1974. White has yet to castle, and Black can gang up on the QN file and/or push in the centre.

But 13 N–B3 is rather polite. White could try **13 N–N5!?**, when **13 . . . Q–B3?** 14 Q–Q5 (or even 14 R–N1) and **13 . . . P–QR3?** 14 N–Q6 are $\pm$. **13 . . . P–Q4!** seems forced, when **14 N–B7** P–Q5 15 R–B3 Q–B3 16 N×R B–N5! recoups Black's material. So critical would be:
b1) **14 P×P** Q–N3 15 Q–N3 P–R3 16 N–Q4 Q–Q3 17 N–B2 P–QN4 18 B–N2 B–N2 19 N–K3 P–B4! ∞;
b2) **14 Q×P** R–Q1 15 Q×BP (15 Q–B3 Q–N3) 15 . . . P–N3 16 Q–K3 (16 Q–N4? Q–B3 Δ . . . P–QR3, . . . Q×R) 16 . . . B–N2 17 P–B3 R–Q2! with a strong attack.

A fascinating variation, and

evidently still another acceptable way for Black to play it.

A23343

7 . . .   **B×Nch**
   8 P×B

The position most often reached. Black can go for a forcing continuation by A233431 8 . . . N–K4, or build up slowly with A233432 8 . . . P–Q3.

8 . . . 0–0 will almost always transpose, and is a good move order. White could try 9 N×N NP×N 10 Q–Q4 P–N4 11 B–N3 P–Q3 12 P–KR4 P–B4 13 Q–Q3, but either 13 . . . Q–K2 or even 13 . . . N–R4!? leaves Black well off.

A233431

8 . . .   **N–K4**

Black decides to break the pin on his KN.
   9 P–B4!

Other moves are inferior:
a) **9 N–N5** P–R3 (or even **9 . . . N×P!** 10 Q–Q4 P–QR3 11 Q×N P×N 12 Q×NP Q–K2 $\mp$ Hult-Vonseca, corres 1949) 10 Q–Q4?! (**10 B×N** P×B 11 N–Q4 ∞) 10 . . . P–Q3 11 B×N P×B 12 N–R3 P–QB4! 13 Q–Q2 Q–R4 14 Q–N2 B–Q2! 15 P–K4 B–B3 $\mp$ Ragozin-Sozin, corres 1936.
b) **9 P–B3?!** N×P! 10 N–B5 (**10 P–K4** N–K4 11 N–B5 N–N3! 12 N×Pch K–B1 $\mp$) 10 . . . P–KN4 11 Q–Q4 P–Q4 12 N–N7ch K–K2 13 B–N3 Carls-Junge, Germany 1942; 13 . . . P–N3! (Shatskes).
c) **9 P–K3** P–Q3 10 B–K2 0–0 11 Q–N3 N–N3 12 B–N3 N–K5 13 R–Q1 Q–K2 14 B–B3 N×B 15

RP×N N–K4 16 N–K2 B–K3 17 B–Q5 B–N5 18 R–Q4 P–B3 19 B–K4 B–K3 20 B–N1 P–QB4 21 R(4)–R4 P–B4! ∓ Volovich-Averbach, Moscow 1968. A fine example of Black play.

9 ...　N–N3

9 ... N×P? 10 P–K4 N–K6 11 Q–K2 N×B 12 P–K5 0–0 13 N–B5! with a terrific onslaught. But now White gains control of d5.

10 B×N　　Q×B
11 P–N3　　0–0

11 ... P–QR3 12 Q–Q3 P–B4 13 N–B2 Q–B3 14 R–KN1 0–0 15 B–N2 Q–B2 16 N–K3 P–Q3 17 K–B2 R–N1 18 N–Q5 Q–Q1 19 P–QR4 ± Byshev-Lissitsin, Leningrad 1956.

12 B–N2　　P–B4!

Slow play is unrewarding e.g. **12 ... P–Q3** 13 0–0 P–QR3 (catastrophic was **13 ... Q–K2** 14 R–N1 Q–K6ch? 15 K–R1 Q×QBP 16 P–KB5 N–K4 17 P–B6 P–KN3 18 R–N3 Q×BP 19 Q–Q2 K–R2 20 R–N4 Q–R3 21 N–B5! 1–0 Kossma-Licman, corres 1947) 14 Q–Q2 N–K2 15 QR–N1 R–N1 16 P–QR4 P–QN3 17 P–R5! ± Alburt-Romanishin, USSR 1973 (1–0, 50).

13 N–N5　　P–QR3

13 ... P–Q4?!, formerly considered effective because of **14 P×P** B–Q2 15 N–B7 (15 R–QN1 N×P!) 15 ... QR–Q1, is practically refuted by **14 Q×P!** P–QR3 15 N–Q6! R–Q1 16 R–Q1 (Shatskes) and not 15 N–B7? N×P!.

14 N–Q6　　Q×Pch
15 K–B2 R–N1 16 P–QR4 P–N3?! (**16 ... N–K2!** Δ ... N–B3 –

Adamski) 17 R–R2 (or 17 R–QN1!) 17 ... N–K2 18 Q–R1 Q×Q 19 R(1)×Q N–B3 20 R–N2 N–N5 21 R–Q1 R–Q1 22 R(2)–Q2 K–B1 23 P–R4 P–QR4 ½–½ Adamski-Uhlmann, Poland-East Germany 1974. Still ±, according to Adamski.

A233432

8 ...　　　　P–Q3 (*73*)

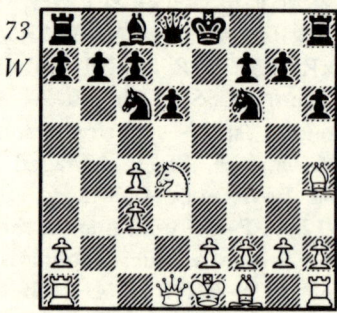

73
W

The modern move, and to all appearances a good one.

9 P–B3

9 P–K3!? develops faster, but allows Black some positional trickery after 9 ... N–K4:

a) **10 B–K2?!** 0–0 (or **10 ... N–N3** 11 B–N3 N–K5. =) 11 0–0 N–N3 12 B×N Q×B. This is Sanz-Tal, a classic example of such positions: 13 R–N1 Q–K2! 14 B–Q3 P–QB4! 15 N–K2 P–N3 16 N–N3 B–N2 17 Q–R5 Q–K3 18 QR–Q1 QR–Q1 (Now Black piles up on the forward QBP.) 19 KR–K1 N–K4 20 P–K4 B–R3! (The knight is a useful defender.) 21 N–B5 P–N3! 22 N×Pch K–N2 23 Q–N5 P–B3 24 Q–B4 R–R1 25 N–B5ch P×N 26 Q–N3ch K–B1 27 P×P Q–N1 0–1. So simple!

b) **10 Q–B2** (at least this prevents ... N–K5) 10 ... 0–0 11 B–K2 R–K1 12 P–B3 N–N3 (**12 ... B–K3!?** and if 13 P–B4 N×P 14 N×B N×KP was interesting.) 13 B–B2 P–B4? (The standard plans of **13 ... P–B3!** △ ... P–Q4 and **13 ... N–Q2**–N3 or N–Q2–B4 were available.) 14 N–B5 P–Q4 15 0–0 R–K4 16 N–N3 N–K2 17 KR–Q1 ± Timman-S. Garcia, Hastings 1973/4. The position is ripe for bishops! (1–0, 31)

        9 ...   N–K4

Or **9 ... 0–0** 10 P–K4 N–K4 11 B–K2 N–N3 (**11 ... B–K3!?** is worth a look. If **12 N×B** P×N, Black has the KB file and excellent posts for his knights. On **12 Q–R4**, 12 ... P–KN4!? 13 B–B2 N(3)–Q2 is a possibility.) 12 B–B2 N–Q2 13 Q–Q2 (13 N–N3!?) 13 ... N–N3 14 N–N3 P–KB4 (**14 ... B–K3?!** 15 P–B5!· ± Botvinnik-Pric, Moscow 1935) 15 P–B5 P×P 16 Q×Q R×Q 17 N×P N–KB5 18 B–N3 N×B 19 B×P? R–K1 20 K×N N–Q4 ∓ Vecsey-Banfalvi Paloc-Kupa, Hungary 1953.

      10 P–K4   N–N3
      11 B–B2   0–0
12 Q–Q2?! (**12 B–K2** is almost equal.) 12 ... P–B3 (Spassky's plan versus Lengyel, Amsterdam 1964. Gipslis analyzes **12 ... R–K1** 13 B–K2 N–R4 14 P–N3 N–K4 15 P–N4 N–KB3 16 P–KR3 B–K3 17 R–N1 N–R2 18 P–KR4 B×BP ∓. He also mentions **12 ... B–K3** 13 B–K2 N–K4, with ideas we have already discussed.) 13 B–K2 P–Q4 14 KP×P P×P 15 P–B5 N–R4 16 0–0 N(4)–B5 17 B–N5 B–R6! (or 17

... **P–QR3** 18 B–R4 B–R6 - Gipslis) 18 B–N3 N×P 19 R–B2 N(7)–R5 20 B–Q6 Q–B3! 21 B×R R×B 22 P–KB4! R–B1 23 R–K1 B–B4 24 N×B N×N 25 Q×P? (25 R–K8ch -Gipslis) 25 ... N×P! 26 Q×NP? (Losing perforce, but **26 R×N?** Q–N4ch 27 K–R1 N–N6ch; **26 Q–B3** P–N4 ∓) 26 ... N–R6ch 27 K–N2 N–K6ch!! 28 K×N Q–K3ch 29 R–B5 (29 K–N3 Q–N5 mate) 29 ... Q×Rch 30 K–N3 Q×P 31 B–Q3 R–K1 32 Q–B3 Q–Q3ch 0–1, Raicević-Gipslis, Vrnjacka Banja 1975.

CONCLUSION:

4 P–Q4 has had its heyday. After 4 ... P×P 5 N×P B–N5 6 B–N5 P–KR3 7 B–R4, **7 ... 0–0, 7 ... P–Q3**, and maybe even **7 ... N–K4** are sufficient for equality, whereas the normal **7 ... B×Nch** 8 P×B P–Q3! (or **8 ... 0–0**) is probably somewhat better for Black.

    White too often assumes permanent weaknesses and/or inferior development as a price for his bishop pair. There are so many good defences that it would be hard to shake the general verdict of easy equality. In fact, even as a surprise weapon, 4 P–Q4 has the drawback that 4 ... P–K5 will level the play without Black needing to know much theory.

B

    4 P–K4

Nimzowitsch. White prevents ... P–Q4, but leaves a hole on d4. In comparison with the Botvinnik systems, White's KN is poorly placed on f3, as it must move again before he can proceed with P–KB4.

Black has two natural replies:
B1 4 . . . B–B4
B2 4 . . . B–N5

And several which allow 5 P–Q4:

a) **4 . . . B–K2** 5 P–Q4 P×P (**5 . . . P–Q3** 6 P–Q5 ±) 6 N×P 0–0 7 B–K2 B–N5 (**7 . . . P–Q3** 8 0–0 R–K1 9 P–B3 ±) 8 P–B3 P–Q3 9 B–N5 ±.

b) **4 . . . P–KN3** 5 P–Q4 P×P 6 N×P B–N2 7 N–B2 0–0 8 P–B3 ±. It's worth noting that the establishment of this kind of central bind often gains effect if Black's knight is on c6; to the extent that, were it on b8 here, 8 . . . P–QB3 and 9 . . . P–Q4 might equalize, even at the cost of a pawn.

c) **4 . . . P–Q3** 5 P–Q4 B–N5! (**5 . . . P×P** 6 N×P P–KN3 is '(b)') 6 P–Q5 N–Q5 7 B–K3 (**7 B–K2** N×B 8 Q×N is Cvetkovic's suggestion. Then Black should probably try 8 . . . B–K2 9 0–0 0–0 e.g. **10 P–KR3** B–B1! 11 N–K1 N–Q2 12 N–Q3 B–N4 =, or **10 B–K3** N–K1 11 P–KR3 B–Q2 Δ . . . P–KN3, . . . P–KB4.) 7 . . . N×Nch 8 P×N B–Q2 9 P–B4?! (**9 P–N4** N–R4 10 P–B5 B–K2 ∞ -Savon) 9 . . . N–N5 10 B–Q2 P×P 11 B×P P–KN4 12 B–N3 (**12 Q–Q4** R–KN1 ∓ -Savon) 12 . . . B–N2 13 P–KR4 P–KR3 14 B–K2 N–K4 ∓ Panno-Savon, Petropolis 1973 (0–1, 37).

B1

4 . . .   B–B4
5 N×P

The only move which aspires to

advantage; otherwise Black consolidates with . . . P–Q3 (and in some instances, . . . N–KN5 Δ . . . P–KB4). Note that 1 P–K4 P–K4 2 N–KB3 N–QB3 3 P–QB4?! B–B4 4 N–B3 P–Q3 runs into this same problem.

Fine gives **5 B–K2**, quoting 5 . . . P–Q3 6 0–0 **B–N5** 7 P–Q3 0–0 8 B–N5 P–KR3 9 B–K3 ± Fine-Adams, USA Ch 1936; but that assessment is debatable and Black had alternatives, e.g. **6 . . . 0–0** 7 P–Q3 N–K2!? and 8 B–N5 P–B3 or 8 P–Q4 P×P 9 N×P N–N3 Δ . . . R–K1, . . . P–B3 etc.

5 . . .   N×N
6 P–Q4   (74)

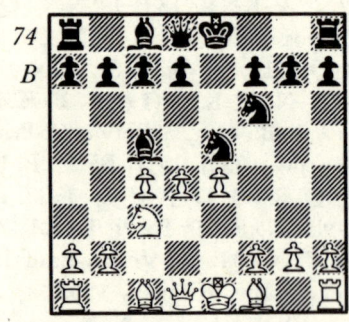

74
B

6 . . .   B–N5

a) **6 . . . B–Q3?** 7 P–B5! B×P 8 P×N N–N1 9 Q–N4 K–B1 10 Q–N3 N–K2 11 B–QB4 N–N3 12 P–B4 (or **12 0–0** Q–K2 13 B–B4) 12 . . . Q–R5 13 N–Q5 P–QB3 14 B–K3! Nimzovich-Reti, Berlin 1928.

b) **6 . . . N×KP** 7 N×N B–N5ch 8 N–B3 (or 8 B–Q2) 8 . . . N–N3 9 B–Q3 0–0 10 0–0 R–K1?! (**10 . . . B×N** 11 P×B P–Q3 -Kotov) 11 Q–R5 B–K2 12 N–Q5 P–Q3 13 B–Q2 B–Q2 14

P–B4! ± K. Grigorian-Zhdanov
USSR Cup, Moscow 1974.

7 P×N   N×P
8 Q–Q4

8 Q–N4? N×N 9 B–Q2 (**9
P–QR3?** B–B1! 10 P×N P–Q3 ∓ -
Pachman) 9 . . . 0–0 10 P×N B–R4
∓ (Savon).

8 . . .   N×N

List-Colle, Berlin 1931 took the
low road: **8 . . . P–KB4** 9 P×Pe.p.
N×P(3) (9 . . . B×Nch 10 P×B
N×P(3) -Tarkatower – 11 P–B5!)
10 P–B5 Q–K2ch 11 B–K3 B×Nch
12 P×B 0–0, and now simply 13
B–B4ch K–R1 14 0–0 ±
(Shatskes).

9 P×N   B–R4

Theory states that **9 . . . B–K2** is
weak due to 10 Q–N4 **K–B1(?)** 11
Q–N3 P–Q3 12 B–K3! P×P 13
R–Q1 Q–K1 14 Q×KP B–Q3 15
Q–KR5 etc. But **10 . . . P–KN3** 11
B–R6 (Shatskes) is not so easy after
11 . . . P–Q3: 12 Q–Q4 P×P 13
Q×KP P–KB3 (Δ . . . Q–Q3) or
12 Q–N3 B–B4! Δ ∴. Q–Q2.

10 B–R3   P–Q3

'?!' (Suetin), who does not offer
an alternative.

11 P×P   0–0

12 0–0–0 P×P 13 Q×QP Q×Q 14
B×Q R–K1 15 K–N2 B–Q2 16
B–Q3 B–B3 17 P–B3 R–K3 18
P–B5 ± Korchnoi-Hübner (2),
Solingen 1973. White has fair
chances to convert his superiority,
and did (1–0, 66).

B2

4 . . .   **B–N5**

Shatskes calls this 'weaker than 4
. . . B–B4', but it is entirely logical.

Without 4 . . . B–N5, we might see 4
P–K4 more often.

5 P–Q3

5 B–Q3!? is worth trying.

5 . . .   P–Q3

6 P–KN3

6 B–K2 0–0 7 0–0 B×N (or **7 . . .
P–KR3** Δ . . . N–R2, . . . P–B4) 8
P×B Q–K2 9 N–K1 (**9 B–N5** N–Q1!
10 P–KN3? N–K3! 11 B–Q2 N–B4
∓ Steinbruck-Kania, 1975) 9 . . .
N–K1 10 N–B2 P–B4 11 P×P B×P
12 N–K3 B–K3 13 P–Q4?! (13
R–N1 or 13 B–B3) 13 . . . B–B2! =
Fine-Dake, Mexico City 1935.

6 . . .   0–0

a) **6 . . . B–N5** 7 P–KR3 (**7 B–K2**
P–KR3 8 B–K3 B×Nch?! – *8 . . .
B–QB4* – 9 P×B Q–Q2 10 Q–B2
0–0 11 Q–Q2 N–R2 12 P–KR3
B×P?? 13 N–N1! B–N5 14 P–B3
B–K3 15 P–Q4 ±± Nimzowitsch-
Sämisch, Dresden 1926) 7 . . . B×N
8 Q×B N–Q5 9 Q–Q1 P–B3 10
B–N2 P–KR4!? 11 0–0 P–R5 12
P–KN4 N–K3 13 N–K2 B–B4 14
B–Q2 Schüssler-Lundin, Gausdal
1978, and now 14 . . . P–KN4 ∞
should be tried.

b) **6 . . . B–QB4** 7 P–KR3 (**7 B–N2**
N–N5?! 8 0–0 P–B4 Nimzowitsch-
Mieses, Hanover 1926, and 9 P×P!
B×P 10 N–KR4 ± wins the light
squares -Taimanov.) 7 . . . B–K3 8
B–N2 P–KR3 9 P–R3 P–QR4 10
Q–R4?! (10 0–0) 10 . . . 0–0 11
N–K2 N–Q2! 12 P–KN4 B–N3 13
B–K3 N–B4 14 Q–Q1 P–R5 ∓
Gabaryn-Alekhine, 1926.

7 B–N2   N–K1

7 . . . N–Q5 8 N×N P×N 9
P–QR3 B×Nch?! 10 P×B P×P 11
Q–B2 ± Nimzowitsch-Spielmann,

Bled 1931. 9 ... B–R4 10 Q–R4 (**10 P–QN4** P×N 11 P×B P–B4) 10 ... P–B4 was better'.

8 0–0   B×N
9 P×B   P–B4

Equal, according to Taimanov. Zagarovsky-Krzyston, corres 1975, tested this assessment: 10 P×P B×P 11 N–R4 B–K3 12 R–QN1 R–N1 **13 B–K3** N–B3 14 Q–R4?! (**14 R–N2!** was better. This position is not analogous to note (b) to 6 ... 0–0, however, because White cannot easily bring a knight to e4.) 14 ... B–Q2 15 P–KR3 Q–K1! 16 K–R2 P–KR3 17 Q–Q1 P–QN3 18 P–N4? N–K2 ∓. Zagarovsky's improvement **13 P–B4** should be met by 13 ... P–KN3 ∞ – Povah.

CONCLUSION:

4 P–K4 doesn't create many problems if Black is careful. 4 ... P–Q3, 4 ... B–B4, and **4 ... B–N5** are all good answers.

C

4 P–Q3

A common sense move. Now if **4 ... P–Q4** 5 P×P N×P, White has a pleasant choice between **6 P–KN3** (Chapter 6), **6 P–K4!?**, and **6 P–K3** with a Scheveningen Reversed (no worry about a Sozin or Keres attack here!). Some samples of the latter possibility can be found in the next section (D 4 P–QR3). Black can do better, however, with:

C1 4 ... P–Q3
C2 4 ... B–N5

a) **4 ... B–B4?!** can be safely answered by **5 P–K3** or **5 P–QR3**, but also by **5 N×P!** B×Pch 6 K×B

N×N 7 P–K4 (or 7 P–Q4!?) 7 ... P–B4 8 B–K2 P–Q3 9 R–B1 with a positional edge. By contrast with 4 P–KN3 B–B4 5 N×P (Chapter 7, C1), White has not weakened his kingside.

b) **4 ... P–KN3** 5 P–KN3 usually transposes to C1 below. 5 ... N–Q5?! 6 N×N! P×N 7 N–N5 P–B4 8 Q–R4! N–R4 9 B–N2 B–K2 10 B–R6! was not a helpful deviation in Ribli-Garcia, Las Palmas 1974.

C1

4 ...   **P–Q3**
5 P–KN3   P–KN3
6 B–N2   B–N2

For **7 0–0** 0–0 see *English II*. But White can set a 'detour' by:

7 R–QN1!?   P–QR4
8 P–QR3   N–Q5

Black has been provoked! If **8 ... 0–0** 9 P–QN4 P×P 10 P×P P–KR3 11 P–N5 N–K2 12 B–N2 B–K3 13 R–R1, White has benefited by his 'saved' tempo (i.e. the omission of ... 0–0), while in this line 10 ... B–B4 runs into 11 N–KR4 forcing the bishop back home because of 12 P–N5.

9 N–Q2   0–0
10 0–0

So all White had achieved by 7 R–QN1 is to transpose into a King's Indian related system of *English II* (quite a limitation of Black's defensive systems, anyway); but 9 N×N P×N 10 N–R4!? 0–0 11 0–0 would have done the same.

We are following Larsen-Portisch, Biel 1977: 10 ... P–B3 11 P–QN4 P×P 12 P×P B–N5?! (**12**

... **P–Q4!** is better; see Chapter 16, G5!) 13 P–KR3 B–Q2 (so as to preserve e6 for the knight e.g. **13 ... B–K3** 14 P–K3 N–B4 15 P–N5 Q–B2 16 N(2)–K4, slightly ±.) 14 K–R2 N–R4 15 P–B5!? P–Q4 16 P–K3 N–K3 17 N–R4 P–B4 (17 ... N–B3!?) 18 N–N6 R–N1 19 P–K4! BP×P 20 P×P N–B2 21 N×B Q×N 22 N–B4 Q–K3 23 N–N6. White has two bishops and is chipping away at Black's centre; he went on to win.

C2

     4 ...   **B–N5**
     5 B–Q2

5 B–N5!? (Petrosian) 5 ... P–KR3 6 B×N B×Nch (**6 ... Q×B(!)** 7 N–Q2 0–0 8 N–Q5?! – *8 P–KN3* – 8 ... Q–Q1 9 P–KN3 B×Nch! 10 Q×B N–Q5 11 B–N2 P–QB3 12 N–B3 P–Q3 13 0–0 B–K3 = Sanguinetti-Benko, Sao Paulo 1977) 7 P×B Q×B 8 N–Q2 (We've seen the ex-world champion use this idea often: emphasis of the light-squared diagonal.) 8 ... 0–0 9 P–KN3 P–Q3 10 B–N2 B–Q2 11 0–0 (±) 11 ... Q–K2 12 K–R1 P–R3 13 Q–B2 QR–N1 14 QR–N1 N–Q1! 15 P–K3 B–B3 16 P–Q4 B×Bch 17 K×B N–B3 18 Q–K4 P–B4 19 Q–Q5ch with minimal pressure. I'd say 'not enough to win', but White did just that in Petrosian-Keene, Nice 1974.

     5 ...   0–0

Now White makes a structural decision:
C21 6 P–KN3
C22 6 P–K3

C21

   6 P–KN3 (*75*)

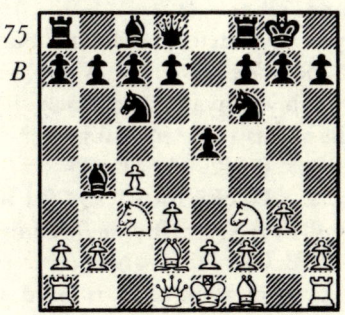

75
B

   6 ...   R–K1

In lieu of this:
a) **6 ... P–Q4?!** 7 P×P N×P 8 B–N2 and Capablanca-Rsheshevsky, Semmering 1937 saw 8 ... N–N3 9 0–0 P–KR3 10 R–K1 (A 'mysterious rook move' – *too* mysterious! **10 P–QR3** or **10 R–B1** would yield an excellent version of Chapter 6: ±) 10 ... Q–K2 11 P–QR3 B–Q3 12 N–QN5 B–K3 13 P–QN4 P–R3 14 N×B P×N 15 P–K4. The play has hardly been critical, and Reshevsky managed to split the point in 51 moves.
b) **6 ... N–Q5** 7 B–N2 (**7 N×P?** Q–K2 8 P–B4 P–Q3 9 P–K3 N–B4 etc.; but also **7 N×N!** P×N 8 N–N5 B×Bch 9 Q×B P–B4 10 N–Q6 ± Benko-L.D.Evans, New York 1976) 7 ... N×Nch 8 B×N P–Q3 9 B–N2 P–B3 10 0–0 B–K3 11 Q–N3! P–QR4 12 P–QR3 B×N 13 Q×B Q–Q2?! (**13 ... R–K1** -Petrosian) 14 B–N5! N–K1 15 P–Q4! P–B3 16 B–K3 B–R6 17 P×P BP×P (**17 ... B×B** 18 K×B QP×P 19 QR–Q1 Q–K3 20 B–B5 R–B2 21 P–QR4 ± -Shamkovich) 18 P–B5!(±) 18 ... N–B3 19 P×P B×B 20 K×B Q×P

21 B–B5 Q–Q4ch 22 P–B3 KR–K1 23 P–K4 ± Petrosian-Bisguier, Lone Pine 1976 (1–0, 51). Typically deft handling! Such positions (i.e. after 6 . . . N–Q5) are probably playable for Black, but who wants to defend all game?

7 B–N2   P–Q3

7 . . . B×N 8 B×B P–Q4 9 P×P N×P 10 B–Q2± (Byrne/Mednis).

8 0–0   N–Q5

A good alternative is hard to find.

9 P–QR3   B×N

10 B×B N×Nch 11 B×N P–B3 12 B–N2 B–Q2?! (**12 . . . P–Q4** 13 P×P P×P ±-Byrne/Mednis; such a centre might counteract the bishops) 13 P–R3 (Δ 14 P–B4) 13 . . . P–KR3 14 K–R2 N–R2 15 P–B4 P×P?! (**15 . . . P–B3** 16 P–KB5 ± -Benko) 16 P×P P–KB4 17 Q–K1 Q–K2 18 Q–N3 (A familiar theme: the KN file and long dark diagonal combine to doom Black's king.) 18 . . . Q–B2 19 B–B3 R–K2 20 R–KN1 N–B3 21 Q–R4 R–KB1 22 R–N2 K–R2 23 R(1)–KN1 Q–K3 24 P–K4 N–K1 25 B–R5 R–B3 26 B–N6ch! R×B 27 R×R 1–0 Benko-Sherwin, Fairfax 1976.

C22

6 P–K3   R–K1

a) **6 . . . P–Q4** 7 P×P N×P 8 B–K2 B–K3 9 0–0 P–B4 10 N×N (**10 Q–N1** is perhaps a better way to exploit the tempo.) 10 . . . Q×N 11 B×B N×B 12 N–N5 ± Larsen-G. Garcia, Las Palmas 1974 (but 0–1, 35). The bishop on b4 really shouldn't fit in here.

b) **6 . . . P–Q3** 7 B–K2 P–QR4 8 0–0 P–R3 9 Q–B2 (bearing a resemblance to E4413 below) 9 . . . B–KB4 10 P–QN3! R–K1 11 P–QR3 B–B4 12 Q–N2 Q–Q2 13 KR–Q1 B–KR2 14 B–K1 (Δ P–Q4) ± Miles-Bisguier, Las Vegas 1976 (1–0, 82).

7 B–K2 (*76*)

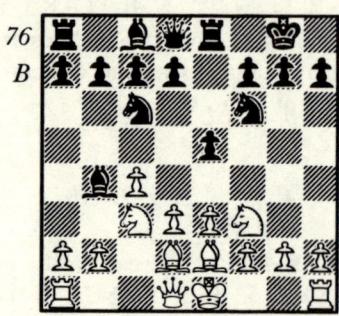

7 . . .   B×N

a) **7 . . . P–Q3** 8 P–QR3 B×N 9 B×B N–K2 10 0–0 P–B4 11 P–QN4 P–QN3 12 P×P (12 Q–B2!?) 12 . . . NP×P 13 R–N1 B–Q2 Polugaevsky-Petrosian, USSR Ch 1977 (½–½, 26).

b) **7 . . . B–B1** seems dull, but looks can belie: 8 0–0 P–Q3 9 N–KN5!? (9 **P–QR3** N–K2 10 P–QN4 N–N3 11 Q–B2 B–B4 = Larsen-Lombardy, Orense 1975) 9 . . . N–Q2 10 P–B4!? P×P 11 P×P N–Q5 12 B–R5 P–KN3 13 P–B5 N–KB3! 14 P×P BP×P 15 N–K2 N–B4! ∓ Möhring-Gipslis, Hradec Kralove 1977/8.

8 B×B   P–Q4

9 P×P   Q×P?!

9 . . . N×P! ± (Polugaevsky) 10 B–Q2 N(4)–N5 11 Q–N1 B–B4 12 P–K4 B–N5; possibly **10 Q–Q2!?**.

10 0–0   B–N5

11 Q–R4!(±) 11 ... QR–Q1 12 KR–Q1 Q–Q2 13 Q–N3 Q–B1 14 QR–B1 Polugaevsky-Osgaard, Manila 1975.

CONCLUSION:

4 P–Q3 is unpretentious but can have some sting if Black does not heed the warning signs. On the other hand, White's pieces are usually confined to three ranks, and he can lose his positional pluses trying to infiltrate Black's domain.

D

4 P–QR3

Eliminating 4 ... B–N5, at any rate. We examine:

D1 4 ... P–KN3
D2 4 ... P–Q4

4 ... P–Q3 5 P–Q4 B–N5 6 P–Q5 N–K2 7 P–KN3 (or 7 P–K4) 7 ... P–KN3 8 B–N2 B–N2 9 N–Q2!? Q–B1? (9 ... 0–0) 10 P–R3 B–Q2 11 P–QN4 P–QR4 12 B–N2 P×P 13 P×P R×R 14 Q×R Marini-Schmid, corres 1954–6. Black is somewhat hemmed in.

D1

4 ... P–KN3

5 P–KN3

The move P–QR3 doesn't fit in well with **5 P–Q4** P×P 6 N×P B–N2 7 P–KN3 0–0 8 N×N NP×N 9 B–N2 R–K1, yet that is playable. Much worse was **5 P–QN4?** P–K5! 6 N–KN5 B–N2 7 Q–B2?! (7 R–R2! ∓) 7 ... N–Q5 8 Q–N1 P–Q4 9 P×P 0–0! 10 P–K3 N×P 11 N(5)×P B–B4 ∓ Martz-Strauss, U.S.A. 1975. After 12 B–N2, however, Black missed 12 ... N–N6! 13 R–R2 N×QP ∓∓ and soon lost. Alas, opening theory will

never guard one against such vicissitudes!

5 ...	B–N2
6 B–N2	0–0
7 0–0	P–Q3
8 P–Q3	

Arriving at a position from *English II ... N–KB3*, Ch 5, but with P–QR3 substituted for R–QN1. White has the option of R–QB1 now, but that isn't much for a tempo. One example: 8 ... N–Q5 (**8 ... P–KR3!** and **8 ... N–KR4!** are good moves.) 9 N×N P×N 10 N–Q5 N–N5?! (**10 ... P–B3 =**) 11 P–N4 P–QB3 12 N–B4 R–K1 13 P–N5 B–Q2 14 R–N1 Q–B1 15 R–K1 ± Seirawan-Bisguier, Lincoln 1975. (1–0,53).

D2

4 ...	P–Q4
5 P×P	N×P
6 P–Q3	B–K2
7 P–K3	0–0
8 B–K2	

8 Q–B2 N–N3?! 9 P–QN4 P–QR3 10 B–K2 B–K3 11 0–0 P–B4 12 B–N2 B–B3 13 QR–N1! Q–Q2 14 B–R1 Q–B2 15 R(B)–B1 ± Nei-Unzicker, Tallin 1977. White has ideal queenside pressure (although 0–1, 47).

8 ... B–K3

After 8 ... B–K3, a 'Reversed Scheveningen', we reach a position that defies exhaustive analysis, but should somewhat favour White. I offer these examples:

a) **9 B–Q2** P–B3 10 P–QN4 N×N 11 B×N B–Q3 12 0–0 Q–Q2 13 Q–B2 P–QR3 14 KR–Q1 Q–B2 15 QR–N1 KR–Q1 16 P–QR4 N–K2

Larsen-Botvinnik, Leiden 1970. Unclear, though White looks a shade better (1–0, 47).

b) **9 0–0** P–B4 10 Q–B2 B–B3 11 N–QR4 B–B2!? 12 R–N1 (or **12 B–Q2** P–QR4 13 QR–B1 ± - Schwarz) 12 ... P–QR4 13 B–Q2 P–K5 14 N–K1! P×P 15 B×QP P–KN3 16 N–KB3 N–K4 17 B–K2 Q–K2 18 KR–Q1 ± Barcza-Bely, Hungarian Ch. 1957.

CONCLUSION

4 P–QR3 would be played more often if it weren't for 4 ... P–KN3.

E

4 P–K3

This modest nudge of the king pawn has introduced some of the most exciting and unique chess in all of the 1 ... P–K4 English! The variations beginning with 4 ... B–N5 5 Q–B2 are continually being enriched with new ideas, a trend which shows no sign of stopping; recent developments like Stean's 7 Q–B5 in the main line are particularly intriguing because of the diversity of chess which results; from mating attacks to prolonged manoeuvreing to double-edged endings! I hope that what follows will give the reader a feeling of that diversity.

The first thing to note is that **4 ... P–Q4** 5 P×P N×P will be found in Chapter 11, B41. Other moves tend not to transpose and, by way of warning, theory has not indicated a clear verdict on any of them! We examine:

E1 4 ... P–KN3

E2 4 ... P–Q3
E3 4 ... B–K2
E4 4 ... B–N5

E1

4 ...	**P–KN3**
5 P–Q4	P–Q3
6 P–QN3	

a) **6 P×P P×P** 7 Q×Qch K×Q 8 B–Q2 with a tiny edge; or **6 ... N×P** 7 N–Q4 ± (Panno).

b) **6 B–K2** P×P? 7 P×P B–N2 8 P–Q5! N–K2 9 P–KR3 0–0 10 0–0 R–K1 11 R–K1 N–Q2 12 B–B1 N–B4 13 B–B4! ± Szabo-Hort, 1973 (1–0, 36).

c) **6 P–QN4(!)** B–N2 7 P–N5 P×P 8 P×P N–K2 9 B–K2 0–0 10 0–0 P–QR3!? 11 P×P P–N3 12 P–QR4 ± Smyslov-Visier, Las Palmas 1972.

6 ...   B–N5!

6 ... B–N2 seems weaker after **7 P×P!** P×P 8 Q×Qch K×Q 9 B–R3 with a very favourable queenless middlegame. Instead, **7 B–N2** 0–0 8 P–Q5 N–K2 brought about play typical of a King's Indian Defence in Nei-Makarichev, Nice 1974.

7 B–K2	B–N2
8 B–N2	0–0
9 P–Q5	

and White has some space advantage: 9 ... N–K2 10 P–K4 N–R4 11 P–N3 B–R3!? (11 ... P–QB3) 12 N–KR4 B×B 13 Q×B N–N2 14 0–0 P–KB4 15 P–B3 R–B2?! (15 ... P–B3) 16 N–N2 Q–Q2 17 P–B4! ± Panno-Hübner, Palma de Mallorca 1970 (1–0, 41).

E2

4 ...   P–Q3

5 P–Q4	B–N5
6 P–Q5	N–QN1
7 P–K4	

Or **7 B–K2** QN–Q2 8 0–0 B–K2 9 N–K1 B×B 10 Q×B with advantage (Shatskes and Taimanov).

7 ...	B–K2
8 P–KR3	B–R4

9 B–K3 P–QR4 10 B–Q3 N–R3 11 P–KN4 B–N3 12 Q–K2 N–Q2 13 P–KR4 P–R4 14 P–N5 N(2)–B4 15 B–B2 P–QB3 16 P–R3 ± Polugaevsky-Hort, Belgrade 1970. 'Self-cramping,' commented Gligorić of Black's play.

E3

4 ...	**B–K2**

More frequently played than **4 ... P–KN3** or **4 ... P–Q3**.

5 P–Q4

There are two noteworthy alternatives:

a) **5 B–K2** 0–0 6 0–0 P–Q4 (**6 ... P–Q3** 7 P–Q4 B–N5 8 P–QR3 – *or 8 P–Q5* – 8 ... P–QR4 9 P–QN3 R–K1, Tiller-Agantysson, Gausdal 1978, is cramped but acceptable.) 7 P×P N×P 8 P–Q3 is another Scheveningen Reversed. See D3.

b) 5 Q–B2 0–0 6 P–QR3 P–Q3 (Now on **6 ... P–Q4** 7 P×P N×P, either **8 B–Q3** P–KN3 9 N×N Q×N 10 B–K4 or simply **8 B–N5** is ±.) 7 B–K2 R–K1 8 0–0 B–B1 9 P–Q4 B–N5 10 P–Q5 N–K2 Tartakower-Dr. E. Lasker, New York 1924. 11 P–K4 Δ B–K3 ± Tartakower.

5 ...	P×P
6 N×P	

Winning ground in the centre. **6**

P×P P–Q4 7 P×P N×P 8 B–QN5 (Taimanov) 8 ... 0–0 =

6 ...	0–0

a) **6 ... N×N?!** 7 Q×N 0–0 8 P–KN3 P–Q3 9 B–N2 P–B3 10 0–0 Q–R4 11 P–N3 Q–R4 12 B–N2 B–R6 13 P–B3! B×B 14 K×B KR–Q1 15 P–K4 ± Fuchs-Gipslis, Budapest 1961. White has a space advantage and better bishop; Black's queen is off-centre.

b) **6 ... P–Q4** is possible; play would probably be similar to the text.

7 B–K2

7 N×N NP×N 8 B–K2 P–Q4 ('?' Keene) 9 0–0 B–Q3 transposes. But if 8 ... 0–0 9 0–0, Black still must find a means of developing, as both **9 ... B–N2** 10 P–QN3 P–B4 11 N–Q5 and **9 ... P–Q3** 10 B–B3 B–Q2 11 P–QN3 look good for White.

7 ...	P–Q4

a) **7 ... N–K4?!** 8 N–B2! P–B3 9 P–K4 P–Q3 10 0–0 R–K1 11 P–QN3 B–B1 12 N–K3 N–N3 13 B–Q3 N–Q2 14 B–B2 N–B4 15 K–R1 P–QR4 16 P–B4 ± Smyslov-Mikenas, USSR Ch 1950 Exemplary piece handling by White.

b) **7 ... B–N5** 8 0–0!? B×N 9 P×B P–Q3 10 B–R3 B–Q2 (10 ... P–QN3!?) 11 P–B5 P–Q4 12 P–QB4 P×P 13 B×P Q–K2 14 Q–B1 ± Filtser-Gasharov, USSR, 1956.

c) **7 ... R–K1** 8 0–0 B–B1 9 P–QN3 P–Q3 10 B–N2 B–Q2 11 R–B1 (**11 N–B2!?; 11 B–B3!?**) 11 ... N×N 12 Q×N P–B3 13 KR–Q1 ± Stean-Garcia, Lone Pine 1978 (½–½, 46).

8 N×N

8 P×P N–QN5! 9 0–0 N(5)×P 10 N×N Q×N 11 N–N5? (11 P–N3) 11 ... P–B3 12 Q×Q N×Q ∓ Mikenas–Keres, 18th USSR Ch 1950.

8 ...   P×N

9 0–0 *(77)*

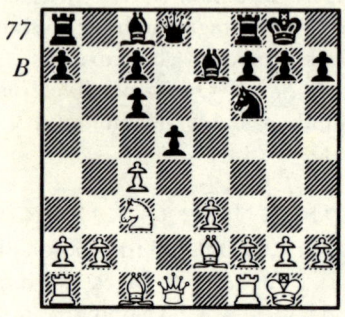

9 ...   B–Q3

Trying to utilize Black's control over e4 to work up kingside chances. It seems clear that White has the advantage if he can develop and swing his rooks to the centre files, so Black must seek counterplay, as in:

a) 9 ... **B–K3** 10 Q–R4 Q–Q3 11 P×P P×P 12 P–QN3 P–B3?! (**12 ... Q–N5!?**; **12 ... KR–Q1** 13 N–N5! Q–Q2 14 Q–R5 ±) 13 B–N2 N–Q2 14 KR–Q1 N–B4 15 Q–Q4 ± Sokolsky–Dragunov, corres 1965. Black will have to defend his centre pawns indefinitely;

b) 9 ... **R–K1!?** 10 Q–R4? (or **10 P–QN3** B–K3!. White should try **10 Q–B2** or **10 B–B3** B–K3 12 Q–R4 ±) 10 ... Q–Q3 11 P–QN3 Q–K4! 12 B–N2 B–Q3 13 P–N3 B–KR6 14 KR–Q1 N–K5, etc. (∓). Black seems on the verge of

equalizing in such lines, but may lack the requisite tempi.

10 P–QN3   Q–K2

11 B–N2   P×P!

If **11 ... Q–K4** 12 P–N3 B–KR6 13 R–K1 Q–B4 15 B–B3 KR–Q1 16 N–N5 ±.

11 ... R–Q1(?) 12 P×P Q–K4 (12 ... P×P 13 N–N5 B–R3 14 N–Q4 B×B 15 Q×B Q–K4 16 P–N3 R–K1 17 QR–B1 ± – Shatskes) 13 P–N3 B–KR6 14 R–K1 B–QN5 15 Q–B2 B–KB4 16 Q–B1 P×P 17 B–B3 Q–K2 18 P–QR3 B–R4 19 P–QN4 B–QN3 20 N×P! ± was Keene–Jansson, Haifa 1976.

12 P×P   R–N1

13 Q–B1 N–N5 14 P–KN3 R–K1 15 N–Q1? (15 P–B5) N×RP 16 P–B5 N×R 17 P×B N×NP! ∓∓, Timman–Karpov, Montreal 1979.

E4

4 ...   **B–N5**

The most active. Now:

E41 5 N–Q5

E42 5 P–Q4

E43 5 B–K2

E44 5 Q–B2

The other queen move is unwieldy: **5 Q–N3** P–QR4! (White threatened N×KP) 6 B–K2 0–0 7 0–0 R–K1 8 P–Q3 P–Q3 9 Q–B2 (an admission of the queen's poor position on b3) 9 ... B–N5 (Clearer is 9 ... P–KR3! Δ ... B–KB4) 10 P–QN3 P–Q4? (10 ... B×N(c3)! 11 Q×B P–K5 12 P×P N×P = was recommended, when 13 Q–B2 (Δ 13 ... N–N5 14 Q–N2) 13 ... P–R5 leaves problems for both sides.) 11 P×P N×P 12 N×N Q×N

13 P–QR3 ± with a favourable Sicilian in reverse, Korchnoi-Lehman, Palma de Mallorca 1968.

E41

> **5 N–Q5**   P–K5
> 6 N–N1!?

6 N×B is usually played here, but does little: 6 . . . N×N 7 N–Q4 0–0 (Possible is **7 . . . P–B4** 8 N–B2 N–Q6ch 9 B×N P×B 10 N–R3 P–Q4 11 Q–N3 B–K3 ∞ Nei-Smyslov, USSR Ch 1960 – eventually drawn.) 8 P–QR3 N–R3 (Also **8 . . . N–B3** 9 P–Q3 N×N 10 P×N P×P can be tried, when 11 B×P is equal, and 11 P–Q5? R–K1ch 12 B–K3 P–Q3 13 P–KR3? R×Bch! led to quick disaster in Ksieski-Pioch, Poland 1976.) 9 B–K2 (**9 P–Q3** P–Q4 10 BP×P Q×P 11 P×P Q×P 12 Q–B3 Q–K4 △ 13 B×N Q–R4ch Shatskes) 9 . . . P–Q4 10 P–Q3 KP×P 11 B×P P–B4 12 N–N5 B–Q2 13 N–B3 P×P 14 B×P N–B2 15 0–0 B–B3 = Swiderski-Marshall, Nüremberg 1906.

> 6 . . .   0–0
> 7 N×B

A new idea was **7 P–QR3** B–Q3 (7 . . . B–K2!?) 8 Q–B2 R–K1 9 KN–K2 ∞, Stean-Lieb, Munich 1979.

> 7 . . .   N×N

8 P–QR3 N–B3 9 P–Q4 P×Pe.p. 10 B×P N–K4 (10 . . . P–Q4 =) 11 B–K2 P–Q3 12 N–B3 B–K3 13 Q–B2 Q–K2 14 N–Q4 B–Q2 15 0–0 P–QR4 16 P–QN3 KR–K1 17 B–N2 ± Flohr-Villard, 1937.

E42

> **5 P–Q4**   P×P
> 6 N×P

6 P×P P–Q4 7 B–N5 B–N5 (Shatskes).

> 6 . . .   0–0
> 7 B–K2   N–K5

Or **7 . . . R–K1** 8 0–0 B×N 9 P×B P–Q3 = (Shatskes).

> 8 Q–B2   R–K1
> 9 0–0?!

9 N×N QP×N (or 9 . . . NP×N) 10 0–0 N×N 11 P×N B–QB4 = Rudakovsky-Lilienthal, USSR Ch 1945

> 9 . . .   N×N(5)

Or **9 . . . N×N(6)** 10 P×N B–B4 11 R–Q1 Q–B3 12 N–N5 Q–Q1 13 B–R3?! (13 N–Q4 = Vaganian) 13 . . . B×B 14 N×B Q–K2 ∓ S. Garcia-Vaganian, Hastings 1974/5.

> 10 P×N   N×N

11 P×N B×P 12 Q×B R×B 13 B–K3 P–Q3! 14 KR–N1 B–B4 15 R×P B–K5 16 R–N5 P–QB3 17 R–N5 P–Q4 with 'dynamic equality' according to Shatskes. Nevertheless, White's eccentric rook and Black's activity lead us to favour the second player.

E43

> **5 B–K2**   0–0
> 6 0–0

6 Q–B2 is E4411. **6 P–QR3?** B×N 7 NP×B P–K5 8 N–Q4 N–K4 ∓ Vordank-Desler, corres 1954.

> 6 . . .   P–K5

Simplest. **6 . . . R–K1** 7 P–QR3?! (**7 Q–B2** is again preferable.) 7 . . . B×N 8 NP×B P–Q3 (or **8 . . . P–K5**) 9 N–K1 N–K2 10 P–Q3 P–B3 11 P–QR4 (or **11 P–K4** N–N3! ± Schwarz) 11 . . . B–K3 12 P–R5 P–Q4 ∓ Nimzowitsch-Reti, Breslau 1925.

7 N–Q4   P–Q4!?

Or **7 . . . R–K1** or **7 . . . B×N!** 8 QP×B P–Q3 (Taimanov).

8 N×QP

Taimanov gives **8 N×N** P×N 9 Q–R4 **B–Q3**('!') 10 Q×BP B–Q2 11 Q–R6 P–B3 and **8 P×P** N×N 9 P×N B–KB4; but the first line seems unclear at best after 12 P×P e.g. **12 . . . . Q–B2** 13 P–KN3 P×P 14 N–N5, or **12 . . . B–B1!?** 13 Q×BP R–N1 14 P–B4. Better is **9 . . . P–QR4 (= /∞)**.

8 . . .   N×N(4)

9 N×N P×N 10 P×N P×P 11 P–Q3 B–Q3 12 P×P P×P 13 Q–B2 R–K1 14 B–Q2 Q–N4 Bobotsov-Szabo, Beverwijk 1966. Black has the attack.

E44

5 **Q–B2** (*78*)

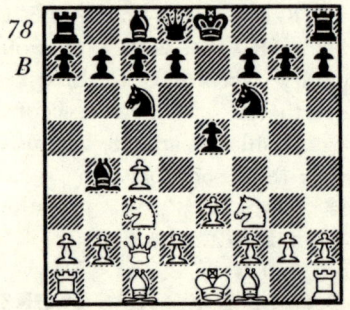

78
B

This prevents doubled pawns and controls key central squares. Now Black makes a major decision:

E441 5 . . . 0–0
E442 5 . . . B×N
E443 5 . . . P–Q3

E441

5 . . .   0–0

Trusting in rapid development. Now White has tried a number of ideas, some very curious indeed. So our analysis again divides:

E4411 6 B–K2
E4412 6 P–QR3
E4413 6 P–Q3
E4414 6 B–Q3
E4415 6 N–Q5

E4411

6 **B–K2**   R–K1

6 B–K2 is slow enough that Black can play several sequences, including **6 . . . B×N!?** 7 Q×B Q–K2 or 7 . . . P–K5 (see E442). Suba-Tompa, Varna 1976 saw **6 . . . P–Q3** and contains some typical themes: 7 0–0 P–QR4 8 P–Q3 P–R3 (Some players like their pawns on black!) 9 P–QN3 B×N?! 10 Q×B N–K2 11 B–N2 P–QN3 (See?! Actually, these structures are characteristic of 4 . . . B–N5.) 12 N–Q2 B–N2 13 P–B4! P×P 14 R×P N–N3 15 R–N4 P–R5 (**15 . . . R–K1** Δ . . . R–K4–N4!?) 16 R–KB1 P×P 17 P×P R–R7 18 R–N3 Q–K2 19 B–Q1 R–R4 20 P–K4 N–K1 21 N–B3 P–QB4 22 R–K1 K–R2 23 P–K5! ± (1–0, 33). Ceding the two bishops is usually appropriate only when Black can enforce . . . P–Q4 or . . . P–K5 soon thereafter.

7 0–0   P–Q3

Solidest. **7 . . . P–K5** (**7 . . . B–B1** – Alekhine – 8 P–Q4 ±) 8 N–K1! (**8 N–Q4?!** N×N 9 P×N P–Q4 10 P×P B–KB4! 11 P–Q3 P×P 12 B×P B×P 13 Q×B N×P ∓ Bobotsov-Portisch, Siegen 1970) 8 . . . B×N 9 NP×B Q–K2 (Or **9 . . . P–QN3** 10 P–B3 B–N2 11 P×P N×P 12 N–Q3 Q–N4 13 N–B4 N–K4 14 P–Q3 Δ

P–K4 ±) 10 P–B3! P–QN3 11 P×P
N×P 12 N–Q3 B–R3 13 N–B4
N–B3 14 P–Q3 N–K4 15 P–K4 ±
Filip-Potuchek, Czechoslovakia
1952.

 8 N–K1

8 P–Q3 will transpose into
E4413.

 8 . . .   B–K3
9 P–QR3 B×N 10 Q×B P–QR4 11
P–N3 Q–Q2 12 P–Q3 P–Q4 =
Flohr-Fine, Nottingham 1936.

E4412

 6 P–QR3?! B×N
 7 Q×B   R–K1
 8 P–Q3   P–QR4

Or **8 . . . P–Q4** 9 P×P Q×P 10
B–K2 P–K5 11 P×P N×P 12 Q–B4
Q–KB4! 13 0–0 B–K3 14 Q–B2
B–Q4! and Black was developing
smoothly in Bielicki-Smyslov,
Havana 1964.

 9 P–QN3   P–Q4
 10 P×P   Q×P
 11 B–N2

Correct is **11 B–K2**, and if 11 . . .
B–N5, 12 0–0; when Black should
play 12 . . . P–K5 13 P×P N×P 14
Q–B2 Q–QB4! =. We are
following Pachman-Bely, 1960,
which ended surprisingly after 11
. . . B–N5 12 B–K2 N–Q5! (79) 13
N×N (13 P×N P×P 14 Q×QP
B×N 15 Q×Q N×Q! ∓) 13 . . .
P×N 14 Q×QP Q×KNP 15 B×B
Q×Rch 16 K–K2 Q–Q4 ∓∓.

E4413

 6 P–Q3

The idea behind this move is to
prevent . . . P–K5 and prepare
B–Q2. If Black opens things up

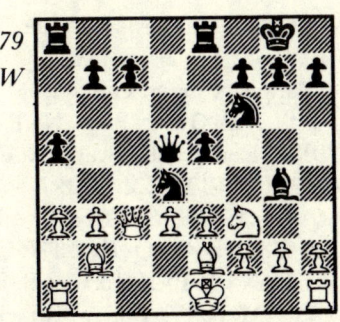

with . . . P–Q4, White should get
Sicilian-like pressure. Taimanov
awards 6 P–Q3 an '!', but it has had
only qualified success.

 6 . . .   R–K1
 7 B–Q2   P–Q3

An enterprising test of White's
strategy is

a) **7 . . . B×N!?** 8 B×B P–Q4 9 P×P
N×P (Fantasy-like is **9 . . . Q×P!?**
10 B–K2 P–K5?! 11 B×N! P×N 12
B×BP N–N5! 13 Q–B3 Q–QR4 14
B×KNP N–B7ch 15 K–Q2 Q×Qch
16 P×Q N×R 17 B–Q4 ± Ribli-
Kavalek, Manila 1976. The two
bishops will wreak havoc.) 10 B–K2
Q–Q3 (Against Taimanov in the
next year's USSR Championship,
Kuzmin varied with **10 . . . B–B4!?**
11 P–K4 N×B 12 P×N B–N5 13
0–0, and now 13 . . . B×N 14 B×B
Q–Q3 would leave White only
minimally better.) **11 0–0** N(3)–N5
12 Q–N1 P–QB4 **13 N–Q2** N–QB3
14 R–Q1 B–K3 15 P–QR3 QR–B1
16 B–B3 Q–K2 17 N–K4 KR–Q1
18 B–Q2 (△ P–QN4) 18 . . . P–B4
19 N–N3 P–QR4 20 Q–B2 P–KN3
∓ Smyslov-Kuzmin, USSR Ch
1973 (0–1, 76). Black achieved a
consolidation of his bind while
White uncharacteristically drifted.

11 P–QR3 improves, and later, **13 R–B1** (=); but in general, 7 . . . B×N appears sound enough.

b) **7 . . . P–Q4** 8 P×P N×P 9 P–QR3 (Remarkable was **9 B–K2** B×N!? 10 P×B P–K5! 11 P×P – *11 N–Q4 N×N Δ . . . B–B4 = /∞ – 11 . . . N–B3* 12 B–Q3 Q–K2 13 N–Q4 N×P 14 N×N P×N 15 0–0 B–B4 = /∞ Martz-Vukić, Vrnjacka Banja 1973.) 9 . . . B–B1 (Here also **9 . . . B×N** 10 P×B P–K5 was feasible.) 10 B–K2 N–B3 (Or **10 . . . B–K3**, but White has all the advantages of a Sicilian Defence) 11 P–QN4 B–KB4 12 N–K4 P–QR3 13 0–0 ± Heinicke-Bogoljubov, W. Germany 1951.

Black had reasonable chances in these lines because, by comparison with C212 above, White's queen comes rather prematurely to c2 and his queen bishop is passively-placed.

8 B–K2

8 P–QR3 B×N 9 B×B B–N5 (9 . . . P–KR3 Δ . . . B–B4) 10 B–K2 B×N!? 11 B×B N–Q5 12 Q–Q1 P–Q4 13 0–0 N×Bch 14 Q×N P–B3 15 P–K4! was barely ±, though White did get the full point in Olafsson-Timman, Lone Pine 1978.

8 . . .   B–KB4

8 . . . P–QR4 9 P–QR3 B–QB4 10 0–0 B–B4 has the advantage of preserving the king's bishop, although after 11 P–QN3 P–K5 (?!) 12 P×P N×P 13 N×N B×N 14 Q–N2(±) N–K4 15 P–QN4 B–QN3 16 B–B3! B×N 17 P×B Q–R5 18 K–R1, White was surprisingly on top since **18 . . .**

R–K3 19 R–KN1 Q×KBP 20 P–B4 N–N3 21 R–N2 and 22 P–KB5 is winning. After **18 . . . P×P** 19 P×P R×R 20 Q×R P–KB3 21 Q–Q1! N–B2 22 P–B4 P–B3 23 B–B3, White had two strong bishops and good kingside prospects, Csom-Jansson, Nice 1974.

9 0–0

9 N–K4 B×N 10 P×B B×Bch 11 N×B Q–K2, Ribli-Portisch, Budapest 1975, gives White control of key central squares, but at the cost of a mediocre bishop and lack of a knight outpost ($\frac{1}{2}$–$\frac{1}{2}$, 16).

9 . . .   P–K5

10 N–K'1 B–N3 11 R–Q1 P–QR4 12 N–Q5 P×P 13 B×P N–K5 14 N–KB3 B×B 15 N×B N–B3 16 B×B RP×B = Panno-Portisch, Petropolis 1973.

E4414

6 B–Q3

This somewhat bizarre-looking move makes its appearance again in E4415. Besides satisfying White's itchiness to develop, it also threatens to fianchetto White's king bishop without allowing . . . P–K5! Well, more or less: after **6 . . . R–K1**, for example, White could play 7 N–Q5 P–KN3 8 N×Nch Q×N 9 B–K4, seizing the long White diagonal – see E4415. **6 . . . P–Q3** saves time on this variation: 7 N–Q5 P–KR3 (or **7 . . . P–KN3**) 8 N×Nch Q×N 9 B–K4 Q–K2! 10 P–QR3 B–R4 11 P–QN4 (**11 P–QN3** is positionally desirable but too slow.) 11 . . .

B–N3 12 B–N2 P–B4 13 B–Q5ch
B–K3 = /∞. But play has usually
gone:

    6 . . .   B×N
    7 QP×B   P–Q3

7 . . . Q–K2! is almost certainly a
good move, forcing White to reveal
his intentions. If **8 P–K4** P–Q3 9
0–0, 9 . . . N–KR4 saves a tempo (9
. . . P–QR4) on the text. Eising-
Haag, 1972, revealed another
point: **8 N–Q2** N–Q1! 9 0–0 P–B3
10 N–K4 (**10 P–B4!?** Haag) 10 . . .
N–K1! 11 N–N3 P–KN3 12 P–B4
P×P 13 P×P P–B4 =; Black will
follow up up with . . . P–Q3 and . . .
Q–KB2.

    8 0–0   Q–K2

Or **8 . . . B–Q2** 9 N–Q2 N–K2 10
R–K1 B–B3?! (**10 . . . P–B3** Δ 11
P–K4 N–N3) 11 P–K4 N–N3 12
P–KN3 Q–Q2 13 N–B1 Q–R6 14
P–B3 P–KR4 15 N–K3 Q–K3 16
N–B5 P–R5 17 B–N5 ± Eising-
Wirtensohn, Mondorf 1973.

    9 N–Q2   P–QR4
    10 R–K1   P–KN3

11 P–K4 N–R4 12 N–B1 N–B5 13
N–K3 (±) Q–N4?! 14 P–B3 N–K2
15 B–B1! P–R4 16 P–KN3 P–KR5
17 N–N4! ± Korchnoi-Szabo,
Amsterdam 1975 (but ½–½, 48).

E4415

    6 N–Q5 (*80*)

The current and probably most
important variation.

    6 . . .   R–K1

At first sight, the move which
keeps options open; but . . . R–K1
has certain inherent disadvantages,
so the alternatives, especially 6 . . .
P–Q3, deserve a look:

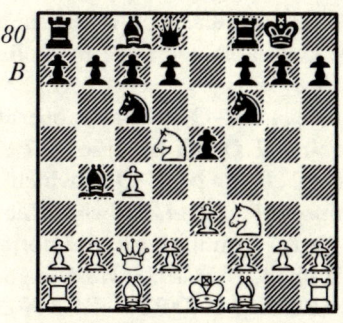

a) **6 . . . B–K2** is plausible, but will
cede the two bishops: 7 P–QR3
P–Q3 8 N×B Q×N 9 P–Q3 B–B4
10 P–QN4 (**10 P–QN3** P–K5 11
P×P Q×P ⨱) 10 . . . P–K5 11
P–N5 P×N (11 . . . N moves 12
N–Q4) 12 P×N P×P(3) 13 P×P ±.
b) **6 . . . P–Q3** avoids problems
connected with Q–KB5. White
may still play
b1) 7 B–Q3 (although the black
rook on f8 is properly behind the
KBP here), or
b2) 7 N×B N×N 8 Q–B3 P–QR4!? 9
P–QR3 N–B3 10 P–QN3 (else 10 . . .
P–R5) 10 . . . B–N5 11 P–Q3 B×N
12 P×B N–R4 13 B–QN2 P–B4 14
0–0–0 P–B5 15 B–K2, probably ±,
though there are many options on
the way. Most likely seems
b3) 7 P–QR3 (which in the text
would be answered by . . . B–B1) 7
. . . B–R4 **8 P–QN4** B–N3 9 N×B
(else 9 . . . N×N) 9 . . . RP×N 10
B–N2 B–N5 11 B–Q3 B–R4 12
N–N5 B–N3 13 0–0 (13 P–KR4
R–K1) 13 . . . Q–K2 14 P–B4 with
pressure. Lastly, sequences such as
7 P–QR3 B–R4 **8 N–N5** P–KN3
are not meaningless e.g. 9 P–KR4
B–B4 10 N×Nch Q×N 11 N–K4
Q–K2 12 P–QN4 B–N3 13 P–Q3

B–K3 14 P–KN3 ∞. All this should be compared with the main lines below.

c) **6 ... P–QR4!?** also operates against **7 Q–B5** because of 7 ... N×N! 8 P×N P–Q3, which is impossible in E44152 below due to 9 Q–K4 winning a piece. Adorjan-Timman, IBM 1978 was also good for Black: **7 P–QR3** B–B4 **8 N–N5** P–KN3 9 N×Nch Q×N 10 N–K4 Q–K2 11 B–K2 P–Q3 12 P–QN3 B–R2! 13 0-0 P–B4 14 N–B3 P–B5! 15 N–Q5 Q–N4 16 K–R1 B–R6! with a strong attack. Instead of 8 N–N5, **8 B–Q3** P–KN3 9 N×Nch Q×N 10 B–K4 would resemble E44151 below, e.g. 10 ... P–Q3 11 P–QN3 Q–K2 12 B–N2 P–B4 13 B–Q5ch B–K3 14 0-0 (± ?).

After 6 ... R–K1, **7 N×B?!** N×N 8 Q–B3 (8 Q–N3 P–B4 =) 8 ... P–QR4! is one way to play it, intending ... P–Q4, e.g. 9 P–QR3? P–Q4 or 9 B–K2 P–Q4 10 0-0 P–Q5! etc. White has two better moves, for which we must ask the reader to tolerate one last fork in the road:

E44151 7 B–Q3
E44152 7 Q–B5

Comparatively dull was **7 N–N5** P–KN3 8 N×Nch (8 P–KR4 B–B1!) 8 ... Q×N 9 N–K4 Q–Q1 10 P–QR3 B–B1 11 P–Q3 B–N2 12 B–K2 N–K2! 13 0-0 P–Q4 14 P×P N×P 15 B–Q2 P–N3= Suba-Suetin, Sochi 1977.

E44151

7 B–Q3   P–KN3
7 ... P–KR3(?) encountered trouble in Miles-Olafsson,

Reykjavik 1978: 8 P–QR3 B–B1 9 P–KR4! (Δ 10 N–N5!) 9 ... N×N (9 ... P–Q3! would be very complex. If 10 N–N5 P×N 11 P×P P–K5 12 P×N P×B 13 Q×P P–KN3 14 P–B4! B–K3 and Black seems able to defend e.g. 15 Q–B3 B×N 16 P×B N–N1 17 P–KN4 Q–Q2 18 R–R4 Q–N4!) 10 P×N N–Q5 (**10 ... N–N1** 11 B–R7ch K–R1 12 N–N5 Q–K2 13 B–N8! ±±) 11 B–R7ch K–R1 12 P×N P×Pch 13 K–Q1 P–KN3 14 B×P P×B 15 Q×NP and although Black drew(!), I do not recommend repeating all his moves!

8 P–QR3	B–B1
9 N×Nch	Q×N
10 B–K4	P–Q3

10 ... Q–K2 11 0-0 B–N2 12 P–QN4 P–QR4 13 P–N5 N–Q1 14 B–N2 N–K3? (Better **14 ... P–QB3** 15 Q–N1 ∞, whereas the seemingly tricky **14 ... P–Q4** is refuted by 15 P×P P–KB4 16 B–Q3 P–K5 17 B–B4 (Keene). 15 P–Q4! ± Keene-Vukcević, 1976.

11 P–QN4	Q–Q1

Or **11 ... Q–K2**, as in two later games, in that case, however, Black's knight does not have e7.

12 B–N2	B–N2
13 0-0	

Things are roughly equal; the modest **13 P–Q3** N–K2 14 N–Q2 would not help much after 14 ... P–QB3.

13 ...	N–K2
14 B–Q3	

Not **14 Q–N3?** P–QB3 15 P–Q4 P–Q4 ∓.

14 ...	P–KB4

We are following Miles-Diesen,

Las Vegas 1976; 15 B–K2 K–R1 16
P–B5 B–K3 17 B–B4 N–Q4 (**17 . . .
Q–Q2!?** 18 N–N5 P–Q4) 18 P–Q3
Q–K2?! (18 . . . P–B3) 19 Q–N3
P–B3 20 P–K4 N–B2 21 P×QP
Q×P and now instead of 22 N–N5
Q–K2 23 P–B4 P×BP! ($\frac{1}{2}$–$\frac{1}{2}$, 47), 22
P×P P×P 23 KR–K1 would have
given Black problems ($\pm$).

E44152
    7 Q–B5(!) (*81*)

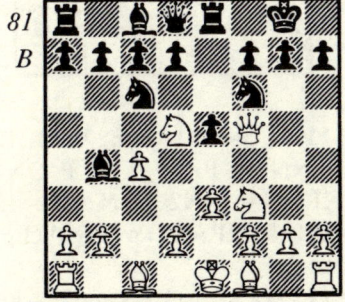

Keene, who should know, attributes this move to Stean. Both **7
B–Q3** and **7 Q–B5** are indicative of
the pragmatism of modern chess,
i.e. the value of a move is not
assessed by its appearance or
conformity to 'general principles,'
but by its ability to score points!
    7 . . .   P–Q3
Black ought not to be limited to
this one move. On the other hand, **7
. . . R–K3?** 8 N–N5 is untenable,
and the gambit idea
a) **7 . . . B–K2?!** 8 N×KP P–Q3
worked out poorly in Diesen-L.D.
Evans, New York 1977: 9 N×N
P×N 10 N×Bch Q×N 11 Q–B4!
P–Q4 12 B–K2 P×P 13 0–0 N–Q4
14 Q×P(4) R–N1 15 P–Q3 and

White was consolidating. A better
version might be
b) **7 . . . N×N** 8 P×N N–K2 9 Q×P
P–Q3 and if **10 Q–Q4**, 10 . . .
B–QB4 11 Q–QB4 P–QN4 12
Q–N3 (**12 Q×P** N×P Δ . . . N–N5)
12 . . . B–N2 13 B×P B×P 14 B–B4
R–N1 15 Q–B2 B×N 16 P×B N–N3
with attacking chances. More
logical is **10 Q–K4!** B–R4 11 B–B4
N–N3 12 Q–B2 B–KN5 13 B–K2
Q–Q2, although that would also be
obscure e.g. **14 0–0?** N–B5! or **14
P–QN3** B–B4 15 Q–Q1 B–K5 etc.
    8 N×Nch   P×N
8 . . . Q×N 9 Q×Q P×Q yields an
intricate ending: 10 P–QR3 (or **10
P–QN3**) 10 . . . B–B4 (After **10 . . .
B–R4**, White can transpose to (a)
by playing 11 P–QN4, or try 11
P–QN3) and now:
a) **11 P–QN4** B–N3 12 B–N2 (**12
P–Q3** N–K2 – *12 . . . P–QR4! 13
P–N5 N–Q1 is preferable* – 13 N–Q2
P–KB4 14 B–N2 P–KB3 15 B–K2
P–B3 16 0–0 B–K3 17 P–Q4 $\pm$
Korchnoi-Hofland, Netherlands
Ch 1977) 12 . . . P–QR4 13 P–N5
N–Q1! (**13 . . . N–K2** 14 B–K2
P–R5?! 15 0–0 P–B3 16 P×P $\pm$
Smejkal-Smyslov, Leningrad 1977)
14 P–QR4 N–K3 15 B–K2 P–B3 16
0–0 B–Q2 17 KR–Q1 P×P! 18
RP×P P–Q4 19 P×P N–B2 =
Keene-Ljubojević, Moscow 1977.
b) **11 P–QN3!** strikes me as best,
e.g. **11 . . . P–B4** 12 B–N2 P–B3 13
0–0–0, when Black has lasting
difficulties due to his crippled (static)
centre pawns and weak KRP.
Given time, White can attack with
e.g. N–KR4, P–KN4, R–KN1 etc.
But after . . . P–KB4, White plays

P–KN3, P–KB4, B–KR3, and so forth. The only example is Piasetski-Rajković, Stip 1977: **11 . . . P–QR4** 12 B–N2 R–R3? 13 0–0–0 P–K5 14 P–Q4! P×N 15 P×B P×NP 16 R–N1 ±.

9 Q–R5!

This must be the move. **9 Q–B2** P–K5 10 N–N1 (instead of **10 N–R4?** P–B4 11 P–KN3 P–Q4 12 P×P N–K4 13 Q–N3 – *better 13 B–K2 P–QB4!? ∞ Timman* – 13 . . . B–K2 14 P–Q4 P×Pe.p. 15 B×P B×N 16 P×B N–B6ch 17 K–Q1 R–K4 18 B–Q2 Q×P! ∓ ∓ Keene-Timman, Bad Lauterberg 1977) 10 . . . P–Q4 11 P×P (or **11 P–QR3?!** P–Q5!? – *11 . . . B–B1* – 12 P×B N×P 13 Q–N3 P–QB4 = /∞ – Timman) 11 . . . Q×P 12 P–QR3 B–Q3 13 N–K2 B–KB4 14 N–B3 Q–K3 ∞ (Timman).

9 . . .   P–Q4

9 . . . P–K5!? 10 P–QR3! P×N (**10 . . . B–R4** 11 P–QN4! B–N3 12 N–R4 R–K4 13 Q–Q1 P–B4 14 P–N3 △ B–QN2 ±) 11 P×B N×P 12 R–R4! ± (Analysis by Keene).

The position after 9 . . P–Q4 is controversial and exciting:

a) **10 P×P?** Q×P 11 B–K2 B–K3 12 0–0 P–K5! 13 Q×Q B×Q 14 N–K1 (14 N–R4!?) 14 . . . QR–Q1 15 P–Q4 B×N! 16 R×B N–N5 ∓ Keene-Korchnoi, Montreux 1977.

b) **10 P–QR3!?** B–B1 11 P–Q4 B–K3! (**11 . . . P×QP?** 12 B–Q3 P–KR3 13 0–0 N–K4 14 N×N P×N – *14 . . . R×N 15 Q–R4 P×BP 16 P×QP!* ± - 15 BP×P Q×P 16 P×P Q×QP 17 B–R7ch! -Keene and Stean) 12 B–Q3 P–KR3 13 P×QP Q×P 14

P–K4 Q–N6! = /∞ Fedorowicz-Tarjan, Hastings 1977/8.

c) I think **10 B–Q3(!)** should be tried: 10 . . . P–K5 (forced) 11 P×P (*82*), with these possibilities:

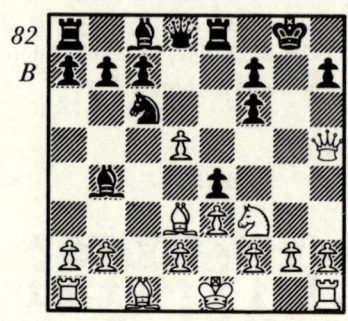

82
B

c1) **11 . . . N–N1** 12 B–B2 B–B1 (12 . . . P×N 13 P×P ±) 13 P–QN3 P–KR3 14 B–N2 P×N (else 15 N–R4) 15 P×P with an overwhelming attack;

c2) **11 . . . P×B** 12 P×N and Black's weak pawns are a liability, e.g. 12 . . . P×P 13 P–QN3 P–R4 (**13 . . . B–B1** 14 Q–R5! △ B–N2, R–QB1) 14 B–N2 B–B1 (White was threatening Q–R6) 15 R–QB1 ± △ **15 . . . R–K3** 16 R–B4, or **15 . . . P–R5** 16 R×P P×P?! 17 R×KBP!, or **15 . . . R–K5** 16 R×P B–KN5 17 Q–R4 B×N 18 Q–N3ch ±.

c3) **11 . . . B–B1!?** is the wierdest line: 12 P–QR3 (!!) (**12 B–N1** N–N5!; **12 B–N5?** P×N 13 P×P – *13 P×N R–K4* – 13 . . . N–K4! etc.; **12 P×N!?** Q×B 13 N–Q4 = /∞) 12 . . . N–N1 (**12 . . . P–KR3** 13 B–B2 P×N 14 P×N ±) 13 B–B2 B–N2 14 P–Q4! P×N 15 Q×RPch K–B1 16 P×P± e.g. 16 . . . P–KB4 17 R–KN1 Q–B3 18 P–K4! P×P 19 R×B P×Pch 20 K–Q1 Q×Pch 21

B–Q2 Q×QP 22 R×Pch! ±±.
Wild and crazy!

E442

5 ...   B×N!?

It may surprise one that Black
wishes to make this capture
unprovoked, but 6 N–Q5 can be
annoying. Moreover, the text looks
toward an early central pawn push
based on the exposed position of
White's queen after it retakes on c3.

6 Q×B

In view of the last note, **6 NP×B**
(∆ P–Q3, P–K4) may be con-
sidered: **6 ... P–K5?!** 7 N–N5
Q–K2 8 P–B3 P×P 9 N×P 0–0 10
B–K2 N–K4 (**10 ... P–QN3** 11
0–0 B–N2 12 N–N5 P–N3 = Timo-
shenko; but 12 N–Q4 N×N – *or 12
... P–N3 13 P–Q3 ∆ P–K4* – 13
BP×N still looks advantageous for
the first player.) 11 0–0 N×Nch 12
P×N (or 12 B×N ±) 12 ... P–Q4
13 P–Q4 B–R6 14 R–B2 P–B3 15
B–Q2 KR–K1 Suba-Timoshenko,
Polanica Zdroj 1976, and now 16
B–Q3 P–KR3 17 R–K1 ± was
correct (Timoshenko). But he also
gives the alternative **6 ... 0–0** 7
P–K4 P–Q3 8 P–Q3 N–K2 =,
when Black can prepare ... P–Q4
by ... P–B3.

6 ...   Q–K2

The point of 5 ... B×N!?: Black
stops P–Q4 from being effective
(... P×P), and prepares to play in
the centre himself. Since one idea of
... P–K5 is ... Q–K4, and one
idea of ... P–Q4 may be ... R–Q1,
6 ... Q–K2 is more efficient than 6
... 0–0 and R–K1.

7 P–QR3

7 B–K2 seems to allow Black his
way: 7 ... 0–0 8 0–0 (Two other
moves: **8 P–Q3** P–Q4 9 0–0 P–K5
10 N–Q2 P×QP 11 B×P Q–K4! 12
Q×Q N×Q 13 B–K2 N×P 14 N×N
P×N   15   B×P   B–K3   ½–½
Polugaevsky-Matanović, Belgrade
1974. This is the~earliest game I
know with 5 ... B×N and 6 ...
Q–K2, for which Matanović
evidently deserves credit. **8 P–N3**
P–Q4 9 P–Q3 P–K5 10 N–Q4
N×N 11 Q×N P–B4 12 Q–N2
P×BP 13 QP×BP B–N5! 14 0–0
QR–Q1 = was another example of
successful Black defence, Pytel-
Rath, Gausdal 1978.) 8 ... P–K5!
(Or **8 ... P–QR4** 9 P–Q3 P–Q4 10
R–K1 P–K5 = Eising-Janatschek,
Copenhagén 1977) 9 N–K1 (**9
N–Q4** N×N 10 Q×N P–B4 11
Q–B3 P–Q4-Gipslis; this variation
examplifies Black's strategy.) 9 ...
P–Q4 10 P–QN3 R–Q1 11 N–B2
B–N5 12 B–R3 Q–K3 13 P–B3
KP×P 14 NP×P B–B4! 15 QR–K1
B×N 16 Q×B P–Q5 ½–½ Smyslov-
Gipslis, Spartakiade 1975. Gipslis
assesses the final position as '±',
perhaps an exaggerated claim after
17 P–K4! (∆ P–Q3, B–B1), but 17
... Q–R6 18 P–Q3 P–KN4! is ∓.

Interesting is **7 P–Q3** e.g. 7 ...
P–Q4 8 P×P N×P 9 Q–Q2! (not 9
Q–B2? N(3)–N5! ∆ 10 ... Q–B4).

7 ...   P–QR4

7 ... 0–0 needs a test. Play might
continue 8 P–QN4 (or 8 P–Q3 ∆ 8
... P–K5 9 N–Q2 or 8 ... P–QR4
9 P–QN3) 8 ... P–Q4 9 B–N2!? (9
P×P N×QP 10 Q–N3 R–Q1 11
B–N2 P–K5 ∆ 12 N–Q4 N–K4 or
12 P–N5 P×N 13 P×N P×NP 14

KB×P N–B5) 9 . . . P–Q5 10 Q–B2
P×P (10 . . . B–N5 11 B–K2
KR–K1!?) 11 QP×P P–K5 12
P–N5!

7 . . . P–Q4!? is also critical, e.g.
8 P×P (8 P–Q4!?) 8 . . . N×P 9
Q–N3 (9 Q–B2 P–K5 10 B–N5
P×N!? or 10 . . . B–Q2) 9 . . . N–N3
10 P–Q3 P–QR4!

8 P–QN3

The sensible move. Keene's **8
P–QN4!?** can also cause Black some
discomfiture:
a) **8 . . . P×P** 9 P×P R×R 10 Q×R
P–K5 (**10 . . . N×P** 11 Q×P ±; **10
. . . Q×P** 11 N×P ±) 11 P–N5! P×N
(**11 . . . N–QN5** 12 N–Q4 P–B4 13
P×Pe.p. QP×P 14 B–R3 P–B4 15
B×N±) 12 P×N P×N P 13 P×Pch±;
b) **8 . . . P–Q4** 9 P×QP N×QP 10
Q–N3 **B–K3** 11 B–B4 **P–R5** 12
Q–B2 ±' These lines are Keene's
analysis, but '(b)' looks suspicious.
What's wrong with **10 . . . N–N3**,
or, for that matter, with the wild **11
. . . P–K5**? The stem game, Keene–
Tisdall, Orense 1977, continued
c): **8 . . . P–Q3** 9 B–N2!? (9 P–N5!?
Keene) 9 . . . B–N5?! (9 . . . P×P
Keene) 10 P–N5 B×N 11 P×B
N–Q5 12 0–0–0! N×BP? (12 . . .
N–K3! Keene) 13 B–N2 P–K5 14
B×N P×B 15 KR–N1 N–K5 (**15
. . . N–R4** 16 Q–Q4! Keene, Δ
Q–Q5. Q–N4) 16 Q×NP R–KB1
17 Q–Q4 Q–K3 18 P–Q3! N–B4 19
Q–B6! ± (1–0, 30).

8 . . .   P–Q4?!

8 . . . 0–0 =, according to Nei,
but we lack examples. 9 P–Q3(!)
P–Q4 (**9 . . . P–K5** 10 N–Q2) 10
P×P N×P 11 Q–N2 is perhaps best,
when Black must work some if he is
to demonstrate that equality.

9 P–Q4!

Less sure was **9 P×P** N×P 10
Q–B2 P–K5! 11 B–N5 B–Q2 (But
11 . . . 0–0! or even **11 . . . P×N!?** –
Tal is fascinating.) 12 B×N P×B
(**12 . . . B×B** 13 N–Q4 ±) 13 N–N1
0–0 14 N–K2 P–KB4 15 B–N2
QR–N1 16 0–0 P–B5 17 N×P N×N
18 P×N R×P 19 QR–K1 Q–K3 20
R–K3 R–N4 21 R(1)–K1 R–N4 22
R–N3 and White's better structure
is   obviously   starting   to   pre-
dominate,   Panno–Gaprindashvili,
Lone Pine 1977 (1–0, 35).

9 . . .   P×QP

9 . . . N×QP 10 N×N P×N 11
Q×P P–QB4 12 Q–B4 ± (Nei).
10 N×P   N–K4
11 P×P   N×P
12 Q–B2 0–0 13 B–K2 (± Nei) 13
. . . N–KN5 14 P–R3 (or **14 0–0!** Δ
14 . . . Q–K4 15 N–B3! Q×R 16
B–N2 Q–R7 17 N–N5! -Nei and
Tal) 14 . . . N(5)–B3 15 0–0 N–K5
16 B–Q3 R–K1 17 B–N2 P–R3 18
QR–Q1 P–QB3 19 KR–K1 B–Q2
20   P–B3   ±   Nei–Tal,   Tallin
1977.

CONCLUSION:

The positions after 5 . . . B×N are
quite unresolved; Black's seventh-
move   alternatives   need   looking
into.

E443
5 . . .   P–Q3
6 P–QR3
6 P–Q3 B–N5 7 B–K2 B×Nch 8
Q×B Q–Q2 9 P–KR3 B–R4 10
P–KN4 B–N3 11 P–K4 P–QR4 12
B–K3 with an interesting fight in

store was Korchnoi-Timman, Netherlands Ch, 1977.

	6 ...	B×N
	7 Q×B	P–QR4
	8 P–QN3	B–N5

8 ... N–K5 9 Q–B2 N–B4 10 P–Q4 ± (Timman). White already looks better after 8 P–QN3.

	9 P–Q3	B×N
	10 P×B	P–Q4?!

Timman suggests '**10...0–0** ∞'. Then the position would be exactly that of E4415, note (b) to 6 ... R–K1! There White took Black's KB via N–Q5, ×B, but the tempi are the same (!), and White should be preferred (±).

	11 P×P	Q×P
	12 R–KN1!	0–0
	13 B–QN2	KR–K1 (*83*)

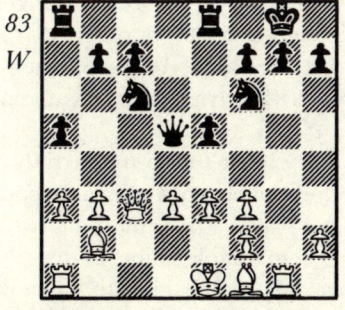

83 W

	14 P–B4	N–Q5

Forced! We are following Miles-Timman, Las Palmas 1977: 15 B–N2 N–B6ch 16 B×N Q×B 17 R–N3 Q–R8ch 18 K–K2 Q×RP 19 R(1)–KN1 N–R4 20 R(3)–N2 Q–R6 21 P×P R–K3. Now, instead of **22 Q×BP?** R–QB3! ($\frac{1}{2}$–$\frac{1}{2}$, 32), **22 Q–Q4!** was still ±, according to Timman.

CONCLUSION

Against 4 P–K3, **4 ... P–Q3** and **4**

... **B–K2** are both reasonable, but fall rather short of equality, while **4 ... P–KN3** seems definitely inferior. Hence the nod has gone to **4 ... B–N5**, against which only 5 Q–B2 sets serious problems in Black's way.

If we accept this as the 'main line,' an assessment is still hard to come by. As things stand, **5 ... B×N** is unclear, and **5...P–Q3** has few advantages over **5...0–0**; so the theoretical fate of 4 P–K3 may hinge upon 5 ... 0–0 6 N–Q5, and **6 ... R–K1** 7 Q–B5!? or **6...P–Q3!?** or some other less-analysed line. My instinct is that Black should be able to equalize; yet if he must grant White the bishop pair without achieving an attack or other concrete compensation, then he should expect a prolonged defensive task. A much closer scrutiny of all these 4 P–K3 lines seems likely in the next few years.

F

4 Q–R4!? (*84*)

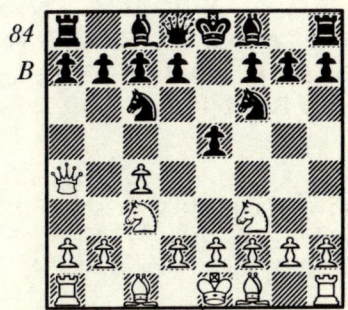

84 B

This queen sortie to the edge of the board makes a fitting conclusion to an often eccentric chapter. 4 Q–R4 has been played by the theoretician Murei, but as far as we know, nobody else has tried it.

The moves serves to discourage 4 ... B–N5 (no small achievement, since 4 ... B–N5 is Black's main defence to 4 P–K4, 4 P–Q3, 4 P–K3, and 4 P–KN3!), and 'pins' Black's QN, Ruy Lopez fashion, so 4 ... P–Q4 is prevented too (see (a) and (b) below). Aside from these defensive roles, the white queen often supports a pawn advance on her side of the board.

Some fairly random possibilities:

a) **4 ... B–N5?** 5 N×P (**5 N–Q5!?** is also interesting 5 ... B–B4?! 6 P–QN4! B–Q5 7 R–QN1 ±) 5 ... B×N 6 N×N B×Pch 7 B×B ±.

b) **4 ... P–Q4?** 5 P×P (**5 N×KP P–Q5!** ±) 5 ... N×P 6 N×P N–N3 7 Q–KB4 ±.

c) **4 ... P–KN3** 5 P–QN4!? (more restrained might be **5 P–K3** e.g. **5 ... P–Q3** 6 P–QN4 or **5 ... B–N2** 6 P–Q4 P×P 7 P×P P–Q4 8 B–N5!) 5 ... B×P (**5 ... P–Q3** 6 P–K3 B–N2 7 B–N2 0–0 8 P–N5 N–K2 9 Q–B2 is a fairly typical English position.) 6 N×P B×N 7 N×N QP×N 8 P×B ... Unclear! For example, **8 ... 0–0** 9 P–B5!? Q–Q4 (**9 ... R–K1** 10 B–N5) 10 B–K3

B–K3 11 Q–R4 N–Q2 12 B–Q4 ∞, or **8 ... N–K5** 9 B–K3 Q–K2 10 B–Q4 0–0 11 P–B3 N–B4 (11 ... P–QB4? 12 Q–R3) 12 Q–B2 ∞.

d) **4 ... B–B4** 5 P–K3 Q–K2 (**5 ... P–Q3??** 6 P–Q4) 6 P–QR3 (**6 N–Q5** N×N! 7 P×N P–K5 =) 6 ... P–K5 7 N–KN5 P–KR3 (**7 ... P–Q3** 8 Q–B2 B–B4 9 P–B3) 8 N–R3 P–KN4 (**8 ... P–Q3** 9 N–B4 ±) 9 P–QN4 B–Q3 10 B–N2 0–0 11 P–B3 with better play for White.

e) **4 ... P–Q3** 5 P–K3! and **5 ... B–Q2** 6 Q–B2 or **5 ... B–N5** 6 B–K2 with a type of game similar to 4 P–K3 P–Q3 (E2) above.

f) **4 ... B–K2** 5 P–KN3?! (**5 P–K3!** 0–0 6 B–K2) 5 ... 0–0 6 B–N2 P–QR3?! 7 0–0 P–Q3 8 P–Q3 R–N1 9 B–Q2 B–N5 10 KR–B1 N–Q5 11 Q–Q1 ∞ Murei-Veinger, Beer-sheva 1978. But here 6 ... P–Q4! was a good choice, when 7 P×P N×P leaves Black threatening ... N–N3.

We expect to see more trials of 4 Q–R4 although it may not appeal to the player who is set in his ways. The remarkable thing is that this obviously interesting 4th (!) move apparently went untried for tens of thousand of master games over a period of 70 years!

9 THE SMYSLOV SYSTEM: 2 N–QB3 P–Q3

1 P–QB4	P–K4
2 N–QB3	P–Q3 (*85*)

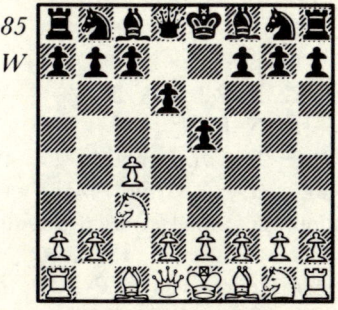

85
W

Taimanov calls this the 'Tchigorin System', but he quotes no Tchigorin games, nor am I aware of any. So, with all due respect to that combatant of days gone by, I have opted for 'Smyslov System' instead. It is Smyslov who, in a manner almost unparalleled in modern opening theory, has contributed the crucial distinguishing ideas in practically every variation, besides playing some very cogent games. Due to his efforts, 2 . . . P–Q3 was brought from *terra incognita* to a place on the theoretical map. This chapter attempts to summarize the results of its recent usage by players such as Larsen, Bronstein, and Polugaevsky.

Black's second move is extremely flexible and may transpose to the King's Indian or Old Indian.

Theory on the purely 'English' variations is often embryonic, and one will find ample opportunity for independent research. We examine:

A 3 P–K3
B 3 P–Q4
C 3 N–B3
D 3 P–KN3

A

3 P–K3

Unassuming but also riskless; White plays a King's Indian Attack reversed after e.g. 3 . . . N–KB3 4 P–Q4 QN–Q2 and 5 . . . P–KN3. For more on these positions, see Chapter 11, B43.

3 . . . P–KB4

a) **3 . . . P–KN3** 4 P–Q4 (**4 N–B3** B–N2 5 B–K2 P–KB4 6 P–Q4 P–K5 7 N–Q2 N–KB3 8 P–QN4 B–K3 ∞ Ribli-Balashov, Leningrad 1977) 4 . . . B–N2 5 P×P B×P (**5 . . . P×P** 6 Q×Qch K×Q 7 P–QN3 △ B–R3 -Larsen. Black's king bishop would then be misplaced for the ending.) 6 Q–Q2 (6 N–B3!? -Larsen) 6 . . . B–N2 7 P–QN3 N–KB3 8 B–N2 0–0 9 N–B3?! (An interesting position, for White is a tempo ahead of section B below! Yet Larsen gives **9 P–N3** QN–Q2 10 B–N2 N–B4 11 KN–K2 P–QR4 ∞ and indeed 12 . . . P–R5

13 P–QN4 P–R6 is threatened. Best is 12 R–Q1 B–B4 13 0–0 N(3)–K5 14 N×N N×N 15 Q–B1 ±.) 9 ... QN–Q2 10 B–K2 N–B4 11 0–0 R–K1 12 QR–Q1 (Here, however, White has lost control over e4. On **12 KR–Q1**, Larsen points out that 12 ... Q–K2! threatens 13 ... N(4)–K5 when ... N×BP! will soon follow.) 12 ... N(3)–K5 13 N×N N×N 14 Q–B1 B×B 15 Q×B Q–B3 Larsen-Tcheskovsky, Ljubljana 1977. Larsen assesses it '=', though he managed to win.

b) **3 ... B–K2** 4 P–Q4 P–KB4 5 P–QN3 N–KB3 6 B–N2 P–B3 7 KN–K2 0–0 8 P–N3 Q–K1 9 B–N2 N–R3 (Black is treating the position like a Dutch. Compare D4 below.) 10 P–QR3 N–B2 11 Q–B2 B–K3 12 P–R3 (Korchnoi has an aversion to early castling on the White side of the many English systems.) 12 ... R–B1 13 P–B4!? N–Q2 14 P–K4 BP×P (**14 ... P–QN4** was suggested) 15 B×P ∞ Korchnoi-Navarovsky, Luhacovice. 1969 ($\frac{1}{2}$–$\frac{1}{2}$, 40).

> 4 P–Q4   N–KB3
> 5 P×P

5 N–B3 would resemble C, and **5 P–KN3** might transpose to D. The text is optimistic.

> 5 ...   P×P
> 6 Q×Qch   K×Q
> 7 P–QN3   P–B3

Here Black has an extra piece out as contrasted with Larsen-Tsheskovsky, note above. Moreover, his bishop is on the correct (i.e. original) diagonal.

> 8 B–N2   K–B2
> 9 0–0–0   QN–Q2

10 B–Q3!?

Trying to provoke a weakening advance on Black's part, though there is the danger that Black's pawn on ... K5 will become a cramping influence. **10 N–B3!?** is another idea, e.g. 10 ... P–K5?! (**10 ... P–QR4?** 11 N–KN5!; **10 ... B–Q3!** 11 B–K2 R–K1) 11 N–KN5 N–B4 12 P–B3, cracking up Black's centre.

> 10 ...   P–K5
> 11 B–B2   P–QR4
> 12 N–R3   B–Q3
> 13 N–K2?!

Intending occupation of the weakened f4, but that only encourages Black's pawn advance on the kingside. **13 R–Q2** is preferable, or even **13 P–B3!?**, e.g. 13 ... P×P 14 P×P R–K1 15 R(Q)–K1 N–B4 16 R–K2, just about holding the balance.

> 13 ...   R–K1

14 N(2)–B4 N–K4 15 R–Q2 B–N5! 16 R–Q4 P–R3 17 R(1)–Q1 B–Q2! (17 ... P–KN4? 18 R–Q8! - Larsen) 18 P–QR3 B–B4 19 R(4)–Q2 QR–Q1 20 N–N1 P–KN4 21 N(4)–K2 N(3)–N5! 22 N–Q4 N×RP 23 N×BP/5 N–Q6ch! 24 B×N B×N 25 B–B2 R×R 26 K×R N–N5 27 K–K1 N–K4 (Δ ... P–KR4–R5 and ... P–QR5) Miles-Larsen, Las Palmas 1977. According to Larsen, the position is ∓.

B

3 P–Q4

A rather controversial move which is again receiving attention since Korchnoi tried it against

Polugaevsky in their 1977 Candidates match. But I doubt its efficacy, at least for winning purposes. After all, Black has not played . . . P–KB4 as in Chapter 10, A3 (2 . . . P–KB4 3 P–Q4 P×P 4 Q×P), and in comparison with those lines he has kept a free diagonal for his queen bishop and better control over key central squares. White hopes nevertheless for a standard bind based primarily on his restraint along the queen file. The question is whether Black's rapid development and active piece play can confute this strategy.

3 . . .   P×P

Of course, **3 . . . N–Q2** may be played, leading in many cases to an Old or King's Indian.

4 Q×P   N–QB3
5 Q–Q2

The idea is to support a bishop on b2 after P–QN3. **5 Q–Q1** has a different intention e.g. 5 . . . P–KN3 6 P–K4 B–N2 7 B–Q3 KN–K2 8 P–B4 0–0 9 N–B3 N–Q5 (or **9 . . . P–B4** =) 10 N–Q2?! (**10 P–KR3**) 10 . . . P–QB3 11 0–0 P–Q4 (or **11 . . . P–KB4**) 12 BP×P P×P 13 P–K5 B–B4?! (**13 . . . N(5)–B4!**) 14 B×B N(5)×B 15 N–B3 P–Q5 16 N–K4 ± Lombardy-Quinteros, Haifa 1976 (½–½, 28). Now:

B1 5 . . . N–B3
B2 5 . . . P–KN3

B1

5 . . .   N–B3
6 P–QN3

The normal plan, but **6 P–KN3!?** is also seen, when there

are evidently three good replies:

a) **6 . . . P–KN3** 7 B–N2 B–N2 is discussed in B2 below.

b) **6 . . . B–K2!?** 7 B–N2 0–0 8 N–R3 N–QN5!? (Good enough, intending . . . N–R3–B4, though 8 . . . N–K4 and 9 . . . P–B3 Δ is more thematic. Black would then prepare . . . P–QN4.) 9 N–B4 P–B3 10 0–0 R–K1 11 P–KR3 B–B1 12 P–N3 N–R3 13 P–K4 N–B4 14 R–K1 Rajkovic-Barcza, Hastings 1972/3. White has developed gracefully, but does not have a convincing plan. By the simple 14 . . . P–QR4, Black could have achieved a fine game.

c) **6 . . . B–K3!?** 7 N–Q5 (At first, **7 P–K4** might seem an improvement, but I haven't found the answer to 7 . . . N–K4 8 P–N3 P–QN4!? e.g. **9 P–B4** P–N5, or **9 P×P** P–Q4! 10 P–B4? B–QN5 or here 10 P×P N×P 11 N×N Q×N etc.) 7 . . . N–K4 8 P–N3 N–K5!? 9 Q–Q4 N–B4 10 P–B4 (**10 B–KN2** P–KN3 11 P–B4 B–N2 12 K–B1 0–0-Shatskes) 10 . . . N–B3 11 Q–K3 B–K2 12 N×B Q×N 13 B–QN2 0–0–0! 14 N–B3 KR–K1 ∓ Taimanov-Smyslov, USSR Ch 1967.

A typical example of Smyslov's crafty piece play.

6 . . .   P–KN3

Now (a) **6 . . . B–K3?!** 7 P–K4 is favourable to White: 7 . . . P–KN3 (**7 . . . P–QR4** is similar to (b), i.e. 8 P–N3 is the correct answer, and not 8 B–Q3 P–R5! = /∞ of Polugaevsky-Techeskovsky, USSR Ch. 1974) 8 P–N3 B–N2 9 B–QN2 N–K4 10 B–N2 0–0 11 P–B4! N(4)–Q2 12 KN–K2 N–B4 13

P–KR3 R–K1 14 0–0 B–QB1 15 P–K5! ± Raičević-Gulko, Sombor 1974.

b) **6 ... P–QR4?!** does not sufficiently emphasize Black's most valuable asset—his lead in devlopment: 7 P–K4 P–R5 8 R–N1! P×P 9 P×P P–KN3 10 P–N3 B–N2 11 B–KN2 0–0 12 KN–K2 N–K4 Korchnoi-Polugaevsky (11), 1977, and 13 0–0 B–R6 14 P–B3! (Keene) maintains White's superiority.

c) **6...B–K2** is plausible although one is reluctant to recommend such a demure move when Black's pieces in the text come out with a vengeance!

    7 B–N2   B–N2
    8 P–N3

White must already be heedful of tactical explosions. In Barcza-Deley, Hungary 1969, White played the innocent-looking **8 P–K3** 0–0 9 KN–K2?, and got cudgelled with 9 ... P–Q4!! 10 N×P N×N 11 B×B N(4)–N5! 12 B×R N–Q6ch 13 K–Q1 N×Pch 14 K–B1 Q×B 15 N–N3 (15 R–KN1 Q–R6ch −+) 15 ... N×R 16 N×N Q–R6ch 17 K–Q1 B–B4 18 K–K1 R–Q1 19 Q–B3 N–N5 20 K–B2 N–B7 21 R–N1 N×KP 22 R–K1 N–Q8ch 0–1.

On 8 **P–K4** 0–0 9 P–B3, Black has **9...R–K1** or **9...N–KR4** (!) Δ ... P–B4.

    8 ...   0–0
    9 B–N2   N–K4

Of the other two ideas, one is very adventurous:

a) **9 ... R–N1?!** 10 N–R3 P–QR3 11 0–0 (or 11 N–B4 ± -Minev) 11 ... P–QN4 12 N–B4 N–K4 (better

12 ... B–Q2 13 P×P P×P 14 QR–B1 N–K2 -Minev) 13 P×P P×P 14 QR–B1 B–N2 15 N(3)–Q5 N–K1 16 KR–Q1 ± Minev-Ornstein, Rimavska Sobota 1974.

b) **9 ... R–K1(!)** is intriguing: 10 N–R3 (**10 N–B3** B–B4 11 0–0 N–K5 12 N×N B×N 13 QR–Q1 Q–K2 = Torre-Shaw, Itoh 1978; or 10 ... R–N1) and now not **10 ... N–K4?!** 11 0–0 R–N1 12 N–B4 ± Benko-Trois, Sao Paulo 1977, but **10 ... P–Q4!**, a suggestion of Ornstein's, when the complications are fantastic. I find Black doing well: **11 N×P** N×N 12 B×B K×B! (12 ... N–K6!? ∞) 13 P×N B×N 14 B×B Q–B3 15 0–0 N–Q5 16 B–N4 (Forced. **16 QR–K1?** R×P! and ... N–B6ch) 16 ... P–KR4 (or **16 ... R–K5** 17 P–B4 QR–K1 Δ ... P–KR4) 17 P–K3 QR–Q1!? 18 B–Q1 (18 P×N =) 18 ... N–B6ch 19 B×N Q×B 20 Q–Q4ch K–N1 21 KR–Q1 R–K5! and 22 ... P–R5 etc. Or **11 P×P** B×N 12 B×B N×P 13 N×N B×B 14 Q×B Q×N 15 0–0 Q–KR4! etc. Although I am reluctant to assess 10 ... P–Q4 without tests, my impression is that it offers excellent counterchances to the second player.

    10 N–B3

10 N–R3(!) may well be a better test of 9 ... N–K4. Then immediate tactical solutions are not available and to avoid getting tied up as in Minev-Ornstein above, Black may have to try the resolute 10 ... P–B3!?, and if 11 R–Q1, 11 ... Q–R4! 12 N–B4 (**12 Q×P??** B×N! and 13 ... N–K5) 12 ...

R–Q1, thinking about . . . P–QR3
and an eventual . . . P–QN4.

   10 . . .   N×Nch
   11 B×N   R–N1
12 0–0 (**12 B–N2** B–B4 13 P–K4?
N×P!) 12 . . . B–R6 13 KR–Q1
N–Q2 14 B–R1 R–K1 15 N–Q5
N–K4 16 P–B4 P–QB3! Stahlberg-
Smyslov, Stockholm 1964. The
threat of . . . Q–N3ch at some
point makes the game at least
equal. A good example of energetic
play in an apparently cramped
position.

B2

   5 . . .   **P–KN3**
Usually this transposes to the
critical B1 lines but can have
independent value if White opts for
an early P–K4.

   6 P–KN3   B–N2
   7 B–N2   N–B3

7 . . . KN–K2 would be
appropriate if White continued **8
P–K4** (Black plays for . . . P–KB4),
but falls short of equality against **8
P–N3**.

   8 P–K4   0–0
   9 KN–K2?!

Kotov suggests **9 P–B3** △
KN–K2 ±, but 9 . . . N–K1(!) 10
KN–K2 P–B4 results in balanced
play anyway e.g. 11 0–0?! P×P 12
N×P B–K3 etc.

   9 . . .   N–K4
   10 P–N3   B–R6!
   11 0–0   R–K1
12 P–B3 B×B 13 K×B P–QR4! 14
B–N2 P–R5 (*86*) 15 N–Q4 (**15
N×P?** R×N! 16 P×R N×QBP 17
Q–B1 N×B 18 Q×N N×P, winning
back the exchange with the better

86
W

game.) 15 . . . P–B3 16 R(B)–K1
Q–R4 (While White has been
catching up on development, Black
has prepared a central and
queenside assault.) 17 Q–QB2
P–R6 18 B–B1 P–Q4! 19 BP×P
P×P 20 B–Q2 QR–B1 21 P–B4
N×KP! 22 R×N (forced) 22 . . .
P×R 23 P×N P–K6! 24 B–K1 B×P
25 N(4)–K2 R(K)–Q1 26 R–B1
P–QN4 27 P–QN4 Q×P 28 R–N1
Q–B5 29 Q–N3 (29 R×P Q×R) 29
. . . Q–B3ch 30 K–N1 Q–B6 31
Q–B2 B×N 32 N×B R–Q7! 33 B×R
Q–B7ch 34 K–R1 Q×B 35 Q×Q
(35 R–QB1 P–N5) 35 . . . P×Q 36
N–K2 R–K1 0–1 Jovanović-
Zatulovska, Menorca 1973. A 27
move sustained initiative!

CONCLUSION:

3 P–Q4 demands precise, often
enterprising countermeasures by
Black; nevertheless, his piece play
seems at least adequate compensation for White's positional
assets.

C

   3 N–B3
A move more committal than it

might at first appear. White strives for P–Q4 without the loss of time that 3 P–Q4 entails. Black has two moves which try to exploit the presence of the knight on f3:

C1 3 . . . B–N5
C2 3 . . . P–KB4

He also has several less acute alternatives, which for convenience are grouped under one section (C3):

C31 3 . . . N–QB3
C32 3 . . . P–KN3
C33 3 . . . N–KB3
C34 3 . . . P–QB4

C1

3 . . .   B–N5

Smyslov's move: As in the Nimzo-Indian, one question is whether White's bishops will make up for his crippled pawn structure. After 4 P–Q4 B×N, however, Black has captured without loss of tempo on White's part (i.e. P–KR3) and without the option of putting his pawns on the opposite colour of his remaining bishop (as he often does in the analogous 'Nimzo' positions). This does not augur well for 3 . . . B–N5, but we shall see that Black has other ideas besides exchanging on f3.

There are two White approaches:

C11 4 P–K3
C12 4 P–Q4

C11

4 P–K3

Preventing the doubled pawns, but walking into a pin and restricting the bishop on c1.

4 . . .   N–KB3
5 B–K2

5 P–KR3 B×N (**5 . . . B–R4** is viable: 6 P–KN4 B–N3 **7 N–KR4** B–K5!? — or just 7 . . . P–QB3! — 8 N×B N×N 9 Q–B3 Q×N 10 Q×N P–QB3 11 P–Q4 N–Q2 = Hamman-Symslov, Skopje 1972; or here **7 Q–N3** Q–B1 8 P–Q4 QN–Q2 =) 6 Q×B P–B3 7 P–Q4 B–K2 8 P–Q5 0–0 9 B–Q3 N–R3 10 0–0 P×P 11 P×P N–B4 12 B–B2 N–K1 = Keres-Spassky, Match (6) 1965.

5 . . .   B–K2

Or **5 . . . P–B3** 6 P–KR3 B–R4 7 0–0 B–K2 **8 P–Q3** 0–0 9 P–QN3 QN–Q2 10 N–KR4 B×B 11 Q×B P–Q4 = Petrosian-Spassky, USSR 1959(?) White should try **8 P–Q4**.

6 P–Q4

6 P–KR3 B–R4 7 P–Q4 QN–Q2 8 0–0 P–B3 9 P–QN3 0–0 10 B–N2 R–K1 11 P–Q5 P–K5 (11 . . . N–B4!?) 12 P×P P×P 13 N–Q4 B×B 14 Q×B N–K4 Larsen-Spassky, Match (6) 1968, and **15 P–B3** P×P 16 N×P = was the game, but **15 QR–Q1** seems to keep a little pressure. Black might have dispensed with . . . P–QB3, as in the text game.

6 . . .	QN–Q2
7 0–0	0–0
8 P–N3	R–K1
9 B–N2	B–B1
10 P×P	

A well-known expediency. Before Black plays . . . P–K5, White lengthens the diagonal of his queen bishop.

| 10 . . . | P×P |
| 11 Q–B2 | P–K5! |

White was getting ideas like R Q1 and N–K4.

12 N–Q4
12 N–KN5 B–KB4 13 P–B3 B–B4! =

12 ...   P–B4!
13 N(4)–N5 P–QR3 14 N–R3 Q–B2 15 QR–Q1 B×B 16 Q×B QR–Q1 17 N–Q5 N×N 18 R×N N–N3 19 R×R R×R ½–½ Uhlmann-Tal, Leningrad 1973.

C12

4 P–Q4 (*87*)

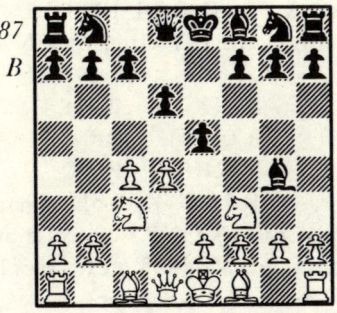

87
B

The only serious try to force the pace. Now:
C121 4 ... N–QB3
C122 4 ... N–Q2
C123 4 ... B×N

C121

4 ...   N–QB3
This alternative is seldom seen.
5 P–Q5   N(3)–K2
a) **5 ... B×N** 6 KP×B N–N1 7 P–B4 N–Q2 8 B–K2 N(1)–B3 9 Q–B2! B–K2 10 B–K3 0–0 11 P–KB5! ± Barcza-Köberl, Hungarian Ch 1957.
b) **5 ... N–N1** 6 P–KN3 (**6 N–Q2!** looks auspicious; **6 P–KR3** B R4?!

7 P–K4?! was less so after 7 ... N–Q2 8 B–K3 B–K2 9 B–K2 B×N 10 B×B B–N4 = Ahues-Sämisch, Berlin 1926.) 6 ... N–KB3 (**6 ... B×N?** 7 P×B grants White two bishops, a lead in development and two natural pawn breaks in the centre. Black should exchange only when he can restrain the doubled pawns.) 7 B–N2 B–K2 8 0–0 (or 8 P–KR3 ±) 8 ... Q–B1·9 R–K1 ± Aramanovich-Smyslov, USSR 1942.

6 P–K4
Or **6 P–KN3**
6 ...   N–N3
6 ... P–KN3 7 P–KR3 B–Q2 (7 ... B×N is a sort of Modern Defence where White has some advantage.) 8 B–Q3 Rovnor-Panov, Moscow-Leningrad 1933, and if 8 ... P–KB4?, 9 P×P P×P 10 N–KR4 N–KB3 11 B–N5 etc.
7 P–KR3   B–Q2
8 B–K3
White's position is well-centralized, and he has a space advantage. I doubt if Rukavina (White in the text) was aware of the prior game Barcza-Lengyel, Hungary, which Schwarz quotes: **8 P–KR4!?** B–K2? (8 ... P–KR4 ±) 9 P–R5 N–B1 10 P–B5 N–B3 11 B–K2 P–KR3 12 P×P B×P 13 N–Q2 N(1)–R2 14 N–B4 Q–K2 15 Q–Q3 ±.
8 ...   B–K2
9 Q–Q2   N–B3
10 B–Q3 0–0 11 N–K2! (**11 0–0** N–R4 12 N–K2 P–KB4 = - Rukavina) 11 ... P–B3 12 N–N3 R–K1 13 0–0 B–KB1 14 P–N4 Rukavina-Mestrović, Yugoslavia

Ch 1975. White is ascendant in every sector of the board.

C122
4 ...   N–Q2

Not as bad as its reputation (e.g. '?' Shatskes, Taimanov).

5 P–KN3(!)

a) **5 P–K4** N(1)–B3 with an Old Indian (Schwarz) but **5 ... B×N!** 6 P×B B–K2 or here **6 ... N–K2** △ ... N–KN3 or even **6 ... P×P** 7 Q×P N–K2 equalizes.

b) **5 P–K3** is like 4 P–K3: 5 ... N(1)–B3 6 B–K2 P–B3 7 P–KR3 B–R4 (or 7 ... B×N =) **8 P×P?** P×P 9 0–0 P–K5 10 N–Q2 B–N3 11 P–QN3 Q–B2 12 Q–B2? Q–K4 13 R–Q1 B–Q3 14 N–B1 0–0 15 B–N2 Q–K2 16 R–Q2 N–K4 17 QR–Q1 N–B6ch! 18 P×N P×P 19 B–Q3 Q–K3! Kaufman-Kavalek, USA Ch 1972. The first improvement would be **8 P–Q5**..

c) **5 B–K3** is the recommendation of the Soviet theoreticians: 5 ... N–K2 (**5 ... P–KN3** 6 P–Q5 B–N2 7 N–Q2! ± -Shatskes) 6 P–Q5 N–KB4(?) 7 B–Q2 B–K2 8 Q–B2! P–KN3 9 N–KN1! and Black pieces can only be saved at some cost, Alburt-Osnos, USSR Ch 1967. On this basis Shatskes and Taimanov faulted 4 ... N–Q2, but that is naturally not the last word. For one thing, Black can play the unassuming **5 ... B–K2!** e.g. 6 P–Q5 P–KB4(!) 7 P–KR3 B–R4, or here just **6 ... N(1)–B3** 7 N–Q2 0–0 with a pleasing position. Aside from that, **5 ... N–K2** 6 P–Q5 P–KN3! 7 P–KN3 B×N led to great

complexities ('= /∞') in Adamski-Bednarski, Poland 1976.·

5 ...   N(1)–B3

5 P–KN3! is a bit subtler than White's attempts of the last note, and this direct a strategy may not equalize. But **5 ... B×N** 6 P×B N(1)–B3 7 B–N2 B–K2 (7 ... P×P!?) 8 0–0 0–0, though solid, is also not quite satisfactory. The position is 'semi-closed', so the knights are not necessarily worse than the bishops, but after 9 P–Q5 (△ P–B4) White has some edge e.g. **9...P–B3?!** 10 P×P P×P 11 P–B4. Best **9 ... P–QR4** 10 P–B4 (10 P–N3!?) 10 ... P×P 11 B×P N–B4 ±.

6 B–N2	B–K2
7 0–0	0–0
8 P–KR3	B×N

8 ... B–R4 9 N–KR4 (Dorfman). Then Black's QNP is en prise and White plays N–B5 next; see D2 below: Smejkal-Balashov.

9 B×B	P×P!

It is logical to create posts in the centre for Black's knights. Otherwise, White might play P–Q5 and P–K4, yielding a rather one-sided structure in which he can patiently prepare P–QB5 and/or P–KB4.

10 Q×P	P–B3
11 P–N3	

'±' Dorfman.

11 ...	R–K1
12 B–QN2	N–B4
13 QR–N1!	P–QR4
14 B–QR1	

Excellent anticipatory manoeuvring, preventing 14 ... P–R5 15 P–N4 P–R6 in the nick of time. We are following Dorfman-Bronstein,

USSR Ch 1975: 14 . . . B–B1 15 B–KN2 Q–B2 16 KR–Q1 R–K3 (?! Black is considering . . . P–KN3.) 17 P–K3 R–Q1 (if **17 . . . P–KN3** 18 N–Q5!) 18 N–K2 R(3)–K1 19 Q–Q2 N(3)–K5 20 Q–B2 Q–K2 21 N–B4 P–B4 (Despite all of Black's efforts, White is still dominant in the centre. His next plan might have been B–Q4 and P–R3 Δ P–QN4, but now that Black has played . . . P–B4, a slight weakening, White switches to central expansion.) 22 N–Q3! N(4)–Q2 23 K–R2 Q–B2 24 R–K1 B–K2 25 P–B3 N(5)–B4 26 N–B2! Q–N3 27 R(N)–Q1 N–B3?! 28 Q–Q2 R–R1 29 B–B3 P–N3 30 B×N! Q×B 31 P–B4 ('±' - Dorfman. By series of forcing moves, White breaks through.) 31 . . . P–Q4 (? **31 . . . QR–B1** 32 P–K4 -Dorfman; but surely that would not be easy to win!) 32 P×P R(R)–Q1 33 Q–B2 P×P 34 R×P and White won in a few moves.

CONCLUSION:

Those employing 3 . . . B–N5 might try 4 . . . N–Q2. Even in the above game, played competently and alertly by White, the first player's advantage was nebulous until the end. Besides, Black could have deviated e.g. at move 5, 8, or (obviously) 27. Finally, other fourth moves do not offer much. For example:

C123
     4 . . .   B×N(?)
Smyslov's idea, but it is difficult to justify.

     5 NP×B
5 KP×B, long recommended, was tested in Uhlmann-Lutikov, Leipzig 1973: 5 . . . P×P? (Uhlmann's notation, and an accurate one. Why open the game so early? **5 . . . N–Q2**) 6 Q×P N–QB3 (**6 . . . N–K2** 7 N–Q5! QN–B3 8 Q–B3 — *8 Q–K4 is the text* — 8 . . . N–K4 9 P–B4 N(4)–N3 10 P–KN3 -Shatskes) 7 Q–K4ch! KN–K2 (Any interpolation is answered by 8 N–Q5.) 8 N–Q5 Q–Q2 9 B–Q2 0–0–0 10 0–0–0 K–N1 11 B–B3 N×N 12 Q×N! R–N1 (**12 . . . Q–K3** 13 R–K1 ± - Uhlmann) 13 P–B5 B–K2 14 B–B4 B–B3 15 Q×BP ± (1–0,37).
     5 . . .   P×P
Now a move like **5 . . . N–Q2** is also playable, but not impressive, since White's pawns are flexible and potentially useful. Soltis gives 6 B–N2 B–K2 7 0–0 N(1)–B3 8 P–N3 with good prospects.
     6 Q×P   N–K2
6 . . . N–QB3 7 Q–K4ch might resemble Uhlmann-Lutikov (note to White's 5th), and **7 Q–Q2** is like the text.
     7 P–N3
Logical, although **7 N–Q5!?** may also be advantageous: 7 . . . N(1)–B3 8 Q–B3 N–K4 9 B–R3! (**9 P–B4?!** N(4)–N3 10 P–B5? N×P 11 Q–R5 P–QB3! 12 N–B7ch K–Q2 13 Q×Nch K×N 14 Q×Pch Q–K2 ∓ O'Kelly-Smyslov, Palma de Mallorca 1967) 9 . . . P–QB3 10 N×N Q×N 11 P–B4 N–N3 12 B–K3 (?), which Taimanov, Shatskes, and Kavalek all like for White without explaining how to

meet 12 . . . Q–R5! e.g. 13 B–Q4 (13 B×RP P–QB4!) 13 . . . P–QB4 (or **13 . . . N×P** 14 B×NP B×B 15 Q×B K–K2 ∓) 14 Q–K3ch K–Q1 15 B–B3 Q×BP ∓. But the spirit is right: 12 B–Q2! leaves Black the problem of getting developed: 12 . . . Q–R5 13 Q–KN3! ±.

7	. . .	N(1)–B3
8	Q–Q2	P–KN3
9	B–N2	B–N2
10	P–KR4	(*88*)

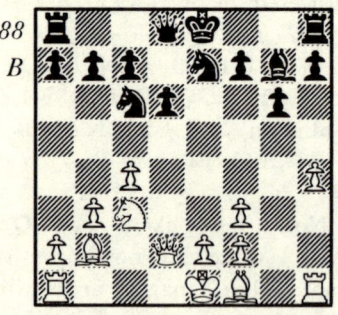

Shatskes (who originally recommended 7 P–N3) gives **10 P–K3** here, but the text seems more direct. The reasoning behind 10 P–KR4 is evidently that **10 N–K4** 0–0 11 N–B6ch K–R1 is unclear, e.g. 12 P–KR4 N–B4 etc. But now 10 P–KR4 **P–KR4?!** 11 N–K4 0–0 12 N–B6ch K–R1? 13 N×RP! is fearsome, destroying Black's haven. Therefore:

10	. . .	N–B4
11	P–R5	R–KN1

12 N–Q5 B×B 13 Q×B N–K4 14 P×P RP×P 15 P–B4 P–QB3 16 P×N P×N 17 0–0–0 Q–N4ch 18 P–K3 P–Q5 19 P×P 0–0–0 20 R×QP! Suba-Mititelu, Romania 1972. After taking the exchange, Black can't cope with White's

many threats based on the open rook file and advanced QP (1–0, 26).

CONCLUSION:

3 . . . B–N5 4 P–Q4 favours White at least moderately in all variations. 4 . . . B×N, although interesting, appears the worst of Black's choices when White pursues his initiative accurately.

C2

3 . . .	P–KB4

This move must be considered one of the drawbacks of 3 N–B3. It is fitting to play . . . P–KB4 when P–Q4 can be met by . . . P–K5 with a gain of tempo.

4 P–Q4

This is, notwithstanding our last comment, the most challenging move, nearly always chosen. **4 P–K3** N–KB3 5 P–Q4 at best transposes. **4 P–Q3** gives up the option for P–Q4 rather early; Black may transpose into another variation with an early . . . P–B3 or . . . N–QB3, or do without those moves for a while so as not to present White a target for P–QN4–N5.

4 P–KN3 is the most independent try. Then:

a) **4 . . . N–KB3** 5 B–N2 (**5 P–Q4!?** see D42) 5 . . . B–K2 (**5 . . . P–B3** 6 P–Q4, see D4, note (b) to 4 . . . N–KB3) 6 0–0 0–0 7 P–Q4 (**7 P–B5** N–B3 8 P×P P×P 9 P–Q4 P–K5 10 N–KN5 P–Q4 11 N–R3 B–K3! and White was getting nowhere, Taimanov-Balashov, 42nd USSR Ch Topl 1974) 7 . . . P–K5 8 N–K1

(△ P–B3) 8 . . . P–B3 9 P–Q5 is complicated, possibly ±.

After 4 P–KN3, Black can enter a known position with **4 . . . P–B3** (or 4 . . . N–KB3 5 B–N2 P–B3). Then on P–Q4, White will always run into . . . P–K5 and . . . P–Q4, a set-up that is stronger here than on the White side of a French Defence; because it is almost impossible to keep Black from playing . . . N–QR3–B2, . . . K–R1, and . . . B–K3–N1 (or . . . Q–Q2) to reinforce his centre, after which he often attacks on the kingside. Therefore, White usually bases his game on P–Q3 e.g. (4 P–KN3):
b) **4 . . . P–B3** 5 P–Q3 N–B3 6 B–N2 B–K2 7 0–0 and:
b1) **7 . . . 0–0!?** 8 P–QN4 (**8 P–B5** QN–Q2 9 P×P B×P Averbach-Matanović, Portoroz 1958) 8 . . . K–R1 9 R–N1 Q–K1?! (9 . . . B–K3! is more watchful of centre points.) 10 P–N5 QN–Q2 11 N–K1 ± Lehmann-Karaklaić, 1958. White intends N–B2–N4 and P–QR4–R5 and B–QR3, etc. He can stanch the kingside with P–B4 if necessary;
b2) **7 . . . N–QR3** 8 R–N1 0–0 9 P–QN4 Q–K1?! (**9 . . . N–B2!** 10 P–QR4 N–K3 = /∞ Behle-Ziese, corres 1976/77) 10 P–N5 N–B4 11 B–QR3 P–K5 12 N–Q4 ± Suttles-Yepez, 1977;
b3) **7 . . . P–QR4!** 8 P–QR3 0–0 9 R–N1 K–R1! (not **9 . . . Q–K1?!** 10 P–QN4 P×P 11 P×P Q–R4 12 P–N5 P–B5 13 P–K3! P×KNP 14 BP×P B–N5 15 Q–B2 ± Sznapik-Schinzel, Poland 1976 (1–0, 39)) 10 P–QN4 P×P 11 P×P B–K3!

12 P–N5 Q–B2 13 Q–N3 QN–Q2 = Averbach-Kotov, USSR 1953?

These '(b)' lines are instructive variations for any English player, since they can arise from several opening sequences.

4 . . .   P–K5

4 . . . N–Q2? 5 N–KN5! Now White has four strategies:
C21 5 B–N5
C22 5 N–KN5
C23 5 N–KN1
C24 5 N–Q2

C21
5 **B–N5**
Not a common development; it may be no worse than 1 P–QB4 P–K4 2 N–QB3 N–QB3 3 N–B3 P–B4 4 P–Q4 P–K5 5 B–N5, which is a popular line from Chapter 10.
5 . . .   N–KB3!?
a) **5 . . . B–K2!** looks satisfactory. Deze gives 6 B×B Q×B 7 N–Q2 △ P–K3, P–KN4, but that is an unwieldy plan, e.g. 7 . . . N–B3 8 P–K3 0–0 or 8 . . . P–B3 9 B–K2 N–R3 △ . . . P–Q4. The bizarre b) **5 . . . Q–Q2!?** is also noteworthy: **6 N–Q2** P–KR3 7 B–K3 P–KN4 8 P–KN3 etc. or **6 N–KR4!?** P–KR3 7 B–B1 ∞.

6 N–Q2
Or **6 N–KN1** P–KR3, Pachman-Tarnovsky, Bucharest 1949. '=' says Schwarz, but 7 B×N Q×B 8 P–K3 poses some complex problems. If Black develops slowly, White gets the standard bind via P–KR4, N–R3–B4 etc., and can expand on the queenside. Yet the violent 8 . . . P–KN4? does not help matters after 9 P–KR4.

6 ...　　　　P–KR3?

Both **6 ... B–K2** and **6 ... QN–Q2** are definite improvements. A recent game saw **6 ... B–K2** 7 P–K3 0–0 8 B–K2 P–B3 9 0–0 N–R3 10 P–B3 P×P 11 B×P N–B2 and White didn't have much, Timman-Ligterink, Lone Pine 1978 ($\frac{1}{2}$–$\frac{1}{2}$, 37).

7 B×N　　　　Q×B
8 P–K3　　　　P–B3

9 P–KN4! (± Deze) 9 ... P×P 10 N(2)×P Q–B2 11 B–K2 P–KR4 12 Q–N3 B–K2 13 0–0–0 Deže-Smejkal, Novi Sad 1976. White broke through on the king's wing (1–0, 34).

C22

5 N–KN5　　　　(*89*)

89　B

This move has been awarded an exclamation point so often it looks lonely without one. Perhaps I should have dared to give it (?!), for the move is very close to a positional error!

Now: C221 5 ... N–KB3
　　　C222 5 ... B–K2
　　　C223 5 ... P–KR3!

C221

5 ...　　　　N–KB3

A common retort.

6 N–R3!

Apparently best. A mistake is the natural

a) **6 P–K3?**, after which we see the first example of correct Black strategy: 6 ... P–KR3 7 N–R3 P–KN4! 8 P–B3 (**8 B–K2** B–N2 9 B–R5ch N×B 10 Q×Nch K–B1 11 0–0 N–Q2 -Browne. 9 ... K–B1! may be even better.) 8 ... P×P 9 P×P B–N2 10 N–B2 0–0 11 B–N2 (**11 B–K2** N–R4 — Δ ... P–B5 — 12 P–B4 P–N5 13 R–KN1 Q–R5! -Browne) 11 ... P–B4 (or 11 ... N–B3 $\mp$) 12 P×P P×P 13 Q×Q R×Q 14 B–Q2 N–B3 and Black was unmistakably better, Hernandez-Browne, Lanzarote 1977 (0–1, 31).

b) **6 P–B3** P–KR3 7 N–R3 P×P and 8 ... P–KN4 is not as dire for White, but there too Black has at least equal prospects.

6 ...　　　　P–B3

6 ... B–K2, see C222. **6 ... P–KN3** is also possible, although 7 B–N5 followed by N–B4, P–KR4, and P–K3. keeps Black on the defensive.

7 P–K3

7 B–N5, exchanging a potentially bad bishop for a good defender, might be more useful. As it is, this bishop is passive for many moves and Black gets time to bulwark his centre.

7 ...　　　　B–K2
8 B–K2

a) **8 N–B4** 0–0 9 P–KR4 N–R3 10 P–R3 N–B2 11 P–Q5(!) N–N5 12 B–K2 N–K4 13 P–KN3 B–B3, Polugaevsky-Larsen, 1974, has been assessed as ±, but Black has many resources.

b) **8 R–QN1** N–R3! 9 P–QN4 N–B2
10 P–N5 P–Q4 (=) transposes into
Petursson-Polugaevsky, Reykjavik
1978; where White gave Black a free
hand to pursue kingside operations:
11 Q–R4? B–Q2 12 B–K2 P×NP! 13
P×NP 0–0 14 0–0 N–K3 15 B–R3
P–N4 ∓ (0–1, 29).

    8 ...   N–R3
    9 0–0   0–0
    10 P–B3   P–Q4

10 ... N–B2 11 P–Q5?! (**11
B–Q2** -Euwe; **11 Q–N3** -Mikenas)
11 ... P×QP 12 P×QP P×P! 13
B×P N–Q2 ∓ Barcza-Fuderer,
Zagreb 1955. Black deploys his
knight to e5 and his bishop to f6.

    11 P×QP   P×QP
    12 P×P   BP×P

13 N–B4 N–B2 14 B–Q2 (Uhlmann
pretends he's in a French Defence!)
14 ... B–Q2 15 B–K1 B–B3 16
B–N3 Q–Q2 17 Q–N3 K–R1 (Both
side are playing normal moves —
here Black might have grabbed
some space with **17 ... P–QN4**.) 18
P–QR4 P–QR3?! 19 P–R5 N–K3
20 N–R4 N×N 21 B×N QR–Q1
Uhlmann-Tseshkovsky, Leipzig.
1975. ±, but the game was drawn.

C222

    5 ...   **B–K2**
    6 N–R3

Here, as in Chapter 10, B342,
Black must reckon with **6
P–KR4!?**, and if **6 ... P–KR3** 7
N–R3 B×P, 8 N–B4 K–B2 (forced)
9 P–K3 P–KN3 10 P–B5!?. Then
10 ... P–KR4! staves off disaster
but it's still complicated. Interesting was **6 ... N–KB3** 7 N–R3 P–B4

('Larsenesque') 8 P–K3 B–K3 9
B–K2 N–R3 10 P–QN3 N–B2 11
B–N2 0–0 12 N–B4 B–B2 13 Q–Q2
Q–Q2 14 0–0–0 P×P? 15 Q×P
N–K3 16 N×N B×N 17 P–B3 R–B2
18 P–R5! ± Watson-Dorsch, Las
Vegas 1976.

    6 ...   P–B3

a) **6 ... N–KB3** 7 B–N5 (**7 P–K3** 0–0
8 B–K2 P–B3 9 0–0 N–R3! 10 P–B3
N–B2 11 Q–N3 K–R1 12 B–Q2
R–QN1 13 B–K1 P–QN4 = /∞
Uhlmann-Rodriguez, Halle 1974) 7
... QN–Q2 8 P–K3 N–B1?! 9 B–K2
N–K3 10 B×N B×B 11 P–KN4!
wrested the initiative in Osnos-
Vasiukov, Riga 1968. Again,
White's B–KN5 helped make
feasible the undermining of Black's
pawn chain.

b) **6 ... P–B4!?** 7 P×P P×P 8
Q×Qch B×Q 9 N–QN5 (**9 B–K3**; **9
P–KN4** -Forintos) 9 ... B–R4ch!
10 B–Q2 B×Bch 11 K×B N–QR3
12 P–K3 N–B3 = /∞ Portisch-
Larsen (8), 1977.

    7 P–KN3

7 . P–K3 N–B3 is (a) of the
preceding note.

    7 ...   N–B3

Or **7 ... N–QR3!**, not allowing 8
B–N5, which White should now
play.

    8 N–B4(?)   0–0
    9 P–KR4   N–R3
    10 P–K3   N–B2
    11 B–Q2   K–R1

Now White's queen bishop lacks
even the route e1–h4 and Black's
centre is safe; 12 Q–B2 B–Q2 13
P–QN4?! P–Q4 14 P–B5 P–QN4!
15 P×Pe.p. P×P ∓. Pachman-
Matanović, Portoroz 1958.

C223
5 ...   P–KR3!

Not that White has had un-restricted good fortune against other moves, but this casts doubt on 5 N–KN5 altogether.

   6 N–R3   P–KN4

Similar to the Browne game in C221, which can now occur by **7 P–K3** N–KB3. The main difference is that this position is forced. And the following attempt to deviate was stifled in Watson-Fritzinger, Saratoga 1976:

   7 P–B3   P×P
   8 KP×P?!

8 NP×P P–B5 is complex (9 Q–Q3 Q–Q2), but the sounder way to advantage is **8 ... B–N2** 9 N–B2 (9 P–K3 N–KB3 is the Browne game) 9 ... N–QB3 ∓.

   8 ...   B–N2

9 N–B2 N–QB3 10 P–Q5 N–Q5 11 B–K2 P–B4 12 P×Pe.p. P×P 13 0–0 N–K2 14 B–K3 P–B4 ∓.

C23
5 N–KN1

The same idea as C22 but in safer form, e.g. **5 ... N–KB3 6 N–R3** is C221, and White has the pleasant alternative **6 B–N5. 5 ... B–K2** can be answered by 6 P–B3 or 6 N–R3.

   5 ...   P–B3
   6 P–KN3

6 N–R3 would be 'normal'. **6 P–QN4** B–K2 (6 ... P–KN3!) 7 P–N5 N–B3 8 N–R3 0–0 9 P–K3 K–R1 10 B–N2 was Miles-Benko, Sao Paulo 1977, with intricate play ahead.

   6 ...   N–B3

   7 N–R3   P–KN3!?
   Or **7 ... N–R3**
   8 N–B4   N–R3
   9 P–KR4   P–Q4
   10 P×P   P×P
11 Q–N3 N–B2 12 B–Q2 B–K2 13 P–K3 (White had to wait to play this until Black could no longer respond with ... B–KR3; thus 7 ... P–KN3!? has had its effect!) 13 ... K–B2 14 R–B1 B–Q2 15 B–K2 B–B3 Portisch-Ivkov, Palma de Mallorca 1970. Drawn in a few moves.

C24
5 N–Q2   N–KB3
   Or **5 ... P–B3** 6 P–K3 N–B3.
   6 P–K3   P–B3

A critical variation. Note that **6 ... N–B3** would be Chapter 10. The alternative of most interest is **6 ... P–KN3(!)** 7 B–K2 and:

a) **7 ... B–N2** 8 P–B3 (**8 0–0** △ P–QN4 -Polugaevsky) 8 ... P×P 9 B×P 0–0 10 0–0 N–B3! 11 R–K1 K–R1 12 R–N1 P–B5!? (**12 ... N–K2** ... P–KN4, ... N–N3 - Polugaevsky) 13 N–B1 P×P, Ribli-Polugaevsky, Budapest, 1975, and with **14 B×P!** (instead of **14 N–N3?**), chances would have been about level (½–½, 20, anyway).

b) **7 ... B–R3!?** 8 P–QN4 0–0 **9 N–N3** (to protect the KP, since Black's king bishop is preventing P–KB3; yet more effective is just **9 B–N2**, intending P–Q5 and at some point P–QB5) 9 ... Q–K2 10 Q–B2 QN–Q2 11 P–QR4 R–K1 12 P–R5?! N–B1 ∓ Furman-Filip. Bucharest 1954.

   7 P–B3

This attempt to commit Black to . . . P–Q4 has been awarded '!' (e.g. Shatskes) and '?' Quinteros). Other moves are **7 P–QN4** (logical, but no examples), and **7 B–K2**, after which Black can play as in the last note (b) with **7 . . . P–KN3** 8 0–0 B–R3! 9 P–QN4 0–0 10 P–N5 R–K1 =, Boleslavsky-Bronstein, Candidates, 1953, or **7 . . . B–K2** 8 P–B3 P–Q4 9 Q–N3 0–0?! (9 . . . P–QR3) 10 P×QP P×QP 11 P×P P×P 12 N(3)×P and Black had little compensation, Ribli-Bilek.

7 . . .   P–Q4 (*90*)

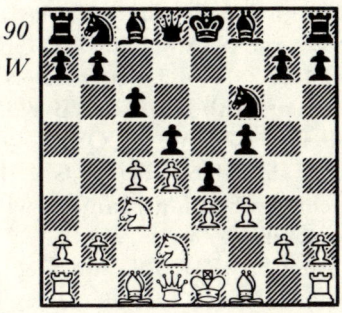

90
W

Very interesting is **7 . . . P×P** 8 Q×P?! (8 N×P Δ B–Q3, 0–0) 8 . . . P–KN3 9 B–Q3 B–N2 10 P–K4 0–0! 11 P×P N–K1! ∓ Schmidt-Nilsson, 1955.

8 Q–N3

If one is dissatisfied with the positions resulting from this move, I suggest **8 Q–R4(!)** for less forcing play. Then **8 . . . B–Q2?** 9 Q–N3 or **8 . . . K–B2** 9 Q–N3! (or 9 P–QN4) is good for White, as is **8 . . . N(1)–Q2** 9 P×QP N–N3 10 Q–N3 P×P 11 P–QR4 Δ 11 . . . P–QR4 12 B–N5ch ±. Better tries are **8 . . . KP×P** 9 N×BP B–K2 10 B–Q3 0–0

11 0–0, although White stands well; and **8 . . . QP×P** 9 P×P (9 Q×P N–Q4! ∞) 9 . . . P–QN4 10 Q–B2, also ±.

8 . . .   P–QR3!

8 . . . KP×P 9 N×BP is favourable for White and **8 . . . Q–N3?** sets the stage for the well-known game Nei-Kuipers, Beverwijk 1966: 9 Q×Q P×Q 10 P×QP P×QP?! (**10 . . . N×P!** and 11 N–B4 ± or 11 K–B2 ±) 11 P–KN4! P–KR3 (**11 . . . B–N5** 12 P–N5 B×N 13 P×B N–Q2 14 P–QB4 ± - Taimanov) 12 P×BP P×P 13 B–Q3 ±±.

9 B–K2?

Allowing . . . P–QN4 must be wrong. **9 P–QR4 P–QR4!?** 10 P×QP P×QP 11 B–N5ch N–B3 is complex, e.g. 12 0–0 (Δ 13 P×P BP×P 14 N(2)×P!) 12 . . . B–K2 13 P–N4!? ∞

Quinteros points out **9 P–B5(!)**, which makes the most sense, since b6 is weak. Then White's best plan is not N–R4 but Q–B2, N–N3, B–Q2, 0–0–0, for Black cannot attack on the queenside without giving White too many good squares for his pieces.

9 . . .   P–QN4

∓, Quinteros.

10 P–B5?

But now that White can't take the QNP en passant, this move loses its point. **10 P×QP**, preserving queenside play, is better.

10 . . .   P–QR4

Black could also immediately advance on the kingside.

11 P–QR4   P–N5
12 N–Q1 P–N4 13 N–B2 P–R4 14

Q–B2 Q–K2 15 N–N3 P–R5 16 B–Q2 B–K3 17 0–0–0 QN–Q2 18 QR–N1 B–R3 19 P–N3? (Waiting is excruciating, but wiser.) 19 . . . P×BP 20 B×P P–N5 21 B–Q1 P–R6 ∓∓ Ribli-Quinteros, Las Palmas 1974. Black put knights on e4 and g5, brought his bishop to a6, and eventually broke through (0–1, 77).

CONCLUSION:

The entire line with 3 . . . P–KB4 has enjoyed fine results thus far. After 4 P–Q4 P–K5, White can only equalize with **5 B–N5** and probably not even achieve that much with **5 N–KN5**. **5 N–KN1** and **5 N–Q2** give White the most positive chances, but Black has plenty of play then, too.

C3

We now look at Black's other third moves. These tend to transpose to another chapter, or to another opening, but White has some very sharp alternatives:

C31

    3 . . .   **N–QB3(?!)**
    4 P–Q4

4 P–KN3 or **4 P–Q3** will transpose, usually to Chapter 1. But **4 P–K3(!)** exploits the position of the knight on c6, as P–Q4–Q5 is not easy to prevent, e.g. 4 . . . P–B4 (4 . . . B–N5!? resembles C11) 5 P–Q4 P–K5, and now **6 N–Q2** and **6 N–KN1** are perfectly reasonable (Black is advised to answer with 6 . . . P–KN3 and . . . B–R3 or . . . B–N2); but the clearest solution is **6**

P–Q5!, when 6 . . . P×N (?! 6 . . . N–K4 ± could be tried.) 7 P×N favours White.

    4 . . .   N–B3

4 . . . P×P 5 N×P ± may lead to Chapter 2; **4 . . . P–KN3?!** 5 P×P (5 **P–KN3** B–N2 6 P×P is similar, and **5 P–Q5** N–K2 6 P–K4 is a Modern Defence position.) 5 . . . P×P? (5 . . . **N×P** 6 N–Q4! B–N2 7 P–K4 ±) 6 Q×Qch K×Q 7 N–KN5! N–R3 8 N(5)–K4 and Black can hardly defend himself.

    5 P–KN3!

5 P×P P×P 6 Q×Qch K×Q 7 **N–KN5** K–K2!. Then White can make no inroads as he did in the last note e.g. 8 N–N5 N–K1 9 P–QN3 P–B4! Δ . . . K–B3. Better **7 B–N5**, although with e.g. 7 . . . B–K3 8 0–0–0ch K–B1 9 N–Q5 N–Q2! Black should be able to face the queenless middlegame with equanimity.

After 5 P–KN3!, we get a position which can also arise in Chapter 8 (via 4 P–Q4 P–Q3).

    5 . . .   B–N5
    6 P–Q5   N–QN1

Uhlmann criticizes this move, but **6 . . . N–K2** is just as unwieldy. Nor is **6 . . . B×N** 7 P×B attractive: 7 . . . N–Q5 (**7 . . . N–K2** 8 P–B4 or **7 . . . N–N1** 8 B–K3) 8 B–N2 (or 8 B–K3 ±) 8 . . . P–KN3 9 0–0 B–N2 10 P–B4 0–0 11 P×P P×P 12 P–B4 ± Lein-Barreras, Cienfuegos 1972.

    7 B–N2   B–K2

Perhaps **7 . . . P–QR4** 8 P–KR3 B–Q2 Δ 9 . . . N–R3 ±

    8 P–KR3   B×N
    9 B×B

9 P×B!? 0–0 10 0–0 P–QR4 11

P–B4 N(1)–Q2 12 P–KR4 (12
Q–B2 △ P–B5) 12 ... R–K1 13
P–N3 (or 13 P–KB5! △ P–KN4) 13
... P×P 14 B×P N–B4 15 P–R3
N(3)–Q2 16 Q–B2 B–B3 17
P–QN4 ± Schmidt-Rosetto, 1975.

    9 ...   0–0
   10 P–K4   KN–Q2

Intending ... B–N4, but: 11
P–KR4! P–QR4 12 0–0 N–B4 13
P–QN3 (After **13 R–N1** or **13
P–R3?** would have come 13 ...
P–R5.) 13 ... N(1)–R3 14 R–N1
P–QB3 15 B–K3 P×P?! (Then
again, White had two bishops and
was staking out terrain everywhere
...) 16 Q×P! N–N5 17 Q–Q2
Q–B1 18 KR–Q1 P–B4 19 P×P (or
19 B×N! -Uhlmann) 19 ... Q×P
20 B–N2 and White was manifestly
better, Uhlmann-Calvo, Madrid
1973 (1–0, 29).

C32
    3 ...   **P–KN3**
Chameleon-like in its ability to
switch from system to system.
    4 P–Q4
    4 P–KN3 could lead to one of
four different chapters or a King's
Indian! Now:
C321 4 ... B–N2
C322 4 ... N–Q2
    4 ... P×P? 5 N×P concedes
White a familiar positional edge,
but **5 Q×P!** is even better e.g. 5 ...
N–KB3 6 B–N5 B–N2 7 Q–K3ch or
5 ... P–KB3 6 B–B4 N–B3 7 Q–Q2
±.

C321
    4 ...   **B–N2**
Now **5 P–K4** B–N5 6 P–Q5 is a

popular Modern Defence position
somewhat favouring White. We
look briefly at another idea which is
also properly a Modern Defence:
    5 P×P   P×P
    6 Q×Qch   K×Q
    7 B–K3
Malich recommends **7 B–N5ch**
P–B3 ('=' Uhlmann) 8 0–0–0ch
B–Q2 9 B–K3 △ P–KN4 ±. But
Black can play the standard 9 ...
B–R3 10 B×B N×B e.g. 11 P–KR3
P–B3 12 P–KN4 N–B2.
    7 ...   P–KR3
Uhlmann also gives **7 ... B–K3**
8 0–0–0ch N–Q2 9 P–B5 P–KR3
10 P–KN3 ∞. Black should be able
to defend. Another thought here is
the direct 9 P–QN3 P–KR3 10
B–B5.
    8 0–0–0ch   B–Q2
    9 P–KN4   K–B1
   10 P–KR3 ±
Uhlmann-Quinteros, Vrsac 1973.
White developed a winning bind,
but ½–½, 58.

C322
    4 ...   N–Q2
Another variety of Modern
Defence.
    5 P–K4
    5 P–KN3 is the author's
preference. **5 B–N5!?** P–KB3 6
B–Q2 N–R3 7 P–KR4?! (7 P–K4!
± -Byrne and Mednis) 7 ... P–B3!
8 P–Q5 Q–N3! 9 R–QN1 P–R4 10
P–R3 N–N5 11 P–K3 B–R3 and
Black had an easy game, Sherwin-
Matera, USA 1977.
    5 ...   B–N2
    6 B–K2   N–K2
    7 P–KR4!?

7 0–0 ±. White should then keep the centre fluid (i.e. avoid P–Q5).

7 ...   P–KR3

A fact of particular interest to blitz players: on either side of the English, P–KR4 is best answered 95% of the time by P–KR3.

8 P–Q5   0–0
9 B–Q2   P–KB4
10 Q–B1   P×P!
11 N×P   N–KB4!

12 P–KN4 N–Q5 13 N×N P×N 14 B×PQ–K2 (Black has plenty of open lines for the pawn.) 15 P–B3 N–K4 16 B–N5 Q–K1 17 0–0 P–Q6 18 B–Q1 N×NP! 19 R–K1 N–K4 20 P–B4 N–N5 21 N–B6ch B×N 22 R×Q B–Q5ch 23 K–N2 R×R 24 B–B3 B–KB4 ∓ Litvinov-Vladimirov, Minsk, 1974 (0–1, 44). A nice conception, and not too speculative, considering White's weakening advances on the kingside.

C33

3 ...   N–KB3 and:
C331 4 P–Q4
C332 4 P–Q3

C331

4 P–Q4

4 P–KN3 reserves this for later.

4 ...   P–K5!?

4 ... QN–Q2 5 P–K4 P–KN3 will be a King's Indian, whereas 5 P–KN3 B–K2 6 B–N2 0–0 is an Old Indian.

5 N–KN5

5 N–Q2 is rather passive: 5 ... B–B4, and a cute example is
a) **6 Q–B2** B–N3 7 N(2)×P? N×N 8 N×N P–Q4! (8 ... Q–R5 -

Schwarz; 9 Q–R4ch! ∞) 9 Q–R4ch (9 P×P B–N5ch) 9 ... P–N4! 10 Q×Pch P–B3 11 Q–N7 P×N 12 Q×R B–N5ch 13 B–Q2 B×Bch 14 K×B Q×Pch 15 K–K1 Q×NP 16 R–Q1 0–0 17 P–K3 B–R4! 18 P–B3 P×P 19 R–Q2 P–B7ch 0–1, Radchenko-Nisman, Candidate Masters, Moscow 1971. Better
b) **6 P–K3** P–B3 7 B–K2 P–Q4 8 Q–N3 (**8 0–0** B–K2 9 P–B4 P×Pe.p.! 10 N×P 0–0 =) 8 ... Q–Q2 9 P×P P×P 10 P–B4 P×Pe.p. 11 N×BP B–Q3! 12 N–K5 B×N 13 P×B N–K5 14 0–0 N–QB3 = Smyslov-Bronstein, 17th USSR Ch. 1949. **14 N×P** is Shatskes' improvement: '14 ... B–K3 15 B–B4 N–B4 16 Q–N5.' But **16 ... B×N!** is at least equal: 17 Q×N B×B 18 Q×B N–B3 or 17 Q×Qch N(1)×Q 18 B×B N×P ∓.

5 ...   B–B4
6 P–KN4 (*91*)

6 Q–B2? P–KR3! 7 N(5)×KP N×N 8 N×N Q–R5! ∓ Boleslavsky-Bronstein, Budapest 1950.

6 ...   B×P
7 B–N2   N–B3
8 N(5)×P   N×N
9 N×N

9 B×N Q–Q2 10 N–Q5!? 0–0–0 11 Q–Q3 R–K1 12 R–KN1? (12 B–K3 ∞ -Raicević) 12 . . . B×P 13 K×B P–B4 14 P–B3 Q–K3! ∓ Polugaevsky-Raicević, Belgrade 1974 (0–1, 62).

9 . . .	**Q–Q2?**
10 P–KR3	B–B4
11 N–N3	B–N3
12 P–KR4	

Schmidt-Westerinen, Helsinki 1966. White threatens P–R5 and can play e.g. P–K4, B–K3, B–KR3 etc. His centre is not a target in this example. But much better was **9 . . . B–K2!** and Black has good play. In the first place, **10 P–KR3** B–B4 11 N–N3 B–N3 12 P–Q5 N–K4 or here 12 P–K4 0–0 achieves nothing, since White's pawns are not mobile. Secondly, the slower **10 N–N3** 0–0 11 P–KR3 B–Q2 12 P–N3 encounters 12 . . . B–R5! (Δ 13 B–N2 Q–N4) 13 Q–Q3 Q–B3 14 B–N2 QR–K1, e.g. 15 R–KB1 Q–N4. Thus Shatskes' statement that either **5 N–Q2** or **5 N–KN5** gains the advantage is by no means correct!

C332

4 P–Q3

As White may not be satisfied with the play after **4 P–Q4** P–K5, we turn our attention to 4 P–Q3 (with Black operating from an Old Indian formation). What follows may arise in various ways, e.g. 1 P–QB4 N–KB3 2 N–QB3 P–Q3 3 P–KN3 P–K4 4 B–N2 P–B3 5 N–B3 N(1)–Q2 6 P–Q3 etc. or 1 P–QB4 P–K4 2 N–QB3 N–KB3 3 P–KN3 B–K2 etc.

4 . . .	QN–Q2

Another example of Black's idea would be **4 . . . P–B3** 5 P–KN3 B–K2 6 B–N2 0–0 7 0–0 B–N5 8 P–KR3 B–R4 9 Q–B2. By transposition we have reached Saidy-Keres, Tallin 1973: 9 . . . QN–Q2 10 P–K4 N–K1 11 B–K3 N–B2 12 P–Q4 B×N 13 B×B P×P 14 B×P N–K3 15 B–K3 B–N4=.

5 P–KN3	P–B3
6 B–N2	B–K2
7 0–0	0–0
8 R–N1	P–KR3

'?!' -Kurajica, who suggests **8 . . . P–QR4** or **8 . . . P–QR3** 9 P–QN4 P–QN4. Black is under no great pressure and can also simply develop with **8 . . . Q–B2** or **8 . . . R–K1**.

9 P–QN4	P–Q4
10 P×P	

10 Q–B2 Δ P–N5 would retain more tension.

10 . . .	P×P

11 Q–N3 P–Q5 12 N–Q5 B–Q3! 13 N×Nch N×N 14 P–K3 B–K3 15 Q–N2 P×P 16 B×P R–K1 17 R(B)–K1 B–Q4 18 B–B5 B×B 19 P×B P–K5 = Andersson-Larsen (8), Stockholm 1975.

C34

3 . . .	**P–QB4**
4 P–K3(!)	P–B4
5 P–Q4	P–K5
6 N–Q2	P×P!?

Freeing White's queen bishop. **6 . . . N–KB3!?**

7 P×P	N–KB3
8 N–N3	P–Q4

9 B–N5 B–N5 10 N–Q2! (±) 10 . . . B–K2 11 P×P N–N5 12 B–N5ch

N–Q2 13 B×B Q×B 14 P–Q6! Q×P 15 N(2)×P ± Portisch-Szabo, Hungary 1974.

CONCLUSION:

Of the four third moves examined in C3, **3 . . . N–QB3** and **3 . . . P–QB4** are difficult at best for Black, but **3 . . . . P–KN3** 4 P–Q4 N–Q2 is playable, and **3 . . . N–KB3** 4 P–Q4 P–K5!? is apparently quite equal. After 3 . . . N–KB3, White should probably content himself with 4 P–KN3, or, a move earlier:

D

3 P–KN3 (*92*)

Now **3 . . . N–KB3** will almost inevitably transpose to D1 through D4, or to another part of the book, or to another opening! We investigate:

D1 3 . . . N–QB3
D2 3 . . . B–N5
D3 3 . . . B–K3
D4 3 . . . P–KB4

3 . . . P–KN3 tends to transpose, e.g. to Chapter 10 although 4 P–Q4 N–QB3!? is independent: 5 P–Q5 (5 **P×P** P×P! 6 Q×Qch K×Q 7 N–B3 P–B3 = Saidy-Kavalek,

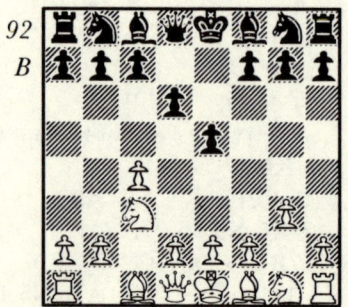

92
B

Lanzarote 1973) 5 . . . N(3)–K2 6 P–K4 B–N2 7 B–N2 P–KB4 8 KN–K2 N–KB3 9 P–B3 0–0 10 P–KR3 P–B3 11 B–K3 P×QP 12 BP×P B–Q2 13 0–0 P–QN4! = Raicević-Ivkov, Madjdanpek 1976.

D1

3 . . .	N–QB3
4 B–N2	N–B3

4 . . . B–K3 is D311. **4 . . . B–Q2?!** 5 P–K3 (or 5 P–QN4 - Schwarz) 5 . . . Q–B1 6 P–Q4 P–KN3 7 P–Q5 N–Q1 8 P–K4 B–N2 9 B–K3 N–KB3 10 P–B3 0–0 11 KN–K2 B–BR6 (not so much to exchange White's mediocre bishop as to get some elbow room before P–QB5 overruns the queenside) 12 0–0 B×B 13 K×B N–K1 14 Q–Q2 P–KB4 15 P–QN4 N–B2 16 P–B5 ± Ilivitsky-Dubinin, Mass, USSR 1961.

  5 P–Q3

Or **5 P–K3** B–K2 (or 5 . . . P–KN3) 6 KN–K2 0–0 7 0–0 ±. P–Q4 is looming.

5 . . .	P–KN3
6 P–B4	

Of course, White could enter *English II . . . N–KB3*, Ch 5 with **6 N–B3** or Chapter 1 with **6 P–K4**.

6 . . .	B–N2
7 N–B3	0–0
8 0–0	P×P

With Black's king knight on e7 this is a good move. Here it is also acceptable, but double-edged. Feasible was **8 . . . N–KR4** or **8 . . . N–Q5**.

9 B×P	B–N5

9 . . . P–KR3 (Botvinnik).

10 Q–Q2   R–K1?

This must be wrong, abandoning the defence of f7. Various commentators suggested **10 ... R–N1** 11 B–N5 B×N, but White is better in that case: 12 B×B N–K4 13 N–Q5 N(4)–Q2 14 B–N2 etc. **10 ... Q–Q2** seems most accurate.

10 ... R–K1 follows Botvinnik-Smyslov (USSR Team Ch) 1966: 11 QR–K1 (or 11 B–N5!) 11 ... R–N1 12 B–N5 B×N 13 B×B N–K4 14 Q–B4 P–KR3 (**14 ... N(4)–Q2** 15 N–K4 R–K3 16 N×Nch B×N 17 B–Q5 ±) 15 B×RP B×B 16 Q×B and White went on to win.

D2

3 ...   **B–N5**

Not logical in a linear sense, but Black develops a piece and may now construct a pawn chain on white squares *behind* his queen bishop, or try to provoke White's pawns to unfavourable squares.

4 B–N2

4 P–Q4 N–QB3?! 5 P–Q5 N–N1 6 B–N2 N–KB3 7 N–B3 B–K2 8 P–KR3 B–Q2 Byrne-Smyslov, 1962. White has territory and better development. But **4 ... N–KB3** (Schwarz), **4 ... N–Q2**, and **4 ... P–QB3** are all practicable.

4 ...   P–QB3
5 N–B3   N–B3

Black proceeds conventionally. In the spirit of 3 ... B–N5 might be **5 ... B–K2** and on **6 0–0**, 6 ... Q–Q2. If **6 P–KR3** B–R4 7 0–0, 7 ... P–KB4! is promising, intending 8 P–Q4 P–K5 and 9 ... N–B3 Δ ... P–Q4. **6 P–Q4** is reliable, when 6 ...

QN–Q2 7 0–0 N(1)–B3 is the text; but 7 ... Q–N3!? is a funny option.

6 0–0   QN–Q2
7 P–Q4   B–K2

7 ... Q–N3 8 P–B5!
8 P–KR3   B–R4

Better **8 ... B×N** (Smejkal). That would transpose to C122, where Bronstein indeed chose that move against Dorfman, and Black was still somewhat worse.

9 N–R4!

Dorfman's suggestion from that game, although here the QNP does not hang. Still, there's nothing very good now about **9 ... B–N3** 10 P–K4! or 9 ... P×P 10 Q×P N–B4 11 N–B5 N–K3 12 Q–Q2.

9 ...   0–0
10 N–B5   R–K1?!

Better **10 ... B–N3** 11 N×B Q×N (Smejkal). Then Black's position appears more flexible than before, but 12 P–Q5! is awkard for him anyway (±).

11 P–Q5!   P×P

11 ... P–B4 12 Q–Q3 Δ P–K4; **11 ... Q–B2?** 12 P×P! P×P 13 N×Bch Δ N–N5 (Smejkal). It is instructive to see how White gets an advantage in this kind of position despite Black's slight lead in development.

12 N(3)×P   N×N

13 B×N Q–B2 14 P–N3 B–B1 15 B–KN2 QR–Q1 16 B–N2 Smejkal-Balashov, Sochi 1973. Smejkal prefers 16 B–R3! here, but he went on to pressure the weak central squares and Black's QP for the point.

D3

3 ...   **B–K3**

Smyslov's idea, which in many instances has equalized the game in a few moves!

White has tried:

D31 4 B–N2
D32 4 P–N3
D33 4 N–B3

D31

4 B–N2

Logical and almost universally played, although by no means clearly best. Black has two main replies:

D311 4 . . . N–QB3
D312 4 . . . P–QB3

D311

4 . . .   N–QB3 *(93)*

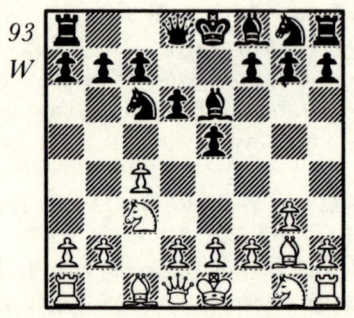

93
W

Dr. Tröger's variation, little investigated. According to Schwarz, the plan is . . . Q–Q2, . . . 0–0–0, and a fierce attack on the kingside; but there are also sane positional motives behind 4 . . . N–QB3. For one thing, Black can threaten . . . P–Q4 with . . . KN–K2 and then react to N–Q5 by . . . Q–Q2, . . . N–Q1, and . . . P–QB3 without losing time to ficchetto his king bishop. Note that the text can arise

also from 2 . . . N–QB3 or 3 . . . N–QB3.

5 P–Q3

a) **5 P–N3** Q–Q2 (or 5 . . . KN–K2) 6 P–K3 KN–K2 7 P–Q4 P×P 8 P×P P–Q4 9 KN–K2 B–R6! 10 B×B (10 P×P N–N5) 10 . . . Q×B 11 N–B4 Q–B4 12 P–KN4 Q–B3 13 B–K3 0–0–0 and Black has good compensation for the pawn he is losing, Niephaus-Tröger, 19?

b) **5 N–Q5** P–KN3 (**5 . . . KN–K2** 6 P–K3 Q–Q2 7 P–QR3?! — 7 Q–R4-Schwarz — 7 . . . N–Q1! 8 P–Q3 P–QB3 9 N–QB3 P–Q4 10 N–B3 P–B3 ∓ Popov-Tröger , Budapest Zonal 1960) 6 P–QN4 (6 Q–R4! - Pytel) 6 . . . B–N2 7 R–N1 Q–Q2 8 P–Q3 N–Q1 9 P–K4 P–KB4 10 N–K2 P–B3 11 N–K3 ∞ Markland-Pytel, Polanica Zdroj 1973.

c) **5 Q–R4** appears logical, Δ P–K3, KN–K2, P–Q4. Black may try 5 . . . Q–Q2 6 P–K3 KN–K2 7 N–Q5 B×N! 8 P×B N–Q1 9 Q×Qch K×Q 10 N–K2, only slightly ±.

5 . . .   Q–Q2

a) **5 . . . B–K2** 6 N–B3! Q–Q2 7 N–Q5 P–B4 8 N–N5! B(2)×N 9 B×B P–KR3 10 B–Q2 ± Analysis by Schwarz. **7 . . . P–KR3** is an improvement.

b) **5 . . . P–B4** 6 P–QN4 (6 P–K3 Δ KN–K2 looks more than adequate.) 6 . . . Q–Q2 7 P–N5 N–Q1 8 P–QR4 ('±' -Pfleger) 8 . . . N–KB3 9 N–Q5 B–K2 (better 9 . . . Q–B2 - Pfleger) 10 N×B Q×N 11 N–B3. White has emerged from the opening with two bishops and excellent queenside prospects. Pfleger-Balinas, Manila 1975.

c) **5 . . . KN–K2** 6 P–B4 (**6 N–B3**
P–B3 7 0–0 Q–Q2 8 Q–R4
P–KR4?! 9 P–KR4 N–B4 10 B–Q2
B–K2 11 P–QN4 ± Filip-Tröger,
Munich 1958. 8 . . . P–Q4 = was
probably too straightforward for
the experimentalist Tröger. Taimanov gives '6 N–Q5!') 6 . . . P–B3
('6 . . . P×P?' -Schwarz, but see the
text) 7 N–B3 Q–Q2 8 P–K4 —
unclear! Dake-Fine, New York
1933.

6 P–B4
a) Benko-Ljubojević, Vrnjacka
Banja 1971, transposed into a
Botvinnik System: **6 P–K4** KN–K2
7 B–K3 P–B4 8 P–N3 P–KN3 9
KN–K2 B–N2 10 0–0 0–0 (∞).
b) Hort-Ilievsky, Skopje 1968 went
6 R–N1 P–KN3?! (why not **6 . . .
KN–K2** 7 N–Q5 N–Q1 etc? or 7
P–QN4 P–Q4 8 P–N5 N–Q1 =) 7
P–QN4 B–N2 8 P–N5 N–Q1 and
White had 'active play of the
queenside', (Taimanov)
c) **6 P–QN4!** saves a tempo on (b): 6
. . . P–KN3 7 P–N5 N–Q1 8
P–QR4 B–N2 — Torre-Chi,
Phillipines-China 1977 — and now
9 B–QR3! looks best.
d) **6 N–Q5** N–Q1 7 N–KB3 P–QB3
8 N–K3 B–R6 9 B×B Q×B 10
P–Q4 ± (but minimally) Portisch-
Buljovcić, Vršac 1971.

6 . . .   P×P
Obviously other moves are possible. **6 . . . P–KN3** is a variant of
Chapter 1, and **6 . . . P–B3** is
similar to note (c) to 5 . . . Q–Q2.

7 P×P!?
A surprising decision; White is
banking on his central majority.
Natural is **7 B×P**, after which Black

doesn't have much latitude for his
pieces, e.g. **7 . . . N–B3** 8 N–Q5
B–K2 (**8 . . . B×N?** 9 P×B N–K2 10
Q–N3 Δ B–R3 ±) 9 N×B Q×N 10
N–B3 (or 10 N–R3) ±. If **7 . . .
KN–K2** 8 N–Q5 N–Q1, 9 P–K4!
P–QB3 10 N–K3 ± (10 . . . P–Q4
11 KP×P P×P 12 Q–N3!).
       7 . . .   B–K2
       8 N–B3   B–R6
9 R–KN1! N–R3 10 P–K4 B×B 11
R×B P–B4 12 N–Q5 0–0–0 13
B–K3 ± Stein-Ljubojević,
Yugoslavia-USSR 1972 (½-½, 35).

D312
      4 . . .   P–QB3
If Black is aiming for this
position, he might play 3 . . .
P–QB3 4 B–N2 B–K3, but then he
must reckon with 4 P–Q4.

4 . . . Q–B1 is not necessarily
bad, but has the drawback that . . .
B×P is still not threatened
(Q–R4ch). White may proceed
simply with 5 P–K3 P–QB3 6
P–N3, intending 7 P–Q4.
      5 P–Q3
5 P–N3 is countered effectively
by 5 . . . P–Q4! 6 P×P P×P 7 N–B3
N–QB3 8 0–0 P–Q5 9 N–QR4 (**9
N–K4?!** P–B4 10 N(4)–N5 B–Q4) 9
. . . N–B3 10 N–N5 B–KN5 = (or
10 . . . B–Q4), Smyslov-Bronstein,
Moscow 1968.
      5 . . .   N–B3
Black may not like to restrict his
options in this way. He can also try:
a) **5 . . . B–K2** 6 P–K4 (**6 N–B3**
P–KB4!?; but **6 P–B4** has its
attraction e.g. **6 . . . N–Q2** 7
P–K4!; or **6 . . . Q–Q2** 7 P×P P×P 8
N–B3 P–B3 9 B–K3 B–R6 10 0–0

±; or **6 . . . P×P(!)** 7 B×P N–B3 8
N–B3 P–KR3 9 0–0 ∞) 6 . . . P–B4
7 Q–R5ch? (7 KN–K2) 7 . . . P–N3
8 Q–K2 N–B3 9 N–B3 P×P 10 P×P
B–N5 11 P–KR3 B×N 12 Q×B
QN–Q2 13 P–KR4 Q–R4 ∓
Sherwin-Weinstein, USA Ch
1962.

b) **5 . . . P–KN3** 6 N–R3!? (**6 P–K4**
is a Botvinnik System; **6 P–B4**
B–N2 7 N–B3 -Schwarz; lastly, **6
B–Q2** B–N2 7 N–B3 N–K2 8
P–KR4 P–KR3 9 Q–B1 P–QR4 10
P–QR3 and 10 . . . N–R3 would
have been =, Ree-Ostojić,
Groningen 1965) 6 . . . P–KR3 7
P–B4 B–N2 8 B–Q2?! (**8 P×P P×P
9 Q–R4!** Δ N–K4, B–K3, Q–N4
must be a better try.) 8 . . . N–K2 9
Q–B1 N–R3 10 0–0 Q–Q2 11
N–B2 P×P 12 P×P?! P–Q4 ∓
Pachman-Szabo, European Team
Ch 1961.

      6 N–B3
6 P–K4!?
      6 . . .   B–K2
      7 0–0   0–0
7 . . . N–R3 8 P–N3 (8 R–N1) 8
. . . P–R3 9 B–N2 0–0 10 Q–B2
B–B4 11 QR–Q1 Q–B1 ∞
Volovich-Bronstein, Moscow 1968.
      8 P–B5!

Ensuring a small advantage. **8
P–QN4** is also thematic, or 8 P–N3
P–KR3 9 P–K4, as in Olafsson-
Smyslov, Candidates 1959. Here 9
B–N2 B–N5? (9 . . . QN–Q2 = -
Boleslavsky) 10 P–KR3 B×N 11
B×B P–Q4 12 P–K3 Q–Q2 13
B–KN2 R–Q1 14 Q–K2 ± was
Mukhin-Bronstein, USSR Ch 1973
(1–0, 47).
      8 . . .   P–KR3

      9 P×P   B×QP
  10 P–N3!   QN–Q2
  11 B–N2   Q–K2
  12 Q–B2 (*94*)

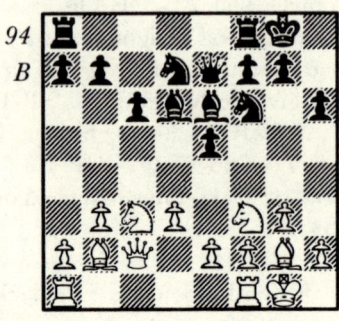

This central formation, reminiscent of a Sicilian Defence, is
slightly better for White here.
Averbach (White) has won more
than one game from similar
structures.
      12 . . .   B–KN5
'? **12 . . . KR–Q1**' (Holmov). Of
course in that case White might hop
his king knight via d2 to c4, after
which K–R1 and P–B4 is one good
plan.
  13 P–KR3   B×N
  14 B×B   B–R6
  15 B×B   Q×B
  16 KR–Q1   QR–Q1
  17 P–QN4!
  A typical type of minority attack
(e.g. *English II,* Ch 1). Particularly
when the dark-squared bishops are
off, a well-timed P–QN4–N5,
enhancing the power of the king
bishop and opening up the
queenside for white rooks, is
surprisingly effective.
      17 . . .   Q×NP
  Otherwise 18 QR–N1 with
threats of P–N5 and possibly

N–R4. **17 ... Q–R3!?** may be a lesser evil.

18 QR–N1 Q–R4 19 R×NP N–B4 20 R–N2 N–K3 21 Q–Q2 N–Q5 22 B–N2 (Black's split, vulnerable pawns now come under fire.) 22 ... Q–R3 23 R–QB1 KR–K1 24 P–K3!? N–K3 25 N–K4 N×N? (25 ... Q×QP ±) 26 B×N P–QB4 27 Q–K2 N–N4 28 B–N2 ± Averbach-Balashov, USSR 1973 (1–0, 72). If 28 ... Q×P, 29 Q×Q R×Q 30 R×P P–K5 31 P–KR4 ± (Holmov).

D32
4 P–N3

Since White only makes the threat of . . . B×P an actual one by 4 B–N2 P–QB3, he opts for protecting the pawn instead. Now on **4 ... P–QB3**, he will play 5 N–B3 and 6 P–Q4 (see also D33).

4 ... P–Q4!

Or **4 ... N–QB3** 5 B–KN2 P–KN3 6 P–K3! B–N2 (**6 ... KN–K2** 7 P–Q4 P×P 8 P×P B–N2 9 KN–K2 P–Q4 10 B–QR3! ±) 7 KN–K2 P–B4 8 P–Q4 B–B2 9 0–0 ±.

5 B–KN2?!

5 P×P B×P 6 N×B Q×N 7 N–B3 N–QB3! (**7 ... P–K5** 8 N–KR4 ±) 8 P–Q3 = /∞.

5 ... P–Q5

Or **5 ... P–QB3** 6 N–B3 P–Q5 7 N–K4 B–K2! Δ ... P–KB4 (Taimanov).

6 N–N1

6 B×NP P×N 7 B×R P–QB3 etc.

6 ... N–QB3 7 P–Q3 Q–Q2 8 P–QR3 P–QR4 9

N–Q2 B–K2 10 B–N2 P–B4 Filip-Tal, Sochi 1973. Black has good attacking chances.

D33
4 N–B3!

A serious alternative to 4 B–N2; White plays for P–Q4, which would be weak immediately, e.g. 4 P–Q4? P×P 5 Q×P N–QB3 6 Q–K3 N–N5!

4 ... P–QB3 (*95*)

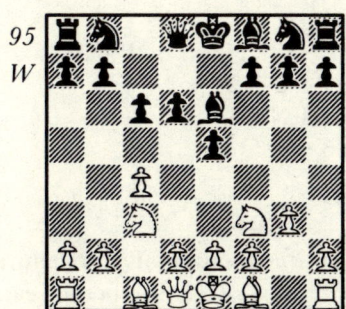

A little investigated position. **4 ... N–Q2** threatens ... B×P, but White can play **5 P–N3**, or probably even **5 P–Q4!?** B×P (**5 ... P×P** 6 Q×P P–QB4 7 Q–B4) 6 Q–R4 B–K3 7 P×P P×P 8 N×P P–QB3 9 B–B4 ±.

This idea seemingly also works after **4 ... N–QB3**: 5 P–Q4! P×P 6 N×P B×P 7 Q–R4 B–K3 8 N×N P×N 9 Q×Pch B–Q2 10 Q–K4ch **B–K2** 11 N–Q5 ±; or **10 ... N–K2?!** 11 B–N2 B–B3? 12 Q×Bch! N×Q 13 B×Nch K–K2 14 N–Q5ch ±±.

5 P–N3

What about **5 P–Q4(!)** here? Then **5 ... Q–B2** 6 P–Q5! and **5 ... B×P** 6 P×P are slightly but definitely better for White.

5 ...   N–B3
6 B–KN2

The minute Black protects his KP in order to play ... P–Q4, White will play P–Q4 himself.

6 ...   P–KR3
7 0–0   Q–B1

8 B–QR3 (8 P–Q4; 8 R–K1) 8 ... B–R6 9 P–Q4 P–K5 10 N–K1 P–KR4(?) 11 P–B3 ± Baukunin-Trapl, 1966. White has more room and better development.

D4

3 ...   **P–KB4** and:

D41 4 B–N2
D42 4 N–B3
D43 4 P–Q4

D41

4 B–N2

It is curious that this natural move is considered second-or even third-best by theoreticians. The question is whether White can build up a specific enough pressure against Black's centre or queenside.

4 ...   N–KB3

a) **4 ... N–QB3** is unnecessarily committal and rules out a possible ... P–B3. An example was Zidkov-Heuer, Moscow 1966: 5 P–K3 P–KN3 6 KN–K2 B–N2 7 P–Q3 (with a rather good variation of the Closed English; but **7 P–Q4!** was thematic and advantageous) 7 ... KN–K2 8 R–QN1 0–0 9 P–B4 B–K3 10 P–QN4 P–Q4? 11 P–N5 ±.

b) **4 ... P–B3** is also unecessary at this stage. **5 P–Q4!?** is possible, or **5 N–B3** N–B3 6 P–Q4! P–K5 7 N–KN5 B–K2 8 P–Q5! P–B4 9 P–B3 P–KR3 10 N–K6 B×N 11 P×B P×P 12 B×P N–B3 13 0–0 0–0

14 B–Q5 ± (a game of the author's).

Now White has essentially two ways to mobilize:
D411 5 P–Q3
D412 5 P–K3

D411

5 P–Q3   B–K2

5 ... P–B3 6 N–B3 is C2 (note (b) to 4 P–Q4). White can also play **6 N–R3** B–K2 7 0–0 0–0 8 P–QN4 P–Q4 9 Q–N3 P×P (9 ... P–Q5 10 N–Q1 Δ P–K3 ±) 10 Q×Pch ± Madsen-L. Schmid, corres 1955.

6 N–B3

6 P–K3 0–0 7 KN–K2 and:

a) **7 ... P–B3** is logical: 8 0–0 K–R1 9 P–Q4 (**9 P–B4!?**) 9 ... P–K5?! (better **9 ... Q–B2** or **9 ... Q–K1**) 10 P–Q5 P–B4 11 P–B3 P×P 12 B×P N–R3 13 N–B4 N–B2 14 Q–K2 R–QN1 15 P–QR4 P–QR3?! 16 P–R5 ± Amos-Allan, Canada 1976;

b) **7 ... Q–K1** 8 0–0 N–B3 (8 ... B–Q1!? Δ ... Q–R4) 9 P–B4 B–Q1 10 P–N3 (10 R–N1) 10 ... K–R1 11 Q–Q2 N–K2 12 P×P P×P 13 P–Q4 N–N3 ∞ Pelts-Donchenko, Ukraine Ch 1970.

6 P–K4 was tested in H. Olafsson-Thibault, Lone Pine 1979: 6 ... P–B3 7 KN–K2 0–0 8 0–0 Q–K1!? (de-centralizing; Simpler was **8 ... N–R3** or **8 ... P–QR4**) 9 P–N3 Q–R4?! (and here 9 ... N–R3!) 10 P–B3! N–R3 11 P×P! Q×P(4) 12 B–QR3 ±.

6 ...   0–0
7 0–0   K–R1

Schwarz calls **7 ... Q–K1** 8 P–B5 '±'.

8 P–QN4   P–QR4?!

9 P–N5 QN–Q2 10 B–QR3! (±) 10
... Q–K1 11 R–B1 R–QN1 12
P–K3 N–N3?! 13 P–B5 P×P 14
N×P ± Benko-Larsen, Winnnipeg
1968 (but 0–1, 39).

D412
5 P–K3

5 **P–Q4 B–K2** transposes. 5
P–Q4 **P×P?** is D43.

5 ...   P–B3

5 ... B–K2 usually transposes,
although 6 P–Q4 0–0 7 KN–K2
K–R1 8 0–0 Q–K1 is possible.

6 P–Q4   B–K2

6 ... P–K5 is a worrisome
alternative: 7 P–Q5 P–KN3! ∞
(White may wish to avoid this by
means of 5 P–Q4). **6 ... Q–B2** 7
KN–K2 B–K2 8 0–0 P–KR4?! is
somewhat brash, and 9 P–K4 P–R5
10 Q–Q3 P–KN3 11 B–N5 (or 11
P–B4!) 11 ... N×KP 12 N×N P×N
13 Q×P B–B4 14 Q–K3 didn't
really justify ... P–KR4–R5 in
Bilek-Zaitsev, Busum 1969.

7 KN–K2   0–0

7 ... B–K3 8 P–N3 QN–Q2 9
0–0 Q–B2 = /∞ Ujteky-Hort,
Czechoslovakia 1960. Leaving g8
open as a bishop retreat square is
one of Hort's pet ideas.

8 P–N3

Prudent, but **8 0–0**, and on **8 ...
Q–K1** or **8 ... QN–Q2**, 9 P–QN4
deserves a look. 8 0–0 **B–K3** 9 P–N3
P–K5? 10 P–Q5 P×P 11 N–B4
B–B2 12 P×P QN–Q2 13 P–B3 ±
Ungureanu-Radovici, Bucharest
1976. A typical motif.

8 ...   QN–Q2

9 B–N2?!

9 P×P P×P 10 B–N2 is correct,
and if 10 ... P–K5, White can play

cautiously with 11 P–KR4 and
N–B4 or less so with 11 0–0 N–B4
12 Q–N1!? N–Q6 13 R–Q1 Q–B2
14 R×N! P×R 15 Q×P with a pawn
and strong position for the
exchange (∞).

9 ...   Q–K1!?

Nunn gives '**9 ... P–K5!** 10
P–Q5? N–K4 ∓; 10 N–B4 N–N3 11
P–Q5 P–N4 12 N–K6 B×N 13 P×B
Q–B1 ∓.' The game Nunn-
Corden, Birmingham 1976 went **9
... R–N1?** 10 Q–B2 P–QN4 11
P×NP P×NP 12 P×P P×P 13 0–0
P–N5 14 N–Q5 ±.

10 P–QR4

'?' (Barcza). **10 P×P** must be
right, extending the scope of
White's queen bishop. We are
following Ujtelky-Barcza, Budapest 1960: 10 ... P–QR4 11
B–QR3 N–N1! 12 Q–Q2 N–R3 13
0–0–0 N–QN5 14 P–Q5 P–B4.
Black has the upper hand.

D42
4 N–B3

This can assume independent
significance:

4 ...   N–KB3

Black could avoid White's idea
by **4 ... P–B3**, or by **4 ... B–K2**,
when 5 P–Q4 P–K5 6 N–KN1
might follow.

5 P–Q4   P–K5

6 N–KR4!?

An original conception. Watson-
Dorsch, Berkeley 1976 continued
more conventionally **6 N–KN5**
P–B3 7 P–KR4 N–QR3 8 N–R3
N–B2 9 B–KN5 B–K2 10 P–K3
B–K3 (**10 ... 0–0**) 11 N–B4 B–B2
12 R–QN1 N–Q2! 13 B×B Q×B 14
P–QN4 P–QR3 15 Q–R4!? 0–0?

(**15 . . . Q–Q1!**) 16 Q–R5, winning
a pawn.

     6 . . .   B–K2
     7 B–R3   P–KN3
     8 0–0

8 **P–B3** P–Q4! seems adequate
for Black

     8 . . .   P–B3
     9 B–N5

9 P–B3 has been recommended,
but 9 . . . P–Q4 Δ 10 Q–N3 QP×P!
11 Q×BP P–QN4 is a good reply.

     9 . . .   N–R3
     10 Q–Q2   N–B2

11 P–B3 P–Q4 12 P×KP QP×P! 13
QR–Q1 0–0 14 P–Q5? (Overlook-
ing the following exchange
sacrifice: **14 B–R6!** R–B2 15 P–Q5
was the correct course, when 15 . . .
P×P 16 P×P N–K1 17 B–B4! is
unclear.) 14 . . . P×P 15 B–R6
P–Q5! 16 B×R Q×B Zhukovitsky-
Vasiukov, USSR Ch 1967. Black's
central pawn mass is worth more
than the exchange (0–1, 40).

D43

     4 P–Q4 *(96)*

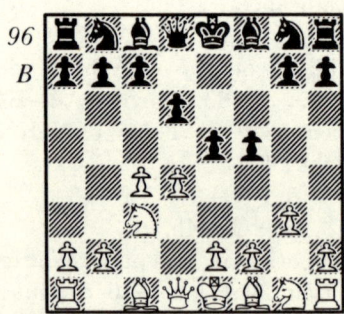

96
B

Favoured by theory. Now:
D431 4 . . . P×P
D432 4 . . . B–K2
D433 4 . . . P–K5

The other try, similar to 4 . . .
B–K2, is **4 . . . N–KB3**. After 5 P×P
P×P 6 Q×Qch K×Q, Euwe opines
that it's equal; but Schwarz takes
exception, giving 7 B–N5 Δ 0–0–0
and commenting that Black players
who use this 'Dutch' set-up are not
aiming to exchange queens
anyway.

I tend to agree with the second
assessment, but not the comment: 7
B–N5 and:

a) **7 . . . B–K2** 8 N–B3! (**8 0–0–0ch**
K–K1 9 N–N5 N–R3) 8 . . . P–K5
(**8 . . . QN–Q2** 9 0–0–0 K–K1 10
B–R3! P–KN3 11 N–N5) 9
0–0–0ch K–K1 10 N–Q4 N–R3
(**10 . . . P–B3?** 11 B–R3 P–KN3 12
B×N B×B 13 N×KP!) 11 B–R3
P–KN3 12 P–B3.

b) **7 . . . B–K3** 8 0–0–0ch K–B1 9
B×N P×B 10 B–R3! P–B3 11 P–N3
Δ N–B3–R4.

In both cases White has a big
advantage, so 4 . . . N–KB3 looks
inferior.

D431

     4 . . .   **P×P?**

Antipositional.

     5 Q×P   N–QB3
     6 Q–Q2   N–B3

7 P–N3 P–KN3 8 B–KN2 B–N2 9
B–N2 0–0 10 N–R3 N–K4 11 0–0
P–B3 12 QR–Q1 N–B2 13 N–KN5!
± Etruk-Arulaid, ESSR 1962.

D432

     4 . . .   **B–K2!**

This is critical for the assessment
of 4 P–Q4.

     5 P×P

5 P–K3 is D412. **5 N–B3** P K5 6

N–KN1, although it seems worse than C23, is still plausible, e.g. 6 . . . N–KB3 7 P–B3 P×P 8 P×P etc.

    5 . . .   P×P
    6 Q×Qch   B×Q

This position is not discussed in any work we know of. White can develop rapidly, but Black has no weaknesses yet. A draw is doubtless the correct result, although a clever player of endings might try his hand on either side. A few lines:

a) **7 B–N2** N–KB3 (**7 . . . P–K3** 8 P–K4! creates an isolated Black KP or, after 8 . . . P–KN3 9 N–B3 B–B2 10 P×P P×P 11 0–0, weak hanging pawns. **7 . . . N–QB3** 8 B×Nch!? P×B 9 N–B3 is interesting.) 8 N–B3 (Now **8 P–K4** N–B3 9 P×P B×P leaves Black actively disposed; but a recent game, Taimanov-Vaganian, Leningrad 1977, went **8 P–N3** P–B3 9 B–N2 QN–Q2 — *9 . . . 0–0 10 N–B3 P–K5!? —* 10 N–B3 0–0 11 0–0 R–K1 12 QR–Q1 B–B2 13 N–KR4! ±, but Black won in 41 moves.) 8 . . . N–B3 (or **8 . . . P–K5** 9 N–Q4 0–0) 9 B–K3 B–K3 =.

b) **7 B–R3** encounters 7 . . . N–KB3! (**7 . . . N–QB3** 8 B–Q2 N–B3 9 0–0–0 0–0 10 N–Q5) 8 P–K4?! (**8 N–B3!?** P–K5 9 N–KR4 P–KN3 10 P–QN3) 8 . . . N–B3!, and if 9 P×P, 9 . . . N–Q5!. exploiting White's drafty center.

D433
    4 . . .   **P–K5**
    5 P–B3

The most direct strategy. **5 P–KR4** △ B–N5, N–R3, P–K3 also deserves consideration.

    5 . . .   N–KB3
    5 . . . P×P 6 P×P! (**6 N×P** is also ±) 6 . . . N–KB3 7 B–N2 P–KN3 8 KN–K2 B–N2 9 0–0 0–0 10 B–K3 R–K1 11 Q–Q2 B–K3 12 P–N3 ± Benko-Formanek, USA 1968 (1–0, 37).

    6 B–N2

Attractive is **6 B–N5** P×P 7 N×P P–KR3?! 8 B–QB1!
    6 . . .   P×P
    7 N×P

Of course **7 P×P** as in Benko-Formanek is good too.

    7 . . .   P–KN3
    8 0–0

Or **8 B–N5** B–N2 9 P–K4 0–0 10 0–0 N–B3 11 P×P B×P 12 N–KR4 ± Biyasis-Schmidt, Lone Pine 1975.
    8 . . .   B–N2
    9 P–K4?!

9 P–Q5! P–B4 10 P×Pe.p. N×P 11 B–B4 ± (Tal). Better **9 . . . 0–0** (Shatskes), but then 10 N–KN5! is strong e.g. 10 . . . R–K1 11 P–K4 P–KR3 12 N–K6 ±.

    9 . . .   P×P
10 N–KN5 0–0 11 N(5)×KP? (**11 N(3)×P!**) 11 . . . N×N 12 R×Rch Q×R 13 N×N N–B3 ∞ Toran-Tal, European Team Ch, 1961. Tal won brilliantly in 25 moves.

CONCLUSION:

3 P–KN3 is a little less committal and probably more effective than **3 N–B3**. White nearly always gets a healthy share of the centre and is generally secure on the kingside. Of the Black responses, **3 . . . N–QB3** 4 B–N2 B–K3!? and **3 . . . B–N5!?** are viable irregular variations which deserve more attention. Smyslov's **3**

. . . B–K3 is intriguing, since 4 B–N2 P–B3 leads to complex positions where, although White may have a slight theoretical edge, the better player will probably win. But for now, 4 N–B3! appears a strong reply. Finally, 3 P–KN3 P–KB4 tends to give White more leeway than 3 N–B3 P–KB4, and he maintains good, though not necessarily better, play after 4 B–N2 or 4 P–Q4. All these lines are tricky and unsettled.

I recommend the Smyslov System (2 . . . P–Q3) to inventive players who like original positions. There are plenty of complications with few forcing lines, and opportunity to hone one's judgement.

10 VARIOUS SYSTEMS WITH ... P–KB4

In the preceding chapter, we discussed 1 P–QB4 P–K4 2 N–QB3 P–Q3 3 N–B3 P–KB4 and 3 P–KN3 P–KB4. Black can also play ... P–KB4 without an early ... P–Q3 i.e. by 2 ... P–KB4, or by 2 ... N–QB3 and 3 ... P–B4. Since the second player has to work so hard to achieve ... P–K4 in a Dutch defence, 'there is a certain logic to placing both KP and KBP on the fourth rank without further ado. The drawback to this strategy, of course, is that it provides White a target of attack: the centre pawns may be provoked to advance, and then be decimated in White's camp. Black naturally prefers it when, by advancing, his pawns cramp the adversary's development.

In each section below, we see different ways in which this conflict of desires can be resolved: 1 P–QB4 P–K4 2 N–QB3
A 2 ... P–KB4
B 2 ... N–QB3 3 N–B3 P–B4
C 2 ... N–QB3 3 P–KN3 P–B4

A

| | 1 P–QB4 | **P–K4** |
| | 2 N–QB3 | **P–KB4** |

Now 3 N–B3 **N–QB3** is B below, and 3 N–B3 **P–Q3** is Chapter 9, C2 (=); but 3 N–B3 **P–K5?** 4 N–Q4

P–Q3 5 P–Q3 P×P 6 Q×P is excellent for White.

The shortcoming of 2 ... P–KB4 (as opposed to 2 ... N–QB3 and 3 ... P–B4) is that White's P–Q4 is not discouraged, while ... P–K5 in reply will not gain a tempo in most cases, because White need not play N–KB3. White can build up to P–Q4 slowly (A1), or try to exploit Black's 'negligence' directly (A2 and A3):
A1 3 P–KN3
A2 3 P–K3
A3 3 P–Q4

Absurd is **3 P–KN4?** P×P 4 B–N2 P–B3! 5 P–KR3 N–B3 6 P×P N×P Δ ... P–Q4 and ... B–QB4 (Schwarz).

3 P–K4?! P×P 4 N×P N–KB3 must be at least equal for Black, since White's d4 and d3 are weak.

A1

| | **3 P–KN3** | **N–KB3** |

3 ... P–Q3 is Chapter 9, D4, and a similar method might be **3 ... B–K2** e.g. 4 P–Q4 P–Q3 5 N–B3 P–K5 6 N–KN1 P–B3 7 P–KR4 N–QR3 8 N–R3 N–B2 9 B–B4 N–B3 10 P–K3 0–0 11 P–QN4 (from a game of the author's). White should be careful to activate his QB in such positions, as it may be trapped behind its own pawn chain, especially as the standard manoeuvre of P–KB3, B–Q2–K1–KN3/KR4 is ruled out here by the pawn on g3.

4 B–N2 (*97*)

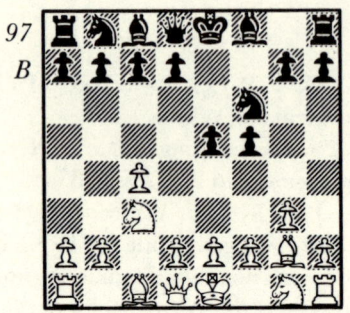

97
B

White can still play **4 N–B3** e.g. 4 . . . P–Q3 5 P–Q4 P–K5 6 N–KN5 (or 6 N–KR4!), transposing to Chapter 9, D42.

4 . . .　　　　P–B3

a) Larsen gives '**4 . . . B–N5?** 5 Q–B2! ±', but Schwarz quotes a game Maicherzik-Ahues, 1953: 5 . . . N–B3! **6 Q×P** P–Q3 7 Q–N1 0–0 ∓. Hmmm . . . anyway, **6 P–QR3(!)** is a safe move, e.g. **6 . . . N–Q5** 7 Q–N1 ±, or **6 . . . B×N** 7 Q×B 0–0 8 P–Q3 ±.

b) **4 . . . P–KN3** 5 P–K3 B–N2 6 KN–K2 0–0 (**6 . . . P–Q3** 7 P–Q4 QN–Q2 8 P–N3 0–0 9 Q–B2 R–K1 **10 0–0?!** P–K5 11 B–QR3 N–B1 12 QR–Q1 P–B3! ∞ Gold-Simagin, Polanica Zdroj 1968 (0–1, 37); better is **10 P×P!** extending the range of White's QB.) 7 P–Q4 P–K5 **8 P–B3** P×P 9 B×P N–R3 (9 . . . P–B3!?) 10 0–0 P–B3 11 B–Q2 P–Q3 12 N–B4 Q–K2 13 P–QR3 N–B2 = Bannik–Zurakhor USSR 1956. More purposeful would be

(after 7 P–Q4 P–K5) **8 0–0** P–Q3 9 P–Q5! Δ 9 . . . P–B4 10 P×Pe.p. and 11 P–N3. White has effectively disturbed the central equilibrium. Also to be considered after 4 . . . P–KN3 is **5 P–Q4!?,** for instance 5 . . . P×P 6 Q×P B–N2 (6 . . . N–B3 7 Q–Q2 B–N2 8 P–N3) 7 P–N3 0–0 8 B–N2 ±.

c) As usual, **4 . . . P–Q3** enters Chapter 9 (D41, this time).

5 P–Q4　　　　P–K5

5 . . . P–Q3 (Larsen) **6 P–K3** B–K2 is another version of Chapter 9 (D412); but **6 P×P(!)** P×P 7 Q×Qch K×Q 8 B–N5 can be rather difficult for Black, e.g. 8 . . . N–Q2 9 0–0–0 K–B2 10 N–B3 (Δ B×N) 10 . . . B–K2 11 N–KR4 P–KN3 12 P–K4! ± (12 . . . P×P 13 KR–K1 N–B4 14 N×KP!).

6 N–R3　　　　N–R3
7 0–0

Since the course of the game is decided by Black's attempt to consolidate at this point, Larsen's note '**7 B–N5!?; 7 P–B3!?**' should be taken seriously (6 P–B3!? was also possible.). For example, **7 B–N5** B–K2 (**7 . . . P–KR3** 8 B×N Q×B and now 9 P–B3 is simplest: 9 . . . P×P 10 B×P B–K2 — *Black must not allow 11 N–B4 and 12 B–R5ch* – 11 0–0 0–0 12 Q–Q2 Δ P–K4 ±) 8 P–B3 **P–Q4(?)** 9 P×QP P×QP 10 N–B4 N–B2 11 Q–N3 and Black is in trouble: 11 . . . N–K3 12 N×N! B×N 13 B×N B×B 14 P×P BP×P 15 B×P B×P 16 R–Q1 etc. But here **8 . . . P×P** is not equal either: 9 B×P 0–0 10 0–0 P–Q3 11 Q–Q2 N–B2 12 P–Q5 ±.

7 P–B3!? will similarly force the

surrender of the centre, or a severe weakening of Black's dark squares after 7 . . . B–N5.

7 . . .	N–B2
8 P–B3	P–Q4
9 P×QP	P×QP

10 B–N5 B–K2 11 N–B4 (Black has an extra tempo to bastion the centre in comparison with the last note, and **11 Q–N3** P–KR3!? is unclear, according to Larsen.) 11. . . N–K3! 12 Q–R4ch K–B2! 13 N×N B×N 14 P×P QP×P 15 K–R1 (**15 QR–Q1!?**—Larsen—looks better timed.) 15 . . . P–KR4! 16 QR–Q1 K–N3 17 P–R4 Q–Q3 18 R–B4?! (**18 B–B4**—Larsen) 18 . . . KR–QB1 19 B–R3 R×N! 20 P×R N–Q4 ∓ Uhlmann-Larsen, Leningrad 1973 (0–1, 39).

A2

3 P–K3

Similar to, and naturally somewhat better than, 2. . . P–K3 in the Sicilian Defence 2 P–KB4 Variation. One might also draw a comparison with 3. . . P–K3 after 1 P–K4 P–QB4 2 N–QB3 N–QB3 3 P–B4, which discourages many players from entering that system.

3 . . .	N–KB3
4 P–Q4	P–K5 (*98*)

a) For **4 . . . P–Q3** 5 N–B3 (**5 P×P** P×P 6 Q×Qch K×Q =) 5 . . . P–K5, refer to Chapter 9, C2.

b) **4 . . . P×P?** 5 P×P B–K2 6 B–Q3 P–Q3 7 Q–B2 N–B3 8 KN–K2 P–KN3 9 P–QR3 0–0 10 P–R3 R–B2 11 B–K3 B–Q2 12 0–0–0 ± (Δ P–B3, P–KN4) O'Kelly-Safvat, Moscow 1956.

5 N–R3

a) Shatskes and Taimanov analyse: **5 P–QR3** ('!') P–B3 6 P–B3 P–Q4 7 N–R3 **B–K2** 8 P×QP P×QP 9 P×P BP×P 10 N–B4 with White better (practically winning, in fact, since 11 N(4)×QP! Δ Q–R5ch as well as 11 Q–N3 is threatened). But **7 . . . B–K3**! improves, when there is a safe way for White to break up the enemy centre (P–KN4 at any point is risky). Best might be 8 P×QP P×QP 9 B–K2 B–K2 10 0–0 N–B3 (10 . . . 0–0 11 Q–N3 Q–Q2 12 N–KN5) 11 B–Q2 with ideas such as N–B4, Q–N3, B–K1–KN3/ KR4.

b) **5 KN–K2** is (by transposition) Euwe-te Kolste, Holland 1926: **5 . . . B–K2?** 6 N–B4 0–0 7 P–KR4 (Δ P–B3 and/or P–B5!?, Q–N3ch, P–R5, etc.) 7 . . . N–N5 8 B–K2 N–KR3 9 N(3)–Q5 P–Q3 10 N×Bch Q×N 11 Q–N3 N–Q2?! 12 P–B5ch K–R1 13 Q–K6 ±±. This oft-quoted game (which arose from 3 P–Q4 P–K5 — see A3) does not convince. **5 . . . P–B3!** grabs more of the centre, e.g. **6 N–B4 B–N5** 7 Q–N3 B×Nch (or 7 . . . P–QR4!?) 8 P×B P–Q3 ∞; and in this line, 6 . . . **N–R3** is also plausible. Another typical idea would be 5 . . . P–B3! **6 P–B3** P–Q4 or 6 . . . P×P) 7

P×QP P×QP 8 P×P BP×P 9 N–B4 B–QN5! 10 Q–N3 N–B3 11 B–N5 0–0 12 0–0 (**12 B×N** B×Nch 13 Q×B P×B 14 Q×P B–Q2 ∞) 12 . . . B×N 13 P×B N–QR4. **6 P–Q5(!)** is again the most unbalancing move, for instance 6 . . . P–Q3 7 N–B4 B–K2 8 P×P P×P 9 B–K2 ± Δ 0–0, P–QN3 etc.

    5 . . .   B–N5

By analogy with the preceding note (b) above, **5 . . . P–B3** could be tried.

    6 Q–N3

6 B–K2 0–0 7 Q–N3 B×Nch 8 P×B **K–R1?** 9 B–R3! P–Q3 10 P–B5 N–B3 11 P×P P×P 12 N–B4 Q–K2 13 0–0 R–Q1 14 P–B4 P–QN3 15 P–B3 ± Simagin-Zagoriansky, Lvov ½F 19th USSR Ch 1951. Black shouldn't let his centre be demolished: **8 . . . P–Q3!** is the proper course, and 9 B–R3 P–B3 10 Q–N4 P–B4! 11 P×P N–R3, etc. or 9 P–B5ch P–Q4 10 P–B4 P–B3 etc.

    6 . . .   B×Nch

    7 Q×B

7 P×B resembles the last note, but White has not wasted time on B–K2 and may be able to resolve the situation favourably with moves like P–B5, B–R3, and N–N5 if necessary.

    7 . . .   N–B3?!

Preferable and less committal is **7 . . . 0–0**, since Black may want to play . . . P–B3 or . . . P–B4.

    8 B–K2   P–Q3
    9 0–0   0–0
10 P–QN3 B–Q2 11 B–N2 Q–K2 12 N–B4 QR–K1 13 QR–B1 B–B1 14 N–Q5 Q–Q1 15 P–B4! Reti-

Romih, London 1927. Either Black gives up the centre and unleashes White's bishops; or, by not capturing *en passant*, he forfeits his chance to block the long/ dark diagonal with . . . N–K4. Then White can prepare R–KN1, P–KN4 etc. (as in the game continuation).

An example of Reti's jet-age style!

A3

    3 P–Q4

Directly attacking the centre without shutting in the B on c1.

    3 . . .   P×P?!

Evidently insufficient, although Black gains time by attacking White's queen. Note the difference between 1 P–QB4 P–K4 2 N–QB3 P–Q3 3 P–Q4 P×P 4 Q×P (Chapter 9, B) and this position. In the first case, . . . P–Q3 helps to develop Black's QB, whereas here . . . P–KB4 only restricts that piece, and weakens e6.

a) **3 . . . P–K5?!** is always condemned as too obliging (it doesn't even gain a tempo), but a refutation is not simple. **4 P–K3** N–KB3 5 KN–K2 and **4 N–R3** N–KB3 5 P–K3 are often given as good for White; these are rather unclear variations discussed in A2 above (note to 5 N–R3). Independent is **4 N–R3 N–KB3** 5 B–N5!, which solves the problem of White's QB and secures his authority over key central squares, e.g. 5 . . . B–K2 6 P–K3 0–0 7 N–B4 P–B3 8 B–K2 (**8 P–KR4** N–R3, = / ∞ according to Schwartz; but then the simple 9 P–B5! looks strong, Δ 10 B–B4ch K–R1 11 P–R5 and 12 N–N6ch. It's not clear how Black meets this idea, so 8 P–KR4 is worth considering.) 8. . . P–Q3 9 Q–N3 N–N5? (**9 . . . K–R1** ± -Palatnik) 10 P–B5ch P–Q4 11 B×B Q×B 12 N(3)×QP P×N 13 B×N! P×B 14 N×P Q–R5 15 N–B7ch K–R1 16 0–0–0 with a winning game, Palatnik-Borngässer, Odessa 1973. Perhaps **4 . . . P–B3!?** is correct.

b) **3 . . . P–Q3** is not mentioned in the books, but keeps Black's pawns healthy. Again, both **4 N–B3** P–K5 and **4 P–KN3** N–KB3 5 B–N2 B–K2 6 P–K3 are lines from Chapter 9 (C2 and D412, respectively). **4 P×P** P×P 5 Q×Qch K×Q naturally gives White some initiative; whether that can be converted to a concrete advantage is hard to say. Compare the ending of Chapter 9, D43, note to 4 . . . B–K2. A sample line: 6 N–B3 P–K5 7 N–Q4 N–KB3 8 P–QN3 P–B3 9 B–N2 K–B2 with good squares for the White pieces (early knight sorties to g5 or b5 were futile), but a solid Black formation.

This needs a test, since 3 . . . P×P lands Black in trouble:

4 Q×P N–QB3

4 . . . N–KB3 waits to see what White is up to. Mikenas-Polugaevsky, 1952 continued: 5 P–KN3 (**5 Q–K5ch** B–K2 6 Q×P(5) P–Q4 ∓ - Schwarz) 5 . . . N–B3 6 Q–K3ch **B–K2?!** 7 B–N2 0–0 8 N–R3 R–K1 9 0–0 B–N5 10 Q–Q3 N–K4 11 Q–B2 P–B3 12 P–R3 B–B1 13 P–N3 P–Q3 14 B–N2 with a firm

grip on the centre. **6 . . . K–B2?!** was not better on account of 7 B–N2 B–N5 8 N–R3 R–K1 9 Q–Q2 (Δ 9 . . . N–K4 10 P–R3!) 9 . . . B×N 10 Q×B P–Q4 11 N–N5ch and 12 P×P ±. Best seems **6 . . . Q–K2**, which was perhaps not played because of Polugaevsky's desire to win. Then **7 N–N5** Q×Q or even **7 . . . K–Q1!?** is about equal, so White should play modestly: **7 B–N2** Q×Q 8 B×Q B–N5 9 B–Q2 0–0 10 N–R3, and if 10 . . . B×N 11 B×B N–K5 12 R–QB1, White's basic advantages have survived, albeit in simplified form.

5 Q–K3ch! (*99*)

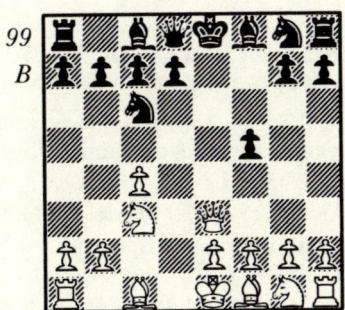

5 Q–Q1 B–N5 6 N–B3 (? **6 B–Q2!** N–B3 7 P–K3 0–0 8 N–R3 promises more.) 6 . . . N–B3 7 Q–B2 (**7 B–Q2** 0–0 8 P–K3 N–K5! 9 N–Q5 N×B 10 N×N P–Q3 11 N×B N×N Δ . . . P–B5 Abramov-Shumlin, Moscow Ch 1957) 7 . . . N–K5 8 B–Q2 B×N 9 B×B Q–K2 10 P–K3 P–Q3 11 B–Q3 0–0 12 0–0 B–Q2 = Δ . . . B–K1–R4 Maslov-Lein, Harkov 1963.

5 . . . K–B2!?

a) **5 . . . B–K2** 6 N–Q5! is held to be strong. Indeed, **6 . . . N–B3** 7

N×Nch and **6 . . . P–Q3** 7 N–R3 are ±; and on **6 . . . K–B2** 7 P–KN3 N–B3 8 B–N2 R–K1 9 Q–B4 (a game of the author's), neither 9 . . . N–QN5? 10 Q×KBP nor 9 . . . P–Q3 10 N–KB3! equalizes.

b) **5 . . . Q–K2** has again been neglected by theory. Some analysis: 6 N–Q5 (**6 Q–N3** N–N5!; **6 Q–Q2** N–B3) 6 . . . Q×Q 7 B×Q and:

b1) **7 . . . K–Q1?** 8 0–0–0 KN–K2 9 N–KB3 P–KR3 10 B–B4 P–Q3 11 P–KR4 ±;

b2) **7 . . . B–Q3!** (Kinabrew) 8 N–KB3 (**8 P–B5?** B–K4 9 N–KB3 N–B3!) 8 . . . KN–K2 9 N–B3! with a bare edge. In view of this last line, **6 N–B3** is a thought.

c) **5 . . . N(3)–K2!?** was tried in Kristič-Puc, Yugoslavia Ch 1970: 6 P–KN3 (6 P–QN3! ±) 6 . . . N–B3 7 B–N2 P–KN3 8 Q–K5 K–B2 and Black has defended against White's immediate threats.

5 . . . K–B2 signals Black's intention to castle by hand:

　6 N–R3

Or **6 N–B3** N–B3 7 N–Q5! N×N (**7 . . . P–Q3** 8 P–KN3 Δ B–N2, N–Q4) 8 P×N B–N5ch 9 B–Q2 R–K1 10 Q–B4 B×Bch 11 N×B N–K2 12 P–Q6! P×P 13 N–B4 (Taimanov and Shatskes).

　6 . . .　　　　N–B3

　7 Q–Q2!

Else . . . P–Q4 comes in powerfully. **7 N–N5ch?!** K–N1 8 P–KN3 P–KR3 9 N–R3 P–Q4 and White's time has been misspent in Bagirov-Nezhmetdinov, Baku 1964.

　7 . . .　　　　B–N5

7 . . . P–KR3 8 N–B4 clearly favours White, who plans P–KN3, B–N2, etc.

　8 P–R3　　　　B×N
　9 Q×B　　　　P–Q4

10 N–N5ch K–N1 11 P×P N×P 12 Q–N3 N–R4 (**12 . . . P–KR3** 13 P–K4! P×P 14 B–QB4 N–K2 15 N×P -Shatskes) 13 Q–B2 P–KR3 14 N–B3 and White stands better (Shatskes and Taimanov).

CONCLUSION:

2 . . . P–KB4 alerts White to his opponent's intentions, apparently prematurely. Thus we encounter moves such as 3 P–Q4, setting the second player some thorny problems. Black might rather play 2 . . . P–Q3 and 3 . . . P–KB4, if that is the kind of set up he wants (i.e. one without . . . N–QB3).

B

　1 P–QB4　　　P–K4
　2 N–QB3　　　**N–QB3**
　3 N–B3　　　P–B4 (*100*)

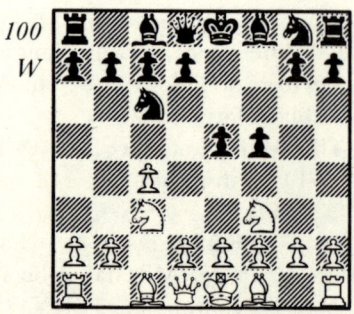

100
W

As usual, the system where . . . P–KB4 is most easily justifiable is one in which a White knight on f3 can be attacked by . . . P–K5. By contrast with 2 . . . P–Q3 3 N–B3

P–KB4 (Chapter 9), Black has an extra knight out and the possibility of developing his king's bishop actively. The emphasis is on piece play, and he will often exchange his advanced KP to that end.

The reader may wish to study 2 . . . N–QB3 and 3 . . . P–B4 (Sections B and C) not only in conjunction with the . . . P–KB4 sections of Chapter 9, but also with those in Chapter 1 (The Closed English). Generally, Black attends to the centre for most of the opening phase; in practice, the failure to establish himself in that sector foredooms a flank advance. Still, one should keep in mind that such an advance (e.g. by . . . P–KN4 and . . . P–KB5) is ofen Black's long-term goal; so that White is under a certain obligation to keep his opponent occupied elsewhere.

To this end, he may choose from:

B1 4 P–Q3
B2 4 P–K3
B3 4 P–Q4

4 P–K4 P×P 5 N×P(4) N–B3 grants Black easy play, and **4 P–KN3** can become perilous after 4 . . . P–K5!? 5 N–KR4?! (5 N–KN1 =) 5 . . . P–Q3 6 B–R3 P–KN4!? 7 N×BP N–B3 8 P–KN4 P–KR4 etc.

B1

4 P–Q3 N–B3

Of course **4 . . . P–Q3** and **4 . . . B–N5** are also playable. If White responds with an early P–KN3, the game may well transpose to C below.

5 N–Q5!?

Most exotic. **5 P–KN3?!** B–B4! and if 6 B–N2, 6 . . . P–K5! 7 P×P P×P 8 N–KN5 P–K6! ∓. **5 P–K3** is slow but sound.

5 . . . P–Q3

5 . . . B–B4 6 B–N5 P–K5 7 B×N P×B 8 N–R4 ±; **5 . . . P–K5!?** succeeds against **6 N–Q2** P×P or **6 P×P** P×P 7 N–Q4? N×N(4) 8 P×N B–N5ch 9 B–Q2 P–K6!; but White should try 6 P×P P×P 7 N–Q2, when 7 . . . N×N 8 P×N P–K6!? is complicated but still a bit better for the first player.

6 P–KN3	B–K3
7 Q–N3	R–QN1
8 B–N2	B–K2

Not **8 . . . P–QN4?** 9 N–N5.

9 0–0	P–KR3

9 . . . Q–Q2 10 N–N5 B–N1 11 P–B4 ±.

10 N–R4!	0–0

10 . . . N–Q5 11 Q–Q1 N×N? 12 P×N B×N 13 NP×B B–Q2 14 P–K3 N–N4 15 P–R4 (Rogoff).

11 N–N6	R–B2
12 P–B4	K–R2
13 N(6)×B	N×N(2)

Rogoff–Tarjan, US Junior Ch 1969. Now, instead of **14 P–K4?** P–QN4!, White should have played **14 N×Nch** R×N 15 Q–B3! P×P 16 P×P (Rogoff) with good bishops (the QB goes to b2) and the dangerous KN file. A noteworthy encounter!

B2

4 P–K3 N–B3

a) **4 . . . P–Q3** 5 P–Q4 P–K5? (better **5 . . . B–K2** or **5 . . . N–B3**) 6 P–Q5! P×N 7 P×N P×BP 8 Q×P ±.

b) **4 . . . P–KN3** makes sense here, e.g. 5 P–Q4 P–K5 **6 N–Q2** and now the most ambitious move is **6 . . . B–R3!**, when Black's central wedge is hard to chip away at. Transposing into B322 by **6 . . . N–B3** 7 P–B3 P×P 8 N×P P–Q3 is less forceful, but roughly equal.

Nor, after 4 . . . P–KN3 5 P–Q4 P–K5, should **6 P–Q5** P×N 7 P×N NP×P 8 Q×P cause Black much difficulty, as his open files and control of the long dark diagonal (8 . . . B–KN2) compensate for his doubleton. More interesting would be **6 N–KN1** B–N2 7 P–KR4! N–B3 8 B–K2, when 8 . . . 0–0 9 P–R5 P–KN4? 10 P–R6 is very strong.

c) **4 . . . P–K5** 5 N–Q4 appears comfortably better for White: 5 . . . N×N 6 P×N N–B3 7 P–Q3 etc.

5	P–Q4	P–K5
6	N–KN1	

6 N–Q2 P–KN3 is similar to the preceding note (b); for **6 N–KN5** P–KR3 7 N–R3 P–KN4!, compare B344 below.

6	. . .	B–N5
7	B–Q2	0–0
8	KN–K2	K–R1(?)
9	N–B4	P–Q3
10	P–KR4	P–QR4

Kottnauer-Steiner, Groningen 1946. Approximately equal, according to Schwarz, although the odds seem in White's favour after 11 P–R5 △ P–QR3 etc. Thus 8 . . . P–Q3 or 8 . . . P–QR4 was more accurate.

B3

4	P–Q4

By far the most common move.

4	. . .	P–K5 (*101*)

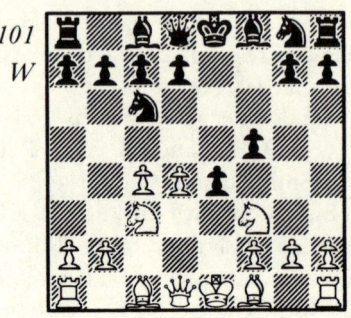

101
W

Clearly best. **4 . . . P×P** 5 N×P exposes the holes in Black's centre, whereas **4 . . . P–Q3** 5 P–Q5 will give White the advantage by P–KN3, B–N2, and an early P–K4 and/or P–QB5.

From the diagram, White has tried everything:

B31 5 P–Q5
B32 5 N–Q2
B33 5 B–N5
B34 5 N–KN5

And of sourse:

a) **5 N–K5** P–Q3 6 N×N P×N 7 P–B3 (**7 P–K3** N–B3, holding e4) 7 . . . P–Q4? (On Schwarz's **7 . . . N–B3**, 8 B–N5 could cause Black difficulty, but Shatskes' **7 . . . P×P!** is the real solution: 8 KP×P P–N3! etc. — perhaps $\overline{\mp}$!) 8 P×KP BP×P 9 Q–R4 B–Q2 10 Q–R5 R–N1 11 P–QR3 N–B3 12 P×P ± Kevitz-Marshall, New York 1935.

b) **5 N–KN1** is not bad, with the usual idea of regrouping via N–KR3 and perhaps developing the QB before playing P–K3. Yet a comparison with A3, note (a) to 3 . . . P×P is not encouraging: Black has the extra move . . . N–QB3 and a tempo besides. 5 . . . P–KN3 is a safe way to proceed.

B31
5 P–Q5
Seldom seen.

5 . . .	P×N
6 P×N	P×NP

6 . . . NP×P is queried by Shatskes, who quotes Reshko-Novotelnov, Leningrad 1966: 7 KP×P B–N5 8 B–Q3 **Q–K2ch** 9 K–Q2! Q–B3 10 K–B2 N–K2 11 P–KR4 **0–0(?)** 12 B–N5 Q–Q5 13 Q–Q2 B×N 14 P×B Q–B4 15 Q–K3 Q×Q 16 P×Q K–B2 17 P–B5! with advantage to White. Apart from the generally improvable character of Black's play, one notes **8 . . . N–K2!?** and, later in the game **11 . . . P–KR3!.**
Of course 6 . . . P×NP is simpler.

7 P×Pch	Q×P
8 Q×Qch	B×Q
9 B×P	P–B3?

The natural **9 . . . 0–0–0!** defends Black's queenside without creating holes. Taimanov continues 10 B–K3 B–N5 11 R–QB1 N–B3 =.
10 B–K3

10 0–0 N–B3 11 B–K3 B–K3 12 P–N3 B–Q3 13 QR–Q1 B–K4 14 B–Q4 B×B 15 R×B R–Q1 = Taimanov–Polugaevsky, 29th USSR Ch 1961.

10 . . .	N–B3

11 B–Q4 (preventing . . . B–Q3–K4) 11 . . . B–K3 12 P–N3 B–R6 13 R–Q1 K–B2 14 0–0 KR–Q1 15 N–R4 ± Mikenas-Furman, Leningrad 1965.
Black must cope with pressure

against his queenside. Hence 9 . . . 0–0–0 was correct.

B32
5 N–Q2
The traditional and most obvious strategy: White plans to force the surrender of e4 by P–K3 and P–B3.

5 . . .	N–B3

Naturally **5 . . . N×P?** 6 N(2)×P favours White, who owns the queen file and d5; and **5 . . . B–N5?!** 6 N–Q5! is not much better. Yet **5 . . . P–KN3** merits attention; a game Kozma–Florian, continued **6 P–K3** P–Q3 7 P–QN3 **B–N2** 8 B–N2 N–B3 9 B–K2 0–0 10 P–QR3 N–K2 11 Q–B2 P–B3 ∞. Here, as in B2, **7 . . . B–R3!?** (or **7 . . . N–B3** 8 B–N2 B–R3) would be promising. White might have played **6 N–N3!?** Δ B–B4, P–K3.
6 P–K3

6 N(2)–N1!? provides for the future of White's QB: 6 . . . P–KN3 (6 . . . P–KR3) 7 B–N5 B–N2 8 P–K3 N–K2 9 B–K2 P–Q3 10 Q–N3 P–KR3 11 B–B4 (or **11 B×N** B×B 12 N–Q5 ±) 11 . . . P–KN4 12 B–N3 N–N3 13 P–KR4 P×P? (13 . . . P–B5!? ±) 14 B×RP ± Suetin-Tseshkovsky, Kislovodsk 1972 (notes by Suetin). Black's kingside pawns are split and vulnerable.
After 6 P–K3:
B321 6 . . . B–N5
B322 6 . . . P–KN3
a) **6 . . . B–K2** gives White a freer hand: 7 B–K2 0–0 8 0–0 Q–K1 9 P–B3 (or even 9 P–B4!) 9 . . . B–N5 L. Schmid-Beni, Amersterdam 1954; 10 N–Q5 ± (Schwarz).

b) **6 . . . P-Q4?!** is a Steinitz French a tempo up for White! After 7 P×P N×P, White seems to be able to play **8 N(2)×P!**. Then if 8 . . . B-N5, 9 B-Q2 holds the pawn: 9 . . . 0-0 (**9 . . . P×N** 10 Q-R5ch) 10 N×N Q×N 11 N-B3 etc. Instead, Palatnik-Kupreichik, USSR 1973 continued **8 N×N?!** Q×N 9 B-B4 Q-Q3 10 P-QR3 B-Q2 11 P-QN4 Q-N3 12 P-N3 B-Q3 13 Q-B2 P-KR4 (13 . . . N-K2 =) with obscure play ahead.

B321
6 . . .   B-N5 (*102*)

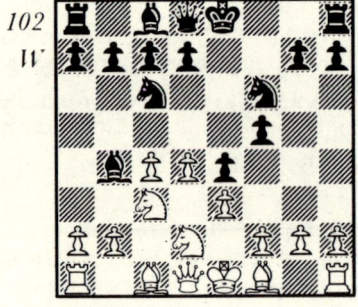

7 B-K2

The alternatives are instructive:
a) **7 Q-N3** P-QR4! (**7 . . . 0-0?** 8 P-Q5 B×N 9 Q×B N-K2 10 P-QN3 P-Q3 11 B-N2 N-N3 12 0-0-0 Q-K2 13 B-K2 ± △ QR-N1, P-B4, etc. Fine-Steiner, Mexico City 1934) 8 B-K2 P-Q3 9 0-0 0-0 10 P-QR3 (10 K-R1!?) 10 . . . B×N 11 Q×B P-R5 = Sokolsky-Smyslov, Kubichev 1943. A handy positional device.
b) **7 N-Q5** 0-0 (or **7 . . . N×N** 8 P×N N-K2 9 Q-N3 B×N 10 B×B P-Q3 11 B-B4 — *11 B-K2!?* 11

. . . 0-0 12 0-0 N-N3 13 P-B4 P-QR4 14 P-QR4 P-QN3 △ . . . B-R3 and Black managed to eke out the draw in Smyslov-Eley, Hasting 1972/3) 8 N×B (**8 Q-N3** P-QR4 △ . . . P-R5) 8 . . . N×N 9 P-Q5?! (The direct **9 P-QR3** N-B3 10 P-QN4 P-Q4 11 P-N5 N-K2 12 P-QR4 △ B-R3 seems preferable.) 9 . . . P-QR4 10 N-N3 P-QN3 11 N-Q4 N-N5! 12 P-QR3 N-QR3 13 P-N4 Q-R5 14 P-N3 Q-B3 with a fine game, Chekover-Rovner, Leningrad 1953.

7 . . .   0-0
8 0-0   R-K1
9 P-B3?!

Since Black is 'lying in wait' for this move, **9 N-Q5** might be tried.
9 . . .   P×P
10 R×P   B×N
11 P×B P-Q3 12 B-Q3 R-K2 13 N-B1 (13 B×P B×B 14 R×B R×P 15 N-B3 R-K1 16 B-N5 Q-Q2! = -Shatskes) 13 . . . N-K5 14 Q-B2 Q-K1 = Holmov-Borisenko, USSR Ch 1954.

B322
6 . . .   P-KN3
The modern move. One idea is that **7 P-B3** can be answered with 7 . . . B-R3! 8 P×P and now Korchnoi gives both **8 . . . P-Q3!?** and **8 . . . B×P** 9 P-K5 N-KN5, with good play in either case. His suggestion of **7 P-B4** is likewise complex after **7 . . . N-KN5** 8 N-N3 P-QR4!, or after **7 . . . P×Pe.p.**, e.g. 8 N×P P-Q3 9 P-QN4 B-N2 10 Q-N3 0-0 11 B-K2 K-R1 12 0-0 N-K2 13

B–Q2 B–K3 14 P–Q5 B–N1 15
N–Q4 Q–Q2 16 K–R1 P–B3 =
Murei-Zaitsev, USSR 1970 (0–1,
39).

7 P–QR3

An alternative is **7 B–K2:** 7 . . .
B–N2 (**7 . . . B–R3!** =) 8 0–0 (**8
QR–N1** P–QR4 9 P–QR3 0–0 10
P–QN4 P×P 11 P×P N–K2 12
Q–N3 P–Q3 13 P–N5 K–R1 14
B–R3? — *14 0–0* — 14 . . . P–B5! 15
N(3)×P P×P 16 P×P N×N 17
N×N B–B4 18 B–Q3 N–Q4! ∓
Miles-Chavez, Sao Paulo 1977) 8
. . . 0–0 9 P–B3 P×P (**9 . . . B–R3!?**
10 P–B4 P–KN4 ∞) 10 B×P P–N3
11 R–K1 B–N2 12 P–QN3 Q–K2
13 B–N2 QR–K1 14 N–N5! P–Q3
15 P–K4 with a very good game,
Hodos-Aronin, USSR 1963. The
main difference between the
examples in this note lies in Hodos's
challenge to (and Miles' dismissal
of) the Black centre.

    7 . . .   B–N2
    8 P–QN4   0–0
    9 P–N3?

Korchnoi himself criticized this,
suggesting **9 P–N5** N–K2 10
P–QR4 P–Q4 11 B–R3 P–B3 12
N–N3 =. Noteworthy are **9
Q–N3** P–B5! and **9 N–Q5** N–K2 10
Q–N3 P–B3 (Aronin).

    9 . . .   P–Q4!

9 . . . P–Q3 10 N–N3 Q–K2 11
Q–B2 N–Q1! 12 P–QR4 N–B2 13
B–QR3 B–Q2 14 0–0–0? (14
P–N5!) 14 . . . P–B3 15 P–R3
P–N3! 16 B–K2 P–QR4 ∓
Korchnoi-Spassky, Match (4) 1968
(0–1, 58).

    10 N–N3

Or **10 P×P** N–K2 11 N–B4

N(2)×P 12 N×N N×N 13 B–QN2
(Korchnoi).

    10 . . .   P–N3
    11 B–Q2   N–K2

12 P–B5 P–KN4 (now that his
centre is secure) 13 P–KR4 P–KR3
14 RP×P RP×P 15 P–B4?! (**15
Q–B2** - Korchnoi- ∓) 15 . . .
P×Pe.p. 16 Q×P B–K3 17 B–K2
Korchnoi-Aronin, USSR Spartakiad 1959. Now both 17 . . .
N–K5 18 Q–N2 R–B2 Δ . . . P–R4,
and 17 . . . K–B2 Δ . . .
N(K)–N1–R3–N5 would have
brought about a clear Black
advantage (Korchnoi).

CONCLUSION:

On 5 N–Q2 N–B3 **6 P–K3**, both
6 . . . B–N5 and **6 . . . P–KN3** seem
to equalize. **6 N(2)–N1?** needs testing.

B33

    5 B–N5

By now a familiar theme: White
deploys his QB before playing P–K3.

    5 . . .   B–K2(!)

a) **5 . . . N–B3** 6 N–Q2 (not **6
P–Q5?** P×N 7 P×N P×NP 8
P×Pch?? N×P! ∓∓, as in e.g.
Razuvaev-Kupreichik, Dubna
1970) 6 . . . B–K2 (**6 . . . B–N5** 7
N–Q5) 7 P–K3 ± Δ P–B3.

b) **5 . . . N(3)–K2** 6 N–Q2 P–KR3 7
B–R4! P–KN4 8 P–K3 N–N3 (**8
. . . N–KB3** 9 B–K2) 9 B–N3 P–B5
10 Q–R5 K–B2 11 N(3)×P! (**11
P×P?** N–B3) 11 . . . P×B 12 B–Q3
K–N2 13 BP×P with two pawns
and a very strong attack for the
piece, Razuvaev-Hodos, Oryel
1967.

6 B×B   N(3)×B

The current preference, but older moves may also be satisfactory:

a) **6 . . . Q×B** 7 N–Q5 Q–Q3 8 N–Q2 N(1)–K2 9 N×N (**9 P–K3?** N×N 10 P×N Q×P 11 B–B4 Q–QR4 gives up a pawn too cheaply.) 9 . . . N×N 10 P–K3 0–0 11 P–KN4!? P–B4?! (**11 . . . P–B5!** looks right: 12 N×P Q–KN3 Δ . . . P×P, . . . P–Q4 and attack) 12 N–N3 P×QP 13 P–B5 Q–KN3 14 Q×P Q×P 15 B–K2 Q–N3 16 0–0–0 ± Bronstein-Dely, Miskole 1963. 11 P–KN4!? is usually given '!', but 11 . . . P–B5! casts doubt on this, so 6 . . . Q×B may be perfectly playable.

b) **6 . . . N(2)×B** 7 N–Q2 (7 N–KN1!?) 7 . . . N×P 8 N(2)×P N–K3 (Shatskes likes **8 . . . N(2)–B3** 9 N–Q2 0–0 **10 P–K3** N–K3 11 B–K2 P–B5 or here **10 P–KN3** P–Q3 11 P–K3 — *11 B–N2 P–B5* — 11 . . . N–K3 12 B–N2 N–B4 13 0–0 B–K3, but White should play on in this last position.) 9 N–Q2 0–0?! (**9 . . . P–Q4!** = -Shatskes) 10 N–B3 ± Katalimov-Cherepkov, Spartak Team Ch 1963.

7 N–Q2	N–KB3
8 P–K3	0–0
9 B–K2	P–Q3

10 P–QN4 K–R1 11 0–0 B–K3 (Here **11 . . . P–B3** Δ . . . P–Q4 is an option. Black's kingside chances with . . . P–KN4, . . . N–N3 etc. are about equal to White's on the queenside.) 12 P–B3 P×P (**12 . . . P–Q4!?** -Tarjan) 13 N×P N–N3 14 B–Q3 Q–K2 15 Q–B2 P–Q4? 16

P–B5 N–K5 17 N–K2! N–N4 18 N–B4 N×Nch 19 R×N ± Tarjan-Gheorghiu, Cleveland 1975 (1–0, 40). Black should not have conceded his opponent the e5 square on move 15; but White was a little better anyway.

B34
5 N–KN5 (*103*)

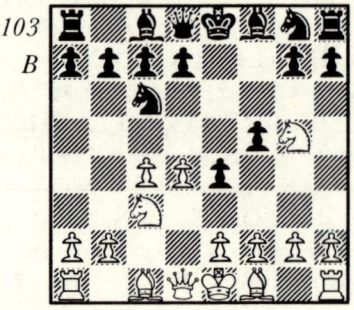

*103
B*

The approved choice, Δ N–R3, B–N5, N–B4, P–K3; however, as in Chapter 9 (2 . . . P–Q3 3 N–B3 P–KB4 4 P–Q4 P–K5 5 N–KN5), the move is rather overrated. In practice thus far, Black's simplest response (B344) has been waived in favour of developing continuations:
B341 5 . . . N–B3
B342 5 . . . B–K2
B343 5 . . . B–N5
B344 5 . . . P–KR3

B341
5 . . .   N–B3
6 N–R3

a) **6 P–KR4!?** prevents . . . P–KR3 and . . . P–KN4 while securing the f4 outpost. If **6 . . . P–KN3**, 7 N–R3 B–N2 8 B–B4 0–0 (**8 . . . N–KR4** 9 P–K3 Q×P 10 B–N5 Q–N5 11 N–Q5!) 9 P–K3 with good prospects; on **6 . . . B–N5**, 7 P–K3 transposes into B343. **6 . . . P–Q3** opts for solidity; a mistreatment of White's position was **7 P–KN3?!** P–KN3 8 N–R3 B–N2 9 B–N5 P–KR3 10 B–B1? (10 B×N =) 10 . . . Q–K2 11 N–B4 Q–B2 12 P–K3 B–Q2 ∓ Δ . . . 0–0–0, . . . P–KN4 Georgadze-Hort, Decin 1977. Better for White to have exchanged his bishop on move 10 than to leave it locked up (at the cost of two tempi!). Best after 6 . . . P–Q3 might be **7 N–R3! P–KN3** 8 B–N5 P–KR3 9 B×N and 10 N–Q5 ±, or here **7 . . . N–KN5!?** 8 B–N5 B–K2 9 B×B N×B 10 P–K3 ±.

b) **6 P–KN3** wastes time, since White's KB is well-placed on e2. A radical answer was **6 . . . P–Q4** 7 P×P N×P 8 Q–N3 **B–N5?** 9 B–Q2 N(3)–K2 10 N(3)×KP! Mochalov-Kupreichik, USSR 1973. **8 . . . N(3)–K2** was better (±). Best after 6 P–KN3 is the unsubtle **6 . . . P–KR3!** 7 N–R3 P–KN4!; compare B344 below.

    6 . . .   P–KN3

6 . . . B–K2 7 P–K3 is B342, and **6 . . . B–N5** is B343 again.

    7 P–K3   B–N2
    8 P–R3

In general, such queenside expansion can wait until the kingside situation is resolved. White should prefer **8 N–B4** 0–0 9 P–KR4.

    8 . . .   P–Q3
    9 P–QN4   N–K2

Black strives for . . . P–Q4.

    10 Q–N3   0–0
    11 B–N2   P–KR3
12 0–0–0?! (**12 N–B4** P–B3 13 P–KR4 ∞ -Minić) 12 . . . P–B3 13

P–B3 P–KN4! 14 P–B4? (14 B–K2 -Minić) 14 . . . N–N3! ∓ Malich-Tcheskovsky, Leipzig 1975. Now White must avoid **15 P×P?** P×P 16 N×P N–N5!, but **15 N–K2** N–N5 16 R–Q2 P–QR4 17 P–N3 P–R5!, as in the game, was also very good for Black (0–1, 29).

B342

    5 . . .   B–K2
    6 N–R3

As in Chapter 9, White can gambit by **6 P–KR4!?** P–KR3 7 N–R3 B×P (**7 . . . P–KN4** 8 P–K3 K–B1! 9 N–Q5! ±) 8 N–B4 K–B2 9 P–K3 P–KN3 10 P–B5! with a nice initiative, e.g. **10 . . . P–Q3** 11 B–B4ch K–N2 12 P–KN3 and 13 N×NP! or **10 . . . P–KR4** 11 P–QN4! Δ P–N5.

    6 . . .   N–B3

6 . . . B–B3 7 P–K3 N(3)–K2?! 8 P–KN4? (As usual, too loosening; **8 P–B3** keeps an edge.) 8 : . . P×P 9 N–B4 N–R3 10 P–KR3 P–Q3 11 N×P 0–0 ∓ Eising-Christoph, West German Ch. 1969 (0–1, 28).

    7 P–K3

Taimanov points out that **7 B–N5!** is still logical.

    7 . . .   0–0
    8 N–B4

White may want to retain the option of N–B2 or wait, as in **8 P–R3** P–QR4 9 B–K2 K–R1 10 0–0 **P–Q3?!** 11 P–B3 Q–K1 12 N–B4 ± Darga-Naranja, Lugano 1968 (1–0, 35). **10 . . . P–Q4** might have been tried.

    8 . . .   P–Q3
    9 B–K2   Q–K1
10 0–0 B–Q1 11 P–B3 N–K2 (**11

. . . P–KN4 12 N(4)–Q5 Q–N3 13
N×Nch △ P×P ±) 12 P×P N×P 13
N×N P×N 14 Q–B2 N–B4 15
B–Q2 P–B3 16 QR–K1 B–Q2 17
Q–N3 Sahović Mestrović, Yugo-
slavia Ch 1974. Now 17 . . . R–N1
± was best (Sahović).

B343

5 . . .   B–N5 *(104)*

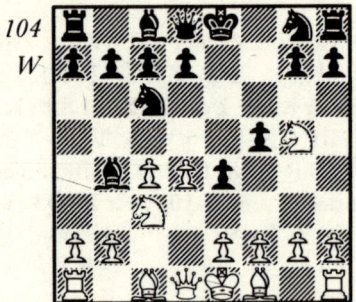

104
W

6 N–R3

White has a wide choice:

a) **6 P–KR4?!** now allows the pawn
snatch 6 . . . P–KR3 7 N–R3 Q×P
($\mp$).

b) **6 P–B5** (Shatskes) has the idea of
Q–N3, but 6 . . . P–KR3 7   N–R3
P–KN4 seems critical, e.g. 8 P–B3
P×P 9 KP×P P–Q4! etc.

c) **6 P–Q5** N–K4 7 Q–Q4 Q–K2
(or **7 . . . Q–B3** △ . . . N–Q6ch -
Shatskes) 8 B–B4 N–N3 9 P–Q6 (**9
B–Q2?** B–B4! -Cafferty) 9 . . . P×P
10 N–R3 N×B 11 N×N Q–K4!
Kotov-Liberzon, Moscow 1972.
Black has good play.

d) **6 P–KN3** N–B3 7 B–N2 **P–Q4** 8
0–0 P×P 9 P–Q5 B×N 10 P×N
Q×Q 11 R×Q B–K4 12 P×P B×P
13 N–K6 P–N3 14 R–N1 △ 15
B–K3 (Cafferty). Among several

alternatives for Black is **7 . . .
P–KR3** and 8 . . . P–KN4.

6 . . .   N–B3
7 P–K3   B×Nch

7 . . . 0–0 8 Q–N3! ±
(Uhlmann). **7 . . . P–QR4!?**, to
reply to a future P–QR3 by . . .
B×N and . . . P–R5.

8 P×B   P–Q3!

8 . . . P–QN3 9 B–R3 B–R3 10
Q–R4 N–QR4 11 B–N4!? (**11
N–B4!** K–B2 12 P–R4 ± -
Uhlmann) 11 . . . B×P 12 B×B
N×B 13 Q–N5! P–QR4! 14 Q×N
P×B 15 P×P R–R2! 16 0–0 P–Q4
Uhlmann-Kärner, Tallin 1977;
approximately equal, though
White has what endgame chances
there are and won after mistakes by
Black.

9 B–R3   0–0
10 B–K2 (**10 P–B5** P–Q4 = was
Szabo-Liberzon, Solingen 1974) 10
. . . N–K2 11 0–0 P–B3 12 Q–N3
N–N3 13 QR–K1 Q–K2 14 Q–N4
R–Q1 Uhlmann-Szabo, Solingen
1974. Black achieved an early
draw.

B344

5 . . .   P–KR3(!)
6 N–R3   P–KN4

I have found no games with, or
even mention of, this straightforward idea, analogous to that in
Chapter 9.

7 P–K3

Natural. Fine for Black are **7
P–Q5** N–K4 8 P–B4 P×Pe.p. 9
KP×P P–B5 and **7 P–B3** P×P 8
KP×P (8 NP×P B–N2 9 P–Q5
N–K4) 8 . . . B–N2 9 P–Q5
Q–K2ch 10 B–K2 N–Q5 11 0–0

N×Bch 12 N×N Q–B4ch 13 K–R1 N–K2.

7 ...	N–B3
8 B–K2	B–N2
9 B–R5ch	K–B1

White has achieved little, as he cannot effectively challenge e4.

CONCLUSION:

While countless move orders are possible, there is much evidence to support the judgment that 2 ... N–QB3 3 N–B3 P–B4 is satisfactory for Black. Both **4 P–Q3** and **4 P–K3** are interesting but not very forceful; and **4 P–Q4** P–K5 grants Black fair prospects after e.g. 5 N–Q2 N–B3 (Δ ... P–KN3), 5 B–N5 B–K2, or 5 N–KN5 P–KR3.

C

1 P–QB4	P–K4
2 N–QB3	**N–QB3**
3 P–KN3	**P–B4**

I believe that this order is on general principle less effective for Black than 3 N–B3 P–B4, and compares rather poorly with the tempo-up 1 P–K4 P–QB4 2 N–QB3 N–QB3 3 P–B4 variation of the Sicilian Defence. Nevertheless, White must play exactly to preserve his first-move advantage.

4 B–N2   N–B3

Worthy of study is **4 ... P–KN3** 5 P–K3 (**5 P–Q3** B–N2 6 B–Q2 — *6 P–K4!?* — 6 ... P–Q3 7 R–N1 P–QR4 8 P–QR3 N–B3 9 P–QN4 P×P 10 P×P 0–0 resembles Chapter 1, C.) 5 ... B–N2 6 KN–K2 N–R3 7 0–0 0–0 8 P–Q4 P–K5 (**8 ... P–Q3** 9 P–B4!? or 9 R–N1) 9 R–N1 (9 P–B3! ±) 9 ...

P–Q3 10 P–QN4 P–KN4 11 P–B3 P×P 12 B×P N–K2 13 P–N5 K–R1 14 P–QR4 B–K3!? 15 B×P!? (15 P–Q5! ±) 15 ... R–QN1 16 B–Q5 N×B 17 N×N Q–Q2 18 P–K4 P×P 19 B×P R×Rch 20 Q×R R–KB1 21 B–B4 B–N5 with a strong attack, Roizman-Osnos, ½F VTs SPS, Ch Leningrad 1970. A good illustration of how mercurial pawn structures (and advantages!) can be in these lines.

4 ... N–B3 sets up an important choice:

C1 5 P–Q3
C2 5 P–K3

5 N–R3!? Δ P–Q3, P–B4 is safe but creates few threats. **5 N–B3** appears normal, yet can turn out strangely, e.g. **5 ... P–K5** 6 N–KR4 P–Q4!? 7 P×P N×P (Δ ... P–KN4) ∞. More cautious was **5 ... B–K2** 6 P–Q4 P–K5 7 N–KN5 0–0 8 0–0 Q–K1 9 P–B5!? P–KR3 10 N–R3 P–Q4 11 R–N1 N–Q1 with chances for both sides, Karpov-Evrosimovski, match game 1969.

C1

5 P–Q3

Emphasizing the light squares. Black may react as follows:

C11 5 ... B–B4
C12 5 ... B–N5

Infrequently seen are:

a) **5 ... P–Q3**, transposing into Karpov-Korchnoi (26), 1978: 6 P–K3 B–K2 7 KN–K2 0–0 8 0–0 Q–K1 9 P–B4 (or **9 R–N1**, Tal's suggestion) 9 ... B–Q1 10 P–QR3 R–N1 (**10 ... N–N1!** -Tal) 11 P–QN4 B–K3 12 N–Q5 P–QN4 13

B–N2 P×P 14 P×P P–K5 and now 15 R–B1 (Tal) would keep White comfortably on top.

b) **5 . . . P–KN3** is very similar to Chapter 1: 6 P–K3 (Other legitimate tries are **6 P–B4** P–Q3 7 N–B3 and **6 P–K4** B–N2 7 KN–K2 0–0 8 0–0 P–Q3 9 P×P P×P 10 P–B4, slightly ±. Petrosian-Hort, European Team Ch 1961 went **6 R–N1** B–N2 7 P–QN4 P–Q3 8 P–N5 N–Q5 — *8 . . . N–K2 9 P–QR4 ±* — 9 N–R3 0–0 10 0–0 P–KR3 11 P–B4 ±.) 6 . . . B–N2 7 KN–K2 0–0 8 Q–Q2 P–Q3 9 P–QN3 (White's queen on d2 will protect the bishop on b2, besides covering f4) 9 . . . N–KR4! 10 P–B4 P×P 11 KP×P N–Q5 (Black's last three moves exploited White's uncastled state, i.e. **11 NP×P** was bad due to 11 . . . Q–R5ch.) 12 B–N2 R–K1 13 0–0–0 P–B3 14 N×N B×N 15 KR–K1 B–Q2 .= Andersson-Uhlmann, Madrid 1973 ($\frac{1}{2}$–$\frac{1}{2}$, 45).

C11

5 . . .   B–B4

A somewhat anti-positional move, recently connected with a gambit idea.

6 P–K3

6 P–QR3 P–QR4 (**6 . . . P–Q3!?** saves a tempo for attack.) 7 P–K3 0–0 (or **7 . . . P–B5!?** — see the text) 8 KN–K2 B–R2 9 0–0 N–K2 10 P–QN4 P–B3 11 B–N2 Q–B2 12 P–Q4 P–Q3 13 R–B1 B–K3 14 N–Q5! Evans-Kramer, U.S.A. 1949. However Black responds, White retains the edge.

6 . . .   P–B5!?

The gambit try, 'although now

Black is a full tempo down on a rather innocuous White variation of the Sicilian Defence. Otherwise: a) **6 . . . P–Q3** 7 KN–K2 0–0 8 0–0 B–N3 9 R–N1 N–K2 10 P–QN4 P–B3 11 P–N5 P–Q4 12 B–QR3 is the modern-looking Blackburne-Schiffers, Vienna 1898 (!), which continued 12 . . . B–K3?! 13 NP×P NP×P 14 P×P P×P 15 P–Q4 P–K5 16 N–B4 ±. b) **6 . . . P–QR3** 7 KN–K2 B–R2 8 0–0 P–Q3 9 N–Q5 0–0 10 P–N3 N–K2 11 B–N2 ± Capablanca-Labatt, New Orleans simul 1915. Another (more typical) example of the pre-theoretical English Opening.

7 KP×P   0–0

7 . . . P–Q3 (transposing) is more accurate, since White could now risk 8 P×P! and probably stand better (e.g. 8 . . . B×Pch is unsound).

8 KN–K2   P–Q3

8 . . . Q–K1 9 P×P N–KN5!? is unclear; best **9 P–KR3!**, when 9 . . . P–Q3 is the next note. Saidy-Fischer, Metropolitan League, New York 1969 saw **9 0–0** P–Q3, transposing to the text.

9 0–0

Reasonable, but **9 N–K4!** is apparently quite strong, e.g. 9 . . . Q–K1 10 N(2)–B3. **9 P–KR3!?** may well be another improvement: 9 . . . Q–K1 10 N–K4 (or **10 P–QR3 P–QR4** 11 N–K4, or here **10 . . . Q–R4** 11 B–K3) 10 . . . P×P (**10 . . . Q–N3?** 11 N×B P×N 12 B×N — *or 12 P–KN4* — 12 . . . P×B 13 P×P; 10 . . . B–Q5 11 N(2)–B3 ±) 11 B×P N×N **12 P×N?!** Q–B2! 13 0–0 Q×P 14 P–K5 K–R1 15

P×P P×P 16 P–R3 P–QR4 =
Sibarević-Kovacević, Yugoslavia
1970 (0–1, 40). Much better was **12
B×N!**, and neither **12 . . . P–KN4**
13 B–K3 nor **12 . . . B×Pch** 13
K×B P–KN4 14 Q–Q2 gives Black
much for his pawn.

>9 . . .   Q–K1
>10 N–R4?!

A mistake in the analogous
Sicilian Variation too, yet both
Karpov and Saidy made this move.
The right way is **10 N–K4!**, when
10 . . . Q–R4 11 N×B P×N 12
N–B3 and **10 . . . N×N** 11 P×N
Q–R4 12 K–R1 deny Black the
attack he wants; also, **10 . . . B–Q5?**
has lost its point here: 11 P×P P×P
12 N×B ± (compare the text).

>10 . . .   B–Q5!
>11 N×B?

Definitely inferior. Karpov
recommends **11 P×P** P×P 12 N×B.
Bellon continues **12 . . . P×N** ±.
Perhaps **12 . . . N×N!?** ±. In either
case, White's advantage would be
smaller than in the last two notes.

>11 . . .   P×N!
>12 P–QR3

12 P–KR3 P–KR4! 13 P–R3
P–R4 14 P–N3 Q–N3 Δ . . . B–B4,
. . . N–Q2–B4 gave Black a strong
attack in the Saidy-Fischer contest
(0–1, 35).

>12 . . .   P–QR4

13 P–N3 B–B4 14 N–N2 Q–N3 15
Q–B2 N–Q2 16 R–K1 N–B4 17
B–B1 R–R3! 18 B–Q2 R–N3 19
B×P Karpov-Bellon, Madrid 1973.
Here Black elected the natural 19
. . . R×P?! and still held the
initiative after 20 B–Q2 R–R1 21
P–QR4 P–KR4; but an even clear-
er solution was 19 . . . N×B! 20

P–QN4 N(R)–N6 21 R–R2 R–R1
22 P×N N×P ∓ (Bellon).

Nonetheless, White's improvements on moves 9, 10, and 11 leave
one suspicious of this variation's
efficacy.

C12

>5 . . .   **B–N5**
>6 B–Q2

6 P–QR3 B×Nch 7 P×B 0–0 8
N–B3 P–Q3 9 0–0 Q–K1 10 P–K3,
Seoyev-Nevidnichy, Moscow 1967,
and now Shatskes' **10 . . . P–K5!**
equalizes. An improved version of
White's plan is **6 N–B3** 0–0 7 0–0
B×N 8 P×B P–Q3 9 R–N1, but 9
. . . Q–K1 (Schwarz) should hold
the balance.

>6 . . .   0–0
>7 N–B3   P–Q3
>8 0–0   P–QR4

9 R–B1 K–R1 10 N–Q5 B–K3 11
B–N5 N–K2! 12 N×N(7) (Doubl-
ing the KBPs only encourages . . .
P–KB5.) 12 . . . Q×N 13 P–Q4
P×P 14 N×P P–B3 15 P–K3
P–KR3 16 B×N Q×B 17 N×B ½–½
Darga-Calvo, Las Palmas 1973.

C2

>5 **P–K3** (*105*)

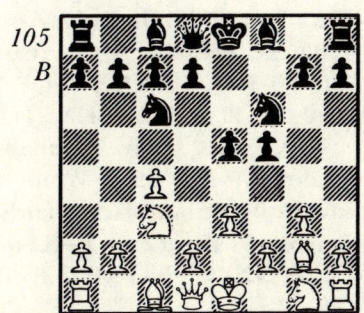

Intending P–Q4. Black replies:
C21 5 . . . P–KN3
C22 5 . . . B–K2

a) **5 . . . B–B4?** 6 KN–K2 and Black cannot transpose to C11 by **6 . . . P–B5** because of 7 P–Q4, whereas **6 . . . P–Q3** 7 P–Q4 B–N3 8 P–QN4! is ±.

b) **5 . . . B–N5** is not appropriate: 6 KN–K2 (or 6 N–Q5 ±) 6 . . . B×N 7 N×B P–Q3 8 0–0 0–0 9 P–Q4 R–K1 10 P–N3 K–R1 11 B–N2 ± Averbach-Chistiakov, Moscow Ch 1957.

c) **5 . . . P–Q3** 6 P–Q4 (**6 KN–K2** transposes to C21 or C22) 6 . . . P–K5 7 P–B3 P×P, and now both **8 Q×P** (Schwarz) and **8 N×P** are attractive for White, who can usually enforce P–K4 and/or P–Q5 and N–Q4.

C21

5 . . .   P–KN3
6 KN–K2

6 P–Q4 P–Q3 (Stolyar-Aronin, Moscow-Leningrad Telephone 1964 went **6 . . . P–K5** 7 KN–K2 N–QN5!? 8 0–0 N–Q6 9 B–Q2! P–B3 — *9 . . . N×P 10 Q–N3 N–Q6 11 P–QR3 Δ P–B3* — 10 N–B1 N×N 11 R×N B–N2 12 P–B3 P×P 13 B×P ±) 7 N–B3 P–K5 8 N–Q2 B–R3 (Plausible, although . . . B–KR3 is more effective when . . . P–KB5 is feasible, i.e. versus White's B–K2.) 9 P–QR3 P–QR4 10 0–0 0–0 11 R–K1 N–KN5 (11 . . . N–K2!?) 12 N–B1 Shatskes-Leonidov, Moscow 1967. White is ready for P–B3, but Black is fairly well deployed after **12 . . . R–K1** or **12 . . . B–N2** 13 P–B3 P×P 14 B×P

N–B3 15 P–N3 R–K1 (light ±).
6 . . .   B–N2
7 P–Q4

White can also play as in Chapter 1, B2: **7 P–Q3** P–Q3 8 R–N1 etc.

7 . . .   P–K5
8 0–0   P–Q3
9 P–B3   P×P

10 B×P (±) 0–0 11 N–B4 K–R1 12 P–N3 P–KN4!? (**12 . . . R–K1** would be less strained, but Black can hardly·complete his development.) 13 N(4)–Q5 N–K2 14 N×N(6) B×N 15 B–QN2 N–N3 16 Q–Q2 P–B3 17 QR–K1 Q–B2 Tal-Klaput, Poland 1966, and 18 P–K4 P–B5 19 P–K5! was recommended. A model game for such positions: White's pressure on the long diagonal and well-posted knights more than compensated for his backward KP.

C22

5 . . .   B–K2
Black prepares . . . 0–0 and perhaps . . . Q–K1–KR4. Then his bishop can drop back to d8 in support of the vulnerable QBP.

White has two approaches:
C221 6 KN–K2
C222 6 P–Q4

C221

6 KN–K2
This gives Black time to maintain his pawn on e5, and therefore may be slightly less accurate than **6 P–Q4** (C222).

6 . . .   0–0
7 P–Q4

Typical White strategy without P–Q4 was demonstrated in Gurevich-Konstantinopolsky, USSR Central Chess Club Ch 1957: **7 0–0** P–Q3 8 N–Q5 N×N 9 P×N N–N1 10 P–Q3 Q–K1 (10 . . . P–QR4!?) 11 B–Q2 N–Q2 12 R–B1 B–Q1 13 P–QN4 N–B3 14 N–B3 B–Q2?! (14 . . . K–R1 △ . . . P–KN4) 15 Q–N3 R–B1 16 P–N5 ±.

    7 . . .   P–Q3
    8 R–QN1

Other plans yield about the same result:

a) **8 0–0** Q–K1 9 B–Q2! (**9 P–Q5?!** N–Q1 10 B–Q2 Q–R4 11 P–QN4 N–B2 12 N–B1 N–N5 13 P–KR3 N–N4! ∓ Kirilov-Alatortsev, 7th USSR Ch 1933. With 9 B–Q2, White can still play in the centre if Black gets ambitious on the king's wing.) 9 . . . Q–R4 10 N–Q5 B–Q1 11 P–QN4 ± Shatskes-Yurkov, Moscow 1967.

b) **8 P–N3** Q–K1 9 B–QR3 R–B2 10 N–Q5 B–B1 11 0–0 N–Q1 12 Q–B2 P–B3 13 P×P P×P 14 B×B Q×B 15 N×Nch R×N 16 QR–Q1 N–B2 17 R–Q2 B–K3 18 R(1)–Q1 R–K1! 19 Q–B3 B–B1 Botvinnik-Alatortsev, Moscow 1935, only minimally better for White.

    8 . . .   P–QR4
    9 P–QR3   Q–K1
    10 P–QN4   RP×P

11 RP×P K–R1 12 N–Q5 B–Q1 13 0–0 P–KN4? (Overambitious. The lesser of evils is **13 . . . N–K2** - Schwarz- 14 N×N(6) R×N 15 P×P P×P 16 B–N2 ±.) 14 B–N2 P–K5 15 N(2)–B3 N×N 16 N×N N–N1 17 R–R1 R×R 18 Q×R ±

Sokolsky-Plater, Poland-Belorussia 1958.

C222
    6 P–Q4   P–K5

Generally an undesirable ⟋ advance if it doesn't gain a tempo and if the pawn can't be supported on e4. Schwarz gives 6 . . . P–Q3 and his reply, **7 KN–K2**, transposes into C221. Indeed, **7 P×P** P×P 8 Q×Qch B×Q should present no real difficulty for Black; but in my opinion 6 . . . P–Q3 creates its own problem, namely **7 P–QN4**(!), which White can play without preparation (i.e. R–QN1, as in C221), because **7 . . . N×NP??** 8 Q–R4ch wins a piece. So play might continue **7 . . . 0–0** 8 P–N5 N–N1 9 P–QR4, staking out a valuable hunk of territory for White, who may then proceed with N–KB3 or KN–K2, P–R5 and/or B–QR3 as he chooses.

    7 P–B3   0–0
    8 N(1)–K2

8 P×P P×P 9 N×P? N×N 10 B×N B–N5ch 11 B–Q2 Q–K2 ruins White's position.

    8 . . .   B–N5
    9 0–0   B×N

On a move like **9 . . . R–K1**, Black must face 10 N–Q5!, followed in some cases by Q–N3; but **9 . . . P×P** would preclude recapture by the queen on f3, for what it's worth.

    10 N×B   P×P
    11 Q×P!   P–Q3 (*106*)

We have seen this pawn structure several times already. Here a world champion shows us how to exploit White's central advantage: 12

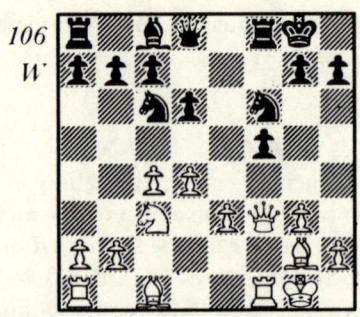

B–Q2 B–Q2 13 QR–K1 Q–K1 14 Q–Q1! (Paradoxically, the queen must retreat in order to emphasize the strength of White's KB. Thus 11 Q×P! has been used as a rank-clearing device. From now on, Black's queenside cannot escape attack.) 14 ... Q–N3 15 N–Q5 N×N 16 P×N N–K2 17 Q–N3 P–N3 18 R–B1 QR–B1 19 R–B3 ± Botvinnik–Simagin, USSR Ch 1952. White doubles rooks on the QB file with enduring pressure, whereas Black's pieces can hardly stir.

CONCLUSION:

After 3 P–KN3 P–B4 4 B–N2 N–B3, White's central and queenside activity, based on his influential KB, seems to obviate Black's hoped-for kingside demonstration. In the variation 5 **P–Q3** B–N5, to be sure, Black probably has enough hold on the middle of the board to equalize; but after **5 P–K3** with an early P–Q4, White can generally gain positional superiority by N–Q5 and/or P–QN4–N5 (or, in the case of . . . P–K5, by P–KB3). All in all, a difficult system to understand *or* play!

11 2 'OTHERS' AND 3 'OTHERS'

In this chapter, we consider a common lament of even strong players: if the Sicilian Defence is so good, how can Black get away with playing the White side (1 ... P–K4) a tempo down? Or, put another way, how can White try to transpose into the Sicilian Defence a tempo up? What follows are analyses, for the most part brief, of the second and third moves by which White attempts to do just that.

2 P–KN3 and 2 N–KB3 have enjoyed sporadic attention over the years; but the rest of the material below is experimental. In particular, the author feels that the sequence 1 P–QB4 P–K4 2 N–QB3 N–KB3 3 P–K3 is well-suited to steer the game in desirable directions, whereas moves such as 2 P–Q3 or 3 Q–B2, although not overtly meanacing, do contain a drop of poison. Both 1 ... P–K4 adherents and players of White in search of new terrain may find these sections thought-provoking, and naturally the commentary here should serve only as a starting point for the reader's investigation.

Section A: 1 P–QB4 P–K4 and:
A1 2 P–KN3
A2 2 N–KB3
A3 2 P–Q3

A4 2 P–K3;
Section B: 1 P–QB4 P–K4 2 N–QB3 N–KB3 and:
B1 3 P–Q3
B2 3 P–K4
B3 3 Q–B2
B4 3 P–K3

A

1 P–QB4   P–K4

Now **2 P–QN3** is a variant of Larsen's Opening (1 P–QN3), the study of which may be fruitful for all English players.

A1

2 P–KN3

The most established of White's choices in this chapter. Among others, Larsen, Petrosian, and Romanishin have experimented with it. Ideally, White achieves an Accelerated Fianchetto Sicilian, tempo in hand.

2 ...   N–KB3

2 ... P–Q3 will transpose, possibly to Chapter 9. Otherwise:
(a) **2...P–KN3** (Not a bad move, as Larsen himself points out, but this game certainly dampened enthusiasm for it!) 3 P–Q4!? (Of course 3 B–N2 and 3 N–QB3 are playable and will transpose to other chapters.) 3 . . . P×P (**3...P–Q3** is also feasible -Larsen) 4 Q×P

N–KB3 (or **4 . . . Q–B3** -Larsen) 5
N–QB3 N–B3 6 Q–K3ch B–K2 (? **6
. . . Q–K2!** e.g. **7 N–N5** Q×Q 8
B×Q K–Q1 ꞊ /∞ -Larsen; **7
N–Q5!?**) 7 N–Q5 N×N 8 P×N
N–N1 9 P–Q6! P×P 10 N–R3 0–0
11 Q–R6 N–B3 12 N–N5 B×N 13
B×B P–B3 (With each manoeuvre
White forces another concession.
The Black QPs are bound to prove
drawbacks in an ending, and in the
meantime White has two bishops
and the attack.) 14 B–Q2 P–N3 15
B–N2 B–N2?! (**15 . . . B–R3** 16
B–QB3 **R–K1** 17 0–0! ± -Larsen.
But in this line Black might try **16
. . . N–K4!**) 16 0–0 N–R4 17 B×N
B×B 18 K×B P×B (more weak
pawns!) 19 QR–Q1 Q–K2 20
R–Q2 QR–N1 21 KR–Q1 ±
Larsen–Gheorghiu, Monaco 1968
(1–0, 38).
   b) **2 . . . N–QB3** 3 B–N2 P–KN3 4
P–K3 (**4 N–QB3** is Chapter 1) 4
. . . B–N2 5 N–K2 P–Q3 6 P–Q4
P×P! (**6 . . . N–B3?!** 7 N(1)–B3 0–0
8 0–0 B–N5?! 9 P–KR3 B–Q2 10
P–N3 N–K1 11 P×P! N×P – *11 . . .
P×P 12 B–QR3 —* 12 B–N2 B–QB3
13 P–K4 — *note how the 'extra'
P–KR3 is helpful for White here* — 13
. . . P–N3 14 Q–Q2 N–B3? 15
P–B4! N(4)–Q2 16 P–K5! B×B 17
P×N B×R 18 P×B ±± Pribyl–
Barreras, Bucharest 1975) 7 P×P
KN–K2 8 0–0 0–0 9 N(1)–B3
Donner–S. Garcia, Cienfuegos
1973. This position is considered in
Chapter 1, B71.
   c) **2 . . . P–QB3** 3 Q–R4!? (**3
N–KB3** P–K5 4 N–Q4 P–Q4 5
P×P Q×P and 5 . . . P×P are
considered in the text below, and **3**

P–Q4 transposes to 4 P–Q4.) 3 . . .
N–QR3!? 4 B–N2 N–B4 5 Q–B2
P–Q4 6 P–QN4 N–K3 7 B–N2 ∞
Hartoch–Korchnoi, Netherlands
Ch 1977.
   3 B–N2
   3 P–Q3!? prepares N–KB3 by
hampering . . . P–K5. Miles–
Littlewood, British Ch 1975, tested
the radical response 3 . . . P–Q4!?: 4
P×P Q×P 5 N–KB3 P–K5!? 6
N–B3 B–QN5 7 Q–R4ch N–B3 (**7
. . . Q–Q2** 8 Q×B N–B3 9 Q–B5
P×N 10 B–N5 ± Suttles–Garcia,
Hastings 1972/3) 8 Q×B Q–K3?!
(**8 . . . N×Q** 9 N×Q N(3)×N 10
P×P N–B7ch 11 K–Q2! ± -Miles)
9 Q–B5 P×N 10 N–N5 K–Q1 11
B–B4 N–Q4 12 P–K4 N×B 13 P×N
± (1–0, 41). Worth trying again!
   Now Black decides between
development and pawn occupation
of the centre:
   A11 3 . . . N–B3
   A12 3 . . . P–B3

   3 . . . P–Q4 4 P×P N×P 5
N–QB3 is Chapter 5.

A11
   3 . . .   N–B3?!
Curiously, this straightforward
development leads to serious
difficulties for Black!
   4 N–QB3   B–N5
What to do? **4 . . . P–KN3** 5
P–K3 B–N2 6 KN–K2 is a position
from Chapter 1, favourable to
White; similarly **4 . . . B–B4**
(Chapter 4 introductory material,
note '(b)') is positionally suspect
after 5 P–K3.
   5 N–Q5! (*107*)
   5 . . .   B–B4

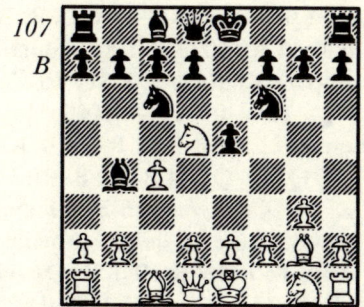

107
B

a) **5 . . . P–QR4** 6 P–QR3 B–B4 7 P–K3 0–0 8 N–K2 P–Q3 9 0–0 R–K1 10 P–KR3 ± Kavalek-Pietzch, Sarejevo 1967.

b) **5 . . . N×N** 6 P×N N–K2 7 N–B3 (or **7 P–K3** 0–0 8 N–B3 B–Q3 9 P–Q4 with advantage -Shatskes) 7 . . . B–Q3 (**7 . . . P–K5** 8 N–N5 P–KB4 9 0–0! N×P 10 P–Q3 ± - Geller) 8 P–K4 P–QB3 9 P–Q4 (or **9 0–0** P×P 10 P–Q4! ± see Chapter 7, D1) 9 . . . BP×P 10 QP×P B–N5ch 11 B–Q2 B×Bch 12 N×B P–Q3 13 P×P(6) Q×P 14 0–0 B–K3 15 P×P N×P 16 N–K4 ± Geller-Debarnot, Las Palmas 1976.

6 P–K3

6 P–Q3 is worse; Black can play either **6 . . . P–KR3** 7 N–B3 P–Q3 = /∞ (see Chapter 7, D12), or **6 . . . N×N!?** 7 P×N N–Q5 8 P–K3 N–B4 9 N–K2 0–0 10 B–Q2 P–Q3 11 0–0 B–Q2 12 B–QB3 B–N3 13 P–Q4 R–K1 14 P–K4 N–R3 15 P–QR4 P–R4 16 Q–Q2 P–KB4! ∞ Street-Browne, California 1976 (0–1, 39).

6 . . .		0–0
7	N–K2	R–K1
8	0–0	B–B1

9 P–Q3 N×N?! (**9 . . . P–Q3** 10 P–QR3 P–QR4 -Mednis and Peters. Still ±.) 10 P×N N–K2

11 P–B4! P×P 12 N×P N–B4 13 Q–B3 Q–K2 14 K–R1 P–Q3 15 B–Q2 B–Q2 16 P–K4! N–R3 17 QR–K1 ± Rogoff-Blumenfeld, Lone Pine 1976.

A12

3 . . .   **P–B3(!)**
   4 N–KB3

4 N–QB3 is Chapter 3, B.

a) **4 P–Q4** P×P 5 Q×P P–Q4 strongly resembles Chapter 3, A, but improves in this respect: White has no knight on c3 to be harassed by . . . P–QB4 and . . . P–Q5. An example is Romanishin-Polugaevsky, USSR Ch 1974: 6 N–KB3 B–K2 7 0–0 0–0 8 P×P P×P 9 N–B3 (White has been able to delay this until his king found a haven.) 9 . . . N–B3 10 Q–QR4 Q–N3 11 Q–N5 P–Q5 (or **11 . . . Q×Q** 12 N×Q B–KB4 - Polugaevsky) 12 Q×Q P×Q 13 N–QN5 R–Q1 14 R–Q1 B–QB4 15 B–N5 R–R4 16 P–QR4 B–B4 (16 . . . B–K3!) 17 B×N P×B 18 N–K1 B–K3 19 B–K4 N–N5 20 P–K3 B–N6 21 R–Q2 R×P? (21 . . . N–B3 = -Bronstein) 22 R×R B×R 23 N×P ± (1–0, 41).

b) **4 P–N3** P–Q4 5 B–N2 P–Q5 (5 . . . QN–Q2) 6 N–KB3 QN–Q2 7 0–0 B–Q3 8 P–K3 P×P 9 QP×P Q–K2 10 Q–B2 ± Cardoso-Naranja, Manila 1973. (1–0, 41).

c) **4 P–K4!?** is Wade's clever suggestion, Δ 4 . . . P–Q4 5 BP×P P×P 6 P×P N×P 7 N–KB3!. A sample line is 7 . . . N–QB3 (7 . . . B–Q3!?) 8 0–0 B–K2 9 R–K1 P–B3 10 P–Q4 B–KN5 11 P×P N×P 12 Q–R4ch, etc. Completely unexplored!

4 . . .   P–K5

If Black likes the Old Indian, he should consider 4 . . . P–Q3.

5 N–Q4   P–Q4
6 P×P

a) **6 N–QB3!?** B–QB4 (6 . . . P×P) 7 N–B2 P×P 8 0–0 B–B4 9 N–K3 B×N 10 BP×B B–N3 11 Q–B2 Q–K2 12 P–N3 P×P 13 Q×NP (13 P×P!?) 13 . . . 0–0 ∞ Bisguier-DeFotis, USA 1972.

b) **6 P–Q3** B–QB4 7 N–N3 B–N5ch 8 B–Q2 B×B 9 Q×B P×BP (**9 . . . B–B4** 10 Q–B4! -Schwarz) 10 P×BP Q–K2 11 N–B3 0–0 12 0–0 P–K6 13 Q×P Q×Q 14 P×Q N–N5 15 N–Q1 R–K1 16 N–B5 (16 B–R3!? P–QR4) 16 . . . N–Q2! 17 N–K4 N(2)–B3 18 N–Q6 R–K3 19 P–B5 N×KP 20 N×N R×N Benko-Tal, Curaçao 1962 ($\frac{1}{2}$–$\frac{1}{2}$, 34). Schwarz recommends 21 B–B3 $\pm$.

6 . . .   Q×P (*108*)

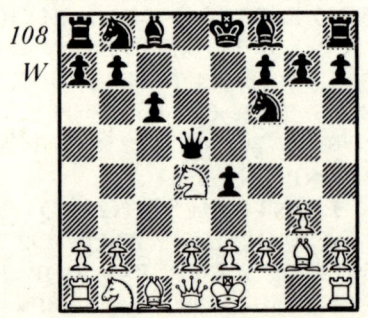

108
W

a) **6 . . . P×P** may be playable, but it is certainly thorny: 7 N–QB3 (or **7 P–Q3!** B–QB4 8 N–N3 B–N5ch 9 B–Q2 B×B 10 Q×B 0–0 11 N–B3 **B–B4?** 12 Q–B4! B–N3 13 P×P $\pm$ Uhlmann-Grägger, East Germany 1961. Better was **11 . . . P×P**, but then White trains his guns on the weak QP.) 7 . . . N–B3 8 N×N P×N 9 P×P P×P 10 Q×P ('$\pm$' -Pomar. Compare Chapter 3, C31) 10 . . . B–K2 11 0–0 (**11 P–K4!?** $\pm$ - Pomar) 11 . . . 0–0 12 P–N3 B–K3 13 R–Q1 Q–Q2 14 B–N2 B–R6 15 QR–B1 (Criticized. **15 B–R1** and **15 B–B3** were suggested instead.) 15 . . . B×B 16 K×B KR–Q1 17 N–R4!? (Very risky. **17 P–K4!** still seems $\pm$.) 17 . . . N–K5 18 P–B3 N–N4 19 Q–B3 Q–R6ch 20 K–R1! N–K3 21 Q×P B–Q3 22 R–KN1 P–KR4 23 R–N2 P–R5 24 P×P QR–B1 25 Q×R R×Q 26 R×Rch K–R2 27 R–B1 P–Q5! 28 R(1)–KN1? (28 R–Q1! -Pomar) 28 . . . P–Q6! 29 N–B3 B–K4 30 N–Q1 B×B 31 R–N3 Q–B4 32 N×B P×P 33 N–B4 Q–Q6 34 P–R5 Q–B6 0–1 Larsen-Pomar, Las Palmas 1975.

b) **6 . . . Q–N3** 7 N–B2 P×P 8 P–Q3 B–QB4 9 0–0 0–0 10 N–B3 Q–B3 Mednis-Reichenbach, Mannheim 1975, and now 11 B–N5! would mount the pressure on Black's centre e.g. 11 . . . QN–Q2 12 R–B1 P–KR3 13 B–K3 etc.

From the diagram, White must meet the threat to his knight:
A121 7 N–B2
A122 7 N–N3

Aside from these retreats, White can remain centralized by **7 P–K3!?**, but at the cost of weakening key light squares e.g. 7 . . . B–QB4 8 N–QB3 Q–K4 9 N–N3 B–N3 10 P–B3 (**10 P–Q3** B–N5 was not to White's liking.) 10 . . . P×P 11 Q×P Q–KB4 12 N–R4 0–0 13 0–0 Q×Q 14 B×Q R–K1 = Hübner-Korchnoi (7), 1973.

A121

7 N–B2 Q–KR4

7 ... B–QB4 8 P–Q4! B–N3 9 N–B3 Q–K3?! (**9 ... Q–KB4 10 0–0** 0–0 11 N–K3 Q–K3 12 P–Q5 P×P 13 N(K)×P N×N 14 Q×N P–B4 = /∞, a game Schwarz gives as 'Haag-Lengyel'. Perhaps **10 B–B4** Δ N–K3 and P–Q5 was a shade more to the point.) 10 0–0 0–0 11 P–B3?! (**11 B–N5!** QN–Q2 12 P–B3 ± -Pytel) 11 ... P×P 12 B×P Q–R6! 13 B–N2 Q–Ṙ4 14 P–K4 B–N5 ∓ Ermenkov-Pytel, Polanica Zdroj 1972.

8 P–KR3

Filip-Portisch, Palma de Mallorca 1970 saw Black's goals of simplification and reinforcement of e4 realized: **8 N–K3?!** B–R6 9 N–B3 (**9 Q–N3!?** -Portisch) 9 ... B×B 10 N×B N–R3 11 Q–B2 Q–K4 12 P–Q4 P×Pe.p. 13 Q×P N–QN5 14 Q–N1 B–K2 15 0–0–0 16 P–K4?! KR–Q1 ∓.

8 ... Q–N3

9 N–B3 B–Q3

10 N–K3 0–0

11 Q–B2 R–K1 12 P–N3 N–R3 13 P–R3 N–B2 14 B–N2 N(2)–Q4 (Black has developed harmoniously and maintains his e4 pawn.) 15 N(K)×N? (Yudovich suggests **15 0–0–0**; and, indeed, 15 ... N×N(K) 16 QP×N B–K4? runs into 17 N×KP!.) 15 ... P×N 16 N–N5 ('?' -Pytel; but a good alternative does not present itself.) 16 ... B×NP! 17 P×B Q×Pch 18 K–B1 P–K6! 19 P×P N–K5 20 B×N R×B ∓∓ Shamkovich-Baumbach, USSR 1970.

A122

7 N–N3

This move, leaving c2 vacant for White's queen, replaced 7 N–B2 on the international circuit, but without much success.

7 ... Q–KR4

8 P–KR3

8 N–B3 B–R6! eliminates the danger to Black's KP. Now White has a potential P–KN4 in response to ... B–KB4.

8 ... Q–N3

9 N–B3 (*109*)

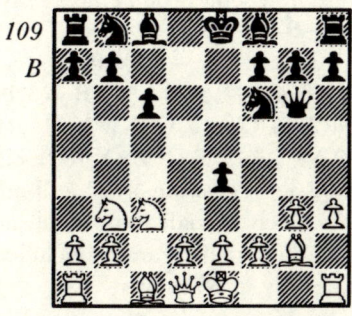

109 *B*

9 ... B–QN5!?

a) **9 ... QN–Q2** 10 Q–B2 (**10 P–Q3** P×P 11 P–K4 N–K4 12 0–0 B–Q3 13 P–B4 Q×NP ∞; **10 K–B1!?** B–N5; **10 0–0** B–Q3!? - analysis by Korchnoi) 10 ... P–K6! 11 Q×Q P×BPch 12 K×P RP×Q 13 P–Q4 N–N3 14 P–K4?! (Speedy development by **14 B–B4** B–K3(?) 15 N–R5 0–0–0 16 QR–B1 -Korchnoi -would have caused more problems.) 14 ... B–K3 15 B–B4 B–QN5 16 N–B5 (**16 QR–B1!** -Osnos) 16 ... 0–0–0 17 N×B P×N 18 P–R3 = /∞ Larsen-Korchnoi, Leningrad 1973 (0–1, 43).

b) **9 ... N–R3** 10 Q–B2? (**10 0–0**

B–KB4 11 P–Q4 P×Pe.p.? 12
P–K4 ± -Karaklaić) 10 . . . N–N5
11 Q–N1 P–K6! 12 Q×Q RP×Q
13 K–B1 P×BP 14 P–R3 N–B7 15
R–QN1 B–K3 16 N–R5 N–K8! ∓
(Δ . . . N×B and . . . R×RP!)
Pribyl-Saidy, Dečin 1974.

10 P–R3

10 Q–B2 is still feasible, and if 10
. . . P–K6, 11 Q×Q P×Pch 12 K×P
RP×Q 13 P–Q4 ±.

10 . . .   B–K2!
11 P–Q3!

White's loose knight on b3 can
cause him some trouble after, say,
11 Q–B2 P–K6.

11 . . .   P×P
12 P–K4 N–R3 13 Q×P B–K3 14
N–R5 R–Q1 15 Q–K2 N–B4 16
0–0 N–N6! 17 N×N B×N 18 B–K3
P–QR3 Petrosian-Pytel, Bath
1973. Neither side has much to
boast of, and the game concluded
peacefully in 36 moves.

CONCLUSION

2 P–KN3 has been on the wane in
grandmaster chess, as Black has
little difficulty defending his spatial
advantage after 6 . . . Q×P. The
interested first player might explore
3 P–Q3!? and/or 4 P–K4.

A2
2 N–KB3

This attempts to get into a
Nimzowitsch Sicilian (1 P–K4
P–QB4 2 N–KB3 N–KB3!?) a
tempo up. Unfortunately (for
White), there's not much comparison. Nimzowitsch himself won
some games with 2 N–KB3 in days
gone by, but realiable defensive

plans have put the move into semi-
retirement.

2 . . .   P–K5
2 . . . N–QB3 is the only
independent option, since **2 . . .
P–Q3** enters other variations after **3
N–B3** or **3 P–Q4.** On 2 . . . N–QB3,
White generally plays 3 P–Q4:
a) **3 . . . P×P** 4 N×P B–N5ch (**4 . . .
B–B4** 5 N×N Q–B3 6 P–K3 Q×N
=-Schwarz; **4 . . . P–KN3 5
P–KN3** B–N2 6 N×N NP×N 7
B–N2 ± is reminiscent of Chapter
2; here **5 P–K4!?** B–N2 6 B–K3
KN–K2 7 N–QB3 0–0 8 Q–Q2
P–Q3 9 B–K2 P–B4 is not so
clearcut.) 5 B–Q2 (For **5 N–B3?**
N–B3, see Chapter 8, A2) 5 . . .
B×Bch 6 Q×B KN–K2 7 P–KN3
0–0 8 B–N2 P–Q3 9 0–0 B–Q2 10
N–QB3 R–K1 11 QR–B1 with the
familiar English bind, Chekhover-
Rabinovich, USSR 1937.
b) **3 . . . P–K5!?** 4 N–N5 (**4
N(3)–Q2** N×P 5 N×P N–K3 6
P–KN3 ± -Minev) 4 . . . B–N5ch 5
N–B3 N–B3 6 P–Q5 B×Nch 7 P×B
N–QN1 (**7 . . . N–K2?** 8 Q–Q4 ±)
8 P–B3?! (8 Q–Q4!?) 8 . . . P–KR3!
9 N×KP N×N 10 P×N Q–R5ch 11
P–N3 Q×KP 12 Q–Q4! Q–N3! 13
B–N2 0–0 = Knezević-Peev,
Albena 1974 (½–½, 28).

3 N–Q4   N–QB3 (*110*)
a) **3 . . . P–QB3?!** 4 P–KN3? P–Q4 5
P×P, see A1: 4 N–QB3! ±.
b) **3 . . . N–KB3 4 N–QB3** N–B3 5
N–N3?! B–N5 6 P–N3 P–QR4 7
P–QR3 B×N 8 QP×B P–Q3 9 B–N2
P–R3 = Holmov-Smyslov, Mos-
cow 1960 (½–½,19). But **5 P–K3!** is
more enterprising, and **4 P–Q3**
comes under consideration also.

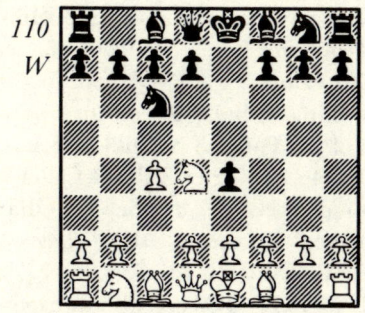

110
W

4 P–K3

a) **4 N–B2** is too timid: 4 . . . N–B3 (or **4 . . . P–Q4** 5 P×P Q×P 6 N–B3 Q–K4 -Fine) 5 N–B3 B–B4 6 P–K3 (**6 P–QN3** 0–0 **7 P–N3?** P–Q4! 8 P×P N–KN5! 9 P–K3 N(3)–K4 10 N×P B–B4 ∓∓ Laurine-Keres, corres 1941 (0–1, 24); better **7 B–N2** or **7 P–K3**) 6 . . . P–Q3 7 P–Q3 P×P 8 B×P B–K3 9 0–0 P–Q4 (Euwe). By judicious exchanges, White may eke out equality.

b) **4 N×N** QP×N 5 N–B3 N–B3 6 P–K3 (**6 P–KN3?** B–QB4 7 B–N2 B–B4 8 0–0 0–0 ∓ Reti-Torre, Moscow 1925; **6 P–Q4** P×Pe.p. 7 Q×P — *7 P–K4?! B–QB4 8 P–KR3 B–K3 9 B×P N–Q2 10 B–K2 Q–R5!* ∓ *Shatskes-Seredenko, Aktyubinsk 1967* — 7 . . . Q×Q 8 P×Q B–KB4 = -Tarkatower-Alekhine, Warsaw 1935) 6 . . . B–KB4! (**6 . . . B–Q3?!** 7 P–Q4 P×Pe.p. 8 B×P Q–K2 9 Q–B2 B–K3 10 P–QN3 0–0–0 11 B–N2 ± Botvinnik-Kan, 22nd USSR Ch 1955), and now 7 P–QN3 B–B4 8 B–N2 Δ Q–B2, as in a Nimzowitsch Sicilian, is at any rate double-edged.
4 . . .   N×N
Or **4 . . . N–B3** 5 N–B3 (**5 N×N**

QP×N **6 P–Q4?** is instructive 6 . . . B–KB4! 7 N–B3 Q–Q2 8 P–KR3 P–KR4 and White is quite tied down, O'Kelly-Portisch, Palma de Mallorca 1966; better **6 N–B3** Δ P–QN3) 5 . . . B–B4 (or **5 . . . B–N5** 6 N×N QP×N 7 B–K2 0–0 8 0–0 Q–K2 9 P–Q3 B×N 10 P×B P×P = Sliwa-Marszalek, Poland Ch 1977) 6 N–N3 B–N5 7 Q–B2 B×N 8 NP×B Q–K2 = Ivlev-Borisenko, RSFSR Ch 1963.
5 P×N   Q–B3!
The difference between our system and Nimzowitsch's 2 . . . N–KB3:, f6 is free for Black's use!
6 P–Q5   B–B4
7 Q–K2   Q–KN3
7 . . . Q–K2?! 8 N–B3 N–B3 9 P–Q3 P×P 10 Q×Qch ± Tarrasch-Grünfeld, 1923.
8 N–B3   N–B3
9 P–Q3 0–0 10 P×P N–N5! 11 N–Q1 P–Q3 12 P–B3 N–K4 Murei-Udov, Moscow 1966. Black has plenty for a pawn, and . . . P–KB4 is coming.

A3
2 P–Q3
Less committal than the above (rather harmless) moves. Here White imagines that he is playing a Sicilian and starts to work on the light squares. Of course, nothing is threatened, but with some time (e.g for N–QB3, P–KN3, B–N2), White can dominate the centre. How should Black reply? On
a) **2 . . . N–QB3**, there is always **3 N–QB3** and a likely transposition to Chapter 1; or **3 P–KN3**.

b) **2 ... P–KN3** can't be bad, yet White can enter acceptable lines by, for example, **3 P–KN3** B–N2 4 B–N2 P–QB3!? 5 N–QB3 N–K2 6 P–K4 0–0 7 KN–K2 etc.

c) **2 ... N–KB3** looks natural. White may try **3 P–KN3** intending **3...P–B3** 4 N–KB3, or **3...P–Q4** 4 P×P Q×P 5 N–KB3 (see A1, note to 3 B–N2). Another answer is simply **3 N–QB3**—see B1. Finally, d) **2 ... P–QB3** may be Black's most subtle choice e.g. 3 N–KB3 P–Q3 4 N–B3 P–KB4!?, a position of the type examined in Chapter 9 (e.g. C2, note (b) to 4 P–Q4). White may aim for an early P–QB5 to create an imbalance.

2 P–Q3 is slow, to be sure, but in no case does Black have a move which devitalizes the game, as he did in A1 and A2.

A4
2 P–K3

Nor is this without point. On a) **2 ... N–KB3**, **3 N–QB3** (probably best) is B4 below. White also has **3 P–QN3** (Larsen's), or even **3 P–QR3!?**, but then 3 ... P–B3! (As usual, **3 ... P–Q4?!** 4 P×P N×P 5 N–KB3 — *and if 5 ... N–QB3, 6 B–N5* — is questionable for the second player.) 4 P–Q4 P×P (**4 ... P–K5** 5 P–Q5!?) 5 P×P (5 Q×P!?) 5 ... P–Q4 6 N–QB3, and although White's 'extra' move P–QR3 is somewhat useful, one cannot speak of any advantage.

b) **2 ... P–QB3** 3 N–KB3 (**3 P–Q4** P×P 4 P×P P–Q4 5 N–QB3 may lead into a kind of Tarrasch French formation.) 3 ... P–K5 4 N–Q4

with an Alapin Sicilian (2 P–QB3) Reversed. For a similar line, see B42 below. 2 ... P–QB3 is safe, but nothing to be afraid of.

c) **2 ... P–Q3** 3 N–QB3 N–KB3 4 P–Q4 QN–Q2 or 3 P–Q4 QN–Q2 might become a King's Indian Attack Reversed (B43 below). Finally,

d) **2 ... N–QB3** can also transpose to B (3 N–QB3 N–B3), or to the Göring Gambit Declined(!) after 3 P–Q4 P×P 4 P×P P–Q4 5 P×P Q×P 6 N–KB3 etc.

Obviously neither **2 P–Q3** nor **2 P–K3** can wrest the advantage against a responsible defence; but they have the virtue of avoiding main lines without allowing simplification.

B

1 P–QB4   P–K4
2 N–QB3   **N–KB3**

Among all these indeterminate moves, we should not neglect Gurgenidze's **2 ... B–N5!?**, which has the motive of playing ... B–QN5 before ... N–QB3, so that White's N–Q5 can be repulsed by ... P–QB3 at some point. This notion receives fulfilment after **3 N–Q5?!** B–B4! 4 P–QN4 B–B1! △ 5 ... P–QB3. Instead, Knezevic-Gurgenidze, Olomouc 1976 continued **3 P–K3** B×N 4 NP×B P–Q3 5 P–K4 P–KB4! 6 P×P B×P 7 P–Q3 KN–K2 8 N–K2 0–0 9 N–N3 B–N3 10 B–K2 B–K1 11 N–K4 N–N3 ∞ (½–½, 20). **3 Q–B2** and **3 N–B3** are natural replies which still await tests.

After 2 ... N–KB3, **3 P–B4**(?)

looks too random. By 3 . . . P×P 4
P–Q4 P–Q4 5 B×P P–B3 ('∓' -
Pachman), Black gains control of
e4 and d5, and White's KP remains
backward. So:
B1 3 P–Q3
B2 3 P–K4
B3 3 Q–B2
B4 3 P–K3

B1

3 P–Q3 and:

a) **3 . . . N–B3** 4 P–KN3 P–Q4 5
P×P etc. is a reversed Dragon—
Chapter 6.

b) **3 . . . P–B3** 4 N–B3 P–Q3 5
P–KN3 P–KN3 (**5 . . . B–K2** is
Chapter 9, C2, note (b) to 4 P–Q4.)
6 B–N2 B–N2 7 0–0 0–0 is *English
II . . . N–KB3*, Ch 6.

c) **3 . . . B–N5** 4 B–Q2 0–0 5
P–KN3 (**5 N–B3** N–B3 is Chapter
8, C2) 5 . . . P–B3 6 N–B3 R–K1 7
P–QR3 B–B1 8 B–N2 P–Q4 9 P×P
P×P 10 P–Q4 P–K5 11 N–K5
N–B3 =.

B2

3 P–K4

Schwarz's explanation of the
'theory' behind 3 P–K4 comes
down to this: White wants to play
P–B4 and mate down the KB file!
3 . . .   B–B4
But can't 3 P–K4 be considered
instead a belated attempt to
play double king pawn? The 'Ruy'
with
a) **3 . . . B–N5** will be ineffective
against both 'Cozio's' (4 KN–K2)
and the 'Improved Exchange
Variation' (4 P–QR3). The
'Ponziani'.

b) **3 . . . P–B3** is best countered by 4
N–B3 (to be dealt with in *English IV*
under 1 . . . N–KB3 2 N–QB3 P–B3
3 P–K4 P–K4).

c) **3 . . . N–B3** ('Three Knights'!?)
is bad, according to Schwarz! 4
P–B4('!') P–Q3 5 P–Q3 B–N5 6
B–K2 P–KR4?! 7 N–B3 B–K2 (**7
. . . B×N** 8 B×B N–Q5) 8 B–K3
Q–Q2 9 P–KR3 B×N 10 B×B P×P
11 B×P N–Q5 12 B–K3 N×Bch 13
Q×N ± Alekhine-Lilienthal,
Hastings 1933/4. But he does not
explain what happens on **4 . . .
P×P!** e.g. 5 P–Q4 B–N5, or **5 N–B3**
B–N5 6 P–Q3 (**6 P–K5** N–KR4) 6
. . . P–Q3 7 B×P 0–0 etc. Possibly **4
P–KN3** should be substituted
for 4 P–B4.
    4 P–Q3   P–Q3
    5 P–KR3   N–B3

5 . . . P–B3 6 B–K3 B×B (**6 . . .
B–QN5** -Schwarz; **6 . . . N(1)–Q2)**
7 P×B P–Q4 8 KP×P P×P 9 N–B3!
P–Q5 10 P×P P×P 11 N–K2 N–B3
12 Q–Q2 0–0 13 0–0–0 Q–N3 (13
. . . R–K1!? Δ 14 Q–B4 N–KR4; 14
P–KN4 B–K3) 14 P–KN4 R–Q1
15 B–N2 B–K3 16 K–N1 P–QR4
17 N–B4 N–N5 18 QR–K1 P–R5
19 R–K5! ± Sliwa-Flohr, Balaton-
jüred 1960 (1–0, 42).
    6 B–K3   0–0
    7 Q–Q2   N–Q5
    8 P–KN4?!

8 P–KN3 was more restrained.
    8 . . .   P–B3
    9 B–N2   P–QR3!
10 KN–K2 P–QN4 11 N–N3
N–K1! 12 0–0 N–B2 13 QR–B1
N(2)–K3 14 N(3)–K2 B–N2 15
N–B5?! (15 P–B4 -Unzicker) 15 . . .
N×Nch 16 Q×N P–N3 17 N–N3

Q–R5 18 Q–Q2 QR–Q1 19 P–N4 B×B 20 Q×B P–QB4! ∓ Sliwa-Keres, Moscow (Alekhine)—1956. Black has refuted White's play; a comparison of the four minor pieces and two queens reveals the extent of his advantage (0–1, 41). Alas, Keres was one of the great double king pawn players: Sliwa should have tried 3 P–K3!

B3

3 Q–B2

The twilight zone. White anticipates the usefulness of his queen development in these variations:

a) **3 ... P–Q4?** 4 P×P N×P 5 Q–K4 ±;

b) **3 ... N–B3** 4 P–K3 B–N5!? (4 ... B–K2) 5 P–QR3 (or 5 KN–K2) 5 ... B×N 6 Q×B ±;

c) **3 ... P–B3** 4 N–B3 P–Q3 5 P–KN3 B–K2 6 B–N2 0–0 7 0–0 Δ P–Q4, R–Q1 etc.;

d) **3 ... P–KN3** 4 N–B3 P–Q3 5 P–K3 B–N2 6 P–QN3 0–0 7 B–N2, a standard King's Indian Attack with colours reversed (objectively equal).

B4

3 P–K3

A favourite of the author's, who at this point must beg the reader's indulgence for devoting too much space to his own games! Unfortunately, although 3 P–K3 is likely the best of White's early attempts to deviate from 3 N–B3 N–B3, there are almost no top-level examples of it; I hope that what follows will illustrate the extent of hidden possibilities in a hitherto un-analysed line.

Black has a handful of plausible replies:

B41 3 ... P–Q4
B42 3 ... P–B3
B43 3 ... P–Q3
B44 3 ... N–B3
B45 3 ... B–N5

For **3 ... B–K2** 4 N–B3 (4 P–Q4?! P×P 5 P×P P–Q4) 4 ... N–B3, see Chapter 8, E3 (±).

B41

3 ...   P–Q4

Obliging, but not necessarily disastrous. The resulting positions are also important for Chapter 8, E (see note to Black's fifth).

4 P×P   N×P
5 N–B3

Or 5 Q–B2 N×N (**5 ... B–K2?** 6 N–B3 N–QB3 7 B–N5 ±; **5 ... P–KN3** 6 Q–K4!; **5 ... N–N5!?** Δ 6 **Q–K4** P–KB4 7 Q×Pch B–K2 ∞ or 6 **Q–N1** P–QB4) 6 NP×N (or 6 Q×N) 6 ... P–QB4 7 N–B3 B–Q3 8 B–K2 0–0 9 0–0 N–B3 10 P–Q3 B–K3 11 B–N2 P–B4 12 P–B4 ±.

5 ...   N–QB3 (*111*)

This often arises from 1 P–QB4 P–K4 2 N–QB3 N–KB3 3 N–B3 N–B3 4 P–K3 P–Q4 5 P×P N×P.

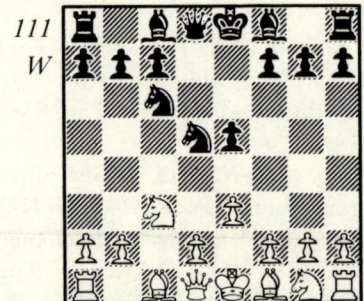

111
W

Instead, **5 . . . N×N** 6 NP×N grants White a central pawn preponderance e.g. 6 . . . B–Q3 (**6 . . . P–K5?** 7 Q–R4ch) 7 P–Q4 N–Q2 (**7 . . . P–K5** 8 N–Q2 B–KB4 9 B–K2 — *9 Q–N3! was also good* — 9 . . . 0–0 10 Q–N3 Q–N4 11 P–N3 B–K3 12 Q×P B–Q4 13 Q–N1 P–KB4 14 Q–N5! B–B3 15 Q–N3ch K–R1 16 P–Q5 ±±, a game of the author's) 8 B–K2 0–0 9 0–0 P–K5?! 10 N–Q2 R–K1 11 N–B4 P–QN3 12 P–B4! (±) P–KB3 13 N×B P×N 14 Q–N3ch 1–0 Watson-Thomas, Texas 1975.

After 5 . . . N–QB3, White has a Two Knights Sicilian with an extra tempo! But how to exploit it?

6 B–N5

Generally considered best, but that remains to be proven. **6 P–Q3** is a Scheveningen Reversed, and a very attractive option is **6 Q–B2**:

a) **6 . . . P–QR3** 7 N×N (**7 P–QR3** is not bad either.) 7 . . . Q×N 8 B–B4 Q–Q1 9 P–QR3 B–N5?! 10 Q–N3! Q–Q2 11 Q×NP R–R2 12 B×Pch K–Q1 (**12 . . . K×B** 13 Q×N!) 13 Q–N3 B–Q3 14 B–Q5 K–B1 15 Q–R4 ±± — a game of the author's.

b) **6 . . . B–K2** 7 P–QR3 N×N ('?' - Schwarz; but **7 . . . B–K3** or **7 . . . 0–0** would run into 8 B–N5!) 8 NP×N 0–0 9 P–Q4 B–Q3 (**9 . . . P×P**, Compare '(c)' 10 B–K2 Q–K2 11 0–0 B–KN5 12 P–R3 B–Q2 13 P–B4 P–QN3 14 B–N2 QR–K1 15 P–B5! P×BP 16 P×KP N×P 17 N×N B×N 18 B×B Q×B 19 KR–B1 ± Flohr-Landau, Kemeri 1937.

c) **6 . . . N×N** 7 NP×N B–Q3 8 P–Q4 0–0 9 B–K2 P×P 10 BP×P B–N5ch 11 B–Q2 B×Bch 12 Q×B B–B4 13 0–0 Q–K2 (Black holds · back the centre, but gets in trouble on the queenside.) 14 QR–B1 KR–B1 15 R–B5 B–K5 16 R(1)–B1 Q–Q3 17 Q–B3 P–KR3 18 N–Q2 B–N3 19 B–B3 ±± Watson-E. McCormick, Nebraska 1975.

d) **6 . . . B–KN5!?** hasn't been tried here. Then **7 Q–K4?!** N–B3 8 Q–R4 B–Q3 is only equal, so either **7 P–Q3** (**7 P–QR3** is similar.) or **7 B–N5** B×N 8 P×B N×N 9 NP×N (9 Q×N Q–Q4!) 9 . . . Q–Q4 10 B–K2 ± is the way to complicate matters.

    6 . . .   N×N

6 . . . Q–Q3 looks mediocre, but is not so easy to refute. Nielson-Pederson, corres 1961 continued 7 P–Q4 P×P 8 N×P?! (8 P×P! - Nielson) 8 . . . N×N 9 P×N B–Q2 10 0–0 0–0–0!? 11 P–QR4? (11 R–N1!?) 11 . . . N–R4! 12 B–R3 P–QB4 13 Q–B2 Q–KN3 14 B–Q3 Q–KB3 ∓. Shatskes recommends **10 N×N: 10 . . . B×N** 11 Q–R4 with the advantage, or **10 . . . P×N** 11 B–Q3, 'in essence a pawn up on the kingside.' In the latter case however, the power of White's majority is rather abstract for the time being (e.g. 11 . . . R–QN1 12 0–0 Q–K4).

    7 NP×N   B–Q2?!

Inferior is

a) **7 . . . P–K5?** 8 N–K5 Q–Q4 (**8 . . . B–Q2** 9 N×B Q×N 10 R–N1 Δ B–R4, P–B3 -Euwe; **8 . . . Q–N4** 9 Q–R4!) 9 Q–R4 B–Q2 10 N×B K×N 11 B–B4 Q–KN4 12 B×P Q×P 13 R–B1 ±± (Euwe).

But

b) **7 . . . B–Q3!** avoids the problems highlighted in the text and the next note, e.g. 8 P–K4 (**8 P–Q4** P–K5; compare note (c) to 8 P–K4.) 8 . . . 0–0! (**8 . . . P–B4** 9 P–Q4! BP×P 10 B–N5 ± -Schwarz; **8 . . . B–Q2!?** 9 P–K4 is the text.) 9 0–0 (**9 P–Q4** P×P 10 P×P R–K1 =) 9 . . . P–B4! ∞.

8 P–K4

a) **8 B×N!?** B×B 9 N×P B×NP and now not **10 Q–R4ch?** P–B3 11 Q–KB4 Q–B2, but **10 R–KN1!** Q–Q4 (**10 . . . B–Q4?** 11 P–QB4 B–K3 12 Q–B3 Δ Q×NP, R–QN1 etc. -Michaelides) 11 Q–R4ch (or **11 P–KB4** B–K2 12 Q–N4) 11 . . . P–B3 12 Q–KB4 B–KR6 13 P–B4 Q–K3 14 B–N2 ± (Michaelides).

b) **8 R–QN1?** P–K5 9 B×N B×B 10 N–K5 Q–N4 11 N×B Q×P ∓∓ (Schwarz).

c) **8 P–Q4** P–K5 (or **8 . . . B–Q3!?**, and if 9 B×N – *9 P–K4 is the text* – 9 . . . B×B 10 P×P B×N 11 Q×B B×P 12 0–0 P–QB3! 13 B–R3 Flohr-Petrov, Kemeri 1937, and now 13 . . . Q–Q4! would have practically levelled things.) 9 N–Q2?! (**9 B×N** B×B 10 N–K5 Q–B3! 11 0–0 B–K2, very slightly ±) 9 . . . Q–N4! 10 B–B1 P–B4 (**10 . . . Q–N3** 11 Q–B2 P–B4 12 P–B3 P×P 13 N×P B–Q3 14 B–B4 N–R4 15 B–Q3 0–0 16 0–0 Q–R4 17 P–B4 ± Watson-Spiller, Los Angeles 1975) 11 P–N3 (? **11 P–KB4!**) 11 . . . B–Q3 12 B–N2 N–R4 13 P–QR4 0–0 ∓ Villegas-Liebstein, Mar del Plata 1944.

8 . . .   B–Q3
9 P–Q4   P×P?!

9 . . . 0–0!? and **9 . . . Q–K2** are improvements.

10 P×P   B–N5ch
11 B–Q2 B×Bch 12 Q×B 0–0 13 0–0 ± (Analysis by Shatskes).

B42

3 . . .   P–B3

An Alapin Sicilian with reversed colours!

4 N–B3

4 P–Q4 P×P 5 P×P (**5 Q×P** P–Q4 6 N–B3 B–K3! =) 5 . . . P–Q4 6 B–Q3 could be a reversed Tarrasch French.

4 . . .   P–K5

4 . . . P–Q3 is a safer move, although complications cannot be permanently avoided e.g. 5 P–Q4 QN–Q2 6 B–K2 B–K2 (**6 . . . P–KN3?!** 7 0–0 B–N2 can be weak when . . . P–QB3 is already in. By 8 P–QN3 0–0 – *8 . . . P×P 9 N×P and d6 is exposed* – 9 P×P P×P 10 B–R3 R–K1 11 Q–B2! Δ QR–Q1, N–KN5–K4 etc., White secures the better prospects.) 7 0–0 0–0 8 Q–B2 R–K1 9 P–QN4 Q–B2 10 P–QR4 N–B1!? 11 P–N5 B–N5 12 P–R5 B–Q1?! (12 . . . P–QR3) 13 P–R6 P–K5 14 P×NP Q×P 15 P×P Q×P 16 P–Q5 Q–B2 17 N–Q4 ± Watson-Gruchacz, Lone Pine 1976.

5 N–Q4   P–Q4

In a weekend Swiss I was surprised by **5 . . . B–N5!?**: 6 Q–B2 B×N (**6 . . . Q–K2** 7 N–B5!? – *7 P–QN3* – 7 . . . Q–K4 8 N–N3 B×N 9 NP×B P–Q3 10 P–Q4 P×Pe.p. 11 B×P – Δ *0–0, P–K4, P–B4* – 11 . . . P–KR4!? ∞/±) 7 Q×B 0–0 8 P–QN3 P–Q3 9 B–N2 QN–Q2 10

B–K2 P–QR4 11 N–B5!? (**11 P–KN4!?**; **11 0–0**) 11 . . . N–B4 12 P–KN4 B×N! 13 P×B N–K1 14 R–KN1 P–B3 15 R–N4! Q–K2! = /∞ Watson-Pope, Berkeley 1977.

    6 P×P   P×P
    7 P–Q3

White's inability to bring his QB to f4 or g5 is more than compensated for by his extra tempo to attack the centre.

    7 . . .   B–K2

7 . . . B–Q3? can be met prudently by **8 B–K2** 0–0 9 P–QN3 ±, or radically by **8 Q–R4ch!** Δ **8 . . . B–Q2** 9 Q–N3 or **8 . . . Q–Q2** 9 N(4)–N5. Not **8 P×P?**, however: 8 . . . N×P 9 B–N5ch B–Q2 10 N×P Q–R5! ∞

    8 B–K2   0–0
    9 0–0   QN–Q2 (*112*)

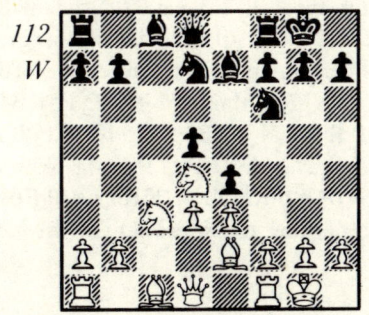

Hanging tough! In other games, **9 . . . P×P?!** 10 Q×P N–B3 11 P–QN3 ± gave White easy play against the isolated QP (or, after N×N, against the backward QBP).

    10 P×P

Lest Black continue . . . N–B4 and recapture on e4 with a knight.

    10 . . .   P×P

    11 P–QN3?!

White should try **11 Q–B2** N–B4 12 R–Q1 (**12 P–QN4** N–Q6! =). Then **12 . . . B–Q2** 13 N–B5 ±, or **12 . . . Q–B2?** 13 P–QN4 N–Q6 14 N×KP! ±. So **12 . . . Q–N3**, and 13 P–QN3 B–Q2 14 B–N2 is best play (∞).

    11 . . .   N–B4

12 B–N2 B–K3?! (**12 . . . B–Q2** Δ . . . Q–N1–K4! was fully equal.) 13 Q–B2 QR–B1 14 QR–Q1 (±) Q–N3 15 Q–N1 KR–Q1 16 K–R1 P–QR3 17 P–B3! N–Q4 (After **17 . . . P×P** 18 P×P, White can gun for Black's king along the long diagonal and KN file.) 18 N×N R×N?! (**18 . . . B×N** 19 N–B5 B–B3 20 Q–R1 ±) 19 P×P R–N4 20 P–K5! P–KR4 21 R–B4 ±± Watson-Mirkin, Providence 1977.

B43
    3 . . .   P–Q3

One of the best moves, preparing to play a King's Indian formation. The subject of 'Reversed King's Indian Attacks' comes up in a variety of English lines, so what follows has more than local relevance.

    4 P–Q4

Almost anything Black does versus a King's Indian Attack can be tried by White over the next few moves, but the extra tempo sometimes proves worthless e.g. **4 P–KN3?!** P–Q4! 5 P×P N×P 6 P–QR3 N×N 7 NP×N Q–Q4 =. More effective is a reversed variation like **4 N–B3** P–KN3 5 P–QN3 B–N2 6 B–N2 0–0 7 B–K2

QN–Q2 8 P–Q4 P–K5?! 9 N–Q2 R–K1 10 Q–B2 Q–K2 11 P–KN4 P–KR3 12 0–0–0 ± (from *Flank Openings*).

    4 ...   QN–Q2

Black may do without this unless White forces things by N–KB3 e.g. **4 ... P–KN3** 5 P–KN3 B–N2 6 B–N2 0–0 7 KN–K2 P–B3 8 0–0 R–K1 9 P–QN4 P–K5! 10 P–N5 B–B4 11 P–QR4 QN–Q2 12 B–QR3 P–B4 = Spiridinov-Matulović, Athens 1969.

    After 4 ... QN–Q2, White decides on a formation:
B431 5 P–KN3
B432 5 B–Q3
B433 5 N–B3

B431
    5 P–KN3   P–KN3
    6 B–N2   B–N2
    7 KN–K2

White plays Petrosian's system versus a King's Indian Attack.
    7 ...   0–0
    8 0–0

8 P–N3!? reserves options for White's king, e.g. 8 ... R–K1 (**8 ... P–B3?!** 9 B–R3 N–K1 10 0–0 P–KB4 – *10 ... Q–R4 11 Q–B1 ±* – 11 P×P N×P 12 Q–Q2 ±) 9 P–QR4 (over-refinement? But **9 B–N2** P–B3 is level, or **9 ... P×P**, or **9 ... P–QR3** Δ ... R–N1, ... P–QN4) 9 ... P–B3 (**9 ... P–K5?!** 10 B–QR3 N–B1 11 Q–B2 B–B4 12 P–KR3 P–KR4 13 0–0–0 P–B3 14 P–KN4! with an attack) 10 B–QR3? (**10 0–0** is best. If then 10 ... P–K5, 11 P–R5 is interesting e.g. 11 ... N–B1 12 P–Q5 P–B4 13 B–Q2 P–R4 14 P–QN4 Δ 14 ...

P×P 15 N–N5 ∞) 10 ... P×P 11 P×P P–Q4! 12 P×P N×P 13 N×N P×N 14 0–0 N–B3 15 N–B3 N–K5! ∓ Watson-Winslow, Vancouver 1976.
    8 ...   R–K1
    9 P–N3   / P–B3
    10 B–N2?!   P–K5

With a good game for Black, since the king pawn cannot be undermined. **10 P×P** was correct, although 10 ... P×P 11 B–QR3 B–B1 is dead equal.

B432
    5 B–Q3   P–KN3

Also **5 ... B–K2** is plausible. Now White sets up as Karpov used to against the King's Indian Attack.
    6 KN–K2   B–N2
    7 0–0

Again, White may want to delay this by 7 P–N3 e.g. 7 ... 0–0 8 B–N2 and if Black plays the 'Fischer plan' (from the K.I.A.) of 8 ... N–R4, then 9 B–K4!? P–KB4 10 B–B3 N(4)–B3 11 P–KN3 P–B3 12 B–N2 (Δ P×P) 12 ... P–K5 13 N–B4 Q–K2 14 P–KR4 would be something to experiment with!
    7 ...   0–0
    8 P–N3

8 Q–B2!? reserves the possibility of P–QN4.
    8 ...   N–K1
a) **8 ... R–K1** 9 B–B2 (9 Q–B2!?) 9 ... P–B3 (**9 ... P–K5?** 10 N–N3; **9 ... N–B1** 10 P×P P×P 11 B–N2) 10 P–QR4!? P×P (**10 ... P–K5** 11 N–N3 P–Q4 12 P×P P×P 13 B–R3 ±) 11 N×P P–QR4 12 P–K4 N–B4 13 P–B3 Q–N3 14 B–K3 Δ 14 ...

P–Q4?! 15 BP×P P×P 16 N(4)–N5.
b) **8 . . . N–R4** 9 P–B4 (9 B–R3!?) 9
. . . P–KB4 10 B–B2 P×QP 11 P×P
R–K1 12 R–B3, about equal.

 9 P×P   N×P
10 B–B2 P–KB4 11 B–N2 N–KB3
12 N–B4 P–B3 13 Q–K2 Q–K2 14
QR–Q1 N–B2 = /∞ Watson-
Diesen, Las Vegas 1976.

B433
  5 N–B3   P–KN3
  6 B–K2   B–N2

This is the 'main line' of the
King's Indian Attack with reverse
colours.

 7 0–0

White should consider **7 P–QN3**,
with play as in the note to 4 P–Q4
(B–N2, Q–B2, and in some cases
0–0–0).

 7 . . .   0–0
 8 P–QN4 R–K1
 9 P–QR4 P–K5 (*113*)

Instead of this advance 9 . . . P×P!?
can be played, e.g. 10 P×P (10
N×P P–B4-Hort) 10 . . . P–B4 11
R–N1 P×NP 12 R×P N–N1! Δ . . .
N–B3 = Spiridonov-Hort, Brno
1975. Should White wish to avoid
this line, he might play 9 P–N5!? or
insert Q–B2 on his eight or ninth
moves; see (c).

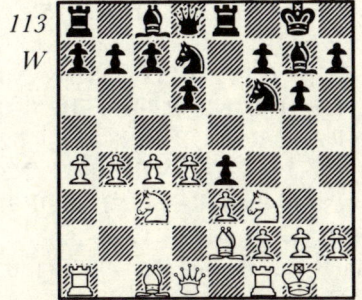

113
W

From the diagrammed position,
we examine a few sketches of
possible strategies. For a further
study of these ideas (with colours
reversed of course) see Keene's
Flank Openings and Weinstein's
King's Indian Attack.
a) **10 N–K1** P–KR4 11 P–R5 N–B1
12 P–N5 (or 12 P–R6) 12 . . .
N(1)–R2 (**12 . . . P–QR3!?** 13
N–B2 N(1)–R2 14 B–N2 P–R5 15
P×P R×P – *15 . . . P×P 16 P–B4!?*
– 16 N–N4 R–R1 17 P–Q5 ∞) 13
P–R6 P–N3 14 P–B4! N–N5 15
N–B2 Q–R5 16 P–R3 N–R3 17
B–Q2 Q–Q1 18 N–N4 B–Q2 19
Q–B2 P–KB4 (**19 . . . N(2)–B3** 20
B–K1 Δ B–R4) 20 B–K1 Δ
N(3)–Q5 (±?).
b) **10 N–Q2** N–B1 11 P–N5 P–KR4
12 P–R5 (**12 B–R3** B–B4 13 P–R5
P–R3 14 B–N4 ∞) 12 . . . P–R3 13
P×P P×P 14 P–B4!? P×Pe.p. 15
B×P R–N1 16 N(2)–K4 = /∞.
c) **10 N–Q2** P–KR4 11 Q–B2
Q–K2 (A position more likely to
arise via 9 Q–B2 Q–K2 10 P–QR4
P–K5 11 N–Q2 P–KR4) 12 B–N2!?
N–B1!? (12 . . . P–R5) 13 N–Q5!
N×N 14 P×N B–B4 15 R–R3 (Δ
R–B3, KR–B1) ∞.
R–N1 P×NP 12 R×P N–N1! Δ
. . . N–B3 = Spiridonov-Hort, Brno
B44
  3 . . .   **N–B3**
Now **4 N–B3** is Chapter 8, E. But
White can go his own way:
  4 P–QR3
 4 KN–K2 is also noteworthy:
a) **4 . . . P–Q3** 5 P–Q4 P–KN3 6
P–KN3 B–N2 7 B–N2 B–Q2
(Black's knight on c6 makes life
difficult for him.) 8 P–Q5 N–K2 9

P–K4 0–0 10 P–KR3 N–K1 11 0–0
P–KB4 12 P×P P×P 13 P–B4
N–N3 14 B–K3 K–R1 15 Q–Q2 ±
Watson-Croushare, Columbus
1977; a standard formation where
White has the option of a queenside
attack or working on Black's centre
after P×P.

b) **4 ... P–Q4** 5 P×P N×P 6
P–QR3 B–K3 7 P–QN4 B–K2 8
B–N2 with a hybrid sort of Sicilian
Reversed, difficult to assess. White
may continue N–B1–N3 etc.; but
Black will have good chances in the
centre and king's wing.

    4 ...   P–QR4

4 ... P–Q4 5 P×P N×P 6 Q–B2
is a tempo-up Taimanov, and **4 ...
P–KN3** may be met by **5 P–Q4**, or
by the modest **5 P–Q3** B–N2 6
B–K2 e.g. 6 ... 0–0 7 B–Q2 P–Q4
(**7 ... R–K1** 8 Q–B2 P–Q3 9 N–B3
B–B4 10 N–KN5!?) 8 P×P N×P 9
N–B3 P–QN3 10 R–B1 N(3)–K2
11 P–QN4 ±.

5 N–B3	B–K2
6 Q–B2	0–0
7 P–QN3	R–K1
8 B–N2	P–Q3

Of course ... P–Q4 on any of
these moves gives White the
'Sicilian' he wants, but now he gets
a powerful attack regardless:

9 B–Q3	P–KR3
10 P–KR4!	

With the naive threat of 11
N–KN5! (e.g. after **10 ... B–K3** or
10 ... B–KN5). Watson-Semakoff,
Gausdal 1978, continued instead
10 ... N–KN5 11 N–Q5 Q–Q2 (Δ
... P–B4) 12 B–R7ch K–B1 13
P–Q4 B–B3 14 0–0–0 P×P 15
N×QP ±.

B45

3 ...   **B–N5** (*114*)

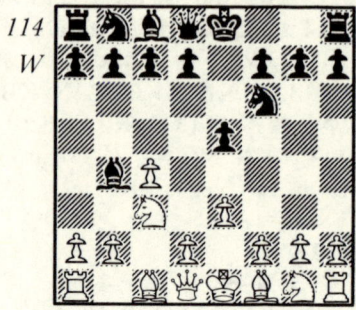

*114
W*

Although White is superficially
well-prepared for it, this move poses
as many problems as any we have
looked at.

    4 KN–K2

Natural, but not necessarily best.
To be considered are

a) **4 N–B3** B×N (**4 ... N–B3** is
Chapter 8, E4) 5 NP×B; and

b) **4 Q–B2** N–B3 (4 ... 0–0 5 N–B3
R–K1 6 P–QR3 B×N 7 Q×B) 5
P–QR3 B×N 6 Q×B P–Q4 7 P×P
N×P (7 ... Q×P!?) 8 Q–B2 0–0 9
N–B3 Q–K2 10 P–Q3 P–QR4 11
P–QN3 N–N3 12 B–N2 ± Watson-
Hillyard, London 1979.

    4 ...   0–0

4 ... P–B3 5 P–Q4 (**5 P–QR3
B×N** 6 N×B P–Q4 7 P–Q4, is
difficult to assess; **5 ... B–R4!** seems
fine, however.) 5 ... P–K5? (**5 ...
P×P** 6 Q×P 0–0 is like the text.) 6
P–Q5! 0–0 7 P–QR3 B–Q3 8 N–N3
R–K1 9 B–K2 P–QR4 10 0–0
N–R3 11 R–N1 P–KN3 12 Q–B2
Q–K2 13 R–Q1 N–B2 14 P–N3
P×P 15 P×P P–N3 16 P–QR4!
B–N2 17 B–B4 ± Torre-Balinas,
Marboro, Phillipines 1977 (1–0,
38).

5 P–QR3

a) **5 Q–N3** is well-answered by 5 ... B–R4! e.g. 6 P–N3 P–B3 7 B–N2 R–K1 8 0–0 P–Q3 9 P–QR3 B–B2 10 P–Q4 = Watson-Burns, Fairfax 1976.

b) **5 P–KN3** P–B3 6 B–N2 P–Q4! 7 P×P P×P 8 Q–N3 N–R3! 9 P–Q4 (**9 N×P?** N–B4!) 9 . . . P–K5 10 0–0 B–N5! =.

5 . . .   B–K2

Or **5 . . . B×N** 6 N×B P–B3 7 P–Q4 P×P 8 Q×P P–Q4 9 P–QN4 P×P! (**9 . . . P–QR4?!** 10 P–N5 B–K3 11 P×QP B×P 12 B–N2 QN–Q2 13 N×B ± Watson-L.D. Evans, New York 1977) 10 Q×Q R×Q 11 B×P QN–Q2 12 B–N2 N–K4 13 B–K2 N–Q6ch? (13 . . . B–B4 =) 14 B×N R×B 15 N–K2! ± Watson-Bloch, London 1978.

6 P–Q4   P×P

7 Q×P

7 N×P P–Q4 8 B–Q3?! (**8 P–QN4** P–QR4) 8 . . . P–B4 9 N–B5 P×P 10 N×Bch Q×N 11 B×P R–Q1 12 Q–K2 N–B3 13 0–0

N–K4 $\mp$ Barcza-Browne, Hastings 1972/3.

7 . . .   N–B3

8 Q–Q1 (**8 Q–Q2?** N–QR4) 8 . . . N–K4! 9 N–B4 P–B3 10 P–QN3 P–Q3 11 B–K2 P–QR3! 12 0–0 P–QN4 13 P×P RP×P 14 B–N2 R–N1 15 N–R2! B–N2 16 N–N4 Q–N3 = Watson-Browne, Berkeley 1976.

CONCLUSION:

With admittedly little evidence to go by, 3 . . . B–N5 represents Black's best bet in this line. Prospective players of 3 P–K3 may want to investigate fourth moves other than 4 KN–K2.

Obviously one cannot reasonably claim a forced advantage from 3 P–K3, or from any of the second and third-move alternatives in this chapter. But they are intriguingly open-ended, and perhaps we shall see a swing toward such ideas as the main lines become more played out.

INDEX OF VARIATIONS
AND TRANSPOSITIONS

In the English Opening, beginning as it does on the very first move, many variations can be reached by more than one route. The following chart is designed to help the reader find his way through such transpositions to the pages covering a particular sequence.

Alternatives to the main part are listed at the beginning of each part; e.g. moves other than 2 N–QB3 (2 P–KN3, 2 N–KB3, etc.) are given in a) through d) immediately below 2 N–QB3.

Unless otherwise indicated, parentheses mean that the enclosed moves are analyzed/discussed in notes to the preceding move. Certain obvious transpositions are not listed. Moreover, the Index does not always note an elementary transposition from one part of a chapter to another (e.g. in (b) under 5 N–B3, 6 P–K4 would transpose to (d) of the same listing). Page numbers are italicised.

II

III

INDEX OF
SIGNIFICANT GAMES

This includes complete games (excepting very short ones) and partial games of respectable length (at least 20 moves, with some exceptions) which are important to theory or particularly well-played.

An asterisk denotes a complete game.